SAS® Programming II: Manipulating Data with the DATA Step

Course Notes

SAS® Programming II: Manipulating Data with the DATA Step Course Notes was developed by J Cheema and Melinda Thielbar. Additional contributions were made by Marty Hultgren, Kent Reeve, Warren Repole, and Roger Staum. Editing and production support was provided by the Curriculum Development and Support Department.

SAS and all other SAS Institute Inc. product or service names are registered trademarks or trademarks of SAS Institute Inc. in the USA and other countries. ® indicates USA registration. Other brand and product names are trademarks of their respective companies.

SAS® Programming II: Manipulating Data with the DATA Step Course Notes

Book code E70307, course code PROG2, prepared date 16Apr2007.   PROG2_008

ISBN 978-1-59994-397-8

Marty. Hultgren@sas.com
Tech Support 919.677.8008
SAS 612.349.9023

Table of Contents

Course Description

This intermediate course focuses on how to manage SAS data set input and output, work with different data types, and manipulate data. Specifically, the course discusses using the DATA step to control SAS data set input and output, combine SAS data sets, summarize data, process data iteratively with DO loops and arrays, and perform data manipulations and transformations.

To learn more...

A full curriculum of general and statistical instructor-based training is available at any of the Institute's training facilities. Institute instructors can also provide on-site training.

For information on other courses in the curriculum, contact the SAS Education Division at 1-800-333-7660, or send e-mail to training@sas.com. You can also find this information on the Web at support.sas.com/training/ as well as in the Training Course Catalog.

For a list of other SAS books that relate to the topics covered in this Course Notes, USA customers can contact our SAS Publishing Department at 1-800-727-3228 or send e-mail to sasbook@sas.com. Customers outside the USA, please contact your local SAS office.

Also, see the Publications Catalog on the Web at support.sas.com/pubs for a complete list of books and a convenient order form.

Prerequisites

Before attending this course, you should have at least six months of experience writing SAS programs or have completed the *SAS® Programming I: Essentials* course and used SAS for at least one month. Specifically, you should be able to

- create and access files in your operating environment

- explain the structure of a SAS program

- explore the structure and contents of a SAS data set

- distinguish between syntax and data errors

- debug a SAS program

- create a SAS data set from a fixed-format external file

- subset the rows and columns of a SAS data set

- create derived variables

- write conditional logic statements

- read and write SAS date values

- access SAS data libraries

- sort a SAS data set

- read one or more SAS data sets using a SET statement

- perform a simple merge using a MERGE statement

- create detail and summary reports from a SAS data set

- place titles and footnotes on reports.

Chapter 1   Introduction

1.1 Overview

Objectives

- Explore the functionality of the DATA step.

3

Why Use the DATA Step?

The DATA step permits true programming functionality.
It is

- flexible
- accessible.

The DATA step is part of Base SAS software, which makes it available on all operating systems and for all SAS users.

4

What Can the DATA Step Do?

You can use the DATA step in the following ways
to transform your information:

- Read from a raw data file into the SAS System.

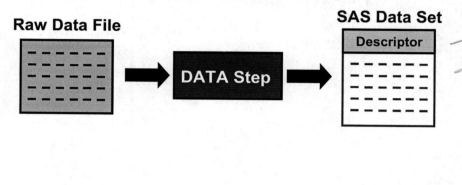

Raw Data File   **SAS Data Set**

metadata
data dictionary

Proc contents to pull
date out

5

What Can the DATA Step Do?

- Create multiple SAS data sets in one DATA step.

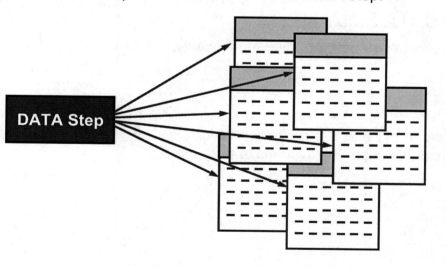

6

What Can the DATA Step Do?

- Rotate a data set.

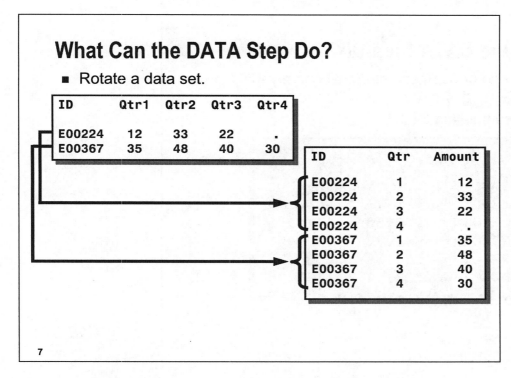

Proc Transpose

7

What Can the DATA Step Do?

- Combine existing data sets.

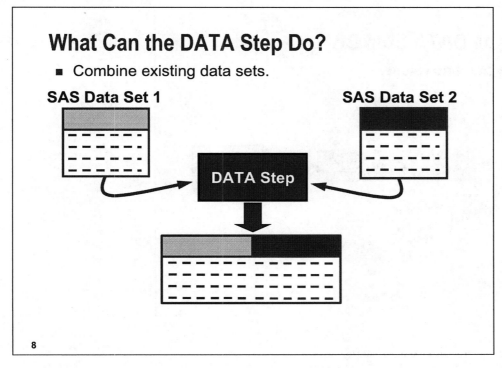

8

What Can the DATA Step Do?

You can also add or augment information in a variety of ways.

- Create accumulating totals.

SaleDate	Sale Amt	Mth2Dte
01APR2001	498.49	498.49
02APR2001	946.50	1444.99
03APR2001	994.97	2439.96
04APR2001	564.59	3004.55
05APR2001	783.01	3787.56

9

What Can the DATA Step Do?

- Manipulate numeric values.

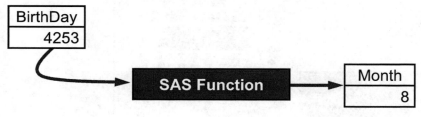

10

What Can the DATA Step Do?

- Manipulate character values.

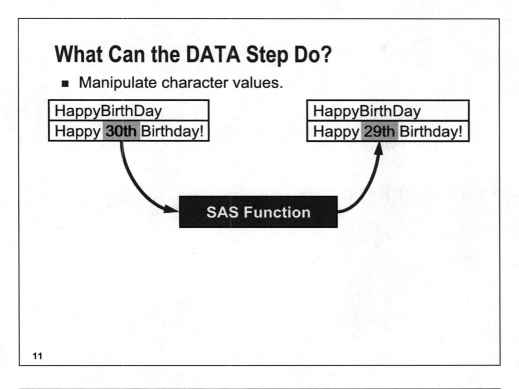

What Can the DATA Step Do?

- Summarize data sets.

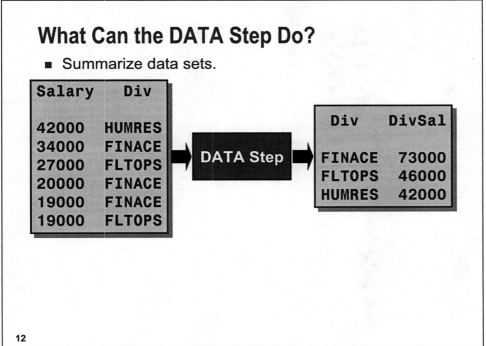

And much, much more.

13

1.2 Review of SAS Basics

Objectives

- Review fundamental SAS concepts.
- Review creating a SAS data set from a raw data file.

15

Industry Terminology Comparison

Data Processing	SAS System	SQL
file	data set	table
record	observation	row
field	variable	column

16

Structure of SAS Data Sets

SAS Data Set

```
                  General Data Set Information

                  Name                    Number of Obs.
                  *Label                  Number of Variables
Descriptor        Date/Time Created
Portion                    Storage Information
                  Information for Each Variable
                       Name    Type   Length   Position
                           *Label *Format *Informat

                  IDNUM   NAME            WAGECAT      WAGERATE

                  1351    Farr, Sue       S            3392.50
                  161                     S            5093.75
Data              212     Moore, Ron      S               .
Portion           2512    Ruth, G H       S            1572.50
                       : : :

                  5151    Coxe, Susan     S            3163.00
```

17

Attributes of SAS Variables

All SAS variables have three required attributes:

- name
- type
- length

18

Variable Names

The rules for naming SAS data sets and variables are the same.

Names

- must be 1 to 32 characters in length
- must start with a letter (A-Z) or an underscore (_)
- can continue with any combination of numbers, letters, and underscores.

19

In SAS Version 8 and higher, SAS variable names are displayed in the case that they are created. However, as in all versions of SAS, variable names are **not** case-sensitive within the program. This enables you to create variable names that are easier to read in reports without worrying about case-sensitivity within your SAS programs.

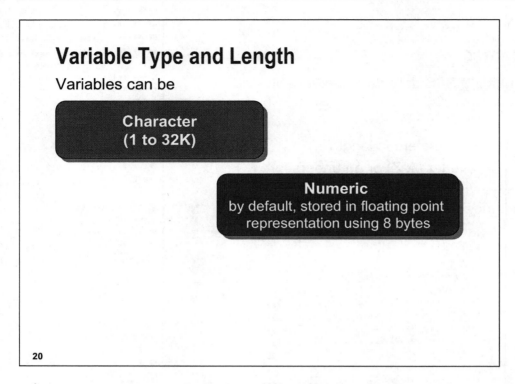

Variable Type and Length

Variables can be

Character
(1 to 32K)

Numeric
by default, stored in floating point
representation using 8 bytes

20

It is possible to store numeric variables using fewer than 8 bytes. However, reducing the length of numeric variables decreases their precision and can yield unexpected results.

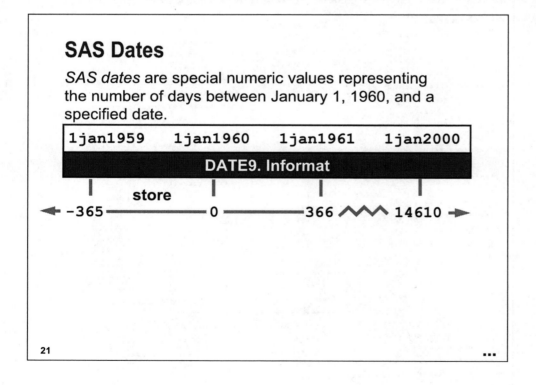

SAS Dates

SAS dates are special numeric values representing the number of days between January 1, 1960, and a specified date.

1jan1959	1jan1960	1jan1961	1jan2000

DATE9. Informat

store

◄— –365 ———— 0 ———— 366 〰〰 14610 —►

21   ...

SAS Dates

SAS dates are special numeric values representing the number of days between January 1, 1960, and a specified date.

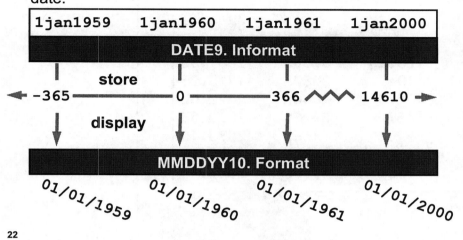

22

Create a SAS Data Set from a Raw Data File

```
E1232  15OCT1999  61065
E2341  01JUN1997  91688
E3452  26OCT1993  32639
E6781  16SEP1992  28305
E8321  26NOV1996  40440
E1052  27FEB1997  39461
E1062  10MAY1987  41463
E8172  06JAN2000  40650
E1091  20AUG1991  40950
```

A raw data file contains employee information for the level 1 flight attendants. Use the raw data file to create the **work.fltat1** SAS data set.

23

Desired Output

Obs	EmpID	Hire Date	Salary	Bonus
1	E1232	14532	61065	3053.25
2	E2341	13666	91688	4584.40
3	E3452	12352	32639	1631.95
4	E6781	11947	28305	1415.25
5	E8321	13479	40440	2022.00
6	E1052	13572	39461	1973.05
7	E1062	9991	41463	2073.15
8	E8172	14615	40650	2032.50
9	E1091	11554	40950	2047.50

Bonus is 5% of the **Salary** value

24

The DATA Statement

A DATA step always begins with a DATA statement.

General form of a DATA statement:

```
DATA SAS-data-set;
```

The DATA statement starts the DATA step and names the SAS data set being created.

25

The INFILE Statement

If you are reading data from a raw data file, you need an INFILE statement.

General form of an INFILE statement:

> **INFILE** '*raw-data-file*' *<options>*;

The INFILE statement points to the raw data file being read. Options in the INFILE statement affect how SAS reads the raw data file.

26

The INPUT Statement

When you read from a raw data file, the INPUT statement follows the INFILE statement.

General form of an INPUT statement:

> **INPUT** *variable-specification ...*;

The INPUT statement describes the raw data fields and specifies how you want them converted into SAS variables.

27

Formatted Input

This input style tells SAS where to find the fields and how to read them into SAS.

INPUT @*n variable-name informat.* ...;

@*n*	moves the pointer to the starting position of the field.
variable-name	names the SAS variable being created.
informat	specifies how many positions to read and how to convert the raw data into a SAS value.

28

The INPUT Statement

Common SAS informats:

$w.	reads a standard character field, where *w* specifies the width of the field in bytes.
w.<d>	reads a standard numeric field, where *w* specifies the width of the field in bytes and *d* specifies the number of implied decimal positions.
DATE9.	reads dates in the form 31DEC2012.

29

An *informat* is a reading instruction. The informat that is used depends on the form of the field in the raw data file. Unless these attributes are specified before the INPUT statement, SAS uses the informat to set the type and length of the variables you read from the raw data file. For a complete list of SAS informats, see the SAS documentation.

The Assignment Statement

To create a new variable in the DATA step, use
an assignment statement:

> *variable-name=expression*;

The assignment statement creates a SAS variable
and specifies how to calculate that variable's value.

30

Create a SAS Data Set from a Raw Data File

```
data work.fltat1;
   infile 'raw-data-file';
   input @1 EmpID $5.
         @7 HireDate date9.
         @17 Salary 5.;
   Bonus=.05*Salary;
run;
```

31

Create a SAS Data Set from a Raw Data File

Partial Log

```
NOTE: 9 records were read from the infile
      'fltat1.dat'.
      The minimum record length was 21.
      The maximum record length was 21.
NOTE: The data set WORK.FLTAT1 has
      9 observations and 4 variables.
```

32   c01s2d1.sas

1.3   Review of DATA Step Processing

Objectives

- Review the two phases of DATA step processing.

34

Create a SAS Data Set from Raw Data

```
data work.fltat1;
    infile 'raw-data-file';
    input @1 EmpID $5.
          @7 HireDate date9.
          @17 Salary 5.;
    Bonus=.05*Salary;
run;
```

35

Processing the DATA Step

The SAS System processes the DATA step in two phases:

- compilation
- execution.

36

Compilation

During compilation, SAS

- checks code for syntax errors
- translates code to machine code
- establishes an area of memory called the *input buffer* if reading raw data
- establishes an area of memory called the *program data vector* (PDV)
- assigns required attributes to variables
- creates the descriptor portion of the new data set.

37

Compiling the DATA Step

```
data work.fltat1;
   infile 'raw-data-file';
   input @1 EmpID $5. @7 HireDate Date9.
         @17 Salary 5.;
   Bonus=.05*Salary;
run;
```

38   ...

Compiling the DATA Step

```
data work.fltat1;
   infile 'raw-data-file';
   input @1 EmpID $5. @7 HireDate Date9.
         @17 Salary 5.;
   Bonus=.05*Salary;
run;
```

Input Buffer

39   ...

Compiling the DATA Step

```
data work.fltat1;
   infile 'raw-data-file';
   input @1 EmpID $5. @7 HireDate Date9.
         @17 Salary 5.;
   Bonus=.05*Salary;
run;
```

Input Buffer

PDV
EmpID
$ 5

40   ...

Compiling the DATA Step

```
data work.fltat1;
   infile 'raw-data-file';
   input @1 EmpID $5. @7 HireDate Date9.
         @17 Salary 5.;
   Bonus=.05*Salary;
run;
```

Input Buffer

PDV
EmpID   HireDate
$ 5   N 8

41   ...

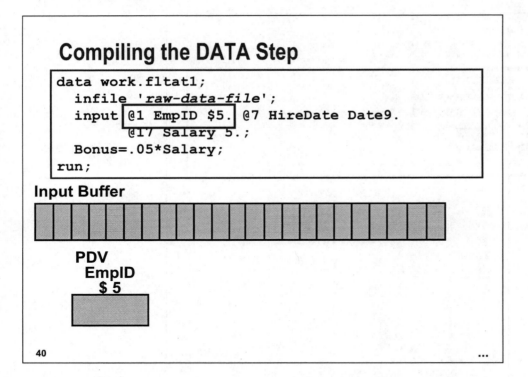

Compiling the DATA Step

```
data work.fltat1;
   infile 'raw-data-file';
   input @1 EmpID $5. @7 HireDate Date9.
         @17 Salary 5.;
   Bonus=.05*Salary;
run;
```

Input Buffer

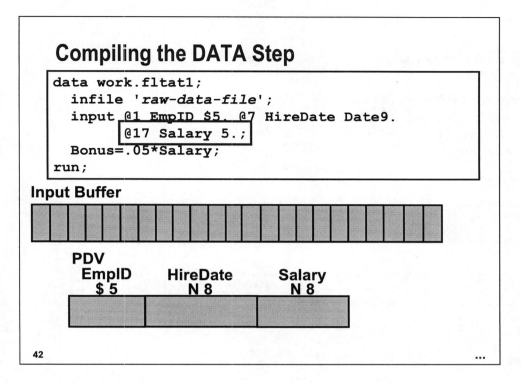

42   ...

Compiling the DATA Step

```
data work.fltat1;
   infile 'raw-data-file';
   input @1 EmpID $5. @7 HireDate Date9.
         @17 Salary 5.;
   Bonus=.05*Salary;
run;
```

Input Buffer

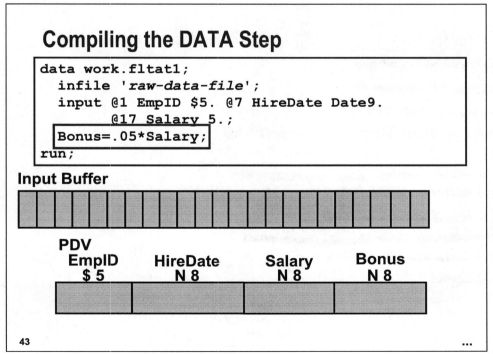

43   ...

Compiling the DATA Step

```
data work.fltat1;
  infile 'raw-data-file';
  input @1 EmpID $5. @7 HireDate Date9.
        @17 Salary 5.;
  Bonus=.05*Salary;
run;
```

Input Buffer

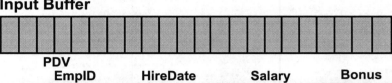

PDV

EmpID	HireDate	Salary	Bonus

fltat1 descriptor portion

EmpID	HireDate	Salary	Bonus
$ 5	N 8	N 8	N 8

44

Execution

During the execution phase, SAS
- initializes the PDV to missing
- reads data values into the PDV
- executes assignment statements and conditional processing
- writes the observation in the PDV to the output SAS data set at the end of the DATA step (by default)
- returns to the top of the DATA step
- initializes any variables that are not read from a SAS data set to missing (by default)
- repeats the process.

45

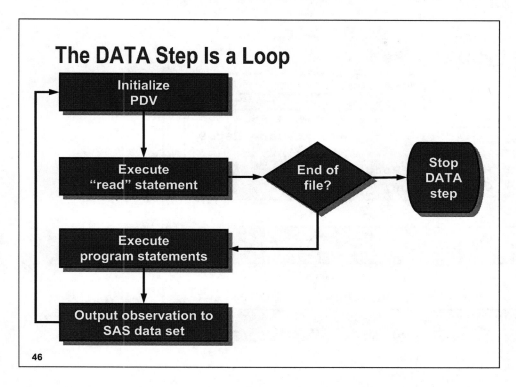

The DATA Step Is a Loop

46

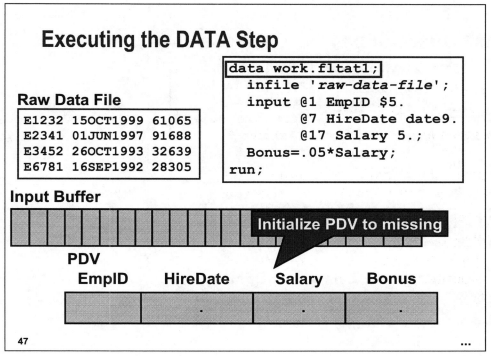

Executing the DATA Step

```
data work.fltat1;
   infile 'raw-data-file';
   input @1 EmpID $5.
         @7 HireDate date9.
         @17 Salary 5.;
   Bonus=.05*Salary;
run;
```

Raw Data File

```
E1232  15OCT1999  61065
E2341  01JUN1997  91688
E3452  26OCT1993  32639
E6781  16SEP1992  28305
```

Input Buffer

Initialize PDV to missing

PDV

EmpID	HireDate	Salary	Bonus

47

Executing the DATA Step

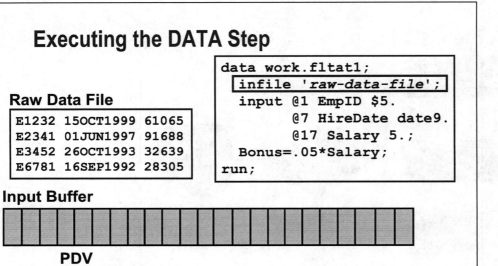

Raw Data File

```
E1232 15OCT1999 61065
E2341 01JUN1997 91688
E3452 26OCT1993 32639
E6781 16SEP1992 28305
```

```
data work.fltat1;
  infile 'raw-data-file';
  input @1 EmpID $5.
        @7 HireDate date9.
        @17 Salary 5.;
  Bonus=.05*Salary;
run;
```

Input Buffer

PDV

EmpID	HireDate	Salary	Bonus
	.	.	.

48   ...

Executing the DATA Step

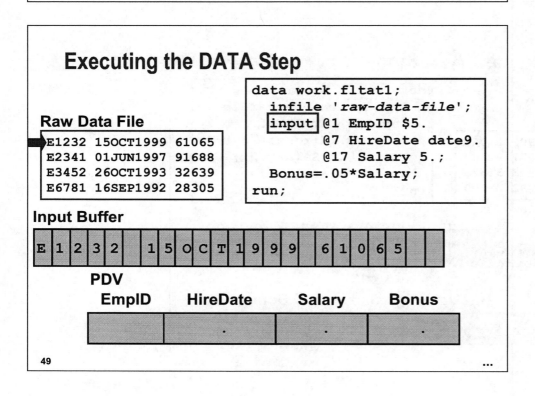

Raw Data File

```
E1232 15OCT1999 61065
E2341 01JUN1997 91688
E3452 26OCT1993 32639
E6781 16SEP1992 28305
```

```
data work.fltat1;
  infile 'raw-data-file';
  input @1 EmpID $5.
        @7 HireDate date9.
        @17 Salary 5.;
  Bonus=.05*Salary;
run;
```

Input Buffer

| E | 1 | 2 | 3 | 2 | | 1 | 5 | O | C | T | 1 | 9 | 9 | 9 | | 6 | 1 | 0 | 6 | 5 | | |

PDV

EmpID	HireDate	Salary	Bonus
	.	.	.

49   ...

Executing the DATA Step

Raw Data File

```
E1232  15OCT1999  61065
E2341  01JUN1997  91688
E3452  26OCT1993  32639
E6781  16SEP1992  28305
```

```
data work.fltat1;
  infile 'raw-data-file';
  input @1 EmpID $5.
        @7 HireDate date9.
        @17 Salary 5.;
  Bonus=.05*Salary;
run;
```

Input Buffer

| E | 1 | 2 | 3 | 2 | | 1 | 5 | O | C | T | 1 | 9 | 9 | 9 | | 6 | 1 | 0 | 6 | 5 | |

PDV

EmpID	HireDate	Salary	Bonus
E1232	.	.	.

50   ...

Executing the DATA Step

Raw Data File

```
E1232  15OCT1999  61065
E2341  01JUN1997  91688
E3452  26OCT1993  32639
E6781  16SEP1992  28305
```

```
data work.fltat1;
  infile 'raw-data-file';
  input @1 EmpID $5.
        @7 HireDate date9.
        @17 Salary 5.;
  Bonus=.05*Salary;
run;
```

Input Buffer

| E | 1 | 2 | 3 | 2 | | 1 | 5 | O | C | T | 1 | 9 | 9 | 9 | | 6 | 1 | 0 | 6 | 5 | |

PDV

EmpID	HireDate	Salary	Bonus
E1232	14532	.	.

51   ...

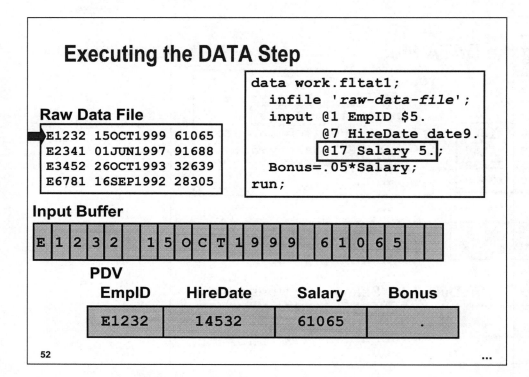

Executing the DATA Step

Raw Data File

```
E1232 15OCT1999 61065
E2341 01JUN1997 91688
E3452 26OCT1993 32639
E6781 16SEP1992 28305
```

```
data work.fltat1;
  infile 'raw-data-file';
  input @1 EmpID $5.
        @7 HireDate date9.
        @17 Salary 5.;
  Bonus=.05*Salary;
run;
```

Input Buffer

| E | 1 | 2 | 3 | 2 | | 1 | 5 | O | C | T | 1 | 9 | 9 | 9 | | 6 | 1 | 0 | 6 | 5 | |

PDV

EmpID	HireDate	Salary	Bonus
E1232	14532	61065	.

52

...

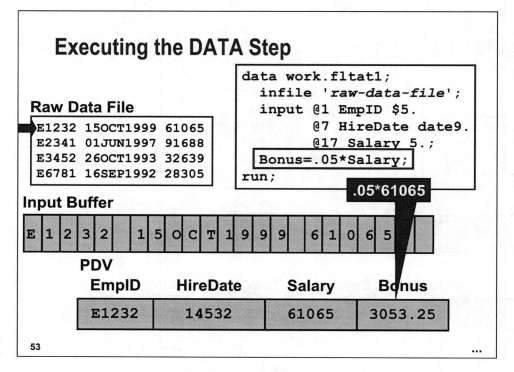

Executing the DATA Step

Raw Data File

```
E1232 15OCT1999 61065
E2341 01JUN1997 91688
E3452 26OCT1993 32639
E6781 16SEP1992 28305
```

```
data work.fltat1;
  infile 'raw-data-file';
  input @1 EmpID $5.
        @7 HireDate date9.
        @17 Salary 5.;
  Bonus=.05*Salary;
run;
```

.05*61065

Input Buffer

| E | 1 | 2 | 3 | 2 | | 1 | 5 | O | C | T | 1 | 9 | 9 | 9 | | 6 | 1 | 0 | 6 | 5 | |

PDV

EmpID	HireDate	Salary	Bonus
E1232	14532	61065	3053.25

53

...

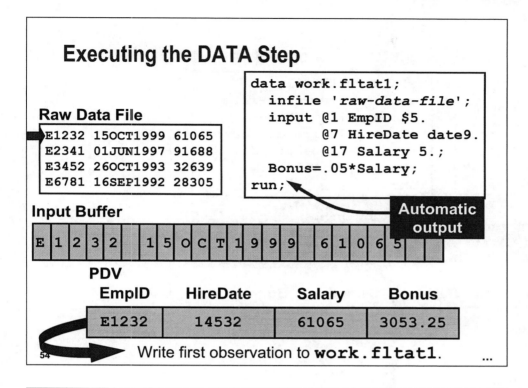

Executing the DATA Step

Raw Data File

```
E1232  15OCT1999  61065
E2341  01JUN1997  91688
E3452  26OCT1993  32639
E6781  16SEP1992  28305
```

```
data work.fltat1;
   infile 'raw-data-file';
   input @1 EmpID $5.
         @7 HireDate date9.
         @17 Salary 5.;
   Bonus=.05*Salary;
run;
```

Automatic output

Input Buffer

E	1	2	3	2		1	5	O	C	T	1	9	9	9		6	1	0	6	5		

PDV

EmpID	HireDate	Salary	Bonus
E1232	14532	61065	3053.25

Write first observation to **work.fltat1**.

54   ...

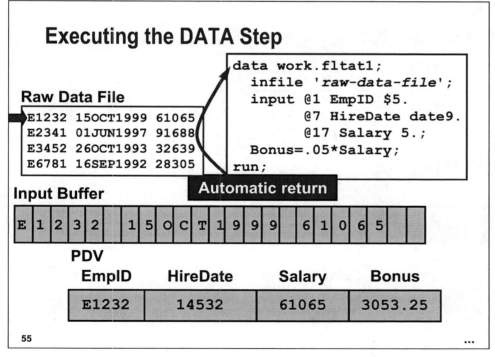

Executing the DATA Step

Raw Data File

```
E1232  15OCT1999  61065
E2341  01JUN1997  91688
E3452  26OCT1993  32639
E6781  16SEP1992  28305
```

```
data work.fltat1;
   infile 'raw-data-file';
   input @1 EmpID $5.
         @7 HireDate date9.
         @17 Salary 5.;
   Bonus=.05*Salary;
run;
```

Automatic return

Input Buffer

E	1	2	3	2		1	5	O	C	T	1	9	9	9		6	1	0	6	5	

PDV

EmpID	HireDate	Salary	Bonus
E1232	14532	61065	3053.25

55   ...

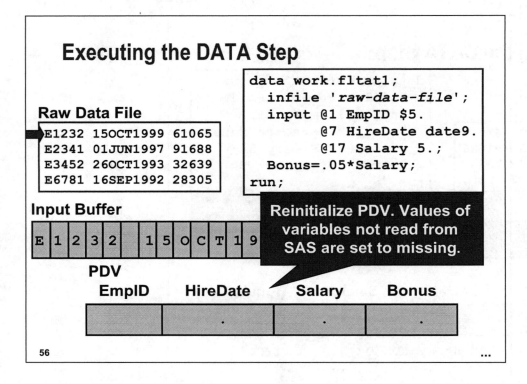

Executing the DATA Step

Raw Data File

```
E1232  15OCT1999 61065
E2341  01JUN1997 91688
E3452  26OCT1993 32639
E6781  16SEP1992 28305
```

```
data work.fltat1;
  infile 'raw-data-file';
  input @1 EmpID $5.
        @7 HireDate date9.
        @17 Salary 5.;
  Bonus=.05*Salary;
run;
```

Reinitialize PDV. Values of variables not read from SAS are set to missing.

Input Buffer

| E | 1 | 2 | 3 | 2 | | 1 | 5 | O | C | T | 1 | 9 |

PDV

EmpID	HireDate	Salary	Bonus
	.	.	.

56

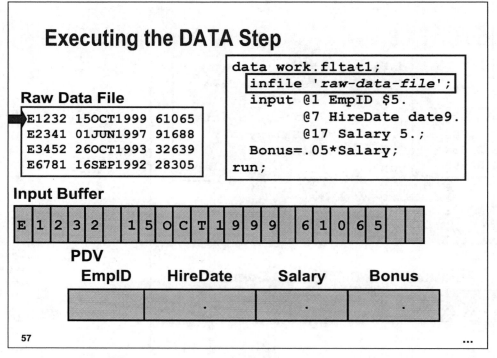

Executing the DATA Step

Raw Data File

```
E1232  15OCT1999 61065
E2341  01JUN1997 91688
E3452  26OCT1993 32639
E6781  16SEP1992 28305
```

```
data work.fltat1;
  infile 'raw-data-file';
  input @1 EmpID $5.
        @7 HireDate date9.
        @17 Salary 5.;
  Bonus=.05*Salary;
run;
```

Input Buffer

| E | 1 | 2 | 3 | 2 | | 1 | 5 | O | C | T | 1 | 9 | 9 | 9 | | 6 | 1 | 0 | 6 | 5 | |

PDV

EmpID	HireDate	Salary	Bonus
	.	.	.

57

Executing the DATA Step

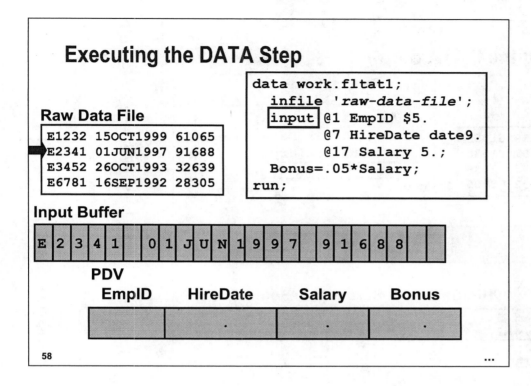

Raw Data File

```
E1232  15OCT1999  61065
E2341  01JUN1997  91688
E3452  26OCT1993  32639
E6781  16SEP1992  28305
```

```
data work.fltat1;
   infile 'raw-data-file';
   input @1 EmpID $5.
         @7 HireDate date9.
         @17 Salary 5.;
   Bonus=.05*Salary;
run;
```

Input Buffer

| E | 2 | 3 | 4 | 1 | | 0 | 1 | J | U | N | 1 | 9 | 9 | 7 | | 9 | 1 | 6 | 8 | 8 | | |

PDV

EmpID	HireDate	Salary	Bonus
	.	.	.

58

...

Executing the DATA Step

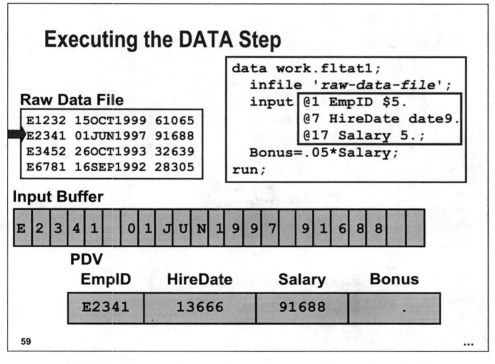

Raw Data File

```
E1232  15OCT1999  61065
E2341  01JUN1997  91688
E3452  26OCT1993  32639
E6781  16SEP1992  28305
```

```
data work.fltat1;
   infile 'raw-data-file';
   input @1 EmpID $5.
         @7 HireDate date9.
         @17 Salary 5.;
   Bonus=.05*Salary;
run;
```

Input Buffer

| E | 2 | 3 | 4 | 1 | | 0 | 1 | J | U | N | 1 | 9 | 9 | 7 | | 9 | 1 | 6 | 8 | 8 | | |

PDV

EmpID	HireDate	Salary	Bonus
E2341	13666	91688	.

59

...

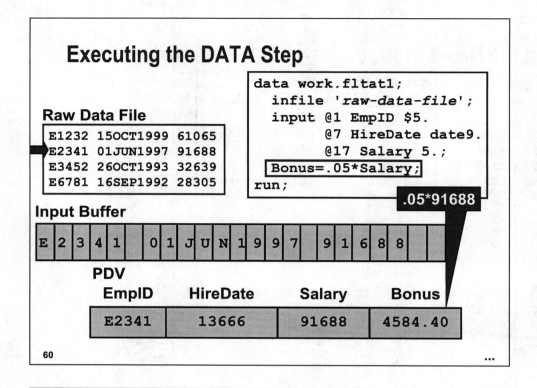

Executing the DATA Step

Raw Data File

```
E1232 15OCT1999 61065
E2341 01JUN1997 91688
E3452 26OCT1993 32639
E6781 16SEP1992 28305
```

```
data work.fltat1;
  infile 'raw-data-file';
  input @1 EmpID $5.
        @7 HireDate date9.
        @17 Salary 5.;
  Bonus=.05*Salary;
run;
```

.05*91688

Input Buffer

| E | 2 | 3 | 4 | 1 | | 0 | 1 | J | U | N | 1 | 9 | 9 | 7 | | 9 | 1 | 6 | 8 | 8 | | |

PDV

EmpID	HireDate	Salary	Bonus
E2341	13666	91688	4584.40

60   ...

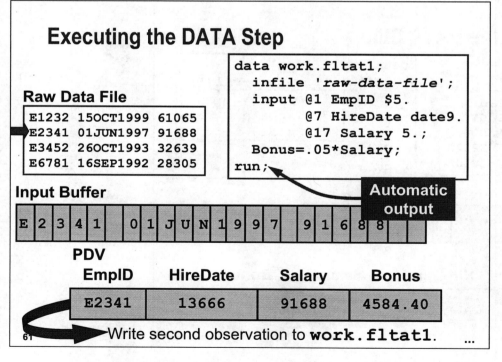

Executing the DATA Step

Raw Data File

```
E1232 15OCT1999 61065
E2341 01JUN1997 91688
E3452 26OCT1993 32639
E6781 16SEP1992 28305
```

```
data work.fltat1;
  infile 'raw-data-file';
  input @1 EmpID $5.
        @7 HireDate date9.
        @17 Salary 5.;
  Bonus=.05*Salary;
run;
```

Automatic output

Input Buffer

| E | 2 | 3 | 4 | 1 | | 0 | 1 | J | U | N | 1 | 9 | 9 | 7 | | 9 | 1 | 6 | 8 | 8 | | |

PDV

EmpID	HireDate	Salary	Bonus
E2341	13666	91688	4584.40

61   Write second observation to **work.fltat1**.   ...

Executing the DATA Step

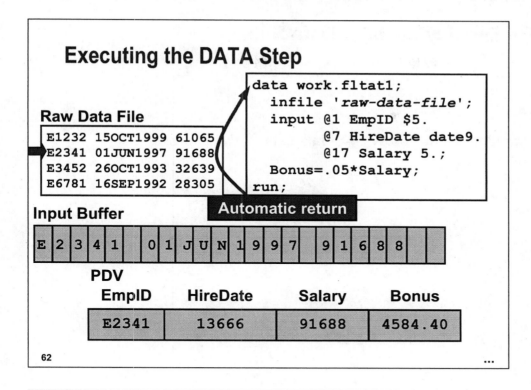

Raw Data File

```
E1232  15OCT1999  61065
E2341  01JUN1997  91688
E3452  26OCT1993  32639
E6781  16SEP1992  28305
```

```
data work.fltat1;
   infile 'raw-data-file';
   input @1 EmpID $5.
         @7 HireDate date9.
         @17 Salary 5.;
   Bonus=.05*Salary;
run;
```

Automatic return

Input Buffer

| E | 2 | 3 | 4 | 1 | | 0 | 1 | J | U | N | 1 | 9 | 9 | 7 | | 9 | 1 | 6 | 8 | 8 | | |

PDV

EmpID	HireDate	Salary	Bonus
E2341	13666	91688	4584.40

62

...

Executing the DATA Step

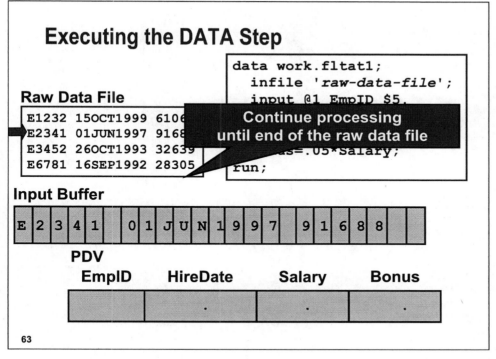

Raw Data File

```
E1232  15OCT1999  6106
E2341  01JUN1997  9168
E3452  26OCT1993  3263
E6781  16SEP1992  28305
```

```
data work.fltat1;
   infile 'raw-data-file';
   input @1 EmpID $5.
```

Continue processing until end of the raw data file

```
   as=.05*Salary;
run;
```

Input Buffer

| E | 2 | 3 | 4 | 1 | | 0 | 1 | J | U | N | 1 | 9 | 9 | 7 | | 9 | 1 | 6 | 8 | 8 | | |

PDV

EmpID	HireDate	Salary	Bonus
	.	.	.

63

1.4 Review of Displaying SAS Data Sets

Objectives

- Review procedures that display SAS data sets.

65

Create a SAS Data Set from Raw Data

```
data work.fltat1;
   infile 'raw-data-file';
   input @1 EmpID $5.
         @7 HireDate date9.
         @17 Salary 5.;
   Bonus=.05*Salary;
run;
```

66

Create a SAS Data Set from Raw Data

Partial Log

```
NOTE: 9 records were read from the infile
      'fltat1.dat'.
      The minimum record length was 21.
      The maximum record length was 21.
NOTE: The data set WORK.FLTAT1 has
      9 observations and 4 variables.
```

67

Viewing a SAS Data Set

You can use the

- CONTENTS procedure to display the descriptor portion of a SAS data set
- PRINT procedure to display the data of a SAS data set.

68

General form of a PROC CONTENTS step:

```
PROC CONTENTS DATA=SAS-data-set;
RUN;
```

General form of a PROC PRINT step:

```
PROC PRINT DATA=SAS-data-set;
RUN;
```

Viewing the Descriptor Portion

```
proc contents data=work.fltat1;
run;
```

Partial Output

```
---Alphabetic List of Variables and Attributes---

        #     Variable    Type      Len

        4     Bonus       Num        8
        1     EmpID       Char       5
        2     HireDate    Num        8
        3     Salary      Num        8
```

69

Viewing the Data Portion

```
proc print data=work.fltat1;
run;
```

Partial Output

Obs	EmpID	Hire Date	Salary	Bonus
1	E1232	14532	61065	3053.25
2	E2341	13666	91688	4584.40
3	E3452	12352	32639	1631.95
4	E6781	11947	28305	1415.25
5	E8321	13479	40440	2022.00

70

The NOOBS Option

The NOOBS option in the PROC PRINT statement suppresses the observation numbers in the list report.

General form of the NOOBS option:

```
PROC PRINT DATA=SAS-data-set NOOBS;
     <additional SAS statements>
RUN;
```

71

Viewing the Data Portion

```
proc print data=work.fltat1 noobs;
run;
```

Partial Output

EmpID	Hire Date	Salary	Bonus
E1232	14532	61065	3053.25
E2341	13666	91688	4584.40
E3452	12352	32639	1631.95
E6781	11947	28305	1415.25

72

The FORMAT Statement

The FORMAT statement applies a SAS format to specified variables. A format controls how data values are displayed.

General form of a FORMAT statement:

> **FORMAT** *SAS-variable(s) format-name. ...;*

You can format as many variables as you need using one FORMAT statement.

73

SAS Formats

General form of a SAS format:

> *<$>FORMAT-NAMEw.<d>*

- $ indicates a character format.
- *FORMAT-NAME* is the name of the format.
- *w* specifies the total number of characters available for displaying the value.
- . is the required delimiter.
- *d* specifies the number of decimal places to be displayed for a numeric value.

74

Common SAS Formats

Examples of formats:

COMMA*w.d*   adds commas to numeric values

                    Example: 46,543

DOLLAR*w.d*   adds commas and a dollar sign
to numeric values.

                    Example: $46,543

MMDDYY10.   writes dates in the form 12/31/2012

75

Applying a Format

```
proc print data=work.fltat1 noobs;
   format HireDate mmddyy10.
           Salary Bonus dollar7.;
run;
```

Partial Output

EmpID	HireDate	Salary	Bonus
E1232	10/15/1999	$61,065	$3,053
E2341	06/01/1997	$91,688	$4,584
E3452	10/26/1993	$32,639	$1,632
E6781	09/16/1992	$28,305	$1,415
E8321	11/26/1996	$40,440	$2,022

76

Formats assigned in a procedure are temporary; they only remain for that procedure. A FORMAT statement in a DATA step assigns the format permanently and makes it available whenever the data set is used.

For example, the following code assigns permanent formats to the variables **Salary**, **Bonus**, and **HireDate**:

```
data work.fltat1;
   infile 'raw-data-file';
   input @1 EmpID $5. @7 HireDate date9. @17 Salary 5.;
   Bonus=Salary*.05;
   format HireDate mmddyy10. Salary Bonus dollar7.;
run;
```

The VAR Statement

To control which variables are displayed and the order in which they are displayed, use the VAR statement.

General form of a VAR statement:

VAR *SAS-variable(s)* ...;

The VAR Statement

```
proc print data=work.fltat1 noobs;
    format Salary Bonus dollar7.;
    var EmpID Bonus Salary;
run;
```

Partial Output

EmpID	Bonus	Salary
E1232	$3,053	$61,065
E2341	$4,584	$91,688
E3452	$1,632	$32,639
E6781	$1,415	$28,305
E8321	$2,022	$40,440
E1052	$1,973	$39,461

c01s4d1.sas

1.5 Working with Existing SAS Data Sets

Objectives

- Review the concept of SAS data libraries.
- Review the LIBNAME statement.
- Review creating a new SAS data set from an existing data set.
- Review conditional processing.

80

SAS Files

SAS data sets and other files are stored in SAS data libraries.

81

SAS Data Libraries

A *SAS data library* is a collection of SAS files that are recognized as a unit by SAS on your operating environment.

- WORK – temporary library

- SASUSER – permanent library

You can create and access your own permanent libraries.

- PROG2 – permanent library

82

SAS Data Libraries

The physical structure of a SAS data library depends on your operating system.

Directory-based operating systems (Windows or UNIX)

- any folder or sub-directory

z/OS (OS/390) systems

- specially formatted sequential file

83

The LIBNAME Statement

The LIBNAME statement establishes the library reference (or *libref*), which is an alias for the SAS data library.

General form of the LIBNAME statement:

> **LIBNAME** *libref* '*SAS-data-library*' *<options>*;

The libref must be eight characters or fewer.

84

Except for the eight-character length limit, the library reference follows the naming conventions for SAS data sets and variables. Specifically, it must

- begin with a letter or underscore
- include no special characters other than the underscore.

The LIBNAME Statement: Examples

Windows

```
libname prog2 'c:\prog2';
```

UNIX

```
libname prog2 '/user/prog2';
```

z/OS (OS/390) Batch and TSO

```
libname prog2 'edu.prog2.sasdata' disp=shr;
```

85

Two-Level SAS Data Set Names

libref.SAS-filename

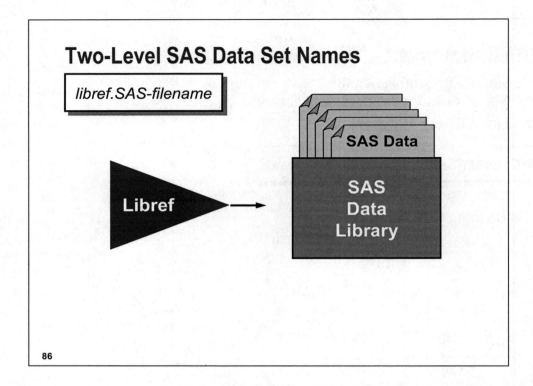

86

The WORK Library

The WORK library is the default library. If you do not specify a library reference on a SAS data set name, SAS assumes the libref is **work**.

work.fltat1 ⟷ fltat1

87

Accessing a Permanent SAS Data Set

There are two steps to accessing a permanent
SAS data set:

1. Use a LIBNAME statement to set up a libref
   that points to the location of the data set.

2. Reference the data set using the libref as the
   first part of the data set name.

If the libref is already assigned in the SAS session,
you do **not** need to assign it again.

88

Viewing a Permanent SAS Data Set
Windows

```
libname prog2 'c:\workshop\winsas\prog2';

proc print data=prog2.test noobs;
run;
```

89

Except for the name of the SAS data library, the SAS code does not change across operating systems.

Viewing a Permanent SAS Data Set

LName	Score
SMITH	0.90
JONES	0.57
MOORE	0.85
LEE	0.98
LONG	0.67
GREEN	0.70
FOREMAN	0.69

90

Viewing a Permanent SAS Data Set

UNIX

```
libname prog2 '/users/prog2';

proc print data=prog2.test noobs;
run;
```

91

Viewing a Permanent SAS Data Set

LName	Score
SMITH	0.90
JONES	0.57
MOORE	0.85
LEE	0.98
LONG	0.67
GREEN	0.70
FOREMAN	0.69

92

Viewing a Permanent SAS Data Set
z/OS (OS/390)

```
libname prog2 '.prog2.sasdata';

proc print data=prog2.test noobs;
run;
```

93

The period at the beginning of the z/OS[1] filename concatenates the user ID to the front.

Viewing a Permanent SAS Data Set

LName	Score
SMITH	0.90
JONES	0.57
MOORE	0.85
LEE	0.98
LONG	0.67
GREEN	0.70
FOREMAN	0.69

94

---

[1] *Any reference to z/OS applies to OS/390, unless otherwise noted.*

Creating a Permanent SAS Data Set

There are two steps when you create a permanent SAS data set:

1. Use a LIBNAME statement to set up a libref that points to the location you want to save to.
2. Use the libref as the first level of the SAS data set name.

If the libref is already assigned in the SAS session, you do **not** need to assign it again.

95

Creating a Permanent SAS Data Set

Windows

```
libname prog2 'c:\workshop\winsas\prog2';

data prog2.fltat1;
   infile 'fltat1.dat';
   input @1 EmpID $5.
         @7 HireDate date9.
         @17 Salary 5.;
   Bonus=.05*Salary;
run;
```

c01s5d1.sas

96

Creating a Permanent SAS Data Set

UNIX

```
libname prog2 '/users/prog2';

data prog2.fltat1;
   infile 'fltat1.dat';
   input @1 EmpID $5.
         @7 HireDate date9.
         @17 Salary 5.;
   Bonus=.05*Salary;
run;
```

97

Creating a Permanent SAS Data Set

z/OS (OS/390)

```
libname prog2 '.prog2.sasdata';

data prog2.fltat1;
   infile '.prog2.rawdata(fltat1)';
   input @1 EmpID $5.
         @7 HireDate date9.
         @17 Salary 5.;
   Bonus=.05*Salary;
run;
```

98

Create a SAS Data Set with SAS Data

LName	Score
SMITH	0.90
JONES	0.57
MOORE	0.85
LEE	0.98
LONG	0.67
GREEN	0.70
FOREMAN	0.69

The scores from a final exam are stored in the SAS data set **prog2.test**. The professor must assign each student a passing grade if the score is 0.7 or above and a failing grade otherwise. The variable **Score** should not appear in the output data set.

99

Desired Output

The data set **work.fnlgrades** should contain only the variables **LName** and **Grade**.

LName	Grade
SMITH	Pass
JONES	Failed
MOORE	Pass
LEE	Pass
LONG	Failed
GREEN	Pass
FOREMAN	Failed

100

The SET Statement

Use a SET statement to read a SAS data set.

General form of a SET statement:

```
SET SAS-data-set <options>;
```

The SET statement points to the SAS data set(s) to be read. Options in the SET statement affect how the data is read.

101

IF-THEN ELSE Statements

One method used to assign values or execute statements conditionally is IF-THEN ELSE statements.

```
IF condition THEN statement;
<ELSE IF condition THEN statement;>
   ...
<ELSE statement;>
```

102

The LENGTH Statement

When you create character variables with conditional logic or functions, it is usually a good idea to assign the lengths explicitly using a LENGTH statement.

General form of a LENGTH statement:

LENGTH *variable-name <$> length-specification ...;*

103

SAS sets the type and length the first time that a variable is referenced in the program. After SAS sets them, the attributes cannot be changed during the DATA step. When you use a LENGTH statement, be certain that it is the first statement to reference the variable.

The DROP Statement

To drop variables that are read or created during the DATA step, use a DROP statement.

General form of a DROP statement:

> **DROP** *SAS-variable(s)*;

Variables dropped with a DROP statement are read into the PDV but are not output to the new SAS data set. They are available for processing during the DATA step.

104

A KEEP statement is also valid for selecting variables to output to a SAS data set:

> **KEEP** *SAS-variable(s)*;

Creating a Variable with Conditional Logic

```
data fnlgrades;
   length Grade $ 6;
   drop Score;
   set prog2.test;
   if Score>=.7 then Grade='Pass';
   else Grade='Failed';
run;
```

105

Compiling the DATA Step

```
data fnlgrades;
  length Grade $ 6;
  drop Score;
  set prog2.test;
  if Score>=.7 then Grade='Pass';
  else Grade='Failed';
run;
```

PDV

Grade
$ 6

106   ...

Compiling the DATA Step

```
data fnlgrades;
  length Grade $ 6;
  drop Score;
  set prog2.test;
  if Score>=.7 then Grade='Pass';
  else Grade='Failed';
run;
```

PDV

Grade	LName	Score
$ 6	$ 8	N 8

107   ...

Compiling the DATA Step

```
data fnlgrades;
  length Grade $ 6;
  drop Score;
  set prog2.test;
  if Score>=.7 then Grade='Pass';
  else Grade='Failed';
run;
```

PDV

Grade $ 6	LName $ 8	D Score N 8

108   ...

Compiling the DATA Step

```
data fnlgrades;
  length Grade $ 6;
  drop Score;
  set prog2.test;
  if Score>=.7 then Grade='Pass';
  else Grade='Failed';
run;
```

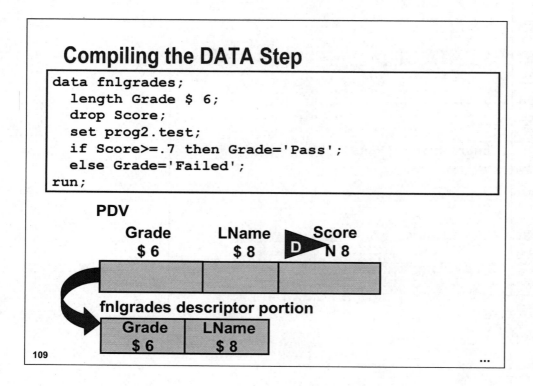

PDV

Grade $ 6   LName $ 8   D Score N 8

fnlgrades descriptor portion

Grade $ 6	LName $ 8

109   ...

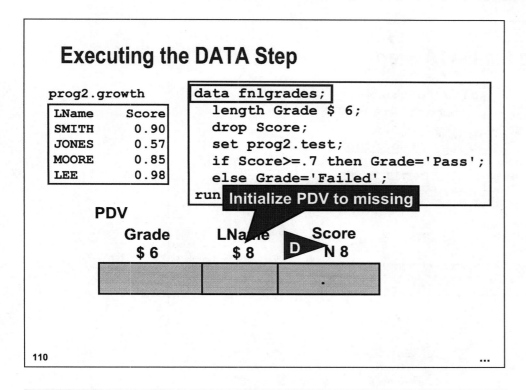

Executing the DATA Step

prog2.growth

LName	Score
SMITH	0.90
JONES	0.57
MOORE	0.85
LEE	0.98

```
data fnlgrades;
   length Grade $ 6;
   drop Score;
   set prog2.test;
   if Score>=.7 then Grade='Pass';
   else Grade='Failed';
run;
```

Initialize PDV to missing

PDV

Grade $ 6	LName $ 8	D Score N 8
		.

110

...

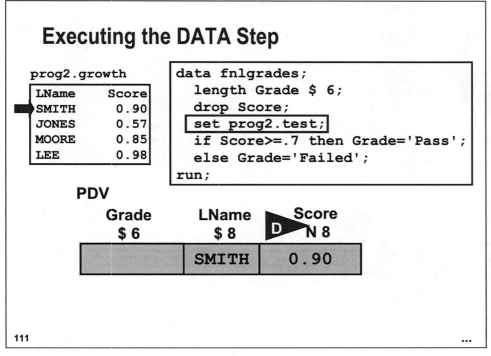

Executing the DATA Step

prog2.growth

LName	Score
SMITH	0.90
JONES	0.57
MOORE	0.85
LEE	0.98

```
data fnlgrades;
   length Grade $ 6;
   drop Score;
   set prog2.test;
   if Score>=.7 then Grade='Pass';
   else Grade='Failed';
run;
```

PDV

Grade $ 6	LName $ 8	D Score N 8
	SMITH	0.90

111

...

Executing the DATA Step

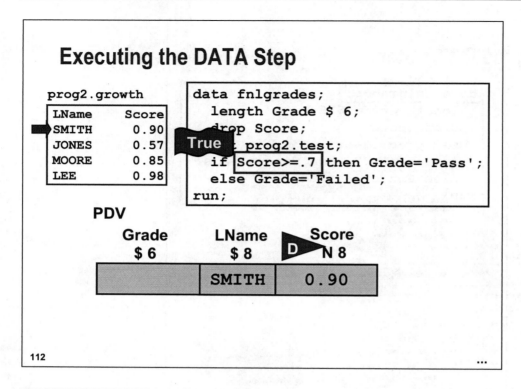

```
data fnlgrades;
   length Grade $ 6;
   drop Score;
   set prog2.test;
   if Score>=.7 then Grade='Pass';
   else Grade='Failed';
run;
```

112   ...

Executing the DATA Step

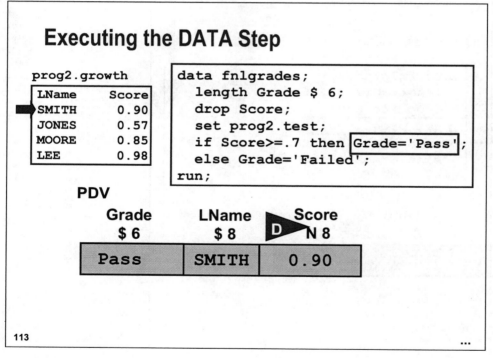

```
data fnlgrades;
   length Grade $ 6;
   drop Score;
   set prog2.test;
   if Score>=.7 then Grade='Pass';
   else Grade='Failed';
run;
```

113   ...

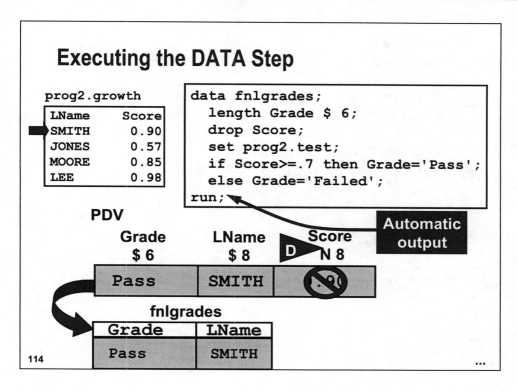

Executing the DATA Step

prog2.growth

LName	Score
SMITH	0.90
JONES	0.57
MOORE	0.85
LEE	0.98

```
data fnlgrades;
   length Grade $ 6;
   drop Score;
   set prog2.test;
   if Score>=.7 then Grade='Pass';
   else Grade='Failed';
run;
```

Automatic output

PDV

Grade $ 6	LName $ 8	D Score N 8
Pass	SMITH	

fnlgrades

Grade	LName
Pass	SMITH

114   ...

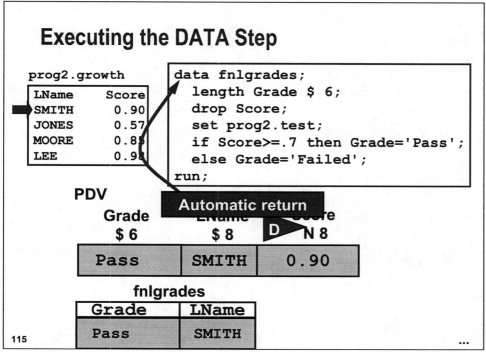

Executing the DATA Step

prog2.growth

LName	Score
SMITH	0.90
JONES	0.57
MOORE	0.85
LEE	0.98

```
data fnlgrades;
   length Grade $ 6;
   drop Score;
   set prog2.test;
   if Score>=.7 then Grade='Pass';
   else Grade='Failed';
run;
```

PDV

Automatic return

Grade $ 6	LName $ 8	D Score N 8
Pass	SMITH	0.90

fnlgrades

Grade	LName
Pass	SMITH

115   ...

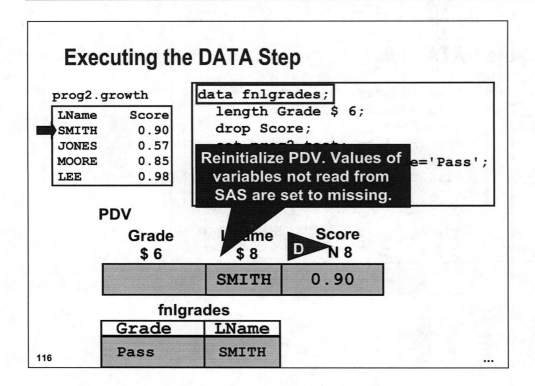

Executing the DATA Step

prog2.growth

LName	Score
➤ SMITH	0.90
JONES	0.57
MOORE	0.85
LEE	0.98

```
data fnlgrades;
  length Grade $ 6;
  drop Score;
  set prog2.test;
                        e='Pass';
```

> Reinitialize PDV. Values of variables not read from SAS are set to missing.

PDV

Grade $ 6	LName $ 8	D ▷ Score N 8
	SMITH	0.90

fnlgrades

Grade	LName
Pass	SMITH

116   ...

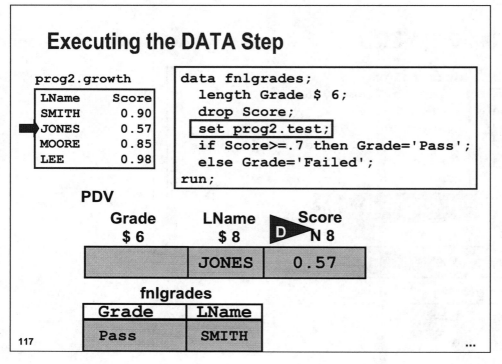

Executing the DATA Step

prog2.growth

LName	Score
SMITH	0.90
➤ JONES	0.57
MOORE	0.85
LEE	0.98

```
data fnlgrades;
  length Grade $ 6;
  drop Score;
  set prog2.test;
  if Score>=.7 then Grade='Pass';
  else Grade='Failed';
run;
```

PDV

Grade $ 6	LName $ 8	D ▷ Score N 8
	JONES	0.57

fnlgrades

Grade	LName
Pass	SMITH

117   ...

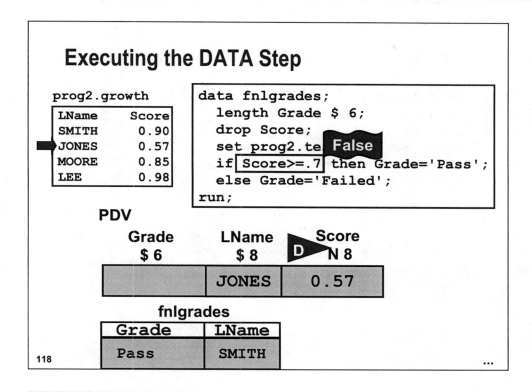

Executing the DATA Step

```
prog2.growth
```

LName	Score
SMITH	0.90
➤ JONES	0.57
MOORE	0.85
LEE	0.98

```
data fnlgrades;
  length Grade $ 6;
  drop Score;
  set prog2.te  False
  if Score>=.7 then Grade='Pass';
  else Grade='Failed';
run;
```

PDV

Grade $ 6	LName $ 8	Score N 8
	JONES	0.57

fnlgrades

Grade	LName
Pass	SMITH

118   ...

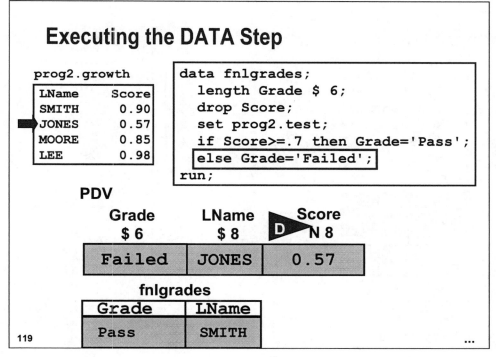

Executing the DATA Step

```
prog2.growth
```

LName	Score
SMITH	0.90
➤ JONES	0.57
MOORE	0.85
LEE	0.98

```
data fnlgrades;
  length Grade $ 6;
  drop Score;
  set prog2.test;
  if Score>=.7 then Grade='Pass';
  else Grade='Failed';
run;
```

PDV

Grade $ 6	LName $ 8	Score N 8
Failed	JONES	0.57

fnlgrades

Grade	LName
Pass	SMITH

119   ...

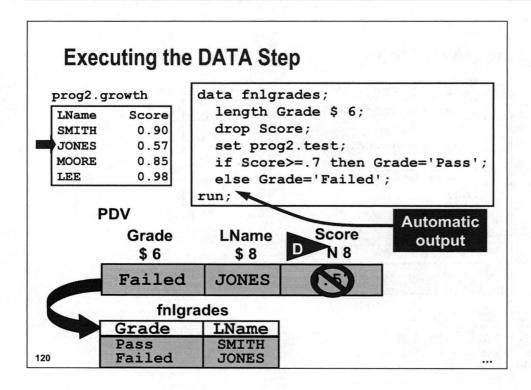

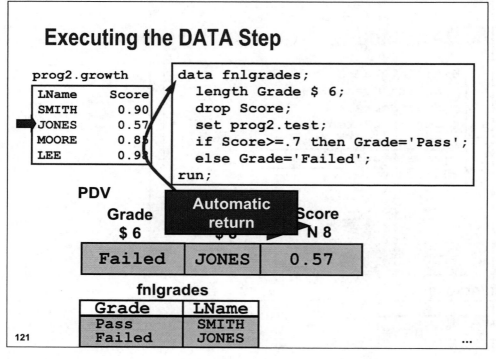

Executing the DATA Step

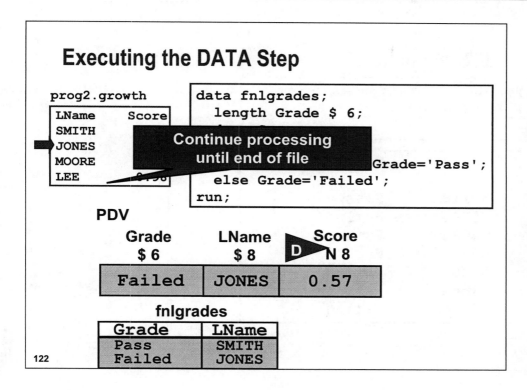

`prog2.growth`

LName	Score
SMITH	
JONES	
MOORE	
LEE	

```
data fnlgrades;
   length Grade $ 6;
```
Continue processing
until end of file
```
                           Grade='Pass';
   else Grade='Failed';
run;
```

PDV

Grade $ 6	LName $ 8	Score N 8
Failed	JONES	0.57

fnlgrades

Grade	LName
Pass	SMITH
Failed	JONES

122

Creating a Variable with Conditional Logic

```
proc print data=fnlgrades noobs;
run;
```

Grade	LName
Pass	SMITH
Failed	JONES
Pass	MOORE
Pass	LEE
Failed	LONG
Pass	GREEN
Failed	FOREMAN

123

Using the VAR Statement

```
proc print data=fnlgrades noobs;
   var LName Grade;
run;
```

LName	Grade
SMITH	Pass
JONES	Failed
MOORE	Pass
LEE	Pass
LONG	Failed
GREEN	Pass
FOREMAN	Failed

c01s5d2.sas

124

1.6 Prerequisite Syntax (Self-Study)

The following is a syntax guide to statements and procedures you should know before you start this class.

Statements Valid Only in a DATA Step

To start the DATA step and name the data set being created:

> **DATA** *SAS-data set*;

To use a raw data file as input:

> **INFILE** '*raw-data-file*' *<options>*;

and

> **INPUT** *variable-specifications*;

To use a SAS data set as input:

> **SET** *SAS-data-set <options>*;

To create a new variable (assignment statement):

> *variable-name=expression*;

To perform conditional processing:

> **IF** *condition* **THEN** *statement*;
> *<***ELSE IF** *condition* **THEN** *statement;>*
>   ...
> *<***ELSE** *statement;>*

DATA Step Compile-Time-Only Statements

To explicitly set the length of a variable:

> **LENGTH** *variable-name <$> length-specification* ...;

To drop a variable or variables on output:

> **DROP** *SAS variable(s) to be dropped*;

or

> **KEEP** *SAS variable(s) to be kept*;

Procedures

To display the descriptor portion of a SAS data set:

> **PROC CONTENTS** DATA=*SAS-data-set*;
> **RUN**;

To create a list report of a SAS data set:

> **PROC PRINT** DATA=*SAS-data-set* <NOOBS>;
> **RUN**;

To control which variables are shown in the PROC PRINT and their order:

> **VAR** *SAS-variable(s)*;

Statements Valid in a Procedure or DATA Step

To apply a format to a variable or variables:

> **FORMAT** *variable-name format. …*;

General form of a format name:

> <$>*FORMAT-NAMEw.<d>*;

where

$ indicates a character format.

FORMAT-NAME   is the name of the format.

w   specifies the total characters available for displaying the value.

.   is the required delimiter.

d   specifies the number of decimal places to be displayed for a numeric value.

Common Numeric Formats

COMMA*w.d*   adds commas to the value.

DOLLAR*w.d*   adds dollar signs and commas to the value.

MMDDYY10.   displays SAS dates in the form 12/31/2012.

DATE9.   displays SAS dates in the form 31DEC2012.

Global Statements

To assign a library reference to a SAS data library:

> **LIBNAME** *libref* '*operating-system-location*';

To assign a header to SAS output:

> **TITLE***n* '*header*';

You can specify up to ten titles. TITLE is equivalent to TITLE1.

When a title is set, it stays in effect until it is changed or canceled, or until the SAS session ends.

1.7   Navigating the SAS Windowing Environment (Self-Study)

These instructions are intended for students navigating the SAS windowing environment on SAS classroom machines. They might not be appropriate for all sites.

Navigating the SAS Windowing Environment on Windows

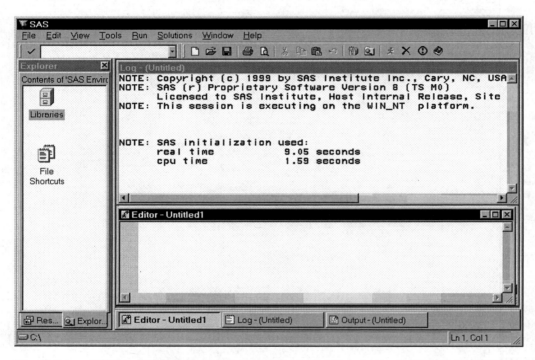

The Enhanced Editor (the default editor on Windows) is only available on the Windows operating system. Unlike the Program Editor, it does not automatically clear when code is submitted, and you can have multiple Enhanced Editor windows open simultaneously. You can use the Program Editor (the default editor in SAS Version 6 and earlier) by selecting **View** ⇨ **Program Editor**.

Navigating the Windows

To navigate to any window, do one of the following:

- Select the window button at the bottom of the screen (if the window is open).
- Select the window name from the View drop-down menu.
- Type the name of the window in the command bar and press the ENTER key.

To close any window, do one of the following:

- Select ☒ in the upper-right corner of the window.
- Type **end** in the command bar, and press the ENTER key.

Opening a SAS Program

To open a SAS program, the Program Editor or the Enhanced Editor must be the active window.

1. Select **File** ⇨ **Open** or select 🖿 . A Windows dialog box appears.

2. Navigate through the folders and highlight the program.

3. Select **OK**.

Submitting a SAS Program

To submit a program, the Program Editor or the Enhanced Editor must be the active window, and the code to be submitted must be in the window.

1. Highlight the code you want to submit. (This is not necessary if you submit the entire contents of the window.)

2. Issue the SUBMIT command by selecting 🏃 , pressing the F3 key, or selecting **Run** ⇨ **Submit**.

Recalling Submitted Code

The Program Editor is cleared automatically every time code is submitted from it. To recall submitted code, make the Program Editor the active window, and do one of the following:

*   Select **Run** ⇨ **Recall**.
*   Type **recall** in the command bar, and press the ENTER key.
*   Use the F4 shortcut key.

🖉   The RECALL command can also be used from the Enhanced Editor to retrieve lost code that was submitted.

Saving a SAS Program

To save a SAS program, the Program Editor or the Enhanced Editor must be the active window, and the code you want to save must be in the window.

1. Select **File** ⇨ **Save As...**. A Windows dialog box appears.

2. Navigate to the folder in which you want to save the program.

3. Type a name for the program in the appropriate box.

4. Select **OK**.

Clearing Windows

To clear a window, do one of the following:

*   Activate the window, type **clear** in the command bar, and press the ENTER key.
*   Activate the window and select **Edit** ⇨ **Clear All**.
*   Type **clear** and the name of the window in the command bar and press the ENTER key.

Issuing Multiple Commands at Once

To issue more than one command at the same time, type the commands in the command bar separated by semicolons.

For example, to clear both the Log and Output windows, type the following in the command bar:

```
clear log; clear output
```

Navigating the SAS Windowing Environment on UNIX

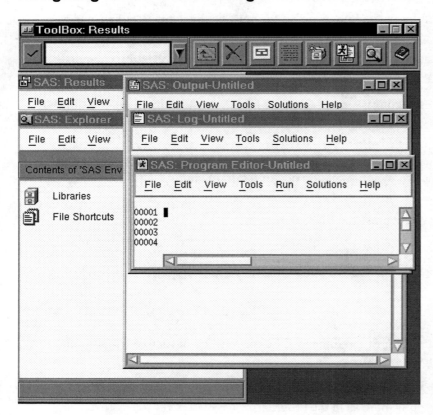

In the UNIX environment, SAS windows are floating, not docked. There is a floating toolbar with a command bar and shortcut icons. Drop-down menus are at the top of each window.

Navigating the Windows

To activate any window, do one of the following:
- Select the window icon at the bottom of the screen.
- Select the window name from the View drop-down menu.
- Type the window name in the command bar, and press the ENTER key.

Submitting a Program

To submit a SAS program, the Program Editor must be the active window and contain the code you want to submit. Do any of the following to submit the contents of the Program Editor:

- Type **submit** in the command bar, and press the ENTER key.
- Use the F3 shortcut key.
- Select [🏃] from the toolbar.
- Select **Run** ⇨ **Submit**.

Recalling Submitted Code

The Program Editor is cleared automatically every time code is submitted from it. To recall submitted code, make the Program Editor the active window, and do one of the following:

- Select **Run** ⇨ **Recall**.
- Type **recall** in the command bar, and press the ENTER key.
- Use the F4 shortcut key.

Saving a SAS Program

To save a SAS program, the Program Editor must be the active window, and the code you want to save must be in the window.

1. Select **File** ⇨ **Save As...**. A dialog box appears.

2. Navigate to the directory in which you want to save the program.

3. Type a name for the program in the appropriate box.

4. Select **OK**.

Clearing Windows

To clear a window, do one of the following:

- Activate the window, type **clear** in the command bar, and press the ENTER key.
- Activate the window and select **Edit** ⇨ **Clear All**.
- Type **clear** and the name of the window at the command bar, and press the ENTER key.

Issuing Multiple Commands at Once

To submit more than one command at the same time, type the commands, separated by semicolons, in the command bar and press the ENTER key.

For example, to clear both the Log and Output windows, type the following in the command bar:

```
clear log; clear output
```

Navigating the SAS Windowing Environment on z/OS

Each time you log on,

1. open the Output window by typing **output** on any command line and pressing the ENTER key.

2. issue the following command from the command line of the Output window. (This prevents suspended output.)

    autoscroll 0

Navigating the Windows

- Each window contains a command line.
- You can open any window by typing its name on any command line and pressing the ENTER key.
- The PageUp and PageDown keys on your keyboard move from one open window to another.
- F7 and F8 enable you to scroll up and down within a window.
- To close any window and return to the Program Editor, issue the END command or use the F3 key. If the Program Editor is active, the F3 key submits the code in the window.
- To maximize a window, type **Z** on the command line and press the ENTER key. To restore the window to normal size, type **Z** on the command line of the maximized window and press the ENTER key.

Including a SAS Program

To include a SAS program in your session, the Program Editor must be the active window.

1. Type **include '*name-of-SAS-program*'** on the command line of the Program Editor window.

2. Press the ENTER key.

Submitting a Program

To submit a SAS program, the Program Editor must be the active window and contain the code you want to submit. To submit code, do one of the following:

- Type **submit** in the command line of the Program Editor, and press the ENTER key.
- Use the F3 shortcut key.

Recalling Submitted Code

The Program Editor is cleared automatically every time code is submitted from it. To recall submitted code, make the Program Editor the active window and do one of the following:

- Type **recall** in the command line of the Program Editor, and press the ENTER key.
- Use the F4 shortcut key.

Saving a SAS Program

To save a SAS program, the Program Editor must be the active window and contain the code you want to save.

1. Type **file '*name-of-SAS-program*'** on the command line of the Program Editor window.

2. Press the ENTER key. A note appears at the top of the window.

Clearing Windows

To clear a window, do one of the following:

- Type **clear** on the command line of that window and press the ENTER key.

- Type **clear** and the name of the window to be cleared on any command line and press the ENTER key.

Editing SAS Program Code in the UNIX and z/OS Environments

Program Editor Line Number Commands

Most Windows users utilize copy and paste commands. However, the Program Editor in all three environments allows the use of line number commands. Use these commands to copy, paste, or delete program code.

I	inserts one line (after) the current line.
I*n*	inserts *n* lines (after) the current line.
IB	inserts one line (before) the current line.
IB*n*	inserts *n* lines (before) the current line.

D	deletes the current line.
D*n*	deletes *n* lines.
DD	deletes a block of lines. Type **dd** on the first and last lines of the block.

R	repeats the current line once.
R*n*	repeats the current line *n* times.
RR	repeats a block of lines once. Type **rr** on the first and last lines of the block.

Moving and Copying Code

To copy or move one line of code, do the following:

1. Type **c** (to copy) or **m** (to move) the line you want to copy or move.

2. Type **a** (for after) or **b** (for before) on the appropriate line to indicate where you want to copy or move the specified line.

To copy or move a block of lines of code, do the following:

1. Type **cc** or **mm** on the first line you want to copy or move.

2. Type **cc** or **mm** on the last line you want to copy or move.

3. Type **a** (for after) or **b** (for before) on the appropriate line to indicate where you want to copy or move the block of lines.

✎   Line number commands are not available in the Windows Enhanced Editor.

Chapter 2   Controlling Input and Output

2.1 Outputting Multiple Observations

Objectives

- Explicitly control the output of multiple observations to a SAS data set.

3

A Forecasting Application

The growth rate of each division of an airline is forecast in **prog2.growth**. If each of the five divisions grows at its respective rate for the next three years, what will be the approximate size of each division at the end of each of the three years?

Partial Listing of **prog2.growth**

Division	Num Emps	Increase
APTOPS	205	0.075
FINACE	198	0.040
FLTOPS	187	0.080

4

A Forecasting Application

The output SAS data set, **forecast**, should contain 15 observations.

Partial Listing of **forecast**

Division	Increase	Year	New Total
APTOPS	0.075	1	220.38
APTOPS	0.075	2	236.90
APTOPS	0.075	3	254.67
FINACE	0.040	1	205.92
FINACE	0.040	2	214.16

5

Automatic Output (Review)

By default, every DATA step contains an automatic OUTPUT statement at the end of each iteration. This automatic OUTPUT statement tells the SAS System to write observations to the data set or data sets that are created.

2. Automatic return

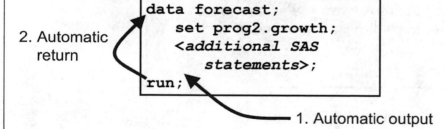

```
data forecast;
    set prog2.growth;
    <additional SAS
        statements>;
run;
```

1. Automatic output

6

The OUTPUT Statement

The explicit OUTPUT statement writes the current contents of the PDV to a SAS data set.

Placing an explicit OUTPUT statement in a DATA step overrides the automatic output, and SAS adds an observation to a data set only when an explicit OUTPUT statement is executed.

> **OUTPUT** <*SAS-data-set-1 ...SAS-data-set-n*>;

`7

Using an explicit OUTPUT statement without arguments causes the current observation to be written to all data sets that are named in the DATA statement.

     Implicit return to the beginning of the DATA step occurs after the bottom of the step is reached; not when an explicit OUTPUT statement is executed.

A Forecasting Application

```
data forecast;
   drop NumEmps;
   set prog2.growth;
   Year=1;
   NewTotal=NumEmps*(1+Increase);
   output;
   Year=2;
   NewTotal=NewTotal*(1+Increase);
   output;
   Year=3;
   NewTotal=NewTotal*(1+Increase);
   output;
run;
```

8
c02s1d1.sas

In years two and three, the existing value of **NewTotal** is used to calculate the new value of **NewTotal**.

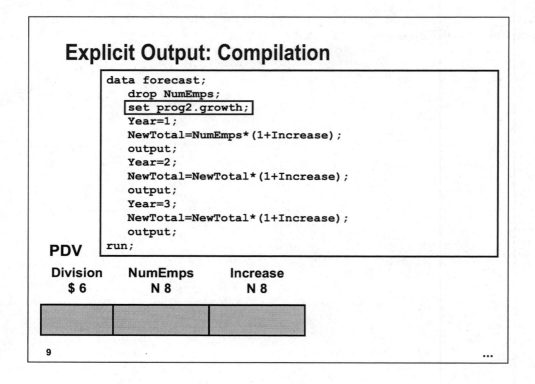

Explicit Output: Compilation

```
data forecast;
   drop NumEmps;
   set prog2.growth;
   Year=1;
   NewTotal=NumEmps*(1+Increase);
   output;
   Year=2;
   NewTotal=NewTotal*(1+Increase);
   output;
   Year=3;
   NewTotal=NewTotal*(1+Increase);
   output;
run;
```

PDV

Division	NumEmps	Increase
$ 6	N 8	N 8

9
...

Explicit Output: Compilation

```
data forecast;
   drop NumEmps;
   set prog2.growth;
   Year=1;
   NewTotal=NumEmps*(1+Increase);
   output;
   Year=2;
   NewTotal=NewTotal*(1+Increase);
   output;
   Year=3;
   NewTotal=NewTotal*(1+Increase);
   output;
run;
```

PDV

Division $ 6	NumEmps N 8	Increase N 8	Year N 8

10   ...

Explicit Output: Compilation

```
data forecast;
   drop NumEmps;
   set prog2.growth;
   Year=1;
   NewTotal=NumEmps*(1+Increase);
   output;
   Year=2;
   NewTotal=NewTotal*(1+Increase);
   output;
   Year=3;
   NewTotal=NewTotal*(1+Increase);
   output;
run;
```

PDV

Division $ 6	NumEmps N 8	Increase N 8	Year N 8	NewTotal N 8

11   ...

Explicit Output: Compilation

```
data forecast;
   drop NumEmps;
   set prog2.growth;
   Year=1;
   NewTotal=NumEmps*(1+Increase);
   output;
   Year=2;
   NewTotal=NewTotal*(1+Increase);
   output;
   Year=3;
   NewTotal=NewTotal*(1+Increase);
   output;
run;
```

PDV

Division $ 6	NumEmps D N 8	Increase N 8	Year N 8	NewTotal N 8

12   ...

Explicit Output: Execution

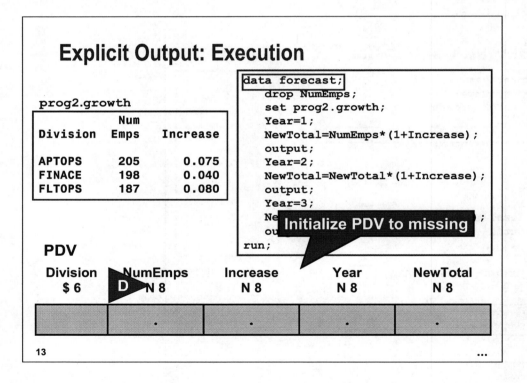

prog2.growth

Division	Num Emps	Increase
APTOPS	205	0.075
FINACE	198	0.040
FLTOPS	187	0.080

```
data forecast;
   drop NumEmps;
   set prog2.growth;
   Year=1;
   NewTotal=NumEmps*(1+Increase);
   output;
   Year=2;
   NewTotal=NewTotal*(1+Increase);
   output;
   Year=3;
   Ne                              ;
   ou
run;
```

Initialize PDV to missing

PDV

Division $ 6	NumEmps D N 8	Increase N 8	Year N 8	NewTotal N 8
	.	.	.	.

13   ...

Explicit Output: Execution

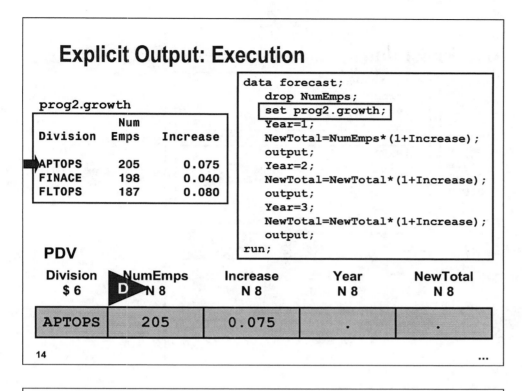

prog2.growth

Division	Num Emps	Increase
APTOPS	205	0.075
FINACE	198	0.040
FLTOPS	187	0.080

```
data forecast;
   drop NumEmps;
   set prog2.growth;
   Year=1;
   NewTotal=NumEmps*(1+Increase);
   output;
   Year=2;
   NewTotal=NewTotal*(1+Increase);
   output;
   Year=3;
   NewTotal=NewTotal*(1+Increase);
   output;
run;
```

PDV

Division $ 6	NumEmps N 8	Increase N 8	Year N 8	NewTotal N 8
APTOPS	205	0.075	.	.

14   ...

Explicit Output: Execution

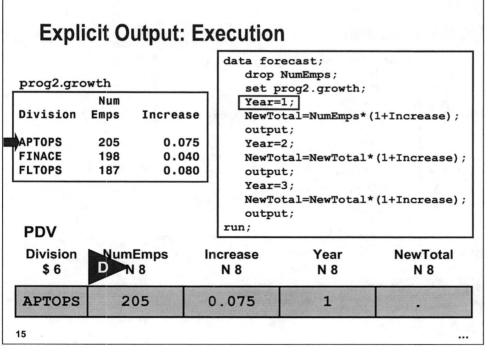

prog2.growth

Division	Num Emps	Increase
APTOPS	205	0.075
FINACE	198	0.040
FLTOPS	187	0.080

```
data forecast;
   drop NumEmps;
   set prog2.growth;
   Year=1;
   NewTotal=NumEmps*(1+Increase);
   output;
   Year=2;
   NewTotal=NewTotal*(1+Increase);
   output;
   Year=3;
   NewTotal=NewTotal*(1+Increase);
   output;
run;
```

PDV

Division $ 6	NumEmps N 8	Increase N 8	Year N 8	NewTotal N 8
APTOPS	205	0.075	1	.

15   ...

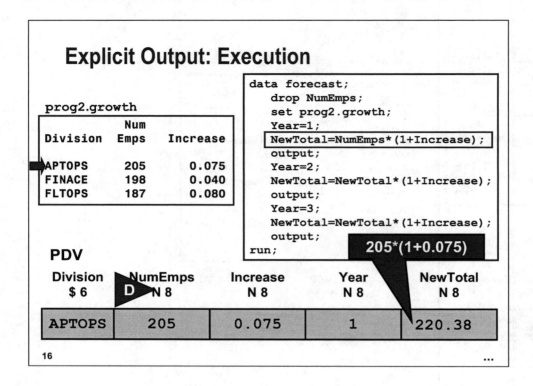

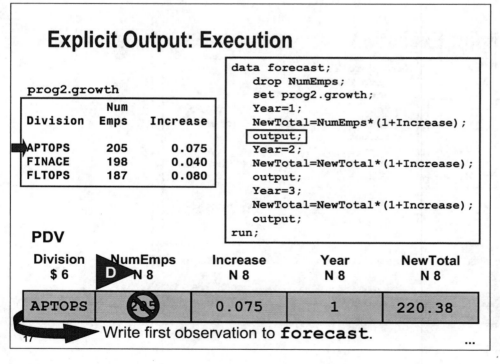

Explicit Output: Execution

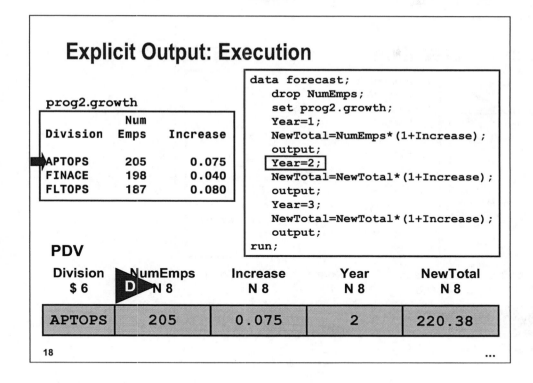

prog2.growth

Division	Num Emps	Increase
APTOPS	205	0.075
FINACE	198	0.040
FLTOPS	187	0.080

```
data forecast;
   drop NumEmps;
   set prog2.growth;
   Year=1;
   NewTotal=NumEmps*(1+Increase);
   output;
   Year=2;
   NewTotal=NewTotal*(1+Increase);
   output;
   Year=3;
   NewTotal=NewTotal*(1+Increase);
   output;
run;
```

PDV

Division $ 6	NumEmps N 8	Increase N 8	Year N 8	NewTotal N 8
APTOPS	205	0.075	2	220.38

18   ...

Explicit Output: Execution

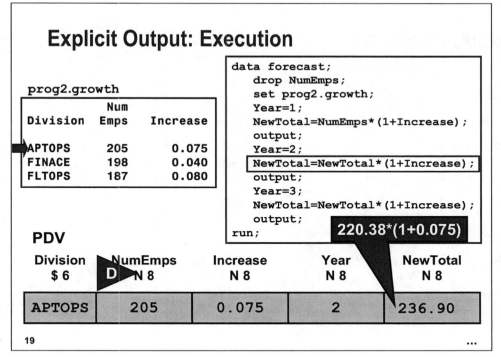

prog2.growth

Division	Num Emps	Increase
APTOPS	205	0.075
FINACE	198	0.040
FLTOPS	187	0.080

```
data forecast;
   drop NumEmps;
   set prog2.growth;
   Year=1;
   NewTotal=NumEmps*(1+Increase);
   output;
   Year=2;
   NewTotal=NewTotal*(1+Increase);
   output;
   Year=3;
   NewTotal=NewTotal*(1+Increase);
   output;
run;
```

220.38*(1+0.075)

PDV

Division $ 6	NumEmps N 8	Increase N 8	Year N 8	NewTotal N 8
APTOPS	205	0.075	2	236.90

19   ...

Explicit Output: Execution

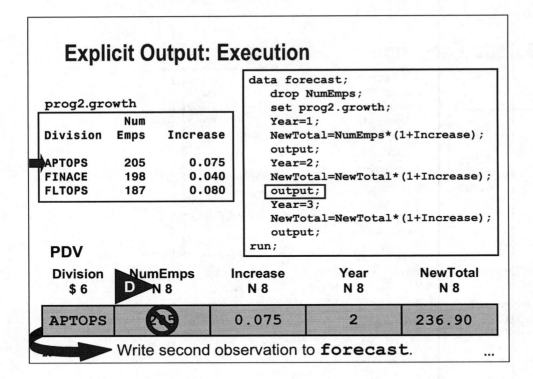

prog2.growth

Division	Num Emps	Increase
APTOPS	205	0.075
FINACE	198	0.040
FLTOPS	187	0.080

```
data forecast;
   drop NumEmps;
   set prog2.growth;
   Year=1;
   NewTotal=NumEmps*(1+Increase);
   output;
   Year=2;
   NewTotal=NewTotal*(1+Increase);
   output;
   Year=3;
   NewTotal=NewTotal*(1+Increase);
   output;
run;
```

PDV

Division $ 6	NumEmps N 8	Increase N 8	Year N 8	NewTotal N 8
APTOPS	205	0.075	2	236.90

Write second observation to **forecast**.   ...

Explicit Output: Execution

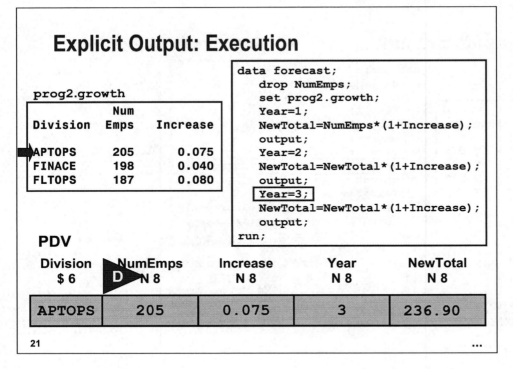

prog2.growth

Division	Num Emps	Increase
APTOPS	205	0.075
FINACE	198	0.040
FLTOPS	187	0.080

```
data forecast;
   drop NumEmps;
   set prog2.growth;
   Year=1;
   NewTotal=NumEmps*(1+Increase);
   output;
   Year=2;
   NewTotal=NewTotal*(1+Increase);
   output;
   Year=3;
   NewTotal=NewTotal*(1+Increase);
   output;
run;
```

PDV

Division $ 6	NumEmps N 8	Increase N 8	Year N 8	NewTotal N 8
APTOPS	205	0.075	3	236.90

21   ...

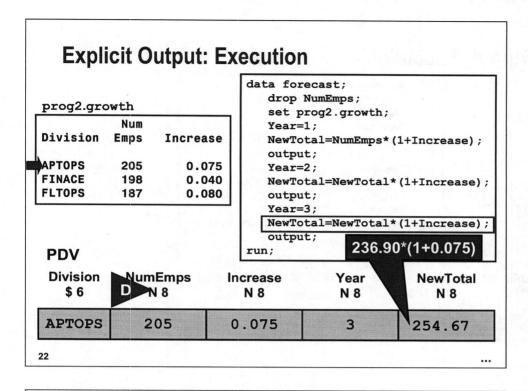

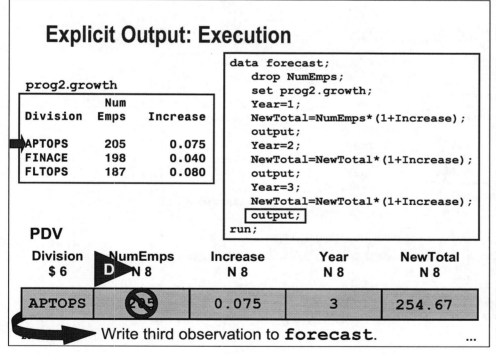

Explicit Output: Execution

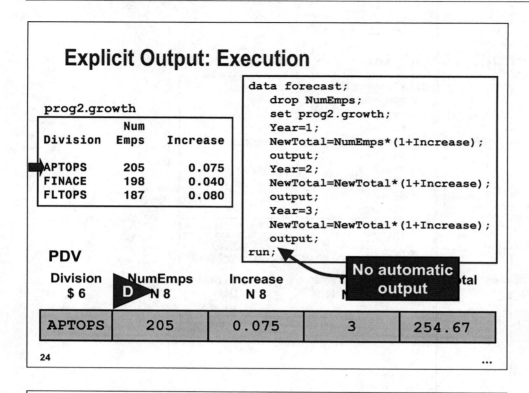

prog2.growth

Division	Num Emps	Increase
APTOPS	205	0.075
FINACE	198	0.040
FLTOPS	187	0.080

```
data forecast;
   drop NumEmps;
   set prog2.growth;
   Year=1;
   NewTotal=NumEmps*(1+Increase);
   output;
   Year=2;
   NewTotal=NewTotal*(1+Increase);
   output;
   Year=3;
   NewTotal=NewTotal*(1+Increase);
   output;
run;
```

No automatic output

PDV

Division $ 6	NumEmps D N 8	Increase N 8	N	tal
APTOPS	205	0.075	3	254.67

24   ...

Explicit Output: Execution

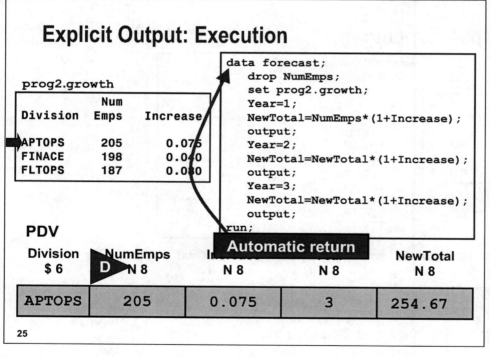

prog2.growth

Division	Num Emps	Increase
APTOPS	205	0.075
FINACE	198	0.040
FLTOPS	187	0.080

```
data forecast;
   drop NumEmps;
   set prog2.growth;
   Year=1;
   NewTotal=NumEmps*(1+Increase);
   output;
   Year=2;
   NewTotal=NewTotal*(1+Increase);
   output;
   Year=3;
   NewTotal=NewTotal*(1+Increase);
   output;
run;
```

Automatic return

PDV

Division $ 6	NumEmps D N 8	Increase N 8	Year N 8	NewTotal N 8
APTOPS	205	0.075	3	254.67

25

Explicit Output: Execution

Contents of the FORECAST data set after the first execution of the DATA step:

```
Division   Increase   Year   NewTotal

APTOPS       0.075      1      220.38
APTOPS       0.075      2      236.90
APTOPS       0.075      3      254.67
```

26

Explicit Output: Execution

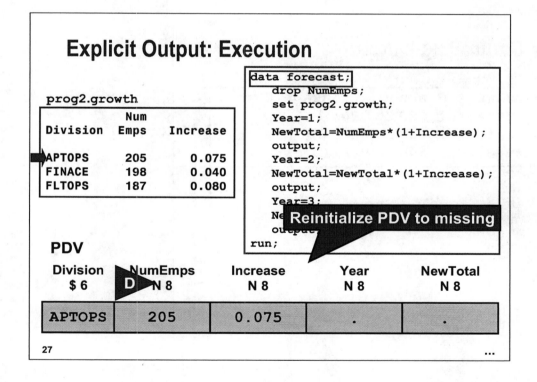

prog2.growth

Division	Num Emps	Increase
APTOPS	205	0.075
FINACE	198	0.040
FLTOPS	187	0.080

```
data forecast;
    drop NumEmps;
    set prog2.growth;
    Year=1;
    NewTotal=NumEmps*(1+Increase);
    output;
    Year=2;
    NewTotal=NewTotal*(1+Increase);
    output;
    Year=3;
    Ne
    ou
run;
```

Reinitialize PDV to missing

PDV

Division $ 6	NumEmps N 8	Increase N 8	Year N 8	NewTotal N 8
APTOPS	205	0.075	.	.

27   ...

Explicit Output: Execution

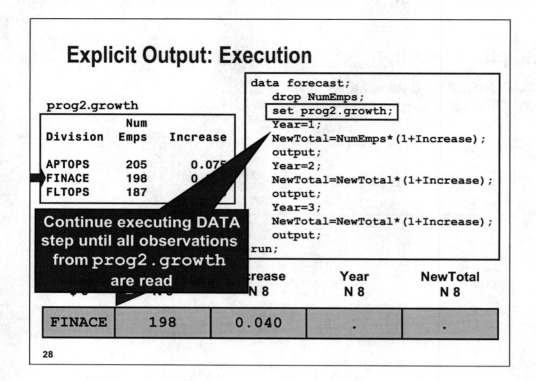

prog2.growth

Division	Num Emps	Increase
APTOPS	205	0.075
FINACE	198	0
FLTOPS	187	

```
data forecast;
   drop NumEmps;
   set prog2.growth;
   Year=1;
   NewTotal=NumEmps*(1+Increase);
   output;
   Year=2;
   NewTotal=NewTotal*(1+Increase);
   output;
   Year=3;
   NewTotal=NewTotal*(1+Increase);
   output;
run;
```

Continue executing DATA step until all observations from `prog2.growth` are read

	crease N 8	Year N 8	NewTotal N 8
FINACE	198	0.040	.	.

28

Explicitly Controlling Output

Partial Log

```
NOTE: There were 5 observations read from
      the data set PROG2.GROWTH.
NOTE: The data set WORK.FORECAST has 15
      observations and 4 variables.
```

29

Explicitly Controlling Output

```
proc print data=forecast noobs;
    format NewTotal 6.;
run;
```

Partial PROC PRINT Output

Division	Increase	Year	New Total
APTOPS	0.075	1	220
APTOPS	0.075	2	237
APTOPS	0.075	3	255
FINACE	0.040	1	206
FINACE	0.040	2	214

30

Exercises

These exercises use SAS data sets stored in a permanent SAS data library.

Fill in the blank with the location of your SAS data library. Submit the LIBNAME statement to assign the libref PROG2 to the SAS data library.

```
libname prog2 '_____';
```

1. Outputting Multiple Observations

Rotating, or transposing, a SAS data set can be accomplished by using explicit OUTPUT statements in a DATA step. When a data set is rotated, the values of an observation in the input data set become values of a variable in the output data set.

Use explicit OUTPUT statements to rotate **prog2.donate** into a data set called **rotate**. Create four output observations in **rotate** from each input observation in **prog2.donate**.

The **rotate** data set should have three variables: **ID**, **Qtr**, and **Amount**. Print the data set to verify your results.

Partial Listing of **prog2.donate**

ID	Qtr1	Qtr2	Qtr3	Qtr4
E00224	12	33	22	.
E00367	35	48	40	30
E00441	.	63	89	90
E00587	16	19	30	29
E00598	4	8	6	1

Partial Listing of **rotate**

Obs	ID	Qtr	Amount
1	E00224	1	12
2	E00224	2	33
3	E00224	3	22
4	E00224	4	.
5	E00367	1	35
6	E00367	2	48
7	E00367	3	40
8	E00367	4	30
9	E00441	1	.
10	E00441	2	63
11	E00441	3	89
12	E00441	4	90

2. **Using Conditional Logic to Output Multiple Observations (Optional)**

The **prog2.ffmethod** data set contains information about the different ways that frequent flyers purchased airline tickets. A value of Y in the **Internet**, **Telephone**, or **TravelAgency** variable indicates that the frequent flyer used that method.

prog2.ffmethod

| | | | Travel |
ID	Internet	Telephone	Agency
F31351	N	Y	Y
F161	Y	Y	N
F212	N	N	Y
F25122	Y	N	N

Use explicit OUTPUT statements to create a data set called **buyhistory**. This data set will contain one observation for each method used by each frequent flyer. There will be two observations in **buyhistory** that refer to F31351, but only one observation that refers to F212.

The **buyhistory** data set should have two variables: **ID** and **Method**. Print the data set to verify your results.

buyhistory

Obs	ID	Method
1	F31351	Telephone
2	F31351	Travel Agency
3	F161	Internet
4	F161	Telephone
5	F212	Travel Agency
6	F25122	Internet

 A DO statement can be used within IF-THEN/ELSE statements to designate a group of statements to be executed, depending on whether the IF condition is true or false.

2.2 Writing to Multiple SAS Data Sets

Objectives

- Create multiple SAS data sets in a single DATA step.
- Use conditional processing to control the data set(s) to which an observation is written.

33

Writing to Multiple SAS Data Sets

The data set **prog2.military** contains information about air facilities maintained by the Army, Navy, Air Force, and Marines.

Create four SAS data sets: **airforce**, **army**, **navy**, and **marines**. Each of the four data sets should contain information about a single branch of the armed forces.

34

Writing to Multiple SAS Data Sets

```
proc print data=prog2.military noobs;
   var Code Type;
run;
```

Partial PROC PRINT Output

Code	Type
SKF	Air Force
DPG	Army
HIF	Air Force
NFE	Naval
DAA	Army

35

The DATA Statement

The DATA statement begins a DATA step and provides names for any output SAS data sets.

You can create multiple SAS data sets in a single DATA step by listing the names of the output data sets separated by at least one space.

```
DATA <data-set-name-1> <...data-set-name-n>;
```

36

If you do not specify a SAS data set name or the reserved name _NULL_ in a DATA statement, then SAS automatically creates data sets with the names **data1**, **data2**, and so on in the **work** library by default.

The OUTPUT Statement (Review)

By default, the explicit OUTPUT statement writes the current observation to every SAS data set listed in the DATA statement.

You can specify the name(s) of a data set or data sets to which SAS writes the observation.

OUTPUT <*SAS-data-set-1*> <*...SAS-data-set-n*>;

37

SAS-data-set-1 through *SAS-data-set-n* must also appear in the DATA statement.

 To specify multiple data sets in a single OUTPUT statement, separate the data set names with a space:

```
output data1 data2;
```

Writing to Multiple SAS Data Sets

```
data airforce army navy marines;
   drop Type;
   set prog2.military;
   if Type eq 'Air Force' then
      output airforce;
   else if Type eq 'Army' then
      output army;
   else if Type eq 'Naval' then
      output navy;
   else if Type eq 'Marine' then
      output marines;
run;
```

38   c02s2d1.sas

An alternate form of conditionally executing statements uses SELECT groups.

SELECT <(*select-expression*)>;
    WHEN-1 (*when-expression-1* <...,*when-expression-n*>)
        statement;
    <...**WHEN**-n (*when-expression-1* <...,*when-expression-n*>)
        statement;>
    <**OTHERWISE** *statement*;>
END;

The DATA step shown above could be rewritten to use SELECT groups as follows:

```
data army navy airforce marines;
   drop Type;
   set prog2.military;
   select (Type);
      when ('Air Force') output airforce;
      when ('Army') output army;
      when ('Naval') output navy;
      when ('Marine') output marines;
      otherwise;
   end;
run;
```

See SAS documentation for more information about using SELECT groups.

Writing to Multiple SAS Data Sets

Partial Log

```
NOTE: There were 137 observations read
      from the data set PROG2.MILITARY.
NOTE: The data set WORK.AIRFORCE has 64
      observations and 5 variables.
NOTE: The data set WORK.ARMY has 41
      observations and 5 variables.
NOTE: The data set WORK.NAVY has 28
      observations and 5 variables.
NOTE: The data set WORK.MARINES has 4
      observations and 5 variables.
```

39

 **Exercises**

3. **Writing to Multiple SAS Data Sets**

    The data set **prog2.elements** contains information about the known elements in the periodic table. Each observation contains an element's name, symbol, atomic number, and state. The value of **State** refers to whether the element is a gas, liquid, solid, or synthetic at room temperature.

    ✎   A *synthetic element* is an element that is not present in nature.

    Create four SAS data sets: **gas**, **liquid**, **solid**, and **synthetic**. Each data set will contain information about those elements that have that state at room temperature. Each of these four data sets should contain three variables; they should not contain the **State** variable.

    ✎   Character values are case-sensitive.

    The **gas** data set should contain 11 observations. The **liquid** data set should contain 4 observations. The **solid** data set should contain 76 observations. The **synthetic** data set should contain 24 observations.

    Partial Listing of **prog2.elements**

    | | | Atomic | |
Name	Symbol	Num	State
Actinium	Ac	89	Solid
Aluminum	Al	13	Solid
Americium	Am	95	Synthetic
Antimony	Sb	51	Solid
Argon	Ar	18	Gas
Arsenic	As	33	Solid
Astatine	At	85	Solid
Barium	Ba	56	Solid
Berkelium	Bk	97	Synthetic
Beryllium	Be	4	Solid
Bismuth	Bi	83	Solid
Bohrium	Bh	107	Solid
Boron	B	5	Solid
Bromine	Br	35	Liquid

Listing of **liquid**

	Obs	Name	Symbol	Atomic Num
	1	Bromine	Br	35
	2	Caesium	Cs	55
	3	Francium	Fr	87
	4	Mercury	Hg	80

 The names of elements and their symbols are approved by IUPAC, the International Union of Pure and Applied Chemistry. IUPAC has not approved names for elements with atomic numbers above 109; therefore, temporary IUPAC names are used.

In 1999, a team of scientists announced the observation of what appeared to be elements 116 (ununhexium) and 118 (ununoctium). In 2001, the team retracted its original paper after several confirmation experiments failed to reproduce the desired results.

In 2004, a team of scientists from the Lawrence Livermore National Laboratory and the Joint Institute of Nuclear Research in Russia announced the discovery of the superheavy elements 113 (ununtrium, uut) and 115 (ununpentium, uup).

Element 117 (ununseptium, uus) is not yet discovered.

4. Writing to Multiple SAS Data Sets (Optional)

A *lanthanide* is any member of the series of elements of increasing atomic numbers beginning with lanthanum (57) and ending with ytterbium (70). An *actinide* is any member of the series of elements that begins with actinium (89) and ends with lawrencium (103).

Create two SAS data sets, **work.lanthanides** and **work.actinides**, from the input data set **prog2.elements**. Each data set should contain information about those elements in its series, with 14 and 15 observations, respectively.

Partial Listing of **lanthanides**

	Obs	Name	Symbol	Atomic Num	State
	1	Cerium	Ce	58	Solid
	2	Dysprosium	Dy	66	Solid
	3	Erbium	Er	68	Solid
	4	Europium	Eu	63	Solid
	5	Gadolinium	Gd	64	Solid

Partial Listing of **actinides**

	Obs	Name	Symbol	Atomic Num	State
	1	Actinium	Ac	89	Solid
	2	Americium	Am	95	Synthetic
	3	Berkelium	Bk	97	Synthetic
	4	Californium	Cf	98	Synthetic
	5	Curium	Cm	96	Synthetic

The lanthanides and actinides are also known as the *rare earth elements*.

2.3 Selecting Variables and Observations

Objectives

- Control which variables are written to an output data set during a DATA step.
- Control which variables are read from an input data set during a DATA step.
- Control how many observations are processed from an input data set during a DATA or PROC step.

42

Controlling Variable Output

By default, the SAS System writes all variables from every input data set to every output data set.

In the DATA step, the DROP and KEEP statements can be used to control which variables are written to output data sets.

43

The DROP and KEEP Statements (Review)

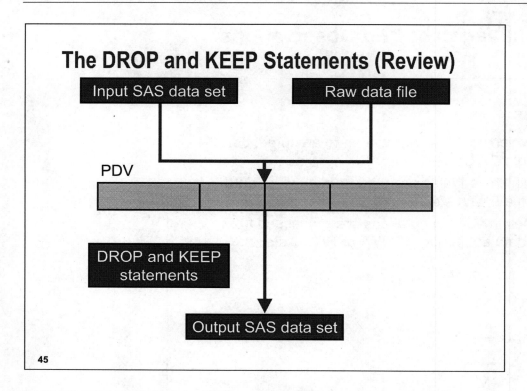

45

Creating Multiple SAS Data Sets (Review)

```
proc contents data=prog2.military;
run;
```

Partial PROC CONTENTS Output

```
---Alphabetic List of Variables and Attributes---

        #     Variable    Type     Len

        6     Airport     Char      40
        3     City        Char      20
        2     Code        Char       3
        5     Country     Char       3
        4     State       Char       2
        1     Type        Char       9
```

46

Creating Multiple SAS Data Sets (Review)

```
data airforce army navy marines;
   drop Type;
   set prog2.military;
   if Type eq 'Air Force' then
      output airforce;
   else if Type eq 'Army' then
      output army;
   else if Type eq 'Naval' then
      output navy;
   else if Type eq 'Marine' then
      output marines;
run;
```

47   c02s3d1.sas

Creating Multiple SAS Data Sets (Review)

Partial Log

```
NOTE: There were 137 observations read
      from the data set PROG2.MILITARY.
NOTE: The data set WORK.AIRFORCE has 64
      observations and 5 variables.
NOTE: The data set WORK.ARMY has 41
      observations and 5 variables.
NOTE: The data set WORK.NAVY has 28
      observations and 5 variables.
NOTE: The data set WORK.MARINES has 4
      observations and 5 variables.
```

48

Controlling Variable Output

The DROP and KEEP statements apply to all output data sets.

However, when you create multiple output data sets, you can use the DROP= and KEEP= data set options to write different variables to different data sets.

49

The DROP= Data Set Option

The DROP= data set option excludes variables from processing or from output SAS data sets.

When the DROP= data set option is associated with an output data set, SAS does not write the specified variables to the output data set. However, all variables are available for processing.

```
SAS-data-set(DROP=variable-1 variable-2 ...variable-n)
```

50

✏️   If the DROP= data set option is associated with an input data set, the specified variables are **not** available for processing.

The KEEP= Data Set Option

The KEEP= data set option specifies variables for processing or for writing to output SAS data sets.

When the KEEP= data set option is associated with an output data set, only the specified variables are written to the output data set. However, all variables are available for processing.

> *SAS-data-set*(KEEP=*variable-1 variable-2 ...variable-n*)

51

If the KEEP= data set option is associated with an input data set, only the specified variables are available for processing.

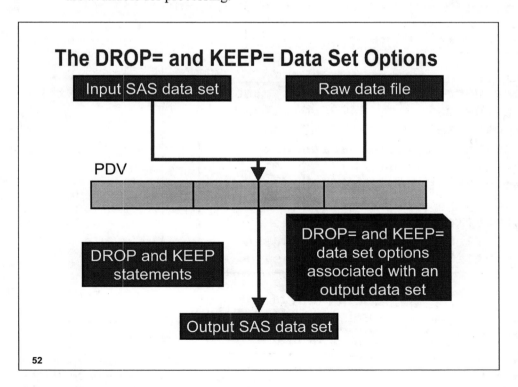

The DROP= and KEEP= Data Set Options

Input SAS data set   Raw data file

PDV

DROP and KEEP statements

DROP= and KEEP= data set options associated with an output data set

Output SAS data set

52

Controlling Variable Output

```
data airforce(drop=Code Type)
     army(drop=City State Country Type)
     navy(drop=Type)
     marines;
   set prog2.military;
   if Type eq 'Air Force' then
      output airforce;
   else if Type eq 'Army' then
      output army;
   else if Type eq 'Naval' then
      output navy;
   else if Type eq 'Marine' then
      output marines;
run;
```

53   c02s3d2.sas

✏ You cannot specify DROP= or KEEP= data set options in the OUTPUT statement.

Controlling Variable Output

Partial Log

```
NOTE: There were 137 observations read
      from the data set PROG2.MILITARY.
NOTE: The data set WORK.AIRFORCE has 64
      observations and 4 variables.
NOTE: The data set WORK.ARMY has 41
      observations and 2 variables.
NOTE: The data set WORK.NAVY has 28
      observations and 5 variables.
NOTE: The data set WORK.MARINES has 4
      observations and 6 variables.
```

54

Controlling Variable Output

```
data airforce(keep=Airport City State Country)
     army(keep=Code Airport)
     navy(keep=Code Airport City State Country)
     marines;
   set prog2.military;
   if Type eq 'Air Force' then
      output airforce;
   else if Type eq 'Army' then
      output army;
   else if Type eq 'Naval' then
      output navy;
   else if Type eq 'Marine' then
      output marines;
run;
```

55   c02s3d3.sas

In many cases, you have a choice between using a DROP= or KEEP= data set option (or DROP or KEEP statements). Typically, choose the data set option or statement that minimizes the amount of typing as in this example:

```
data airforce(drop=Code Type)
     army(keep=Code Airport)
     navy(drop=Type)
     marines;
   set prog2.military;
   if Type eq 'Air Force' then
      output airforce;
   else if Type eq 'Army' then
      output army;
   else if Type eq 'Naval' then
      output navy;
   else if Type eq 'Marine' then
      output marines;
run;
```

Controlling Variable Output

Partial Log

```
NOTE: There were 137 observations read
      from the data set PROG2.MILITARY.
NOTE: The data set WORK.AIRFORCE has 64
      observations and 4 variables.
NOTE: The data set WORK.ARMY has 41
      observations and 2 variables.
NOTE: The data set WORK.NAVY has 28
      observations and 5 variables.
NOTE: The data set WORK.MARINES has 4
      observations and 6 variables.
```

56

Controlling Variable Input

In the DATA step, the DROP and KEEP statements apply only to output SAS data sets.

However, the DROP= and KEEP= data set options can apply to both input and output SAS data sets.

57

Controlling Variable Input

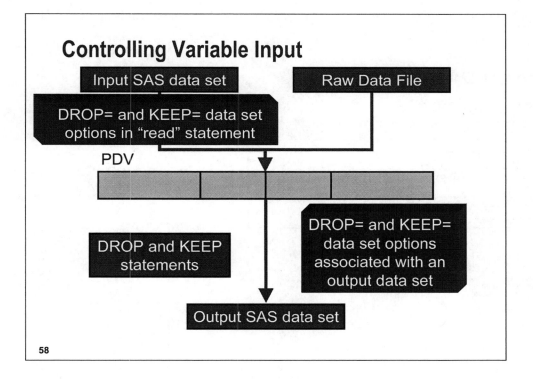

58

Controlling Variable Input

SAS applies data set options to input data sets before it

- evaluates programming statements
- applies data set options to output data sets.

```
data army(keep=Code Airport);
   set prog2.military(drop=City State
                           Country);
   if Type eq 'Army' then output;
run;
```

c02s3d4.sas

59

If a DROP or KEEP statement is used at the same time as a data set option, the statement is applied first.

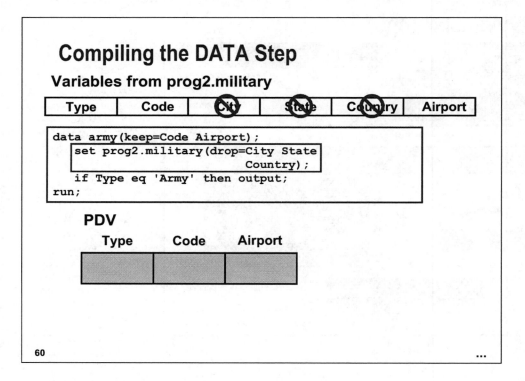

Compiling the DATA Step

Variables from prog2.military

| Type | Code | City | State | Country | Airport |

```
data army(keep=Code Airport);
   set prog2.military(drop=City State
                           Country);
   if Type eq 'Army' then output;
run;
```

PDV

| Type | Code | Airport |

60

Compiling the DATA Step

Variables from prog2.military

Type	Code	City	State	Country	Airport

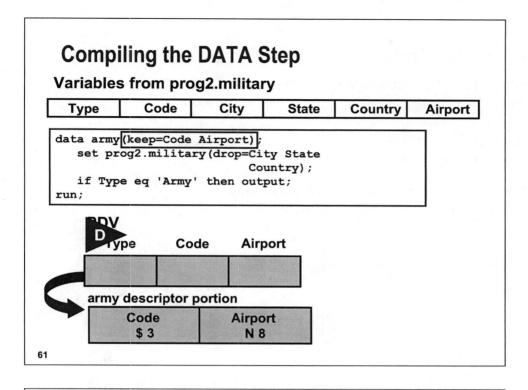

```
data army(keep=Code Airport);
   set prog2.military(drop=City State
                           Country);
   if Type eq 'Army' then output;
run;
```

61

Controlling Which Observations Are Read

By default, SAS begins processing a SAS data set with the first observation and continues processing until end of file.

The FIRSTOBS= and OBS= data set options can be used to control which observations are processed.

You can use FIRSTOBS= and OBS= with **input data sets**. You cannot use either data set option in the DATA statement.

62

FIRSTOBS= and OBS= can also be used with INFILE statements.

The OBS= Data Set Option

The OBS= data set option specifies an ending point for processing an input data set.

SAS-data-set(OBS=*n*)

This option specifies the number of the last observation to process, **not** how many observations should be processed.

63

n   specifies a positive integer that is less than or equal to the number of observations in the data set, or zero.

✎   The OBS= data set option overrides the OBS= system option for the individual data set.

To guarantee that SAS processes all observations from a data set, you can use the following syntax:

SAS-data-set(OBS=MAX)

Controlling Which Observations Are Read

The OBS= data set option in the SET statement stops reading after observation 25 in the **prog2.military** data set.

```
data army;
   set prog2.military(obs=25);
   if Type eq 'Army' then output;
run;
```

64

Controlling Which Observations Are Read

Partial Log

```
60    data army;
61        set prog2.military(obs=25);
62        if Type eq 'Army' then output;
63    run;

NOTE: There were 25 observations read
      from the data set PROG2.MILITARY.
NOTE: The data set WORK.ARMY has 10
      observations and 6 variables.
```

65

The FIRSTOBS= Data Set Option

The FIRSTOBS= data set option specifies a starting point
for processing an input data set.

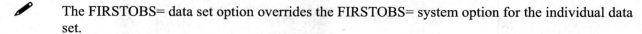

SAS-data-set(FIRSTOBS=n)

FIRSTOBS= and OBS= are often used together to define
a range of observations to be processed.

66

n   specifies a positive integer that is less than or equal to the number of observations in the data set.

        The FIRSTOBS= data set option overrides the FIRSTOBS= system option for the individual data
        set.

Controlling Which Observations Are Read

The FIRSTOBS= and OBS= data set options
in the SET statement read 15 observations from
prog2.military. Processing begins with
observation 11 and ends after observation 25.

```
data army;
   set prog2.military(firstobs=11 obs=25);
   if Type eq 'Army' then output;
run;
```

c02s3d5.sas

Controlling Which Observations Are Read

Partial Log

```
67    data army;
68       set prog2.military(firstobs=11 obs=25);
69       if Type eq 'Army' then output;
70    run;

NOTE: There were 15 observations read from the
      data set PROG2.MILITARY.
NOTE: The data set WORK.ARMY has 5 observations
      and 6 variables.
```

Controlling Which Observations Are Read

The FIRSTOBS= and OBS= data set options can also be used in a PROC step.

The following PROC PRINT step begins processing the **army** data set at observation 2 and stops processing the **army** data set after observation 4.

```
proc print data=army(firstobs=2 obs=4);
   var Code Airport;
run;
```

69

The DROP= and KEEP= data set options can be used to exclude variables from processing during a PROC step:

```
proc print data=army(drop=City State Country Type);
run;
```

However, DROP= and KEEP= do **not** affect the order in which the variables are processed.

Controlling Which Observations Are Read

Partial Log

```
75    proc print data=army(firstobs=2 obs=4);
76       var Code Airport;
77    run;

NOTE: There were 3 observations read from
      the data set WORK.ARMY.
```

70

Controlling Which Observations Are Read

PROC PRINT Output

Obs	Code	Airport
2	LGF	Laguna Army Air Field
3	SYL	Roberts Army Air Field
4	HGT	Tusi Army Heliport

71

 **Exercises**

5. Controlling Input and Output Size

Recall that the **prog2.elements** data set contains information about the known elements on the periodic table. Each observation contains an element's name, symbol, atomic number, and state. The value of **State** refers to whether the element is a gas, liquid, solid, or synthetic at room temperature.

Partial Listing of **prog2.elements**

Name	Symbol	Atomic Num	State
Actinium	Ac	89	Solid
Aluminum	Al	13	Solid
Americium	Am	95	Synthetic
Antimony	Sb	51	Solid
Argon	Ar	18	Gas

Create two SAS data sets: **natural** and **synthetic**.

The **natural** data set should contain information about elements that are solids, liquids, or gases at room temperature. It should contain three variables (**Name**, **AtomicNum**, and **State**) and 91 observations.

The **synthetic** data set should contain two variables (**Name** and **AtomicNum**) and 24 observations.

Partial Listing of **natural**

Obs	Name	Atomic Num	State
1	Actinium	89	Solid
2	Aluminum	13	Solid
3	Antimony	51	Solid
4	Argon	18	Gas
5	Arsenic	33	Solid

Partial Listing of **synthetic**

Obs	Name	Atomic Num
1	Americium	95
2	Berkelium	97
3	Bohrium	107
4	Californium	98
5	Curium	96

2.4 Writing to an External File

Objectives

- Write observations from a SAS data set to a comma-delimited external file.
- Insert header and footer records into an external file.

74

Introduction

The **prog2.maysales** data set contains information about houses. Read this data set and write the data to an external file.

prog2.maysales

Description	List Date	Sell Date	Sell Price
Colonial	13803	14001	355200
Townhouse	13894	14016	241200
Townhouse	14108	14392	238100
Ranch	14585	14736	219400
Victorian	14805	15106	358200

75

The ODS CSVALL Statement

ODS statements are global in most respects. They enable you to manage output objects produced by procedures or the DATA step.

The ODS CSVALL statement creates a comma-delimited file from output objects with these characteristics:

- values containing letters or special characters are enclosed in matching quotes
- titles and footnotes are preserved.

> **ODS CSVALL** FILE=*file-specification*;
> *<additional code>*
> **ODS CSVALL CLOSE;**

    CSVALL is a SAS®9 option.

76

The additional code can be any DATA or PROC step that produces output objects.

The ODS CSVALL Statement

To create the desired external file, place a PRINT procedure step between the ODS statements.

```
ods csvall file='raw-data-file';

title1;
footnote1 'Data: PROG2.MAYSALES';
proc print noobs data=prog2.maysales;
     format listdate
             selldate date9.;
run;

ods csvall close;
```

77   c02s4d1.sas

The ODS CSVALL Statement

raw-data-file

```
"Description","ListDate","SellDate","SellPrice"
"Colonial","16OCT1997","02MAY1998",355200
"Townhouse","15JAN1998","17MAY1998",241200
"Townhouse","17AUG1998","28MAY1999",238100
"Ranch","07DEC1999","06MAY2000",219400
"Victorian","14JUL2000","11MAY2001",358200

Data: PROG2.MAYSALES
```

78

In order to view the external file from an interactive SAS session, you can use the Results Viewer or the FSLIST procedure (described later in this section).

If a dialog box prompts you to choose to either open or save the file, save it and then open the file with an appropriate application. Opening the file in response to the prompt might inadvertently leave the file open and locked against further processing.

The DATA Step

You can use the DATA step to write

- a custom report
- data to an external file to be read by other programming languages or software.

79

You can also use the EXPORT procedure to read data from a SAS data set and write it to an external data source. External data sources can include database tables, PC files, spreadsheets, and delimited external files.

    PROC EXPORT is available in the following operating environments: UNIX, OpenVMS, and Windows.

The DATA Step

READING FROM AN EXTERNAL FILE	WRITING TO AN EXTERNAL FILE
The **DATA** statement begins the DATA step.	The **DATA** statement begins the DATA step.
The **INFILE** statement identifies an external file to read with an INPUT statement.	The **FILE** statement identifies an external file to write with a PUT statement.
The **INPUT** statement describes the arrangement of values in the input data record.	The **PUT** statement describes the arrangement of values in the output data record.

82

The DATA Statement

Usually, the DATA statement specifies at least one data set name that the SAS System uses to create an output data set.

Using the _NULL_ keyword as the data set name causes SAS to execute the DATA step without writing observations to a data set.

```
DATA   _NULL_;
```

83

The FILE Statement

The FILE statement can be used to specify the output destination for subsequent PUT statements.

General form of the FILE statement:

> **FILE** *file-specification* *<options>*;

You can use the FILE statement in conditional processing (IF-THEN/ELSE or SELECT) because it is executable.

84

file-specification   identifies an external file that the DATA step uses to write output from a PUT statement. It can have these forms:

'*external-file*'   specifies the physical name of an external file, which is enclosed in quotation marks. The physical name is the name by which the operating environment recognizes the file.

fileref   specifies the file reference for an external file. You must have previously associated a *fileref* with an external file in a FILENAME statement or function, or in an appropriate operating environment command.

LOG   is a reserved file reference that directs the output from subsequent PUT statements to the log.

PRINT   is a reserved file reference that directs the output from subsequent PUT statements to the same print file as the output that is produced by SAS procedures.

The default *file-specification* is LOG.

You can use multiple FILE statements to write to more than one external file in a single DATA step.

You can use PRINT as your initial *file-specification* to verify the contents of your output file before creating an external file.

The FILENAME statement associates a SAS file reference with an external file or an output device.

> **FILENAME** *fileref* *<device-type>* '*external-file*' *<host-options>*;

fileref	specifies any SAS name.
device-type	specifies the type of device or the access method that is used if the fileref points to an input or output device or location that is not a physical file.
'*external-file*'	specifies a physical name of an external file. The physical name is the name that is recognized by the operating environment.
host-options	specify details, such as file attributes and processing attributes, that are specific to your operating environment.

The PUT Statement

The PUT statement can write lines to the external file that is specified in the most recently executed FILE statement.

General form of the PUT statement:

> **PUT** *variable-1 variable-2 ... variable-n*;

With *simple list output*, you list the names of the variables whose values you want written. The PUT statement writes a variable value, inserts a single blank, and then writes the next value.

85

In addition to variable values, you can also use a quoted character string to specify a string of text to write. When a quoted character string is written, SAS does **not** automatically insert a blank space. The output pointer stops at the column that immediately follows the last character in the string.

The values of character variables are left-aligned in the field; leading and trailing blanks are removed.

A null PUT statement can be used to output a blank line:

```
put;
```

Modified List Output

Modified list output increases the versatility of the
PUT statement because you can specify a SAS format
to control how the variable values are written.

To use modified list output, use the colon (:) format
modifier in the PUT statement between the variable
name and the format.

PUT *variable-1 : format-1.*
 variable-2 : format-2.
 ...
 variable-n : format-n.;

86

format-1. through *format-n.*   specify formats to use when the data values are written. You can specify
either SAS formats or user-defined formats.

The colon format modifier enables you to specify a format that the PUT statement uses to write the
variable value. All leading and trailing blanks are deleted, and each value is followed by a single blank.

    See SAS documentation for a complete list of SAS formats and their usage.

Writing to an External File

```
data _null_;
   set prog2.maysales;
   file 'raw-data-file';
   put Description
       ListDate : date9.
       SellDate : date9.
       SellPrice;
run;
```

Why is the $ omitted after **Description** in the
PUT statement?

87   c02s4d2.sas

A FILENAME statement can be used to associate the fileref EXTFILE with the raw data file:

```
filename extfile 'raw-data-file';
```

The FILE statement can be subsequently revised:

```
file extfile;
```

Writing to an External File

Partial Log

```
NOTE: 5 records were written to the file
      'raw-data-file'.
      The minimum record length was 32.
      The maximum record length was 36.
NOTE: There were 5 observations read from
      the data set PROG2.MAYSALES.
```

Can you use PROC PRINT to view the raw data file?

88

The FSLIST Procedure

The FSLIST procedure enables you to browse external files within an interactive SAS session. You cannot use the FSLIST procedure to browse SAS data sets.

```
PROC FSLIST FILEREF=file-specification <option(s)>;
RUN;
```

Remember to close the FSLIST window when you finish browsing your external file.

89

file-specification	specifies the external file to browse. You must specify *file-specification*. It can be one of the following:
'external-file'	is the complete operating environment file specification for the external file. You must enclose the name in quotation marks.
fileref	specifies the fileref of an external file. You must have previously associated the fileref with an external file in a FILENAME statement or function, or in an appropriate operating environment command.

✎   Aliases for FILEREF= include FILE=, DDNAME=, and DD=.

You can use any text editor available for your operating environment to view the external file. For instance, Windows users can use Notepad or Microsoft Word, UNIX users can use emacs or vi, and z/OS users can use ISPF.

Reading from an External File

```
proc fslist fileref='raw-data-file';
run;
```

PROC FSLIST Output

```
Colonial 16OCT1997 02MAY1998 355200
Townhouse 15JAN1998 17MAY1998 241200
Townhouse 17AUG1998 28MAY1999 238100
Ranch 07DEC1999 06MAY2000 219400
Victorian 14JUL2000 11MAY2001 358200
```

How can you add a single row of column headers before the rows of data?

90

The _N_ Automatic Variable

The _N_ automatic variable is created by every DATA step.

Each time that the DATA step loops past the DATA statement, _N_ is incremented by 1. Therefore, the value of _N_ represents the number of times that the DATA step iterated.

_N_ is added to the Program Data Vector, but it is not output.

91

Writing to an External File

```
data _null_;
   set prog2.maysales;
   file 'raw-data-file';
   if _N_=1 then
      put 'Description ' 'ListDate '
          'SellDate ' 'SellPrice';
   put Description
      ListDate : date9.
      SellDate : date9.
      SellPrice;
run;
```

Why is the second PUT statement not contained in an
ELSE statement?

92   c02s4d3.sas

The IF-THEN statement shown above could also be written as follows:

```
if _N_=1 then
   put 'Description ListDate SellDate SellPrice';
```

Exercise caution when indenting or breaking lines within a quoted string. The following PUT statement
produces unexpected results:

```
if _N_=1 then
   put 'Description ListDate SellDate
       SellPrice';
```

Because of the indention within the quoted string, the following results are produced:

```
Description ListDate SellDate      SellPrice
```

Writing to an External File

```
proc fslist fileref='raw-data-file';
run;
```

PROC FSLIST Output

```
Description ListDate SellDate SellPrice
Colonial 16OCT1997 02MAY1998 355200
Townhouse 15JAN1998 17MAY1998 241200
Townhouse 17AUG1998 28MAY1999 238100
Ranch 07DEC1999 06MAY2000 219400
Victorian 14JUL2000 11MAY2001 358200
```

How can you add a footer record after the rows of data?

93

The END= Option in the SET Statement

The END= option in the SET statement creates and names a temporary variable that acts as an end-of-file indicator.

SET *SAS-data-set* END=*variable <options>*;

This temporary variable is initialized to 0. When the SET statement reads the last observation of the data set listed, the value of the variable is set to 1.

The variable is not added to any new data set.

94

END= is an option in the SET statement. It is not a data set option; it is not enclosed in parentheses.

Writing to an External File

```
data _null_;
   set prog2.maysales end=IsLast;
   file 'raw-data-file';
   if _N_=1 then
      put 'Description ' 'ListDate '
          'SellDate ' 'SellPrice';
   put Description
      ListDate : date9.
      SellDate : date9.
      SellPrice;
   if IsLast=1 then
      put 'Data: PROG2.MAYSALES';
run;
```

95   c02s4d4.sas

```
if IsLast=1 then
   put 'Data: PROG2.MAYSALES';
```

could be replaced with

```
if IsLast then
   put 'Data: PROG2.MAYSALES';
```

Writing to an External File: Compilation

```
data _null_;
   set prog2.maysales end=IsLast;
   file 'raw-data-file';
   if _N_=1 then
      put 'Description ' 'ListDate '
          'SellDate ' 'SellPrice';
   put Description
      ListDate : date9.
      SellDate : date9.
      SellPrice;
   if IsLast=1 then
      put 'Data: PROG2.MAYSALES';
run;
```

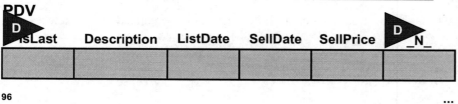

96   ...

Writing to an External File: Execution

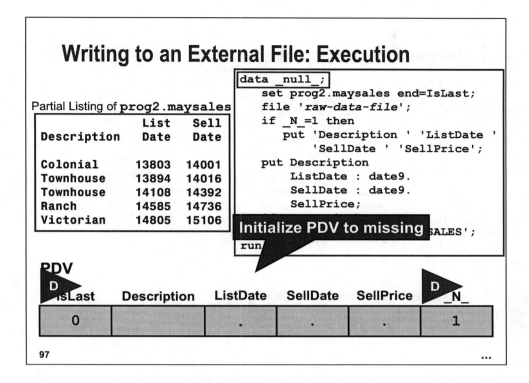

Partial Listing of **prog2.maysales**

Description	List Date	Sell Date
Colonial	13803	14001
Townhouse	13894	14016
Townhouse	14108	14392
Ranch	14585	14736
Victorian	14805	15106

```
data _null_;
   set prog2.maysales end=IsLast;
   file 'raw-data-file';
   if _N_=1 then
      put 'Description ' 'ListDate '
          'SellDate ' 'SellPrice';
   put Description
      ListDate : date9.
      SellDate : date9.
      SellPrice;
```
Initialize PDV to missing `SALES';`
```
   run
```

PDV

IsLast	Description	ListDate	SellDate	SellPrice	_N_
0		.	.	.	1

97   ...

Writing to an External File: Execution

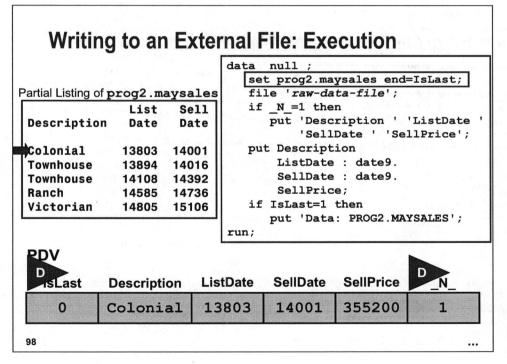

Partial Listing of **prog2.maysales**

Description	List Date	Sell Date
Colonial	13803	14001
Townhouse	13894	14016
Townhouse	14108	14392
Ranch	14585	14736
Victorian	14805	15106

```
data _null_;
   set prog2.maysales end=IsLast;
   file 'raw-data-file';
   if _N_=1 then
      put 'Description ' 'ListDate '
          'SellDate ' 'SellPrice';
   put Description
      ListDate : date9.
      SellDate : date9.
      SellPrice;
   if IsLast=1 then
      put 'Data: PROG2.MAYSALES';
run;
```

PDV

IsLast	Description	ListDate	SellDate	SellPrice	_N_
0	Colonial	13803	14001	355200	1

98   ...

Writing to an External File: Execution

Partial Listing of **prog2.maysales**

Description	List Date	Sell Date
►Colonial	13803	14001
Townhouse	13894	14016
Townhouse	14108	14392
Ranch	14585	14736
Victorian	14805	15106

```
data _null_;
  set prog2.maysales end=IsLast;
  file 'raw-data-file';
  if _N_=1 then
    put 'Description ' 'ListDate '
         'SellDate ' 'SellPrice';
  put Description
     ListDate : date9.
     SellDate : date9.
     SellPrice;
  if IsLast=1 then
    put 'Data: PROG2.MAYSALES';
run;
```

PDV

D IsLast	Description	ListDate	SellDate	SellPrice	D _N_
0	Colonial	13803	14001	355200	1

99   ...

Writing to an External File: Execution

Partial Listing of **prog2.mays...** **True**

Description	List Date	Sell Date
►Colonial	13803	14001
Townhouse	13894	14016
Townhouse	14108	14392
Ranch	14585	14736
Victorian	14805	15106

```
data _null_;
  set prog2.maysales end=IsLast;
  file 'raw-data-file';
  if _N_=1 then
    put 'Description ' 'ListDate '
         'SellDate ' 'SellPrice';
  put Description
     ListDate : date9.
     SellDate : date9.
     SellPrice;
  if IsLast=1 then
    put 'Data: PROG2.MAYSALES';
run;
```

PDV

D IsLast	Description	ListDate	SellDate	SellPrice	D _N_
0	Colonial	13803	14001	355200	1

Write header information to external file.

...

Writing to an External File: Execution

Partial Listing of **prog2.maysales**

Description	List Date	Sell Date
Colonial	13803	14001
Townhouse	13894	14016
Townhouse	14108	14392
Ranch	14585	14736
Victorian	14805	15106

```
data _null_;
   set prog2.maysales end=IsLast;
   file 'raw-data-file';
   if _N_=1 then
      put 'Description ' 'ListDate '
          'SellDate ' 'SellPrice';
   put Description
       ListDate : date9.
       SellDate : date9.
       SellPrice;
   if IsLast=1 then
      put 'Data: PROG2.MAYSALES';
run;
```

PDV

IsLast	Description	ListDate	SellDate	SellPrice	_N_
0	Colonial	13803	14001	355200	1

Write first line of data to external file.

Writing to an External File: Execution

Partial Listing of *raw-data-file*

```
Description ListDate SellDate SellPrice
Colonial 16OCT1997 02MAY1998 355200
```

Writing to an External File: Execution

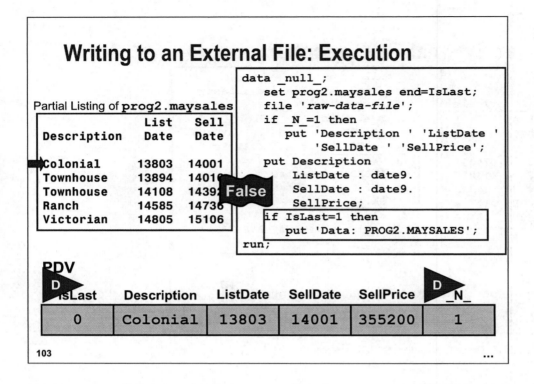

Partial Listing of **prog2.maysales**

Description	List Date	Sell Date
Colonial	13803	14001
Townhouse	13894	14016
Townhouse	14108	14392
Ranch	14585	14736
Victorian	14805	15106

```
data _null_ ;
   set prog2.maysales end=IsLast;
   file 'raw-data-file';
   if _N_=1 then
      put 'Description ' 'ListDate '
          'SellDate ' 'SellPrice';
   put Description
       ListDate : date9.
       SellDate : date9.
       SellPrice;
   if IsLast=1 then
      put 'Data: PROG2.MAYSALES';
run;
```

False

PDV

IsLast	Description	ListDate	SellDate	SellPrice	_N_
0	Colonial	13803	14001	355200	1

103   ...

Writing to an External File: Execution

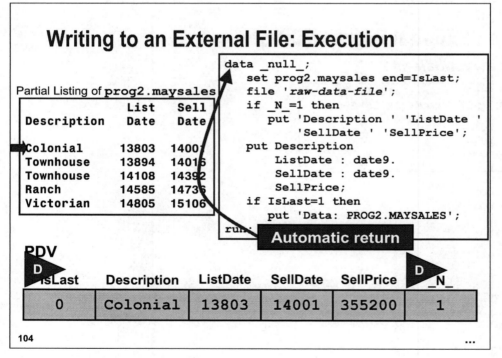

Partial Listing of **prog2.maysales**

Description	List Date	Sell Date
Colonial	13803	14001
Townhouse	13894	14016
Townhouse	14108	14392
Ranch	14585	14736
Victorian	14805	15106

```
data _null_ ;
   set prog2.maysales end=IsLast;
   file 'raw-data-file';
   if _N_=1 then
      put 'Description ' 'ListDate '
          'SellDate ' 'SellPrice';
   put Description
       ListDate : date9.
       SellDate : date9.
       SellPrice;
   if IsLast=1 then
      put 'Data: PROG2.MAYSALES';
run;
```

Automatic return

PDV

IsLast	Description	ListDate	SellDate	SellPrice	_N_
0	Colonial	13803	14001	355200	1

104   ...

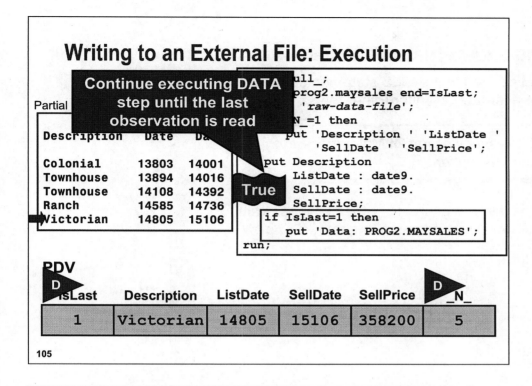

Writing to an External File: Execution

Continue executing DATA step until the last observation is read

Partial

Description	Date	Da...
Colonial	13803	14001
Townhouse	13894	14016
Townhouse	14108	14392
Ranch	14585	14736
Victorian	14805	15106

```
          ull_;
          rog2.maysales end=IsLast;
          'raw-data-file';
          N_=1 then
          ut 'Description ' 'ListDate '
              'SellDate ' 'SellPrice';
    put Description
        ListDate : date9.
        SellDate : date9.
        SellPrice;
    if IsLast=1 then
        put 'Data: PROG2.MAYSALES';
run;
```

True

PDV

IsLast	Description	ListDate	SellDate	SellPrice	_N_
1	Victorian	14805	15106	358200	5

105

Writing to an External File

```
proc fslist fileref='raw-data-file';
run;
```

PROC FSLIST Output

```
Description ListDate SellDate SellPrice
Colonial 16OCT1997 02MAY1998 355200
Townhouse 15JAN1998 17MAY1998 241200
Townhouse 17AUG1998 28MAY1999 238100
Ranch 07DEC1999 06MAY2000 219400
Victorian 14JUL2000 11MAY2001 358200
Data: PROG2.MAYSALES
```

106

Specifying an Alternate Delimiter

Use the DLM= option in the FILE statement to create
a file with an alternate delimiter (other than a blank).

> **FILE** *file-specification* DLM='*quoted-string*'
> <*other-options*>;

You can also specify a character variable whose value
contains your delimiter, instead of a quoted string.

🖊 DLM= is an alias for DELIMITER=.

107

'*quoted-string*'   specifies an alternate delimiter (other than the default, a blank) to be used for simple
or modified list output. Although a character string or character variable is accepted,
only the first character of the string or variable is used as the output delimiter.

To specify a tab character on a PC or on UNIX, use **dlm='09'x**. To specify a tab character on z/OS,
use **dlm='05'x**.

Writing to an External File

```
data _null_;
    set prog2.maysales end=IsLast;
    file 'raw-data-file' dlm=',';
    if _N_=1 then
        put 'Description,ListDate,'
            'SellDate,SellPrice';
    put Description
        ListDate : date9.
        SellDate : date9.
        SellPrice;
    if IsLast=1 then
        put 'Data: PROG2.MAYSALES';
run;
```

108   c02s4d5.sas

The IF-THEN statement shown above can also be written as follows:

```
if _N_=1 then
    put 'Description,ListDate,SellDate,SellPrice';
```

Writing to an External File

```
proc fslist fileref='raw-data-file';
run;
```

PROC FSLIST Output

```
Description,ListDate,SellDate,SellPrice
Colonial,16OCT1997,02MAY1998,355200
Townhouse,15JAN1998,17MAY1998,241200
Townhouse,17AUG1998,28MAY1999,238100
Ranch,07DEC1999,06MAY2000,219400
Victorian,14JUL2000,11MAY2001,358200
Data: PROG2.MAYSALES
```

109

 **Exercises**

6. Writing to an External File

The data set **prog2.visits** contains information about patients who visited a physician's office. Create a comma-delimited external file containing the information from **prog2.visits**. The name of your external file will depend on your operating environment.

The values of **Date** should be output using the MMDDYY10. format.

The first record in the external file should contain column headers. The last record in the external file should contain a footer.

✐   If you elect to use the DATA step to create the external file, use the FSLIST procedure to view your external file. Remember to close the FSLIST window when you finish viewing the file.

✐   If you elect to use ODS to create the external file, and a dialog box prompts you to choose to either open or save the file, save it and then open the file outside the SAS environment (using Microsoft Excel or another appropriate application). Opening the file in response to the prompt might leave the file open and locked against further processing.

Listing of **prog2.visits**

SSN	Date	Fee
243-88-4364	22JUL2001	864.15
193-27-9815	22JUL2001	621.50
278-80-5793	23JUL2001	1228.75
926-36-3948	24JUL2001	897.25
618-96-1764	24JUL2001	897.25
679-72-1759	25JUL2001	952.50
618-96-1764	26JUL2001	731.50
679-72-1759	26JUL2001	1781.25
236-76-1574	29JUL2001	897.25
345-10-3912	29JUL2001	1228.75
679-72-1759	30JUL2001	1339.25
278-80-5793	30JUL2001	676.25

✐   The values of **Date** are displayed with a permanently assigned DATE9. format. The values of **Date** should **not** be output using this format.

Desired Output (External File)

```
SSN,Date,Fee
243-88-4364,07/22/2001,864.15
193-27-9815,07/22/2001,621.5
278-80-5793,07/23/2001,1228.75
926-36-3948,07/24/2001,897.25
618-96-1764,07/24/2001,897.25
679-72-1759,07/25/2001,952.5
618-96-1764,07/26/2001,731.5
679-72-1759,07/26/2001,1781.25
236-76-1574,07/29/2001,897.25
345-10-3912,07/29/2001,1228.75
679-72-1759,07/30/2001,1339.25
278-80-5793,07/30/2001,676.25
Data: PROG2.VISITS
```

2.5 Solutions to Exercises

1. Outputting Multiple Observations

```
data rotate;
   drop Qtr1 Qtr2 Qtr3 Qtr4;
   set prog2.donate;
   Qtr=1;
   Amount=Qtr1;
   output;
   Qtr=2;
   Amount=Qtr2;
   output;
   Qtr=3;
   Amount=Qtr3;
   output;
   Qtr=4;
   Amount=Qtr4;
   output;
run;

proc print data=rotate;
run;
```

2. Using Conditional Logic to Output Multiple Observations (Optional)

```
data buyhistory(keep=ID Method);
   length Method $ 13;
   set prog2.ffmethod;
   if Internet eq 'Y' then
      do;
         Method='Internet';
         output;
      end;
   if Telephone eq 'Y' then
      do;
         Method='Telephone';
         output;
      end;
   if TravelAgency eq 'Y' then
      do;
         Method='Travel Agency';
         output;
      end;
run;

proc print data=buyhistory;
   var ID Method;
run;
```

3. **Writing to Multiple SAS Data Sets**

```
data gas liquid solid synthetic;
   drop State;
   set prog2.elements;
   if State eq 'Gas' then
      output gas;
   else if State eq 'Liquid' then
      output liquid;
   else if State eq 'Solid' then
      output solid;
   else if State eq 'Synthetic' then
      output synthetic;
run;

proc print data=liquid;
run;
```

4. **Writing to Multiple SAS Data Sets (Optional)**

```
data lanthanides actinides;
   set prog2.elements;
   if AtomicNum ge 57 and AtomicNum le 70 then
      output lanthanides;
   else if AtomicNum ge 89 and AtomicNum le 103 then
      output actinides;
run;

proc print data=lanthanides;
run;

proc print data=actinides;
run;
```

5. Controlling Input and Output Size

```
data natural(keep=Name AtomicNum State)
     synthetic(keep=Name AtomicNum);
   set prog2.elements;
   if State eq 'Synthetic' then
      output synthetic;
   else
      output natural;
run;

proc print data=natural;
run;

proc print data=synthetic;
run;
```

Alternate Solution:

```
data natural(keep=Name AtomicNum State)
     synthetic(keep=Name AtomicNum);
   set prog2.elements;
   if State in ('Solid','Liquid','Gas') then
      output natural;
   else
      output synthetic;
run;

proc print data=natural;
run;

proc print data=synthetic;
run;
```

6. Writing to an External File

```
data _null_;

   /* The END= option in the SET statement is
      used to determine when SAS reads the last
      observation from PROG2.VISITS. */

   set prog2.visits end=IsLast;

   /* The DLM= option in the FILE statement separates
      the data values with commas. */

   file 'visits.csv' dlm=',';

   /* The _N_ automatic variable is used to write
      column headers at the top of the raw data
      file. */

   if _N_ = 1 then
      put 'SSN,Date,Fee';
   put SSN
      Date : mmddyy10.
      Fee;

   /* The value of ISLAST, created using the END=
      option in the SET statement, is used to
      create a footer at the bottom of the raw
      data file. */

   if IsLast = 1 then
      put 'Data: PROG2.VISITS';
run;

   /* The FILE statement is applicable to the Windows
      and UNIX operating environments. z/OS users
      should use:

      file '.prog2.rawdata(visits)' dlm=','; */

proc fslist fileref='visits.csv';
run;

   /* The PROC FSLIST statement is applicable to the
      Windows and UNIX operating environments. z/OS
      users should use:

      proc fslist fileref='.prog2.rawdata(visits)';
      run */
```

Alternate Solution (SAS®9):

```
/* The file 'visits.csv' is applicable to the Windows
and UNIX operating environments. z/OS users should use
'.prog2.rawdata(visits)' in both the ODS and PROC FSLIST statements.
*/

ods csvall file='visits.csv';

title1;
footnote1 'Data: PROG2.VISITS';
proc print noobs data=prog2.visits;
   format Date mmddyy10.;
run;

ods csvall close;
```

Chapter 3   Summarizing Data

3.1 Creating an Accumulating Total Variable

Objectives

- Understand how the SAS System initializes the value of a variable in the PDV.
- Prevent reinitialization of a variable in the PDV.
- Create an accumulating variable.

3

Creating an Accumulating Variable

SaleDate	SaleAmt
01APR2001	498.49
02APR2001	946.50
03APR2001	994.97
04APR2001	564.59
05APR2001	783.01
06APR2001	228.82
07APR2001	930.57
08APR2001	211.47
09APR2001	156.23
10APR2001	117.69
11APR2001	374.73
12APR2001	252.73

The SAS data set **prog2.daysales** contains daily sales data for a retail store. There is one observation for each day in April showing the date (**SaleDate**) and the total receipts for that day (**SaleAmt**).

4

Creating an Accumulating Variable

The store manager also wants to see a running total
of sales for the month as of each day.

Partial Output

SaleDate	Sale Amt	Mth2Dte
01APR2001	498.49	498.49
02APR2001	946.50	1444.99
03APR2001	994.97	2439.96
04APR2001	564.59	3004.55
05APR2001	783.01	3787.56

5

 The input SAS data set must be sorted by **Date** for the following method to work.

Creating Mth2Dte

By default, variables created with an assignment
statement are initialized to missing at the top of
the DATA step.

```
Mth2Dte=Mth2Dte+SaleAmt;
```

An accumulating variable must retain its value
from one observation to the next.

6

The RETAIN Statement

General form of the RETAIN statement:

> **RETAIN** *variable-name* *<initial-value>* ...;

The RETAIN statement prevents SAS from re-initializing the values of new variables at the top of the DATA step.

Previous values of retained variables are available for processing across iterations of the DATA step.

7

The RETAIN Statement

The RETAIN statement

- retains the value of the variable in the PDV across iterations of the DATA step
- initializes the retained variable to missing before the first execution of the DATA step if an initial value is not specified
- is a compile-time-only statement.

8

The RETAIN statement has no effect on variables that are read with SET, MERGE, or UPDATE statements; values read from SAS data sets are automatically retained.

A variable referenced in the RETAIN statement appears in the output SAS data set only if it is given an initial value or referenced elsewhere in the DATA step.

Retain Mth2Dte and Set an Initial Value

```
retain Mth2Dte 0;
```

If you do not supply an initial value, all the values
of **Mth2Dte** will be missing.

9

Creating Accumulating Variables: Compilation

```
data mnthtot;
   set prog2.daysales;
   retain Mth2Dte 0;
   Mth2Dte=Mth2Dte+SaleAmt;
run;
```

PDV

SaleDate	SaleAmt	Mth2Dte

R

10   ...

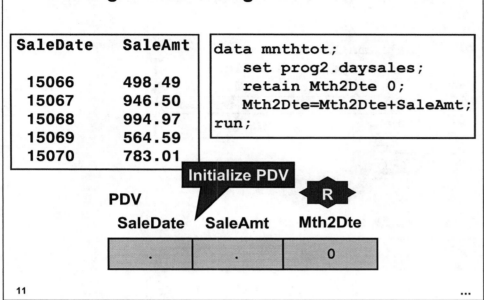

Creating Accumulating Variables: Execution

SaleDate	SaleAmt
15066	498.49
15067	946.50
15068	994.97
15069	564.59
15070	783.01

```
data mnthtot;
   set prog2.daysales;
   retain Mth2Dte 0;
   Mth2Dte=Mth2Dte+SaleAmt;
run;
```

Initialize PDV

R

PDV

SaleDate	SaleAmt	Mth2Dte
.	.	0

11   ...

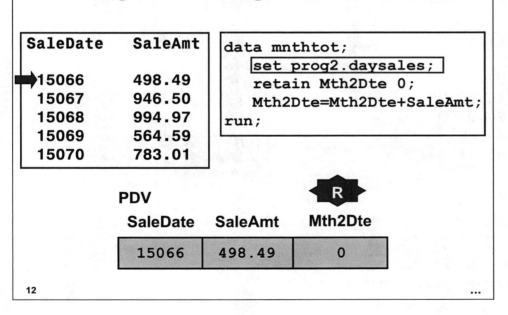

Creating Accumulating Variables: Execution

SaleDate	SaleAmt
→15066	498.49
15067	946.50
15068	994.97
15069	564.59
15070	783.01

```
data mnthtot;
   set prog2.daysales;
   retain Mth2Dte 0;
   Mth2Dte=Mth2Dte+SaleAmt;
run;
```

R

PDV

SaleDate	SaleAmt	Mth2Dte
15066	498.49	0

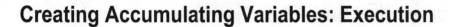

12   ...

Creating Accumulating Variables: Execution

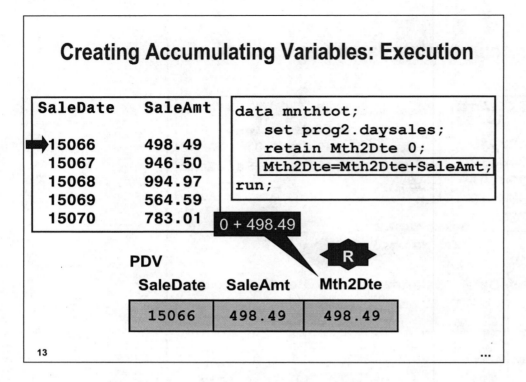

Creating Accumulating Variables: Execution

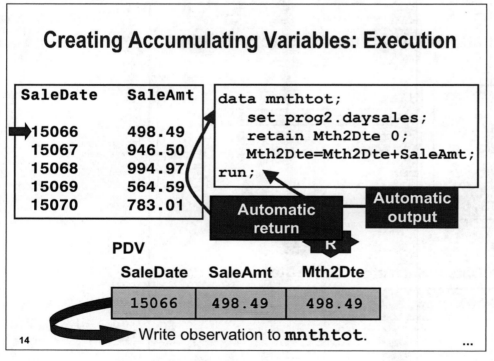

Creating Accumulating Variables: Execution

SaleDate	SaleAmt
➤ 15066	498.49
15067	946.50
15068	994.97
15069	564.59
15070	783.01

```
data mnthtot;
    set prog2.daysales;
    retain Mth2Dte 0;
    Mth2Dte=Mth2Dte+SaleAmt;
run;
```

Do not re-initialize PDV to missing

R

PDV

SaleDate	SaleAmt	Mth2Dte
15066	498.49	498.49

15

...

Creating Accumulating Variables: Execution

SaleDate	SaleAmt
15066	498.49
➤ 15067	946.50
15068	994.97
15069	564.59
15070	783.01

```
data mnthtot;
    set prog2.daysales;
    retain Mth2Dte 0;
    Mth2Dte=Mth2Dte+SaleAmt;
run;
```

R

PDV

SaleDate	SaleAmt	Mth2Dte
15067	946.50	498.49

16

...

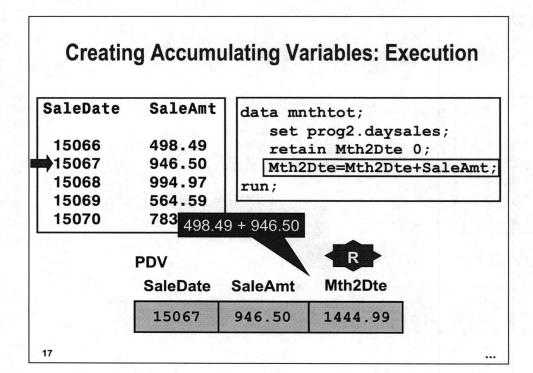

Creating Accumulating Variables: Execution

SaleDate	SaleAmt
15066	498.49
→ 15067	946.50
15068	994.97
15069	564.59
15070	783

```
data mnthtot;
   set prog2.daysales;
   retain Mth2Dte 0;
   Mth2Dte=Mth2Dte+SaleAmt;
run;
```

498.49 + 946.50

R

PDV

SaleDate	SaleAmt	Mth2Dte
15067	946.50	1444.99

17

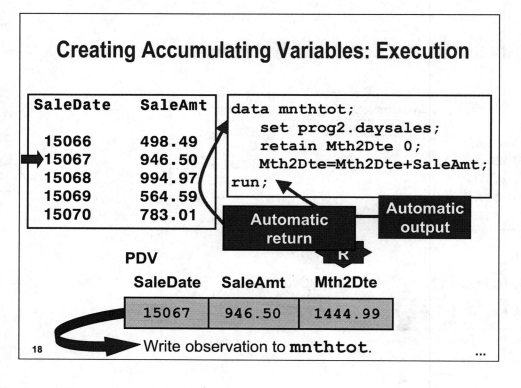

Creating Accumulating Variables: Execution

SaleDate	SaleAmt
15066	498.49
→ 15067	946.50
15068	994.97
15069	564.59
15070	783.01

```
data mnthtot;
   set prog2.daysales;
   retain Mth2Dte 0;
   Mth2Dte=Mth2Dte+SaleAmt;
run;
```

Automatic return

Automatic output

R

PDV

SaleDate	SaleAmt	Mth2Dte
15067	946.50	1444.99

Write observation to **mnthtot**.

18

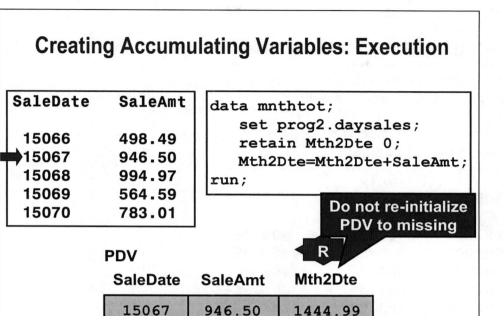

Creating Accumulating Variables: Execution

SaleDate	SaleAmt
15066	498.49
→15067	946.50
15068	994.97
15069	564.59
15070	783.01

```
data mnthtot;
   set prog2.daysales;
   retain Mth2Dte 0;
   Mth2Dte=Mth2Dte+SaleAmt;
run;
```

Do not re-initialize PDV to missing

R

PDV

SaleDate	SaleAmt	Mth2Dte
15067	946.50	1444.99

19 ...

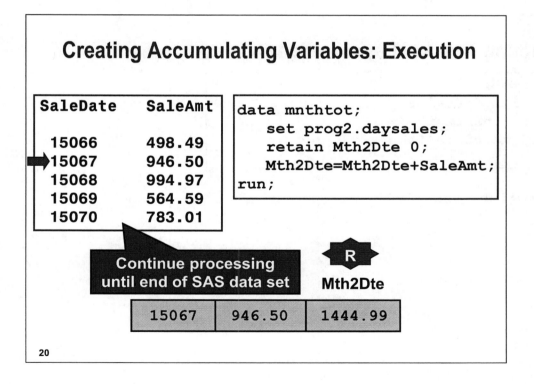

Creating Accumulating Variables: Execution

SaleDate	SaleAmt
15066	498.49
→15067	946.50
15068	994.97
15069	564.59
15070	783.01

```
data mnthtot;
   set prog2.daysales;
   retain Mth2Dte 0;
   Mth2Dte=Mth2Dte+SaleAmt;
run;
```

Continue processing until end of SAS data set

R

Mth2Dte

15067	946.50	1444.99

20

Creating Accumulating Variables

```
proc print data=mnthtot noobs;
   format SaleDate date9.;
run;
```

Partial PROC PRINT Output

SaleDate	Sale Amt	Mth2Dte
01APR2001	498.49	498.49
02APR2001	946.50	1444.99
03APR2001	994.97	2439.96
04APR2001	564.59	3004.55
05APR2001	783.01	3787.56

21

Accumulating Totals: Missing Values

```
data mnthtot;
   set prog2.daysales;
   retain Mth2Dte 0;
   Mth2Dte=Mth2Dte+SaleAmt;
run;
```

What happens if there are missing values for **SaleAmt**?

22

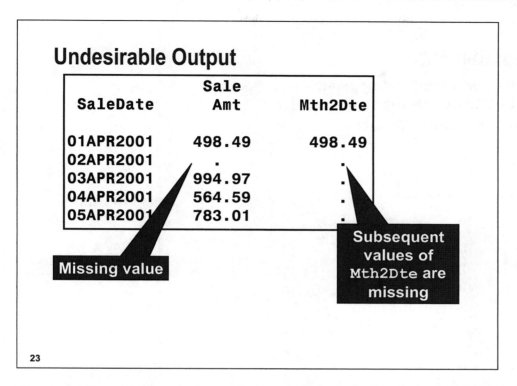

The result of any mathematical operation on a missing value is missing. With the above code, one missing value for **SaleAmt** causes all subsequent values of **Mth2Dte** to be missing. You can solve this problem by using the SUM function in the assignment statement:

```
Mth2Dte=sum(Mth2Dte,SaleAmt);
```

See Chapter 5, "Data Transformations," for details.

However, the sum **statement** is a more efficient solution because it does not require SAS to invoke the SUM function.

The Sum Statement

When you create an accumulating variable, an alternative to the RETAIN statement is the sum statement.

General form of the sum statement:

> *variable* **+** *expression*;

24

    Like the assignment statement, the sum statement does not begin with a keyword.

The Sum Statement

The sum statement

- creates the variable on the left side of the plus sign if it does not already exist
- initializes the variable to zero before the first iteration of the DATA step
- automatically retains the variable
- adds the value of *expression* to the variable at execution
- ignores missing values.

25

Accumulating Totals: Missing Values

```
data mnthtot2;
   set prog2.daysales2;
   Mth2Dte+SaleAmt;
run;
```

26

Accumulating Totals: Missing Values

```
proc print data=mnthtot2 noobs;
   format SaleDate date9.;
run;
```

Partial PROC PRINT Output

SaleDate	SaleAmt	Mth2Dte
01APR2001	498.49	498.49
02APR2001	.	498.49
03APR2001	994.97	1493.46
04APR2001	564.59	2058.05
05APR2001	783.01	2841.06

27   c03s1d1.sas

Exercises

1. Creating an Accumulating Total Variable

The data set **prog2.states** contains the state name (**State**), the date the state entered the United States (**EnterDate**), and the size of the state in square miles (**Size**) for all 50 U.S. states. The data set is sorted by **EnterDate**.

Partial Listing of **prog2.states**

State	EnterDate	Size
Delaware	07DEC1787	1955
Pennsylvania	12DEC1787	44820
New Jersey	18DEC1787	7418
Georgia	02JAN1788	57918
Connecticut	09JAN1788	4845
Massachusetts	06FEB1788	7838
Maryland	28APR1788	9775
South Carolina	23MAY1788	30111

The variable **EnterDate** has the permanent format DATE9.

Create the SAS data set **work.usarea** that contains the new variable **TotArea**, which is a running total of the size of the United States as each state was added, and the new variable **NumStates**, which shows how many states were in the United States at that point.

Partial Listing of **work.usarea**

Obs	State	EnterDate	Size	TotArea	Num States
1	Delaware	07DEC1787	1955	1955	1
2	Pennsylvania	12DEC1787	44820	46775	2
3	New Jersey	18DEC1787	7418	54193	3
4	Georgia	02JAN1788	57918	112111	4
5	Connecticut	09JAN1788	4845	116956	5
6	Massachusetts	06FEB1788	7838	124794	6
7	Maryland	28APR1788	9775	134569	7
8	South Carolina	23MAY1788	30111	164680	8

3.2 Accumulating Totals for a Group of Data

Objectives

- Define First. and Last. processing.
- Calculate an accumulating total for groups of data.
- Use a subsetting IF statement to output selected observations.

30

Accumulating Totals for Groups

EmpID	Salary	Div
E00004	42000	HUMRES
E00009	34000	FINACE
E00011	27000	FLTOPS
E00036	20000	FINACE
E00037	19000	FINACE
E00048	19000	FLTOPS
E00077	27000	APTOPS
E00097	20000	APTOPS
E00107	31000	FINACE
E00123	20000	APTOPS
E00155	27000	APTOPS
E00171	44000	SALES

The SAS data set **prog2.empsals** contains each employee's identification number (**EmpID**), salary (**Salary**), and division (**Div**). There is one observation for each employee.

31

Desired Output

Human resources wants a new data set that shows the total salary paid for each division.

Div	DivSal
APTOPS	410000
FINACE	163000
FLTOPS	318000
HUMRES	181000
SALES	373000

32

Grouping the Data

You must group the data in the SAS data set before you can perform processing.

33

Review of the SORT Procedure

You can rearrange the observations into groups using the SORT procedure.

General form of a PROC SORT step:

```
PROC SORT DATA=input-SAS-data-set
          <OUT=output-SAS-data-set>;
    BY <DESCENDING> BY-variable ...;
RUN;
```

34

The SORT Procedure

The SORT procedure

- rearranges the observations in a DATA set
- can sort on multiple variables
- creates a SAS data set that is a sorted copy of the input SAS data set
- replaces the input data set by default.

35

Sorting by Div

```
proc sort data=prog2.empsals out=salsort;
   by Div;
run;
```

36

Processing Data in Groups

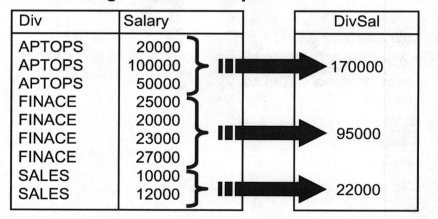

Div	Salary		DivSal
APTOPS	20000		
APTOPS	100000		170000
APTOPS	50000		
FINACE	25000		
FINACE	20000		
FINACE	23000		95000
FINACE	27000		
SALES	10000		
SALES	12000		22000

37

BY-Group Processing

General form of a BY statement used with the SET statement:

```
DATA output-SAS-data-set;
    SET input-SAS-data-set;
    BY BY-variable ...;
    <additional SAS statements>
RUN;
```

The BY statement in the DATA step enables you to process your data in groups.

38

When a BY statement is used with a SET statement, the data must

- be sorted or grouped in order by the BY variable(s), **or**
- have an index based on the BY variable(s), **or**
- reside in a DBMS table.

BY-Group Processing

```
data divsals(keep=Div DivSal);
    set salsort;
    by Div;
    <additional SAS statements>
run;
```

39

BY-Group Processing

A BY statement in a DATA step creates temporary variables for each variable listed in the BY statement.

General form of the names of BY variables in a DATA step:

First.*BY-variable*
Last.*BY-variable*

40

First. and Last. Values

- The **First.** variable has a value of 1 for the first observation in a BY group; otherwise, it equals 0.
- The **Last.** variable has a value of 1 for the last observation in a BY group; otherwise, it equals 0.

Use these temporary variables to conditionally process sorted, grouped, or indexed data.

41

First. / Last. Example

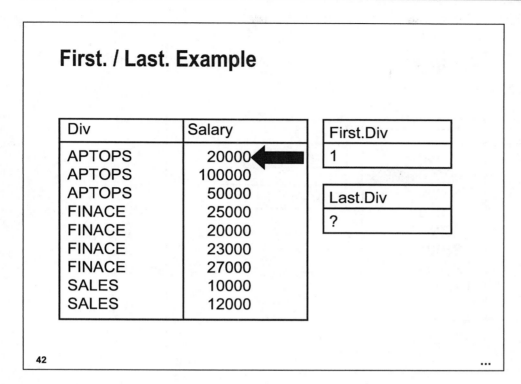

42   ...

First. / Last. Example

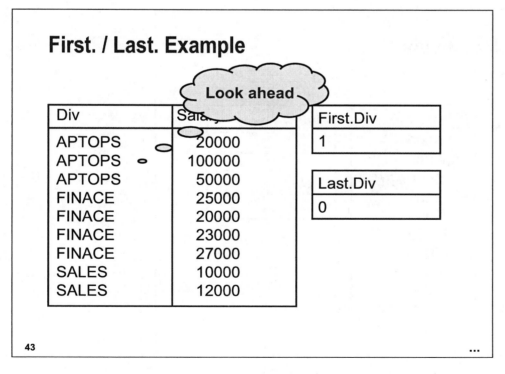

43   ...

First. / Last. Example

Div	Salary
APTOPS	20000
APTOPS	100000
APTOPS	50000
FINACE	25000
FINACE	20000
FINACE	23000
FINACE	27000
SALES	10000
SALES	12000

First.Div
0

Last.Div
0

44   ...

First. / Last. Example

Div	Salary
APTOPS	20000
APTOPS	100000
APTOPS	50000
FINACE	25000
FINACE	20000
FINACE	23000
FINACE	27000
SALES	10000
SALES	12000

First.Div
0

Last.Div
1

45   ...

First. / Last. Example

Div	Salary
APTOPS	20000
APTOPS	100000
APTOPS	50000
FINACE	25000 ←
FINACE	20000
FINACE	23000
FINACE	27000
SALES	10000
SALES	12000

First.Div
1

Last.Div
0

46

What Must Happen When?

There is a three-step process for accumulating totals.

1. Set the accumulating variable to zero at the start of each BY group.

2. Increment the accumulating variable with a sum statement (automatically retains).

3. Output only the last observation of each BY group.

47

Accumulating Totals for Groups

1. Set the accumulating variable to zero at the start of each BY group.

```
data divsals(keep=Div DivSal);
   set salsort;
   by Div;
   if First.Div then DivSal=0;
   <additional SAS statements>
run;
```

48

Accumulating Totals for Groups

2. Increment the accumulating variable with a sum statement (automatically retains).

```
data divsals(keep=Div DivSal);
   set salsort;
   by Div;
   if First.Div then DivSal=0;
   DivSal+Salary;
   <additional SAS statements>
run;
```

49

First. / Last. Example

Div	Salary	DivSal
APTOPS	20000	20000
APTOPS	100000	120000
APTOPS	50000	170000
FINACE	25000	25000
FINACE	20000	45000
FINACE	23000	68000
FINACE	27000	95000
SALES	10000	10000
SALES	12000	22000

50

Subsetting IF Statement

The subsetting IF defines a condition that the observation must meet to be further processed by the DATA step.

General form of the subsetting IF statement:

IF *expression*;

- If the expression is true, the DATA step continues processing the current observation.
- If the expression is false, SAS returns to the top of the DATA step.

51

Accumulating Totals for Groups

3. Output only the last observation of each BY group.

```
data divsals(keep=Div DivSal);
   set salsort;
   by Div;
   if First.Div then DivSal=0;
   DivSal+Salary;
   if Last.Div;
run;
```

52

The statement **if Last.*BY-variable*;** means if Last.*BY-variable* is **true**. A numeric value is considered true if it is not equal to zero and not missing.

Subsetting IF Statement

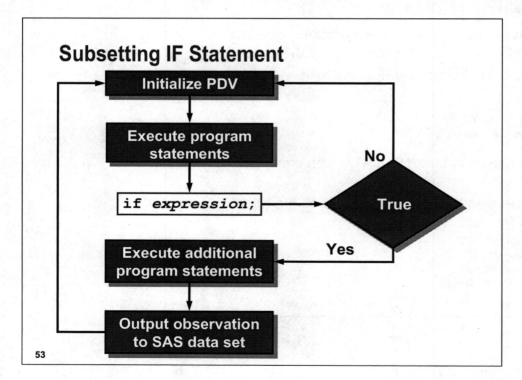

53

Accumulating Totals for Groups

Partial Log

```
NOTE: There were 39 observations read
      from the data set WORK.SALSORT.
NOTE: The data set WORK.DIVSALS has 5
      observations and 2 variables.
```

54

Accumulating Totals for Groups

```
proc print data=divsals noobs;
run;
```

PROC PRINT Output

Div	DivSal
APTOPS	410000
FINACE	163000
FLTOPS	318000
HUMRES	181000
SALES	373000

55   c03s2d1.sas

Input Data

EmpID	Salary	Region	Div
E00004	42000	E	HUMRES
E00009	34000	W	FINACE
E00011	27000	W	FLTOPS
E00036	20000	W	FINACE
E00037	19000	E	FINACE
E00077	27000	C	APTOPS
E00097	20000	E	APTOPS
E00107	31000	E	FINACE
E00123	20000	NC	APTOPS
E00155	27000	W	APTOPS
E00171	44000	W	SALES
E00188	37000	W	HUMRES
E00196	43000	C	APTOPS
E00210	31000	E	APTOPS
E00222	250000	NC	SALES
E00236	41000	W	APTOPS

The SAS data set `prog2.regsals` contains each employee's ID number (`EmpID`), salary (`Salary`), region (`Region`), and division (`Div`). There is one observation for each employee.

56

Desired Output

Human Resources wants a new data set that shows the total salary paid and the total number of employees for each division in each region.

Partial Output

Region	Div	DivSal	Num Emps
C	APTOPS	70000	2
E	APTOPS	83000	3
E	FINACE	109000	4
E	FLTOPS	122000	3
E	HUMRES	178000	5
NC	APTOPS	37000	2
NC	FLTOPS	28000	1

57

Sorting by Region and Div

The data must be sorted by **Region** and **Div**.

Region is the primary sort variable. **Div** is the secondary sort variable.

```
proc sort data=prog2.regsals out=regsort;
   by Region Div;
run;
```

58

Sorting by Region and Div

```
proc print data=regsort noobs;
   var Region Div Salary;
run;
```

Partial PROC PRINT Output

Region	Div	Salary
C	APTOPS	27000
C	APTOPS	43000
E	APTOPS	20000
E	APTOPS	31000
E	APTOPS	32000
E	FINACE	19000
E	FINACE	31000

59

Multiple BY Variables

```
data regdivsals;
   set regsort;
   by Region Div;
   additional SAS statements
run;
```

60

Multiple BY Variables: Example

Region	Div
C	APTOPS
C	APTOPS
C	APTOPS
E	APTOPS
E	FINACE
E	FINACE
NC	FINACE
NC	SALES
NC	SALES
NC	SALES
NC	SALES

First.Region
1

First.Div
1

Last.Region
?

Last.Div
?

61   ...

Multiple BY Variables: Example

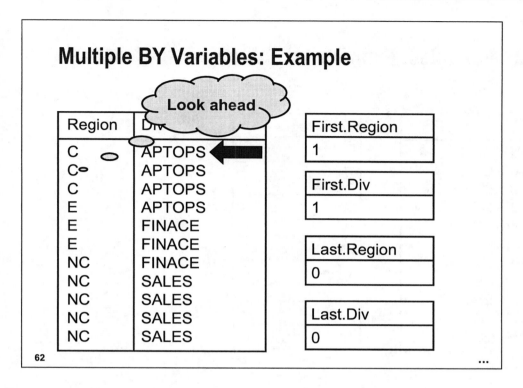

Region	Div
C	APTOPS
C	APTOPS
C	APTOPS
E	APTOPS
E	FINACE
E	FINACE
NC	FINACE
NC	SALES
NC	SALES
NC	SALES
NC	SALES

First.Region
1

First.Div
1

Last.Region
0

Last.Div
0

62   ...

Multiple BY Variables: Example

Region	Div
C	APTOPS
C	APTOPS
C	APTOPS
E	APTOPS
E	FINACE
E	FINACE
NC	FINACE
NC	SALES
NC	SALES
NC	SALES
NC	SALES

First.Region
0

First.Div
0

Last.Region
0

Last.Div
0

63   ...

Multiple BY Variables: Example

Region	Div
C	APTOPS
C	APTOPS
C	APTOPS
E	APTOPS
E	FINACE
E	FINACE
NC	FINACE
NC	SALES
NC	SALES
NC	SALES
NC	SALES

First.Region
0

First.Div
0

Last.Region
1

Last.Div
1

64   ...

Multiple BY Variables: Example

Region	Div
C	APTOPS
C	APTOPS
C	APTOPS
E	APTOPS
E	FINACE
E	FINACE
NC	FINACE
NC	SALES
NC	SALES
NC	SALES
NC	SALES

First.Region
1

First.Div
1

Last.Region
0

Last.Div
1

65   ...

Multiple BY Variables: Example

Region	Div
C	APTOPS
C	APTOPS
C	APTOPS
E	APTOPS
E	FINACE
E	FINACE
NC	FINACE
NC	SALES
NC	SALES
NC	SALES
NC	SALES

First.Region
0

First.Div
1

Last.Region
0

Last.Div
0

66

Multiple BY Variables

When you use more than one variable in the BY statement, a **change in the primary variable** forces `Last.BY-variable`=1 for the secondary variable.

Region	Div	First. Region	Last. Region	First. Div	Last.Div
C	APTOPS	1	0	1	0
C	APTOPS	0	0	0	0
C	APTOPS	0	1	0	1
E	APTOPS	1	0	1	1
E	FINACE	0	0	1	0

67

Multiple BY Variables

```
data regdivsals(keep=Region Div
                        DivSal NumEmps);
   set regsort;
   by Region Div;
   if First.Div then do;
      DivSal=0;
      NumEmps=0;
   end;
   DivSal+Salary;
   NumEmps+1;
   if Last.Div;
run;
```

68

Multiple BY Variables

Partial Log

```
NOTE: There were 39 observations read
      from the data set WORK.REGSORT.
NOTE: The data set WORK.REGDIVSALS has
      14 observations and 4 variables.
```

69

Multiple BY Variables

```
proc print data=regdivsals noobs;
run;
```

Partial PROC PRINT Output

Region	Div	DivSal	Num Emps
C	APTOPS	70000	2
E	APTOPS	83000	3
E	FINACE	109000	4
E	FLTOPS	122000	3

c03s2d2.sas

70

if last.div=1; does subsetting if

 **Exercises**

2. Accumulating Totals for a Group of Data

The data set **prog2.flymiles** has one observation for each trip that a frequent flyer made with an airline. It shows the frequent flyer number (**ID**) and the number of miles earned for that trip (**Miles**).

Partial Listing of **prog2.flymiles**

ID	Miles
F212	763
F161	272
F31351	800
F25122	733
F25122	859
F31351	437
F31351	1553
F31351	312
F161	2245

The data set is not sorted by **ID**.

Create a data set named **work.freqmiles** that has one observation for each frequent flyer as well as a new variable named **TotMiles**, which shows the total number of frequent flyer miles the person earned.

Listing of **work.freqmiles**

Obs	ID	Tot Miles
1	F161	5813
2	F212	6454
3	F25122	10208
4	F31351	5090

3. **Accumulating Totals for Groups of Data Using More than One BY Variable**

The data set **prog2.flydays** has one observation for each trip that a frequent flyer made with an airline. It contains the frequent flyer number (**ID**), the number of miles earned for that trip (**Miles**), and a variable that indicates whether the miles were earned on a weekday flight (**Code='MF'**) or a weekend flight (**Code='SS'**).

Partial Listing of **prog2.flydays**

ID	Code	Miles
F212	SS	763
F161	MF	272
F31351	SS	800
F25122	SS	733
F25122	MF	859
F31351	SS	437
F31351	SS	1553
F31351	MF	312
F161	SS	2245

Create a SAS data set named **work.daymiles** that shows how many total miles each frequent flyer earned for each type of flight.

Listing of **work.daymiles**

Obs	ID	Code	Tot Miles
1	F161	MF	2633
2	F161	SS	3180
3	F212	MF	976
4	F212	SS	5478
5	F25122	MF	7007
6	F25122	SS	3201
7	F31351	MF	2100
8	F31351	SS	2990

4. Detecting Duplicate Observations Using BY-Group Processing (Optional)

The data set **prog2.dupsals** has the variables **EmpID** and **Salary**.

Partial Listing of **prog2.dupsals**

EmpID	Salary
E00290	37000
E00379	25000
E00037	19000
E00037	27526
E00236	41000
E00236	59978
E00372	36000
E00372	41011
E00421	31000
E00424	17000

The data set should contain only one observation per employee (that is, all employee ID numbers should be unique). However, a SAS programmer discovered some duplicate observations. Write a DATA step that sends all observations that are not unique on EmpID to a data set named **work.baddata,** and all unique observations to a data set named **work.gooddata**.

Partial Listing of **work.gooddata**

	Non-Duplicate EmpIDs		
Obs	EmpID	Salary	
1	E00048	19000	
2	E00077	27000	
3	E00107	31000	
4	E00123	20000	
5	E00155	27000	
6	E00188	37000	
7	E00196	43000	
8	E00210	31000	
9	E00259	32000	
10	E00272	22000	
11	E00290	37000	
12	E00379	25000	
13	E00388	25000	
14	E00421	31000	
15	E00424	17000	
16	E00427	27000	

Partial Listing of **work.baddata**

```
                         Duplicate EmpIDs

                  Obs     EmpID      Salary

              1   E00004      42000
              2   E00004      62902
              3   E00009      34000
              4   E00009      49761
              5   E00011      27000
              6   E00011      38193
              7   E00036      20000
              8   E00036      27057
              9   E00037      19000
             10   E00037      27526
             11   E00097      20000
```

Hint: To create two data sets, list both in the DATA statement. To control to which data set an observation is written, use the OUTPUT statement. (Refer to Chapter 2, "Controlling Input and Output.")

5. Rotating a Data Set (Optional)

A bookstore sells three types of products: books, cards, and periodicals. The SAS data set
prog2.salesbyday has an observation for each product each day that the store is open (three
observations for each day). The variable **Sales** shows the total sales for that product on each day.

Partial listing of **prog2.salesbyday**

Date	MerchType	Sales
01APR2001	Books	1602.27
01APR2001	Cards	669.49
01APR2001	Periodicals	1651.49
02APR2001	Books	2818.33
02APR2001	Cards	217.19
02APR2001	Periodicals	87.62
03APR2001	Books	751.67
03APR2001	Cards	125.78
03APR2001	Periodicals	72.20

 The variable **Date** is a SAS date, but it has a permanent DATE9. format applied. The data
set is already sorted by **Date**.

Rotate the data set so that it has only one observation per day, and a variable for each type of
merchandise. The value for each merchandise type should be the sales for that product on that day.

Partial Output

Obs	Date	Books	Cards	Periodicals
1	01APR2001	1602.27	669.49	1651.49
2	02APR2001	2818.33	217.19	87.62
3	03APR2001	751.67	125.78	72.20
4	04APR2001	890.87	2370.92	587.84
5	05APR2001	1926.04	165.25	265.96
6	06APR2001	141.11	1739.46	3725.15
7	07APR2001	1406.71	117.76	706.78
8	08APR2001	153.18	78.77	171.64

3.3 Solutions to Exercises

1. **Creating an Accumulating Total Variable**

```
data usarea;
   set prog2.states;
   TotArea+Size;
   NumStates+1;
    /*Sum statements create TotArea and NumStates,
       retain, set initial values to 0, and ignore
       missing values of size*/
run;

proc print data=usarea;
run;
```

2. **Accumulating Totals for a Group of Data**

```
   /*Data must be sorted or indexed for
     BY-group processing*/
proc sort data=prog2.flymiles out=milesort;
   by ID;
run;

data freqmiles(drop=miles);
   set milesort;
   by ID;
    /*BY statement create First.ID and Last.ID*/
   if First.ID then TotMiles=0;
    /*Set TotMiles to 0 when ID changes*/
   TotMiles+Miles;
    /*Sum statement creates TotMiles, retains it,
       sets initial value to 0, and ignores missing
       values of miles*/
   if Last.ID;  /*Output only the last of
                                each BY group*/
run;

   /*Create a list report of the data set to verify
     the output*/

proc print data=freqmiles;
run;
```

3. Accumulating Totals for a Group of Data Using More than One BY Variable

```
      /*Data must be sorted or indexed for
        BY-group processing*/
proc sort data=prog2.flydays out=daysort;
   by ID Code;
run;

data daymiles(drop=Miles);
   set daysort;
   by ID Code;
     /*BY statement creates First.ID, Last.ID
                            First.Code, and Last.Code*/
   if First.Code then TotMiles=0;
   /*Set TotMiles to 0 when subgroup changes*/
   TotMiles+Miles;
      /*Sum statement creates TotMiles, retains it,
         sets initial value to 0, and ignores missing
         values of miles*/
   if Last.Code then output;/*Output only the last of
                              each BY group*/
run;

   /*Create a list report of the data set to verify
     the output*/

proc print data=daymiles;
run;
```

4. Detecting Duplicate Observations Using BY-Group Processing (Optional)

```
/*Data must be sorted or indexed for
  BY-group processing*/
proc sort data=prog2.dupsals out=dupsort;
   by EmpID;
run;

data gooddata baddata;
    /*Both new data sets must be listed
      on the DATA statement*/
   set dupsort;
   by EmpID;
      /*BY statement creates First.EmpID and
        Last.EmpID*/
   if First.EmpID and Last.EmpID
      /*first and last of this ID means it's unique*/
      then output gooddata;
   else output baddata;
run;

/*Create list reports to verify results*/

proc print data=gooddata;
   title 'Non-Duplicate EmpIDs';
run;

proc print data=baddata;
   title 'Duplicate EmpIDs';
run;
```

5. Rotating a Data Set (Optional)

```
data widebooks(drop=MerchType Sales);
   set prog2.salesbyday;
   by date;
   retain Books Cards Periodicals;
   if MerchType='Books' then Books=Sales;
   else if MerchType='Cards' then Cards=Sales;
   else if MerchType='Periodicals' then
        Periodicals=Sales;
   if last.date then output;
run;

proc print data=widebooks;
   title 'Rotating a Data Set';
run;
```

Chapter 4   Reading and Writing Different Types of Data

4.1   Reading Delimited Raw Data Files

Objectives

- Read a space-delimited raw data file.
- Read a comma-delimited raw data file.
- Read a raw data file with missing data at the end of a row.
- Read a raw data file with missing data represented by consecutive delimiters.

3

List Input with the Default Delimiter

```
50001  4feb1989 132 530
50002  11nov1989 152 540
50003  22oct1991 90 530
50004  4feb1993 172 550
50005  24jun1993 170 510
50006  20dec1994 180 520
```

- The data is not in fixed columns.
- The fields are separated by spaces.
- There is one nonstandard field.

4

List Input

Raw data with fields that are not in fixed columns is called *free format*. Use list input to read free-format data.

The list input style signals to the SAS System that fields are separated by delimiters.

SAS then reads from non-delimiter to delimiter instead of from a specific location on the raw data record.

5

Delimiters

Common delimiters are

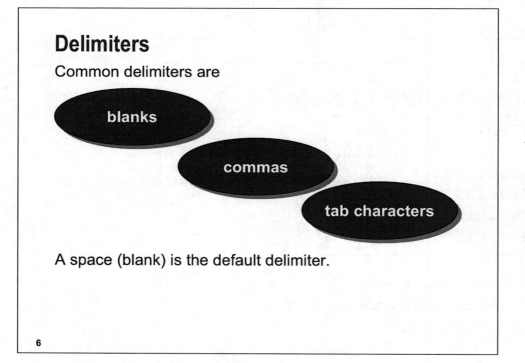

A space (blank) is the default delimiter.

6

List Input

General form of the INPUT statement for list input:

> **INPUT** *var-1* $ *var-2* . . . *var-n*;

You must specify the variables in the order that they appear in the raw data file.

Specify a $ after the variable name if it is character. No symbol after the variable name indicates a numeric variable.

7

Input Data

The second field is a date. How does SAS store date values?

```
50001  4feb1989  132  530
50002  11nov1989  152  540
50003  22oct1991  90  530
50004  4feb1993  172  550
50005  24jun1993  170  510
50006  20dec1994  180  520
```

8

Standard Data

The term *standard data* refers to character and numeric data that SAS recognizes automatically.

Examples of standard **numeric** data:

- 35469.93
- 3E5 (exponential notation)
- -46859

Standard **character** data is any character you can type on your keyboard. Standard character values are always left-justified by SAS.

9

The following are the only acceptable characters in a standard numeric field:

```
0 1 2 3 4 5 6 7 8 9 . E e D d - +
```

 E, e, D, and **d** represent exponential notation in a standard numeric field. For example, **3E5** is an alternative way of writing **300000**.

Nonstandard Data

The term *nonstandard data* refers to character and numeric data that SAS does not recognize automatically.

Examples of nonstandard numeric data:

- 12/12/2012
- 29FEB2000
- 4,242
- $89,000

10

Examples of nonstandard character data include preserving leading blanks in character values, hexadecimal characters, and values surrounded by matching quotes.

Informats

To read nonstandard data, you must apply an informat.

General form of an informat:

$$<\$>INFORMAT\text{-}NAME<w>.<d>$$

Informats are instructions that specify how SAS reads raw data.

11

$	indicates a character informat.
INFORMAT-NAME	is the name of the informat.
w	is an optional field width. If no width is specified, SAS uses the default width for that informat.
.	is the **required** delimiter.
d	is an optional decimal specification for numeric informats.

Informats

Examples of informats are

COMMA*w*.	reads numeric data ($4,242) and strips out selected nonnumeric characters, such as dollar signs and commas.
MMDDYY*w*.	reads dates in the form 12/31/2012.
DATE*w*.	reads dates in the form 29Feb2000.

12

With date **informats**, SAS uses the specified width to determine how far to read. With the list input style, the length of the informat is not important because the delimiter determines how far SAS reads.

With date **formats**, the specified width determines

- whether SAS displays a two- or four-digit year
- whether SAS displays dividers if they are valid for that format.

Specifying an Informat

To specify an informat when using list input, use the colon (:) format modifier in the INPUT statement between the variable name and the informat.

General form of a format modifier in an INPUT statement:

read & store

```
INPUT variable : informat;
```

13

Without the Colon

The colon signals that SAS should read from non-delimiter to delimiter.

If the colon is omitted, SAS reads the width of the **informat**, which might cause it to read past the end of the field or to stop reading before the end of the field.

- No error message is printed.
- You might see invalid data messages or unexpected data values.

14

Example: Suppose that you have the following data record:

```
Cheema,3May1975,F
```

and the programmer forgot the colon in the INPUT statement, as follows:

```
data new;
    infile 'birthdays.dat' dlm=', ';
    input Name $ Birthday date9. Gender $;
run;
```

For **Birthday**, SAS reads exactly nine characters, starting at the first position of the Date field. This results in the following value:

```
3May1975,
```

Commas are not valid in a date field. When SAS attempts to convert this value to a SAS date value, it prints an invalid data message to the log and sets the value of **Birthday** to missing.

Reading a Delimited Raw Data File

```
data airplanes;
   infile 'raw-data-file';
   input ID $
         InService : date9.
         PassCap CargoCap;
run;
```

How does SAS determine the lengths of these variables?

15

Lengths of Variables

When you use list input, the default length for character and numeric variables is eight bytes.

You can set the length of variables with a LENGTH statement or with an informat.

General form of a LENGTH statement:

LENGTH *variable-name(s)* <$> *length-specification ...;*

16

You do not need to set the lengths of numeric variables when reading with list input because the default width of eight bytes is sufficient. You cannot store a numeric in more than eight bytes. Storing a numeric in less than eight bytes reduces its precision and can cause unexpected results.

Setting the Length of a Variable

```
data airplanes;
   length ID $ 5;
   infile 'raw-data-file';
   input ID $
         InService : date9.
         PassCap CargoCap;
run;
```

17   c04s1d1.sas

An informat can also set the length of a character variable. The following code produces the same result as the code used in the example:

```
data airplanes;
   infile 'raw-data-file';
   input ID : $5.
         InService : date9.
         PassCap CargoCap;
run;
```

 If you use this method to set the lengths of character variables, be certain to use the colon modifier.

Using List Input: Compilation

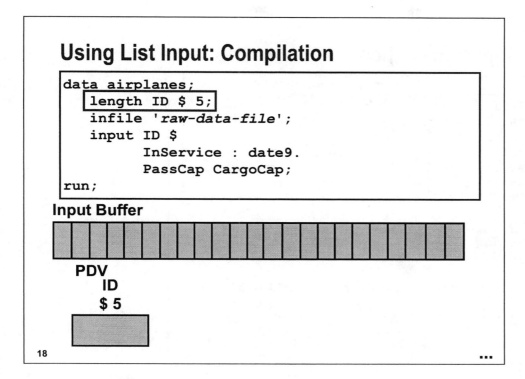

```
data airplanes;
   length ID $ 5;
   infile 'raw-data-file';
   input ID $
         InService : date9.
         PassCap CargoCap;
run;
```

Input Buffer

PDV
ID
$ 5

18

...

Using List Input: Compilation

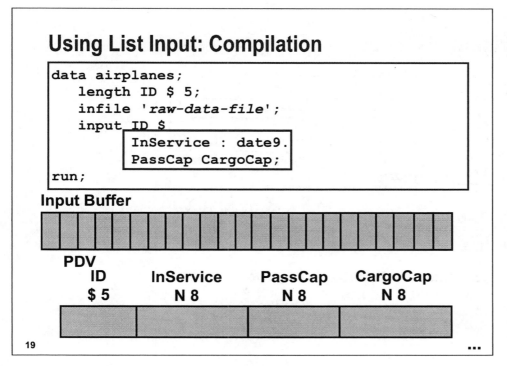

```
data airplanes;
   length ID $ 5;
   infile 'raw-data-file';
   input ID $
         InService : date9.
         PassCap CargoCap;
run;
```

Input Buffer

| PDV ID $ 5 | InService N 8 | PassCap N 8 | CargoCap N 8 |

19

...

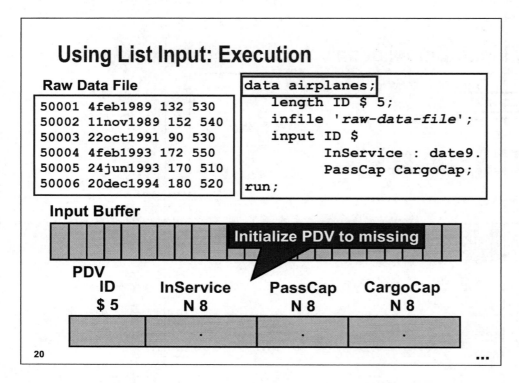

Using List Input: Execution

Raw Data File

```
50001  4feb1989 132 530
50002  11nov1989 152 540
50003  22oct1991 90 530
50004  4feb1993 172 550
50005  24jun1993 170 510
50006  20dec1994 180 520
```

```
data airplanes;
   length ID $ 5;
   infile 'raw-data-file';
   input ID $
          InService : date9.
          PassCap CargoCap;
run;
```

Input Buffer

Initialize PDV to missing

PDV ID $ 5	InService N 8	PassCap N 8	CargoCap N 8
	.	.	.

20   ...

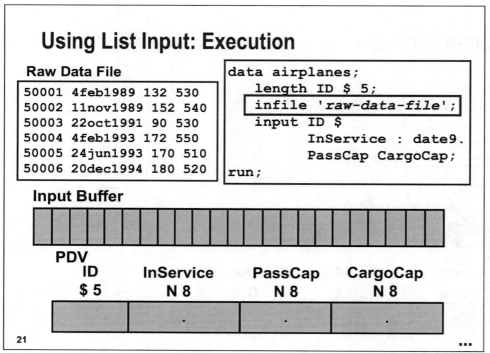

Using List Input: Execution

Raw Data File

```
50001  4feb1989 132 530
50002  11nov1989 152 540
50003  22oct1991 90 530
50004  4feb1993 172 550
50005  24jun1993 170 510
50006  20dec1994 180 520
```

```
data airplanes;
   length ID $ 5;
   infile 'raw-data-file';
   input ID $
          InService : date9.
          PassCap CargoCap;
run;
```

Input Buffer

PDV ID $ 5	InService N 8	PassCap N 8	CargoCap N 8
	.	.	.

21   ...

Using List Input: Execution

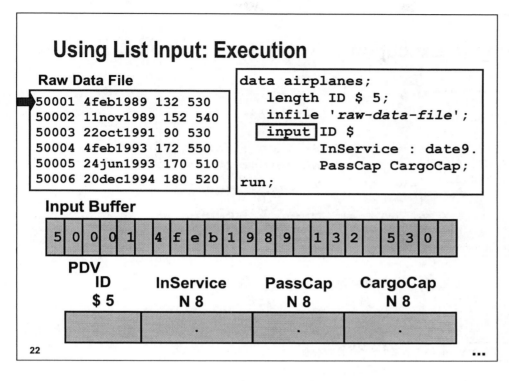

Raw Data File

```
50001 4feb1989 132 530
50002 11nov1989 152 540
50003 22oct1991 90 530
50004 4feb1993 172 550
50005 24jun1993 170 510
50006 20dec1994 180 520
```

```
data airplanes;
   length ID $ 5;
   infile 'raw-data-file';
   input ID $
         InService : date9.
         PassCap CargoCap;
run;
```

Input Buffer

| 5 | 0 | 0 | 0 | 1 | 4 | f | e | b | 1 | 9 | 8 | 9 | 1 | 3 | 2 | 5 | 3 | 0 | |

PDV

ID $ 5	InService N 8	PassCap N 8	CargoCap N 8
	.	.	.

22

...

Using List Input: Execution

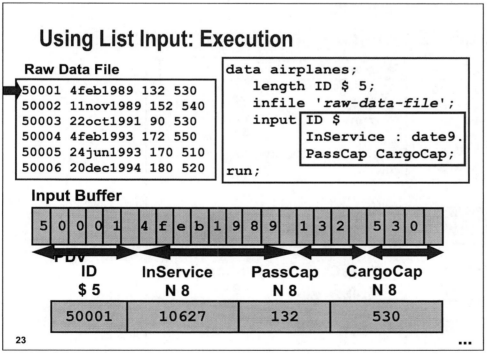

Raw Data File

```
50001 4feb1989 132 530
50002 11nov1989 152 540
50003 22oct1991 90 530
50004 4feb1993 172 550
50005 24jun1993 170 510
50006 20dec1994 180 520
```

```
data airplanes;
   length ID $ 5;
   infile 'raw-data-file';
   input ID $
         InService : date9.
         PassCap CargoCap;
run;
```

Input Buffer

| 5 | 0 | 0 | 0 | 1 | 4 | f | e | b | 1 | 9 | 8 | 9 | 1 | 3 | 2 | 5 | 3 | 0 | |

PDV

ID $ 5	InService N 8	PassCap N 8	CargoCap N 8
50001	10627	132	530

23

...

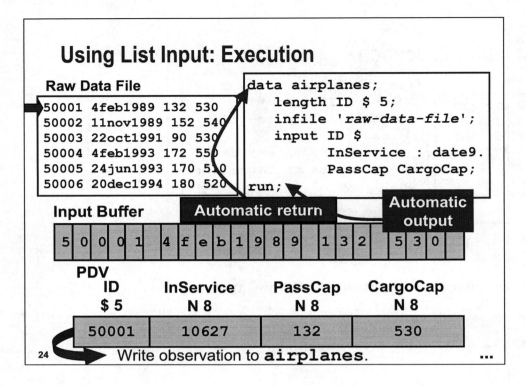

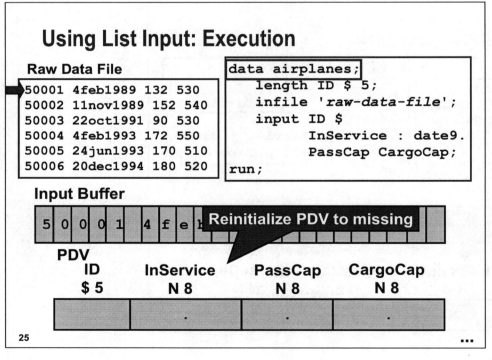

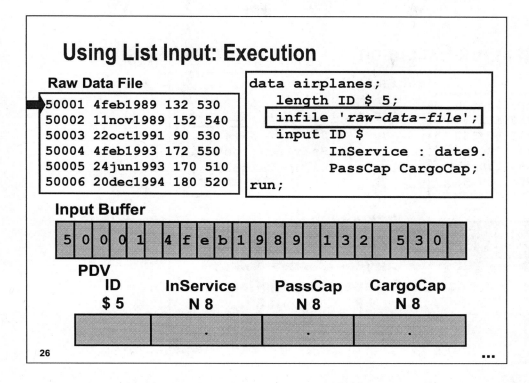

Using List Input: Execution

Raw Data File

```
50001  4feb1989 132 530
50002  11nov1989 152 540
50003  22oct1991  90 530
50004  4feb1993 172 550
50005  24jun1993 170 510
50006  20dec1994 180 520
```

```
data airplanes;
   length ID $ 5;
   infile 'raw-data-file';
   input ID $
           InService : date9.
           PassCap CargoCap;
run;
```

Input Buffer

5	0	0	0	1	4	f	e	b	1	9	8	9	1	3	2	5	3	0

PDV

ID $ 5	InService N 8	PassCap N 8	CargoCap N 8
	.	.	.

26   ...

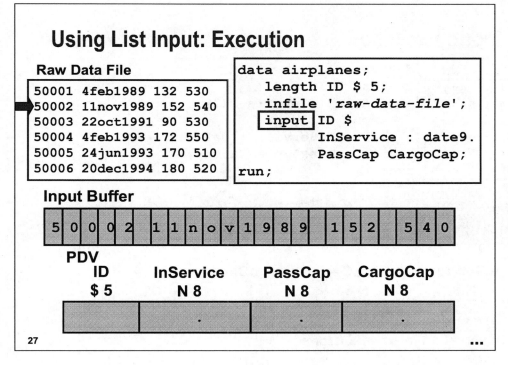

Using List Input: Execution

Raw Data File

```
50001  4feb1989 132 530
50002  11nov1989 152 540
50003  22oct1991  90 530
50004  4feb1993 172 550
50005  24jun1993 170 510
50006  20dec1994 180 520
```

```
data airplanes;
   length ID $ 5;
   infile 'raw-data-file';
   input ID $
           InService : date9.
           PassCap CargoCap;
run;
```

Input Buffer

5	0	0	0	2	1	1	n	o	v	1	9	8	9	1	5	2	5	4	0

PDV

ID $ 5	InService N 8	PassCap N 8	CargoCap N 8
	.	.	.

27   ...

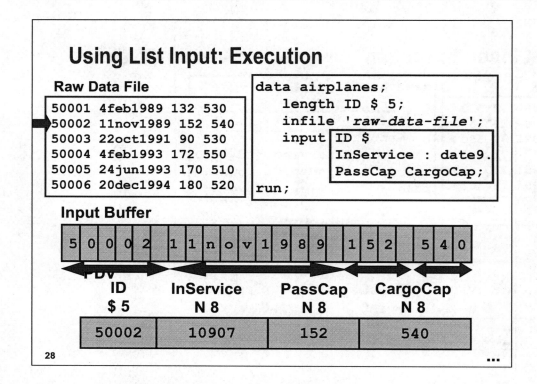

Using List Input: Execution

Raw Data File

```
50001  4feb1989 132 530
50002  11nov1989 152 540
50003  22oct1991 90 530
50004  4feb1993 172 550
50005  24jun1993 170 510
50006  20dec1994 180 520
```

```
data airplanes;
   length ID $ 5;
   infile 'raw-data-file';
   input ID $
         InService : date9.
         PassCap CargoCap;
run;
```

Input Buffer

| 5 | 0 | 0 | 0 | 2 | | 1 | 1 | n | o | v | 1 | 9 | 8 | 9 | | 1 | 5 | 2 | | 5 | 4 | 0 |

PDV

ID $ 5	InService N 8	PassCap N 8	CargoCap N 8
50002	10907	152	540

28   ...

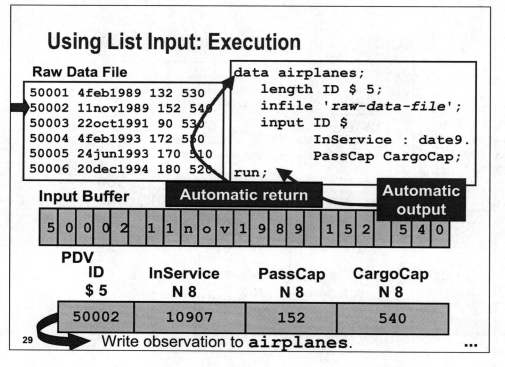

Using List Input: Execution

Raw Data File

```
50001  4feb1989 132 530
50002  11nov1989 152 540
50003  22oct1991 90 530
50004  4feb1993 172 550
50005  24jun1993 170 510
50006  20dec1994 180 520
```

```
data airplanes;
   length ID $ 5;
   infile 'raw-data-file';
   input ID $
            InService : date9.
            PassCap CargoCap;
run;
```

Automatic return   **Automatic output**

Input Buffer

| 5 | 0 | 0 | 0 | 2 | | 1 | 1 | n | o | v | 1 | 9 | 8 | 9 | | 1 | 5 | 2 | | 5 | 4 | 0 |

PDV

ID $ 5	InService N 8	PassCap N 8	CargoCap N 8
50002	10907	152	540

29   Write observation to **airplanes**.   ...

Using List Input: Execution

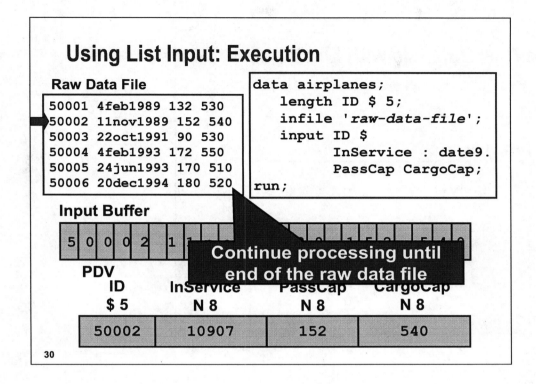

Raw Data File

```
50001  4feb1989 132 530
50002  11nov1989 152 540
50003  22oct1991 90 530
50004  4feb1993 172 550
50005  24jun1993 170 510
50006  20dec1994 180 520
```

```
data airplanes;
   length ID $ 5;
   infile 'raw-data-file';
   input ID $
         InService : date9.
         PassCap CargoCap;
run;
```

Input Buffer

| 5 | 0 | 0 | 0 | 2 | 1 | 1 | | | | | | | 1 | 5 | 2 | 5 | 4 | 0 |

**Continue processing until
end of the raw data file**

PDV

ID $ 5	InService N 8	PassCap N 8	CargoCap N 8
50002	10907	152	540

30

Reading a Raw Data File with List Input

```
proc print data=airplanes noobs;
run;
```

PROC PRINT Output

ID	In Service	Pass Cap	Cargo Cap
50001	10627	132	530
50002	10907	152	540
50003	11617	90	530
50004	12088	172	550
50005	12228	170	510
50006	12772	180	520

31   c04s1d1.sas

 InService appears as a SAS date, that is, the number of days since January 1, 1960. To change the date's appearance, apply a SAS date format with a FORMAT statement in the PRINT procedure. You can also use a FORMAT statement in the DATA step to permanently associate a format with a variable.

Non-Default Delimiter

The fields are separated by commas.

```
50001 , 4feb1989,132, 530
50002, 11nov1989,152, 540
50003, 22oct1991,90, 530
50004, 4feb1993,172, 550
50005, 24jun1993, 170, 510
50006, 20dec1994, 180, 520
```

32

Using the DLM= Option

The DLM= option sets a character or characters that SAS recognizes as a delimiter in the raw data file.

General form of the INFILE statement with the DLM= option:

> **INFILE** *'raw-data-file'* DLM=*'delimiter(s)'*;

Any character you can type on your keyboard can be a delimiter. You can also use hexadecimal characters.

33

If you specify more than one delimiter in the DLM= option, **any** of those characters is recognized as a delimiter. For example, DLM = ',!' indicates that either a comma or an exclamation point acts as a delimiter. By default, two or more consecutive delimiters are treated as one; therefore, a comma and an exclamation point together are also treated as a delimiter.

One example of a hexadecimal character is a tab character. To specify a tab character on a PC or on UNIX, type **dlm='09'x**. To specify a tab character on z/OS, type **dlm='05'x**.

 You can find the hexadecimal representation of a printable character using the HEX*w*. or $HEX*w*. format in SAS. For nonprintable characters like a tab character, you should consult a programming reference for your operating system.

Specifying a Delimiter

```
data airplanes2;
   length ID $ 5;
   infile 'raw-data-file' dlm=',';
   input ID $
         InService : date9.
         PassCap CargoCap;
run;
```

34   c04s1d1.sas

Missing Data at the End of a Row

```
50001 , 4feb1989,132
50002, 11nov1989,152, 540
50003, 22oct1991,90, 530
50004, 4feb1993,172
50005, 24jun1993, 170, 510
50006, 20dec1994, 180, 520
```

35

Missing Data at the End of a Row

By default, when there is missing data at the end of a row, the following occurs:

1. SAS loads the next record to finish the observation.
2. A note is written to the log.

36

Missing Data at the End of a Row: Execution

Raw Data File

```
50001 , 4feb1989,132
50002, 11nov1989,152, 540
50003, 22oct1991,90, 530
50004, 4feb1993,172
50005, 24jun1993, 170, 510
50006, 20dec1994, 180, 520
```

```
data airplanes3;
   length ID $ 5;
   infile 'raw-data-file'
        dlm=',';
   input ID $
        InService : date9.
        PassCap CargoCap;
run;
```

Input Buffer

Initialize PDV to missing

```
PDV
  ID        InService    PassCap      CargoCap
 $ 5          N 8          N 8          N 8
```

37   ...

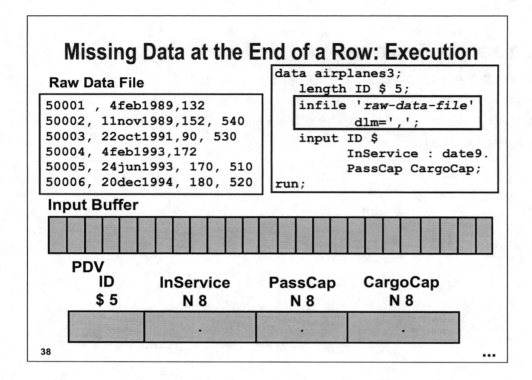

Missing Data at the End of a Row: Execution

Raw Data File

```
50001 , 4feb1989,132
50002, 11nov1989,152, 540
50003, 22oct1991,90, 530
50004, 4feb1993,172
50005, 24jun1993, 170, 510
50006, 20dec1994, 180, 520
```

```
data airplanes3;
   length ID $ 5;
   infile 'raw-data-file'
        dlm=',';
   input ID $
        InService : date9.
        PassCap CargoCap;
run;
```

Input Buffer

PDV

ID $ 5	InService N 8	PassCap N 8	CargoCap N 8
	.	.	.

38

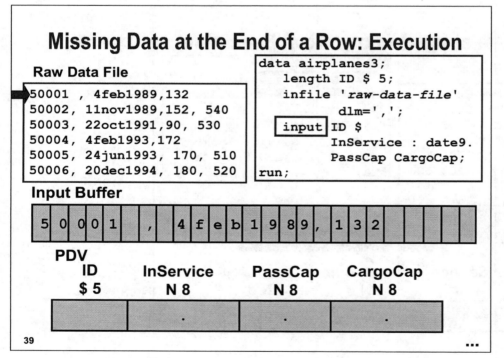

Missing Data at the End of a Row: Execution

Raw Data File

```
50001   , 4feb1989,132
50002, 11nov1989,152, 540
50003, 22oct1991,90, 530
50004, 4feb1993,172
50005, 24jun1993, 170, 510
50006, 20dec1994, 180, 520
```

```
data airplanes3;
   length ID $ 5;
   infile 'raw-data-file'
        dlm=',';
   input ID $
        InService : date9.
        PassCap CargoCap;
run;
```

Input Buffer

| 5 | 0 | 0 | 0 | 1 | | , | | 4 | f | e | b | 1 | 9 | 8 | 9 | , | 1 | 3 | 2 | | | | |

PDV

ID $ 5	InService N 8	PassCap N 8	CargoCap N 8
	.	.	.

39

Missing Data at the End of a Row: Execution

Raw Data File

```
50001 , 4feb1989,132
50002, 11nov1989,152, 540
50003, 22oct1991,90, 530
50004, 4feb1993,172
50005, 24jun1993, 170, 510
50006, 20dec1994, 180, 520
```

```
data airplanes3;
   length ID $ 5;
   infile 'raw-data-file'
          dlm=',';
   input ID $
         InService : date9.
         PassCap CargoCap;
run;
```

Input Buffer

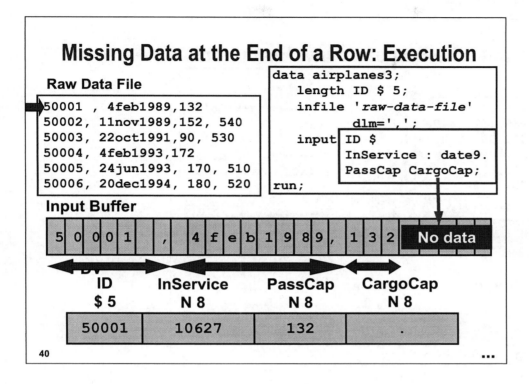

40

...

Missing Data at the End of a Row: Execution

Raw Data File

```
50001 , 4feb1989,132
50002, 11nov1989,152, 540
50003, 22oct1991,90, 530
50004, 4feb1993,172
50005, 24jun1993, 170, 510
50006, 20dec1994, 180, 520
```

```
data airplanes3;
   length ID $ 5;
   infile 'raw-data-file'
          dlm=',';
   input ID $
         InService : date9.
         PassCap CargoCap;
run;
```

Input Buffer

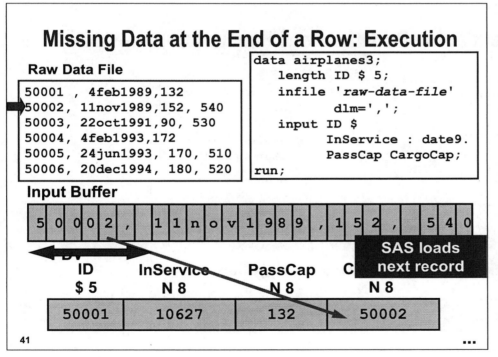

41

...

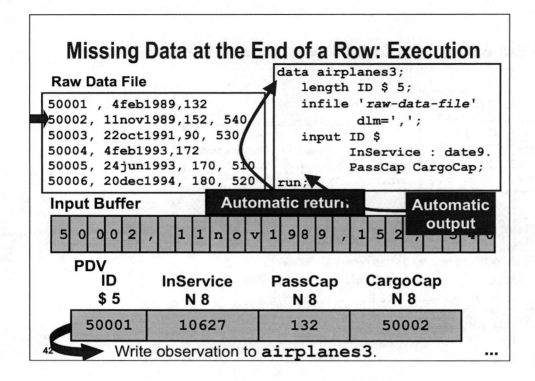

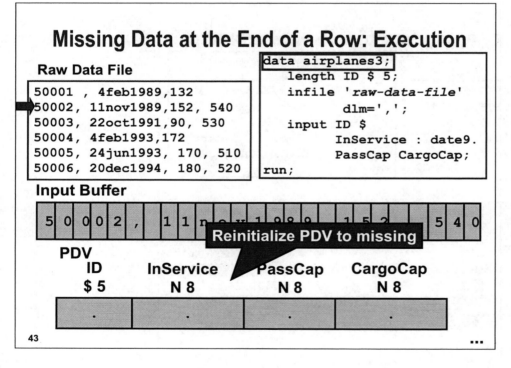

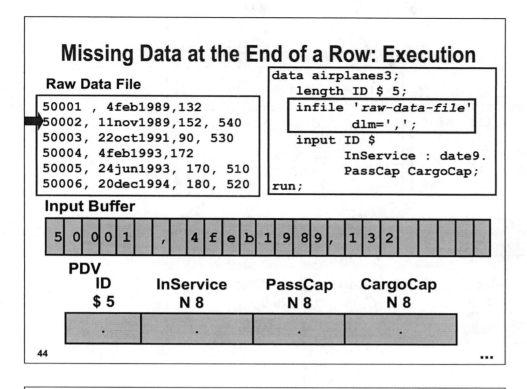

Missing Data at the End of a Row: Execution

Raw Data File

```
50001 , 4feb1989,132
50002, 11nov1989,152, 540
50003, 22oct1991,90, 530
50004, 4feb1993,172
50005, 24jun1993, 170, 510
50006, 20dec1994, 180, 520
```

```
data airplanes3;
   length ID $ 5;
   infile 'raw-data-file'
          dlm=',';
   input ID $
          InService : date9.
          PassCap CargoCap;
run;
```

Input Buffer

| 5 | 0 | 0 | 0 | 1 | | , | | 4 | f | e | b | 1 | 9 | 8 | 9 | , | 1 | 3 | 2 | | | | |

PDV

ID $ 5	InService N 8	PassCap N 8	CargoCap N 8
.	.	.	.

44   ...

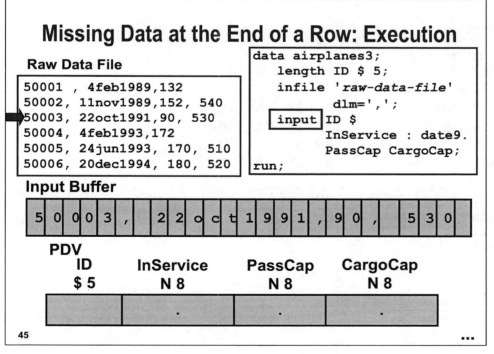

Missing Data at the End of a Row: Execution

Raw Data File

```
50001 , 4feb1989,132
50002, 11nov1989,152, 540
50003, 22oct1991,90, 530
50004, 4feb1993,172
50005, 24jun1993, 170, 510
50006, 20dec1994, 180, 520
```

```
data airplanes3;
   length ID $ 5;
   infile 'raw-data-file'
          dlm=',';
   input ID $
          InService : date9.
          PassCap CargoCap;
run;
```

Input Buffer

| 5 | 0 | 0 | 0 | 3 | , | | 2 | 2 | o | c | t | 1 | 9 | 9 | 1 | , | 9 | 0 | , | | 5 | 3 | 0 |

PDV

ID $ 5	InService N 8	PassCap N 8	CargoCap N 8
	.	.	.

45   ...

Missing Data at the End of a Row: Execution

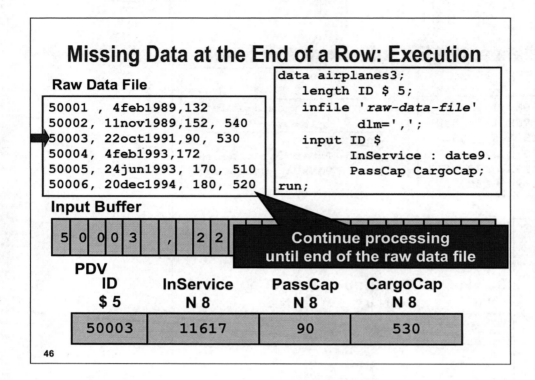

Raw Data File

```
50001 , 4feb1989,132
50002, 11nov1989,152, 540
50003, 22oct1991,90, 530
50004, 4feb1993,172
50005, 24jun1993, 170, 510
50006, 20dec1994, 180, 520
```

```
data airplanes3;
   length ID $ 5;
   infile 'raw-data-file'
       dlm=',';
   input ID $
       InService : date9.
       PassCap CargoCap;
run;
```

Input Buffer

| 5 | 0 | 0 | 0 | 3 | | , | | 2 | 2 |

Continue processing
until end of the raw data file

PDV

ID $ 5	InService N 8	PassCap N 8	CargoCap N 8
50003	11617	90	530

46

Partial SAS Log

```
NOTE: 6 records were read from the infile
      'aircraft3.dat'.
      The minimum record length was 19.
      The maximum record length was 26.
NOTE: SAS went to a new line when INPUT
      statement reached past the end of
      a line.
NOTE: The data set WORK.AIRPLANES3 has 4
      observations and 4 variables.
```

47

Missing Data at the End of the Row

```
proc print data=airplanes3 noobs;
run;
```

PROC PRINT Output

ID	In Service	Pass Cap	Cargo Cap
50001	10627	132	50002
50003	11617	90	530
50004	12088	172	50005
50006	12772	180	520

48

The MISSOVER Option

The MISSOVER option prevents SAS from loading a new record when the end of the current record is reached.

General form of the INFILE statement with the MISSOVER option:

INFILE *'raw-data-file'* MISSOVER;

If SAS reaches the end of the row without finding values for all fields, variables without values are set to missing.

49

Using the MISSOVER Option

```
data airplanes3;
   length ID $ 5;
   infile 'raw-data-file' dlm=',' missover;
   input ID $
         InService : date9.
         PassCap CargoCap;
run;
```

50   c04s1d1.sas

Using the MISSOVER Option

Partial SAS Log

```
NOTE: 6 records were read from the infile
      'aircraft3.dat'.
      The minimum record length was 19.
      The maximum record length was 26.
NOTE: The data set WORK.AIRPLANES3 has 6
      observations and 4 variables.
```

51

Using the MISSOVER Option

```
proc print data=airplanes3 noobs;
run;
```

PROC PRINT Output

ID	In Service	Pass Cap	Cargo Cap
50001	10627	132	.
50002	10907	152	540
50003	11617	90	530
50004	12088	172	.
50005	12228	170	510
50006	12772	180	520

52   c04s1d1.sas

The MISSOVER option is also valid in formatted and column input and can be used when you want to ensure that incomplete fields are set to missing. Suppose there is a raw data file with the following values:

```
1
22
333
```

If the shorter records are not padded with blanks, reading the file with the following code produces all missing values:

```
data nums;
    infile 'raw-data-file' missover;
    input num 4.;
run;
```

Notice the informat. This specifies that SAS is to look for exactly four bytes of data. In this case, the MISSOVER option indicates the variable is to be set to missing if the field is three bytes or less.

The TRUNCOVER option enables SAS to read variable-length records without setting incomplete fields to missing. If the same raw data file is read with the code

```
data nums;
    infile 'raw-data-file' truncover;
    input num 4.;
run;
```

the resulting values are 1, 22, 333.

When used with list input and without informats, the MISSOVER and TRUNCOVER options produce the same results.

Another INFILE statement option that deals with variable length records is the PAD option. The PAD option instructs SAS to make all records the same length by adding spaces to the end of shorter records. All records are padded to either the default record length or the record length specified by the LRECL= option. It is often used in the Windows operating environment with column or formatted input to prevent carriage returns from affecting how raw data is read.

The PAD option is **not** appropriate for reading delimited files with list input because it can cause unexpected results. This is especially true if the data is delimited with spaces or if there is potentially more than one missing field at the end of some rows.

Missing Values without a Placeholder

There is missing data represented by two consecutive delimiters.

```
50001 , 4feb1989,, 530
50002, 11nov1989,132, 540
50003, 22oct1991,90, 530
50004, 4feb1993,172, 550
50005, 24jun1993,, 510
50006, 20dec1994, 180, 520
```

53

Missing Values without a Placeholder

By default, SAS treats two consecutive delimiters as one. Missing data should be represented by a placeholder.

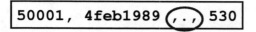

```
50001, 4feb1989 (,.,) 530
```

A placeholder can be a period if the data is numeric, or a space if the data is character and the file is not space-delimited.

Missing Values without a Placeholder

```
data airplanes4;
   length ID $ 5;
   infile 'raw-data-file' dlm=',';
   input ID $
         InService : date9.
         PassCap CargoCap;
run;
```

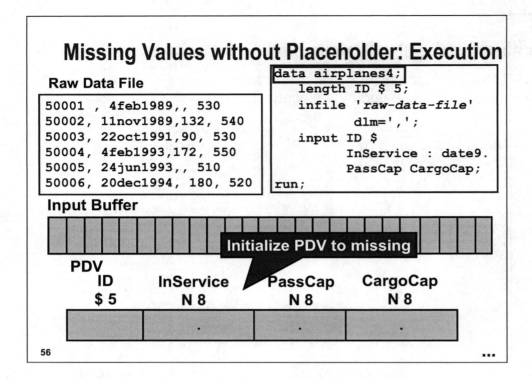

Missing Values without Placeholder: Execution

Raw Data File

```
50001 , 4feb1989,, 530
50002, 11nov1989,132, 540
50003, 22oct1991,90, 530
50004, 4feb1993,172, 550
50005, 24jun1993,, 510
50006, 20dec1994, 180, 520
```

```
data airplanes4;
    length ID $ 5;
    infile 'raw-data-file'
            dlm=',';
    input ID $
            InService : date9.
            PassCap CargoCap;
run;
```

Input Buffer

Initialize PDV to missing

PDV ID $ 5	InService N 8	PassCap N 8	CargoCap N 8
	.	.	.

56

...

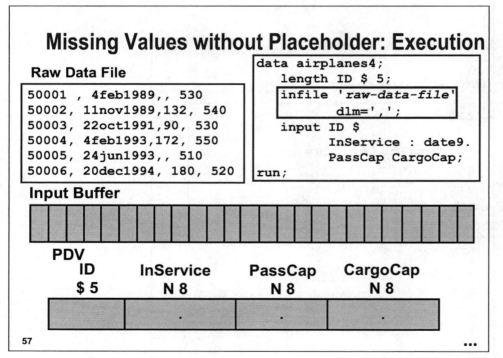

Missing Values without Placeholder: Execution

Raw Data File

```
50001 , 4feb1989,, 530
50002, 11nov1989,132, 540
50003, 22oct1991,90, 530
50004, 4feb1993,172, 550
50005, 24jun1993,, 510
50006, 20dec1994, 180, 520
```

```
data airplanes4;
    length ID $ 5;
    infile 'raw-data-file'
            dlm=',';
    input ID $
            InService : date9.
            PassCap CargoCap;
run;
```

Input Buffer

PDV ID $ 5	InService N 8	PassCap N 8	CargoCap N 8
	.	.	.

57

...

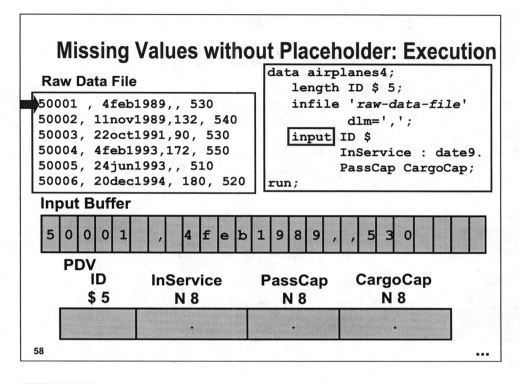

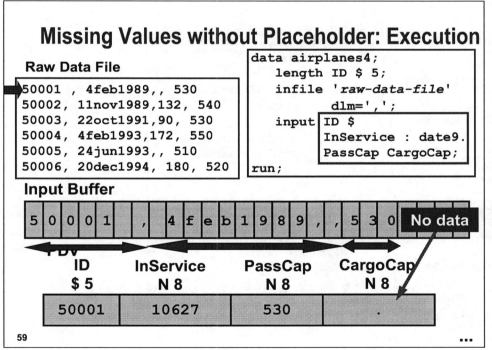

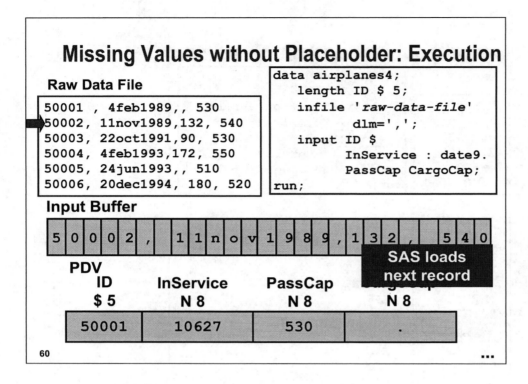

Missing Values without Placeholder: Execution

Raw Data File

```
50001 , 4feb1989,, 530
50002, 11nov1989,132, 540
50003, 22oct1991,90, 530
50004, 4feb1993,172, 550
50005, 24jun1993,, 510
50006, 20dec1994, 180, 520
```

```
data airplanes4;
    length ID $ 5;
    infile 'raw-data-file'
        dlm=',';
    input ID $
        InService : date9.
        PassCap CargoCap;
run;
```

Input Buffer

| 5 | 0 | 0 | 0 | 2 | , | | 1 | 1 | n | o | v | 1 | 9 | 8 | 9 | , | 1 | 3 | 2 | , | | 5 | 4 | 0 |

PDV

SAS loads next record

ID $ 5	InService N 8	PassCap N 8	CargoCap N 8
50001	10627	530	.

60   ...

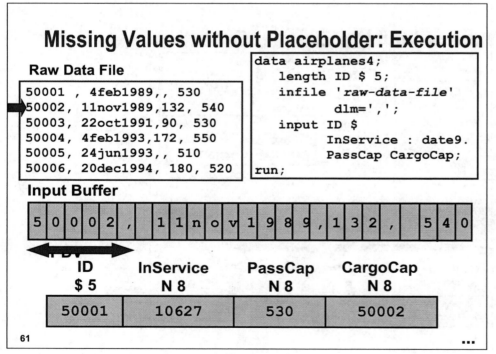

Missing Values without Placeholder: Execution

Raw Data File

```
50001 , 4feb1989,, 530
50002, 11nov1989,132, 540
50003, 22oct1991,90, 530
50004, 4feb1993,172, 550
50005, 24jun1993,, 510
50006, 20dec1994, 180, 520
```

```
data airplanes4;
    length ID $ 5;
    infile 'raw-data-file'
        dlm=',';
    input ID $
        InService : date9.
        PassCap CargoCap;
run;
```

Input Buffer

| 5 | 0 | 0 | 0 | 2 | , | | 1 | 1 | n | o | v | 1 | 9 | 8 | 9 | , | 1 | 3 | 2 | , | | 5 | 4 | 0 |

PDV

ID $ 5	InService N 8	PassCap N 8	CargoCap N 8
50001	10627	530	50002

61   ...

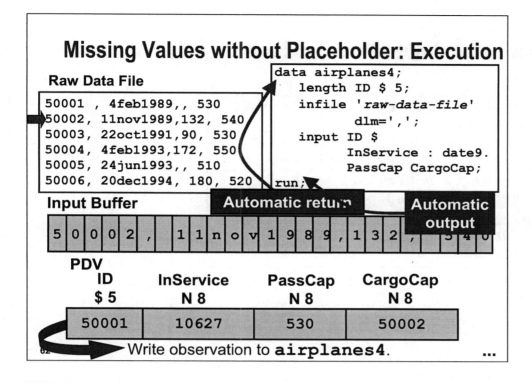

Missing Values without Placeholder: Execution

Raw Data File

```
50001 , 4feb1989,, 530
50002, 11nov1989,132, 540
50003, 22oct1991,90, 530
50004, 4feb1993,172, 550
50005, 24jun1993,, 510
50006, 20dec1994, 180, 520
```

```
data airplanes4;
   length ID $ 5;
   infile 'raw-data-file'
         dlm=',';
   input ID $
         InService : date9.
         PassCap CargoCap;
run;
```

Input Buffer

| 5 | 0 | 0 | 0 | 2 | , | | 1 | 1 | n | o | v | 1 | 9 | 8 | 9 | , | 1 | 3 | 2 | , | 5 | 4 | 0 |

Automatic return   **Automatic output**

PDV

ID $ 5	InService N 8	PassCap N 8	CargoCap N 8
50001	10627	530	50002

Write observation to `airplanes4`.   ...

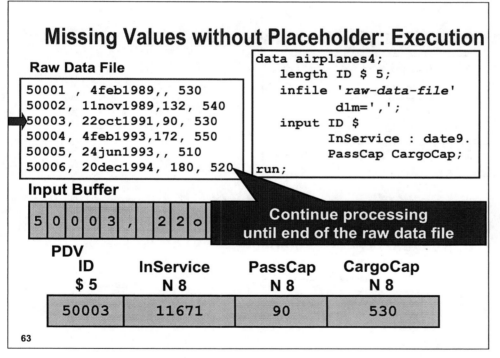

Missing Values without Placeholder: Execution

Raw Data File

```
50001 , 4feb1989,, 530
50002, 11nov1989,132, 540
50003, 22oct1991,90, 530
50004, 4feb1993,172, 550
50005, 24jun1993,, 510
50006, 20dec1994, 180, 520
```

```
data airplanes4;
   length ID $ 5;
   infile 'raw-data-file'
         dlm=',';
   input ID $
         InService : date9.
         PassCap CargoCap;
run;
```

Input Buffer

| 5 | 0 | 0 | 0 | 3 | , | | 2 | 2 | o | | | | | | |

Continue processing until end of the raw data file

PDV

ID $ 5	InService N 8	PassCap N 8	CargoCap N 8
50003	11671	90	530

63

Missing Values without a Placeholder

Partial SAS Log

```
NOTE: 6 records were read from the infile
      'aircraft4.dat'.
      The minimum record length was 21.
      The maximum record length was 26.
NOTE: SAS went to a new line when INPUT
      statement reached past the end of a
      line.
NOTE: The data set WORK.AIRPLANES4 has 4
      observations and 4 variables.
```

64

Missing Values without a Placeholder

```
proc print data=airplanes4 noobs;
run;
```

PROC PRINT Output

| | In | Pass | Cargo |
ID	Service	Cap	Cap
50001	10627	530	50002
50003	11617	90	530
50004	12088	172	550
50005	12228	510	50006

65

Missing Values without a Placeholder

If your data does not have a placeholder, use the
DSD option.

```
50001 , 4feb1989  ,,   530
```

66

The DSD Option

General form of the DSD option in the INFILE statement:

INFILE '*raw-data-file*' DSD;

67

The DSD Option

The DSD option

- sets the default delimiter to a comma
- treats consecutive delimiters as missing values
- enables SAS to read values with embedded delimiters if the value is surrounded by matching quotation marks.

68

For example, the following record is comma-delimited, but the salary value has an embedded comma.

```
Zoellner, Jane, "$55,000"
```

The DSD option signals SAS to ignore delimiters that are surrounded by matching quotation marks.

Using the DSD Option

```
data airplanes4;
   length ID $ 5;
   infile 'raw-data-file' dsd;
   input ID $
         InService : date9.
         PassCap CargoCap;
run;
```

69   c04s1d1.sas

Missing Values without a Placeholder

Partial SAS Log

```
NOTE: 6 records were read from the infile
      'aircraft4.dat'.
      The minimum record length was 22.
      The maximum record length was 25.
NOTE: The data set WORK.AIRPLANES4 has 6
      observations and 4 variables.
```

70

Using the DSD Option

```
proc print data=airplanes4 noobs;
run;
```

PROC PRINT Output

ID	In Service	Pass Cap	Cargo Cap
50001	10627	.	530
50002	10907	132	540
50003	11617	90	530
50004	12088	172	550
50005	12228	.	510
50006	12772	180	520

c04s1d1.sas

71

INFILE Statement Options

Problem	Option
Non-blank delimiters	DLM='*delimiter(s)*'
Missing data at end of row	MISSOVER
Missing data represented by consecutive delimiters **and/or** Embedded delimiters where values are surrounded by matching quotation marks	DSD

These options can be used separately or together in the INFILE statement.

 **Exercises**

1. Reading Nonstandard Data

The **STATES** raw data file contains information on state name, state population, state size, and date of statehood.

The order and layout of the fields are as follows:

Order	Field	Notes
1	State Name	Longest value is 14 characters
2	State Population	Written in COMMA10.
3	State Size	Square miles (numeric field)
4	Date of Statehood	Written in DATE9.

Sample Records

```
Alabama! 4,447,100! 50750! 14DEC1819
Alaska! 626,932! 570374! 03JAN1959
Arizona! 5,130,632! 113642! 14FEB1912
Arkansas! 2,673,400! 52075! 15JUN1836
California! 33,871,648! 155973! 09SEP1850
Colorado! 4,301,261! 103729! 01AUG1876
Connecticut! 3,405,565! 4845! 09JAN1788
```

Use the **STATES** raw data file to create the **work.states** data set listed below.

Partial Listing of **work.states**

```
                                             Enter
      Obs     State        Population    Size    Date

       1    Alabama          4447100    50750   -51152
       2    Alaska            626932   570374     -363
       3    Arizona          5130632   113642   -17488
       4    Arkansas         2673400    52075   -45124
       5    California      33871648   155973   -39925
       6    Colorado         4301261   103729   -30467
       7    Connecticut      3405565     4845   -62813
       8    Delaware          783600     1955   -62846
       9    Florida         15982378    53997   -41941
      10    Georgia          8186453    57918   -62820
```

  The variable **EnterDate** is a SAS date, and it is displayed as the number of days since January 1, 1960 by default. To view the values as calendar dates, apply a SAS date format. (See Section 1.4, "Review of Displaying SAS Data Sets.") You can apply the format with a FORMAT statement in either the DATA step or the PROC PRINT step.

2. Using INFILE Statement Options to Change Defaults

The **AROMAS** raw data file contains information on different conditions and possible aromatherapy cures. For each record, the condition is listed first and followed by as many as three possible cures.

Order	Field	Notes
1	Condition	Longest value is 11 characters.
2	Possible Cure	Longest value is 11 characters.
3	Possible Cure	Longest value is 11 characters.
4	Possible Cure	Longest value is 11 characters.

Sample Records

```
ANGER "Ylang Ylang"
ANXIETY Bergamot Petitgrain
BOREDOM Lemongrass
DEPRESSION Basil Bergamot Immortelle
DULLNESS Grapefruit Lemongrass Lime
GRIEF Melissa
HEADACHE Chamomile Lavender
FATIGUE Basil Peppermint Rosemary
INSOMNIA Chamomile Lavender Marjoram
```

✎   The fields are separated by spaces, and one field has embedded delimiters with quotes around the value. All the records do not have values for all fields.

Use the **AROMAS** raw data file to create the **work.aromas** data set listed below.

```
                        Aromatherapy Data Set

        Obs    Condition    Cure1           Cure2         Cure3

         1     ANGER        Ylang Ylang
         2     ANXIETY      Bergamot        Petitgrain
         3     BOREDOM      Lemongrass
         4     DEPRESSION   Basil           Bergamot      Immortelle
         5     DULLNESS     Grapefruit      Lemongrass    Lime
         6     GRIEF        Melissa
         7     HEADACHE     Chamomile       Lavender
         8     FATIGUE      Basil           Peppermint    Rosemary
         9     INSOMNIA     Chamomile       Lavender      Marjoram
        10     MIGRAINE     Lavender
        11     STRESS       Benzoin         Bergamot      Chamomile
        12     VERTIGO      Lavender        Peppermint
        13     SHOCK        Peppermint      Petitgrain
```

✎   This data set is not intended as medical advice or as a guide to aromatherapy.

3. Reading a Fixed-Column Raw Data File with Variable Length Records (Optional)

The **AROMASF** raw data file is a fixed-column version of the **AROMAS** raw data file. It has the following layout:

Field	Starting Position	Field Length
Condition	1	10
Cure 1	11	11
Cure 2	22	11
Cure 3	33	11

Sample records

```
ANGER       Ylang Ylang
ANXIETY     Bergamot    Petitgrain
BOREDOM     Lemongrass
DEPRESSIONBasil         Bergamot    Immortelle
DULLNESS    Grapefruit  Lemongrass  Lime
GRIEF       Melissa
HEADACHE    Chamomile   Lavender
FATIGUE     Basil       Peppermint  Rosemary
INSOMNIA    Chamomile   Lavender    Marjoram
MIGRAINE    Lavender
STRESS      Benzoin     Bergamot    Chamomile
VERTIGO     Lavender    Peppermint
SHOCK       Peppermint  Petitgrain
```

Read the **AROMASF** raw data file, using column or formatted input, and create the **work.aromasf** SAS data set. Verify the data carefully. You should have the same output as in Exercise 2.

✎   For help on reading raw data with formatted input, review Chapter 1, Section 2. For help on options for fixed-column raw data files, read the notes about MISSOVER, TRUNCOVER, and PAD.

✎   This exercise is only appropriate for Windows and UNIX users.

4.2   Controlling when a Record Loads

Objectives

- Read a raw data file with multiple records per observation.
- Read a raw data file with mixed record types.
- Subset from a raw data file.
- Read a raw data file with multiple observations per record.

75

Multiple Records Per Observation

```
Farr, Sue
Anaheim, CA
869-7008
Anderson, Kay B.
Chicago, IL
483-3321
Tennenbaum, Mary Ann
Jefferson, MO
589-9030
```

A raw data file has three records per employee. Record 1 contains the first and last names, record 2 contains the city and state of residence, and record 3 contains the employee's phone number.

76

Desired Output

The SAS data set should have one observation per employee.

LName	FName	City	State	Phone
Farr	Sue	Anaheim	CA	869-7008
Anderson	Kay B.	Chicago	IL	483-3321
Tennenbaum	Mary Ann	Jefferson	MO	589-9030

77

The INPUT Statement

The SAS System loads a new record into the input buffer when it encounters an INPUT statement.

You can have multiple INPUT statements in one DATA step.

```
DATA SAS-data-set;
    INPUT var-1 var-2 var-3;
    INPUT var-4 var-5;
    <additional SAS statements>
```

Each INPUT statement ends with a semicolon.

78

Multiple INPUT Statements

```
data address;
   length LName FName $ 20
          City $ 25 State $ 2
          Phone $ 8;
   infile 'raw-data-file' dlm=',';
   input LName $ FName $;
   input City $ State $;
   input Phone $;
run;
```

Load Record →
Load Record →
Load Record →

81

Line Pointer Controls

You can also use line pointer controls to control when SAS loads a new record.

```
DATA SAS-data-set;
     INPUT var-1 var-2 var-3 /
           var-4 var-5;
     <additional SAS statements>
```

SAS loads the next record when it encounters a forward slash.

82

Reading Multiple Records per Observation

```
data address;
    length LName FName $ 20
            City $ 25 State $ 2
            Phone $ 8;
    infile 'raw-data-file' dlm=',';
    input LName $ FName $ /
            City $ State $ /
            Phone $;
run;
```

Load Record → (input LName $ FName $ / ← Load Record)
(City $ State $ / ← Load Record)

85

The forward slash is known as a *relative* line pointer control that moves the pointer relative to the line on which it currently appears. There is also an *absolute* line pointer control that moves the pointer to a specific line. Example:

```
data example;
    infile 'raw-data-file';
    input #1 LName $ FName $
          #2 City $ State $
          #3 Phone $;
run;
```

LName and **FName** are read from record 1, **City** and **State** from record 2, and **Phone** from record 3 on the first iteration of the DATA step. Then, **LName** and **FName** are read from record 4, **City** and **State** from record 5, and **Phone** from record 6 on the second iteration of the DATA step, and so on.

Reading Multiple Records per Observation

Partial SAS Log

```
NOTE: 9 records were read from
      the infile 'addresses.dat'.
      The minimum record length was 8.
      The maximum record length was 20.
NOTE: The data set WORK.ADDRESS has
      3 observations and 5 variables.
```

86

Reading Multiple Records per Observation

```
proc print data=address noobs;
run;
```

PROC PRINT Output

LName	FName	City	State	Phone
Farr	Sue	Anaheim	CA	869-7008
Anderson	Kay B.	Chicago	IL	483-3321
Tennenbaum	Mary Ann	Jefferson	MO	589-9030

c04s2d1.sas

87

Mixed Record Types

Not all records have the same format.

```
101 USA 1-20-1999 3295.50
3034 EUR 30JAN1999 1876,30
101 USA 1-30-1999 2938.00
128 USA 2-5-1999 2908.74
1345 EUR 6FEB1999 3145,60
109 USA 3-17-1999 2789.10
```

The dates are represented differently and the decimal places and commas are reversed for the USA and European sales figures.

88

Desired Output

Sales ID	Location	Sale Date	Amount
101	USA	14264	3295.50
3034	EUR	14274	1876.30
101	USA	14274	2938.00
128	USA	14280	2908.74
1345	EUR	14281	3145.60
109	USA	14320	2789.10

89

The INPUT Statement

Multiple INPUT statements are needed.

```
input SalesID $ Location $;
if Location='USA' then
    input SaleDate : mmddyy10.
         Amount;
else if Location='EUR' then
    input SaleDate : date9.
         Amount : commax8.;
```

90

Multiple Input Statements: Execution

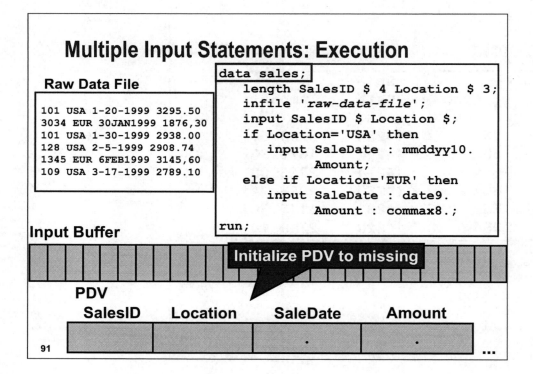

Raw Data File

```
101  USA  1-20-1999  3295.50
3034 EUR  30JAN1999  1876,30
101  USA  1-30-1999  2938.00
128  USA  2-5-1999   2908.74
1345 EUR  6FEB1999   3145,60
109  USA  3-17-1999  2789.10
```

```
data sales;
    length SalesID $ 4 Location $ 3;
    infile 'raw-data-file';
    input SalesID $ Location $;
    if Location='USA' then
        input SaleDate : mmddyy10.
             Amount;
    else if Location='EUR' then
        input SaleDate : date9.
             Amount : commax8.;
run;
```

Input Buffer

Initialize PDV to missing

PDV

SalesID	Location	SaleDate	Amount
		.	.

91

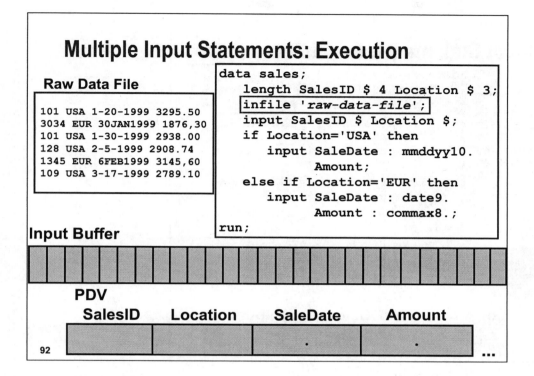

Multiple Input Statements: Execution

Raw Data File

```
101 USA 1-20-1999 3295.50
3034 EUR 30JAN1999 1876,30
101 USA 1-30-1999 2938.00
128 USA 2-5-1999 2908.74
1345 EUR 6FEB1999 3145,60
109 USA 3-17-1999 2789.10
```

```
data sales;
   length SalesID $ 4 Location $ 3;
   infile 'raw-data-file';
   input SalesID $ Location $;
   if Location='USA' then
      input SaleDate : mmddyy10.
            Amount;
   else if Location='EUR' then
      input SaleDate : date9.
            Amount : commax8.;
run;
```

Input Buffer

PDV

SalesID	Location	SaleDate	Amount
		.	.

92

...

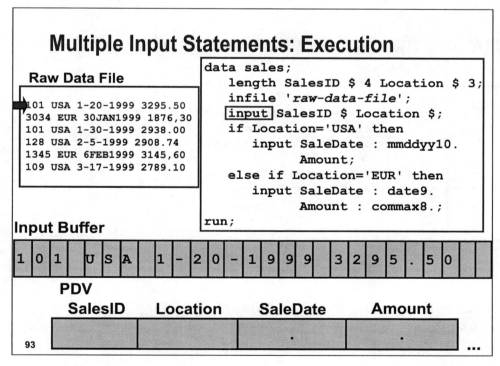

Multiple Input Statements: Execution

Raw Data File

```
101 USA 1-20-1999 3295.50
3034 EUR 30JAN1999 1876,30
101 USA 1-30-1999 2938.00
128 USA 2-5-1999 2908.74
1345 EUR 6FEB1999 3145,60
109 USA 3-17-1999 2789.10
```

```
data sales;
   length SalesID $ 4 Location $ 3;
   infile 'raw-data-file';
   input SalesID $ Location $;
   if Location='USA' then
      input SaleDate : mmddyy10.
            Amount;
   else if Location='EUR' then
      input SaleDate : date9.
            Amount : commax8.;
run;
```

Input Buffer

| 1 | 0 | 1 | | U | S | A | | 1 | - | 2 | 0 | - | 1 | 9 | 9 | 9 | | 3 | 2 | 9 | 5 | . | 5 | 0 | | |

PDV

SalesID	Location	SaleDate	Amount
		.	.

93

...

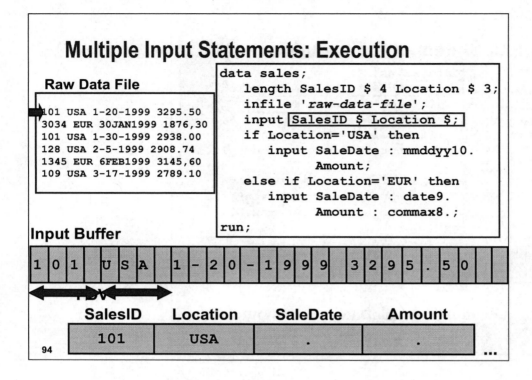

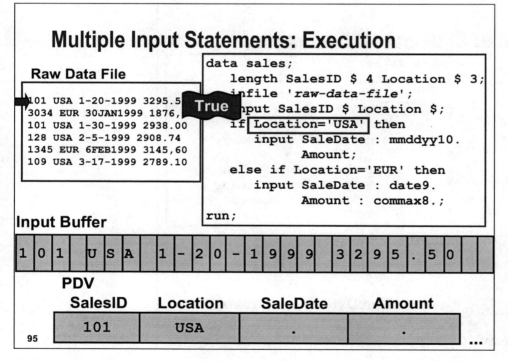

Multiple Input Statements: Execution

Raw Data File

```
101 USA 1-20-1999 3295.50
3034 EUR 30JAN1999 1876,30
101 USA 1-30-1999 2938.00
128 USA 2-5-1999 2908.74
1345 EUR 6FEB1999 3145,60
109 USA 3-17-1999 2789.10
```

```
data sales;
   length SalesID $ 4 Location $ 3;
   infile 'raw-data-file';
   input SalesID $ Location $;
   if Location='USA' then
      input SaleDate : mmddyy10.
           Amount;
   else if Location='EUR' then
      input SaleDate : date9.
           Amount : commax8.;
run;
```

Input Buffer

| 3 | 0 | 3 | 4 | | E | U | R | | 3 | 0 | J | A | N | 1 | 9 | 9 | 9 | | 1 | 8 | 7 | 6 | , | 3 | 0 |

PDV

SalesID	Location	SaleDate	Amount
101	USA	.	.

96

...

Multiple Input Statements: Execution

Raw Data File

```
101 USA 1-20-1999 3295.50
3034 EUR 30JAN1999 1876,30
101 USA 1-30-1999 2938.00
128 USA 2-5-1999 2908.74
1345 EUR 6FEB1999 3145,60
109 USA 3-17-1999 2789.10
```

```
data sales;
   length SalesID $ 4 Location $ 3;
   infile 'raw-data-file';
   input SalesID $ Location $;
   if Location='USA' then
      input SaleDate : mmddyy10.
           Amount;
   else if Location='EUR' then
      input SaleDate : date9.
           Amount : commax8.;
run;
```

Input Buffer

| 3 | 0 | 3 | 4 | | E | U | R | | 3 | 0 | J | A | N | 1 | 9 | 9 | 9 | | 1 | 8 | 7 | 6 | , | 3 | 0 |

PDV

SalesID	Location	SaleDate	Amount
101	USA	.	.

97

...

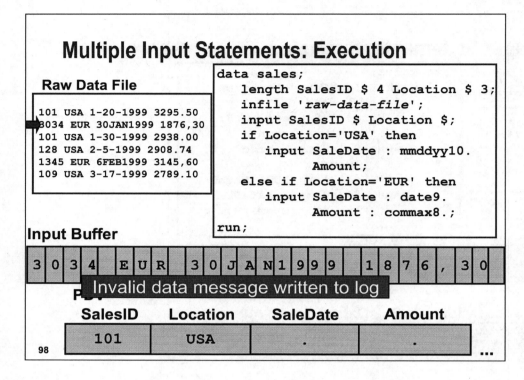

Multiple Input Statements: Execution

Raw Data File

```
101 USA 1-20-1999 3295.50
3034 EUR 30JAN1999 1876,30
101 USA 1-30-1999 2938.00
128 USA 2-5-1999 2908.74
1345 EUR 6FEB1999 3145,60
109 USA 3-17-1999 2789.10
```

```
data sales;
   length SalesID $ 4 Location $ 3;
   infile 'raw-data-file';
   input SalesID $ Location $;
   if Location='USA' then
      input SaleDate : mmddyy10.
            Amount;
   else if Location='EUR' then
      input SaleDate : date9.
            Amount : commax8.;
run;
```

Input Buffer

| 3 | 0 | 3 | 4 | | E | U | R | | 3 | 0 | J | A | N | 1 | 9 | 9 | 9 | | 1 | 8 | 7 | 6 | , | 3 | 0 |

Invalid data message written to log

PDV

SalesID	Location	SaleDate	Amount
101	USA	.	.

98

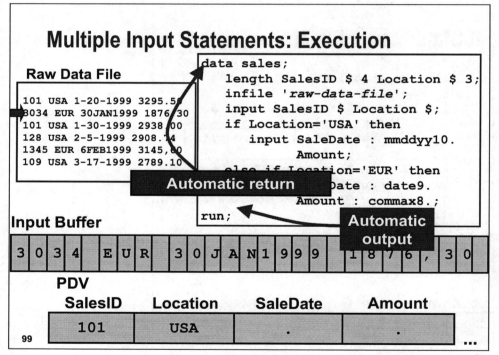

Multiple Input Statements: Execution

Raw Data File

```
101 USA 1-20-1999 3295.50
3034 EUR 30JAN1999 1876,30
101 USA 1-30-1999 2938.00
128 USA 2-5-1999 2908.74
1345 EUR 6FEB1999 3145,60
109 USA 3-17-1999 2789.10
```

```
data sales;
   length SalesID $ 4 Location $ 3;
   infile 'raw-data-file';
   input SalesID $ Location $;
   if Location='USA' then
      input SaleDate : mmddyy10.
            Amount;
   else if Location='EUR' then
      input SaleDate : date9.
            Amount : commax8.;
run;
```

Automatic return

Automatic output

Input Buffer

| 3 | 0 | 3 | 4 | | E | U | R | | 3 | 0 | J | A | N | 1 | 9 | 9 | 9 | | 1 | 8 | 7 | 6 | , | 3 | 0 |

PDV

SalesID	Location	SaleDate	Amount
101	USA	.	.

99

Multiple Input Statements: Execution

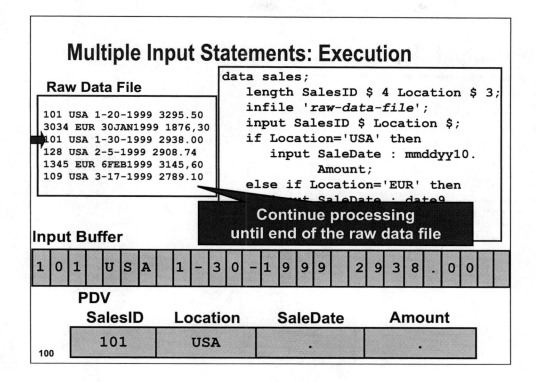

Raw Data File

```
101 USA 1-20-1999 3295.50
3034 EUR 30JAN1999 1876,30
101 USA 1-30-1999 2938.00
128 USA 2-5-1999 2908.74
1345 EUR 6FEB1999 3145,60
109 USA 3-17-1999 2789.10
```

```
data sales;
   length SalesID $ 4 Location $ 3;
   infile 'raw-data-file';
   input SalesID $ Location $;
   if Location='USA' then
      input SaleDate : mmddyy10.
              Amount;
   else if Location='EUR' then
      ut SaleDate : date9.
```

Continue processing
until end of the raw data file

Input Buffer

| 1 | 0 | 1 | | U | S | A | | 1 | - | 3 | 0 | - | 1 | 9 | 9 | 9 | | 2 | 9 | 3 | 8 | . | 0 | 0 | | |

PDV

SalesID	Location	SaleDate	Amount
101	USA	.	.

100

Multiple INPUT Statements

Partial SAS Log

```
NOTE: 6 records were read from the
      infile 'sales.dat'.
      The minimum record length was 24.
      The maximum record length was 26.
NOTE: The data set WORK.SALES has
      3 observations and 4 variables.
```

101

Undesirable Output

Sales ID	Location	Sale Date	Amount
101	USA	.	.
101	USA	.	.
1345	EUR	.	.

102

The Single Trailing @

The single trailing @ holds a raw data record in the input buffer until SAS

- executes an INPUT statement with no trailing @ or
- begins the next iteration of the DATA step.

General form of an INPUT statement with the single trailing @:

INPUT *var1 var2 var3 ... @;*

103

Processing the Single Trailing @

Hold record for next INPUT statement

Load next record

```
input SalesID $ Location $ @;
if location='USA' then
    input SaleDate : mmddyy10.
         Amount;
else if Location='EUR' then
    input SaleDate : date9.
         Amount : commax8.;
```

105   ...

Single Trailing @: Execution

Raw Data File

```
101 USA 1-20-1999 3295.50
3034 EUR 30JAN1999 1876,30
101 USA 1-30-1999 2938.00
128 USA 2-5-1999 2908.74
1345 EUR 6FEB1999 3145,60
109 USA 3-17-1999 2789.10
```

```
data sales;
    length SalesID $ 4 Location $ 3;
    infile 'raw-data-file';
    input SalesID $ Location $ @;
    if Location='USA' then
        input SaleDate : mmddyy10.
             Amount;
    else if Location='EUR' then
        input SaleDate : date9.
             Amount : commax8.;
run;
```

Input Buffer

SalesID	Location	SaleDate	Amount
		.	.

106   ...

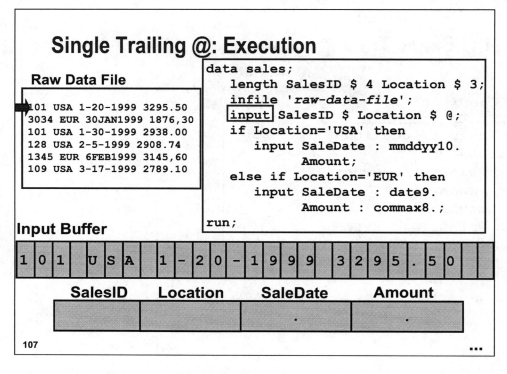

Single Trailing @: Execution

Raw Data File

```
101 USA 1-20-1999 3295.50
3034 EUR 30JAN1999 1876,30
101 USA 1-30-1999 2938.00
128 USA 2-5-1999 2908.74
1345 EUR 6FEB1999 3145,60
109 USA 3-17-1999 2789.10
```

```
data sales;
   length SalesID $ 4 Location $ 3;
   infile 'raw-data-file';
   input SalesID $ Location $ @;
   if Location='USA' then
      input SaleDate : mmddyy10.
         Amount;
   else if Location='EUR' then
      input SaleDate : date9.
         Amount : commax8.;
run;
```

Input Buffer

| 1 | 0 | 1 | | U | S | A | | 1 | - | 2 | 0 | - | 1 | 9 | 9 | 9 | | 3 | 2 | 9 | 5 | . | 5 | 0 | | |

SalesID	Location	SaleDate	Amount
		.	.

107   ...

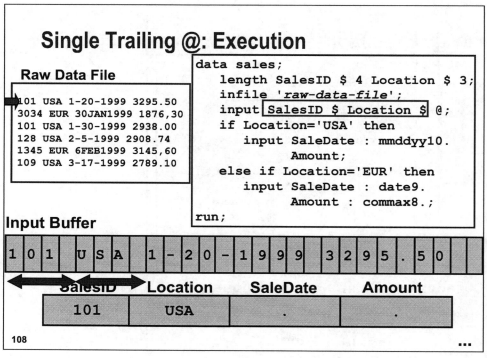

Single Trailing @: Execution

Raw Data File

```
101 USA 1-20-1999 3295.50
3034 EUR 30JAN1999 1876,30
101 USA 1-30-1999 2938.00
128 USA 2-5-1999 2908.74
1345 EUR 6FEB1999 3145,60
109 USA 3-17-1999 2789.10
```

```
data sales;
   length SalesID $ 4 Location $ 3;
   infile 'raw-data-file';
   input SalesID $ Location $ @;
   if Location='USA' then
      input SaleDate : mmddyy10.
         Amount;
   else if Location='EUR' then
      input SaleDate : date9.
         Amount : commax8.;
run;
```

Input Buffer

| 1 | 0 | 1 | | U | S | A | | 1 | - | 2 | 0 | - | 1 | 9 | 9 | 9 | | 3 | 2 | 9 | 5 | . | 5 | 0 | | |

SalesID	Location	SaleDate	Amount
101	USA	.	.

108   ...

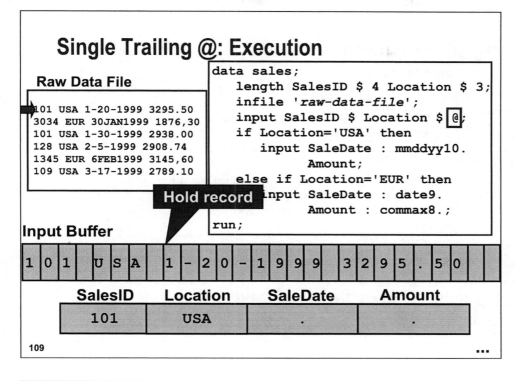

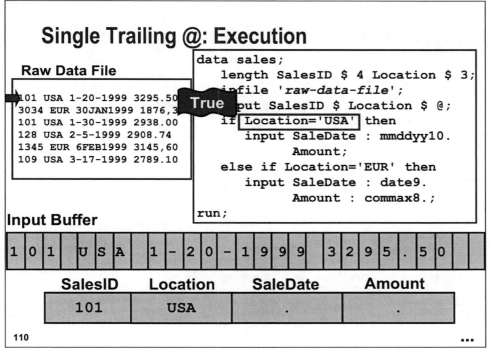

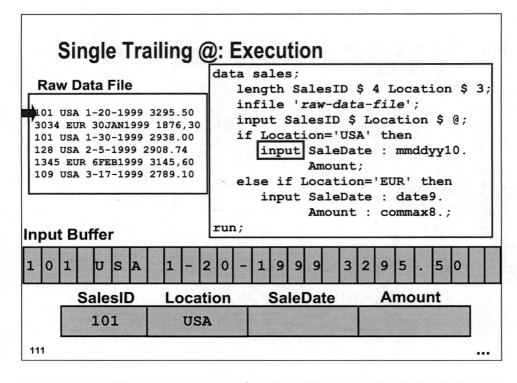

Single Trailing @: Execution

Raw Data File

```
101 USA 1-20-1999 3295.50
3034 EUR 30JAN1999 1876,30
101 USA 1-30-1999 2938.00
128 USA 2-5-1999 2908.74
1345 EUR 6FEB1999 3145,60
109 USA 3-17-1999 2789.10
```

```
data sales;
   length SalesID $ 4 Location $ 3;
   infile 'raw-data-file';
   input SalesID $ Location $ @;
   if Location='USA' then
      input  SaleDate : mmddyy10.
             Amount;
   else if Location='EUR' then
      input SaleDate : date9.
            Amount : commax8.;
run;
```

Input Buffer

| 1 | 0 | 1 | | U | S | A | | 1 | – | 2 | 0 | – | 1 | 9 | 9 | 9 | | 3 | 2 | 9 | 5 | . | 5 | 0 | |

SalesID	Location	SaleDate	Amount
101	USA		

111

...

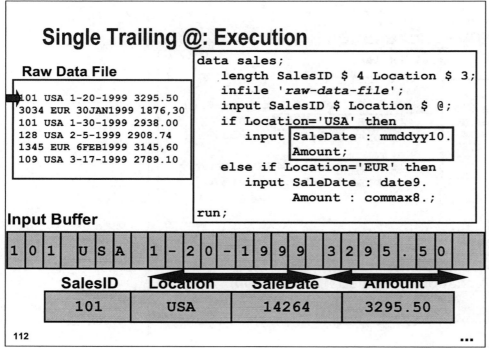

Single Trailing @: Execution

Raw Data File

```
101 USA 1-20-1999 3295.50
3034 EUR 30JAN1999 1876,30
101 USA 1-30-1999 2938.00
128 USA 2-5-1999 2908.74
1345 EUR 6FEB1999 3145,60
109 USA 3-17-1999 2789.10
```

```
data sales;
   length SalesID $ 4 Location $ 3;
   infile 'raw-data-file';
   input SalesID $ Location $ @;
   if Location='USA' then
      input SaleDate : mmddyy10.
            Amount;
   else if Location='EUR' then
      input SaleDate : date9.
            Amount : commax8.;
run;
```

Input Buffer

| 1 | 0 | 1 | | U | S | A | | 1 | – | 2 | 0 | – | 1 | 9 | 9 | 9 | | 3 | 2 | 9 | 5 | . | 5 | 0 | |

SalesID	Location	SaleDate	Amount
101	USA	14264	3295.50

112

...

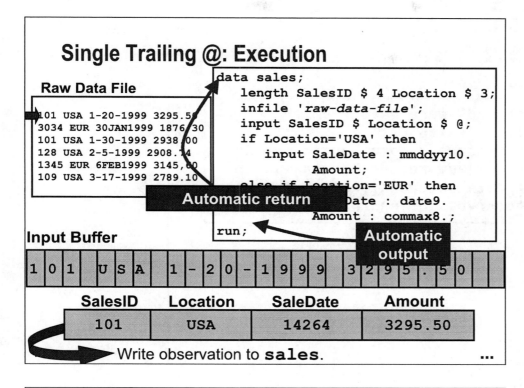

Single Trailing @: Execution

Raw Data File

```
101 USA 1-20-1999 3295.50
3034 EUR 30JAN1999 1876,30
101 USA 1-30-1999 2938.00
128 USA 2-5-1999 2908.74
1345 EUR 6FEB1999 3145,60
109 USA 3-17-1999 2789.10
```

```
data sales;
   length SalesID $ 4 Location $ 3;
   infile 'raw-data-file';
   input SalesID $ Location $ @;
   if Location='USA' then
      input SaleDate : mmddyy10.
           Amount;
   else if Location='EUR' then
           Date : date9.
           Amount : commax8.;
run;
```

Automatic return

Automatic output

Input Buffer

| 1 | 0 | 1 | | U | S | A | | 1 | - | 2 | 0 | - | 1 | 9 | 9 | 9 | | 3 | 2 | 9 | 5 | . | 5 | 0 | | |

SalesID	Location	SaleDate	Amount
101	USA	14264	3295.50

Write observation to **sales**.   ...

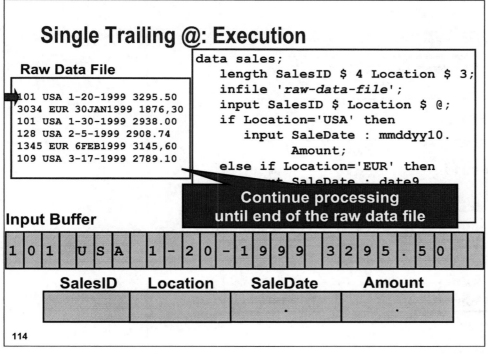

Single Trailing @: Execution

Raw Data File

```
101 USA 1-20-1999 3295.50
3034 EUR 30JAN1999 1876,30
101 USA 1-30-1999 2938.00
128 USA 2-5-1999 2908.74
1345 EUR 6FEB1999 3145,60
109 USA 3-17-1999 2789.10
```

```
data sales;
   length SalesID $ 4 Location $ 3;
   infile 'raw-data-file';
   input SalesID $ Location $ @;
   if Location='USA' then
      input SaleDate : mmddyy10.
           Amount;
   else if Location='EUR' then
           SaleDate : date9
```

Continue processing until end of the raw data file

Input Buffer

| 1 | 0 | 1 | | U | S | A | | 1 | - | 2 | 0 | - | 1 | 9 | 9 | 9 | | 3 | 2 | 9 | 5 | . | 5 | 0 | | |

SalesID	Location	SaleDate	Amount
		.	.

114

Mixed Record Types

Partial SAS Log

```
NOTE: 6 records were read from the
      infile 'sales.dat'.
      The minimum record length was 24.
      The maximum record length was 26.
NOTE: The data set WORK.SALES has
      6 observations and 4 variables.
```

115

Mixed Record Types

```
proc print data=sales noobs;
run;
```

PROC PRINT Output

Sales ID	Location	Sale Date	Amount
101	USA	14264	3295.50
3034	EUR	14274	1876.30
101	USA	14274	2938.00
128	USA	14280	2908.74
1345	EUR	14281	3145.60
109	USA	14320	2789.10

c04s2d2.sas

116

Subsetting from a Raw Data File

This scenario uses the raw data file from the previous example.

```
101  USA  1-20-1999  3295.50
3034 EUR  30JAN1999  1876,30
101  USA  1-30-1999  2938.00
128  USA  2-5-1999   2908.74
1345 EUR  6FEB1999   3145,60
109  USA  3-17-1999  2789.10
```

The dates are represented differently and the decimal places and commas are reversed for the USA and European sales figures.

117

Desired Output

The sales manager wants to see sales for the European branch only.

Sales ID	Location	Sale Date	Amount
3034	EUR	14274	1876.30
1345	EUR	14281	3145.60

118

The Subsetting IF Statement

```
data europe;
   length SalesID $ 4
          Location $ 3;
   infile 'raw-data-file';
   input SalesID $ Location $ @;
   if Location='USA' then
      input SaleDate : mmddyy10.
            Amount;
   else if Location='EUR' then
      input SaleDate : date9.
            Amount : commax8.;
   if Location='EUR';
run;
```

119

The Subsetting IF Statement

The subsetting IF should appear as early in the program as possible but after the variables have been assigned values.

120

The Subsetting IF Statement

```
data europe;
   length SalesID $ 4
          Location $ 3;
   infile 'raw-data-file';
   input SalesID $ Location $ @;
   if Location='EUR';
   input SaleDate : date9.
          Amount : commax8.;
run;
```

Because the program reads only European sales,
the INPUT statement for USA sales is not needed.

121

Subsetting Observations: Execution

Raw Data File

```
101 USA 1-20-1999 3295.50
3034 EUR 30JAN1999 1876,30
101 USA 1-30-1999 2938.00
128 USA 2-5-1999 2908.74
1345 EUR 6FEB1999 3145,60
109 USA 3-17-1999 2789.10
```

```
data europe;
   length SalesID $ 4
          Location $ 3;
   infile 'raw-data-file';
   input SalesID $ Location $ @;
   if Location='EUR';
   input SaleDate : date9.
          Amount : commax8.;
run;
```

Input Buffer

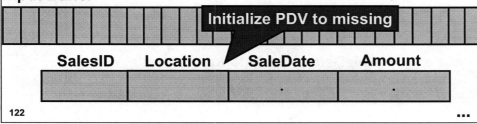

Initialize PDV to missing

SalesID	Location	SaleDate	Amount

122   ...

Subsetting Observations: Execution

Raw Data File

```
101 USA 1-20-1999 3295.50
3034 EUR 30JAN1999 1876,30
101 USA 1-30-1999 2938.00
128 USA 2-5-1999 2908.74
1345 EUR 6FEB1999 3145,60
109 USA 3-17-1999 2789.10
```

```
data europe;
  length SalesID $ 4
         Location $ 3;
  infile 'raw-data-file';
  input SalesID $ Location $ @;
  if Location='EUR';
  input SaleDate : date9.
        Amount : commax8.;
run;
```

Input Buffer

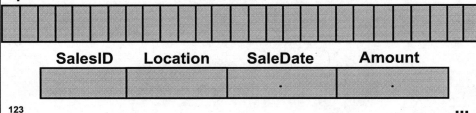

SalesID	Location	SaleDate	Amount
		.	.

123   ...

Subsetting Observations: Execution

Raw Data File

```
101 USA 1-20-1999 3295.50
3034 EUR 30JAN1999 1876,30
101 USA 1-30-1999 2938.00
128 USA 2-5-1999 2908.74
1345 EUR 6FEB1999 3145,60
109 USA 3-17-1999 2789.10
```

```
data europe;
  length SalesID $ 4
         Location $ 3;
  infile 'raw-data-file';
  input SalesID $ Location $ @;
  if Location='EUR';
  input SaleDate : date9.
        Amount : commax8.;
run;
```

Input Buffer

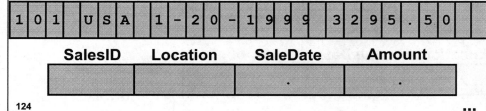

SalesID	Location	SaleDate	Amount
		.	.

124   ...

Subsetting Observations: Execution

Raw Data File

```
101 USA 1-20-1999 3295.50
3034 EUR 30JAN1999 1876,30
101 USA 1-30-1999 2938.00
128 USA 2-5-1999 2908.74
1345 EUR 6FEB1999 3145,60
109 USA 3-17-1999 2789.10
```

```
data europe;
   length SalesID $ 4
          Location $ 3;
   infile 'raw-data-file';
   input SalesID $ Location $ @;
   if Location='EUR';
   input SaleDate : date9.
         Amount : commax8.;
run;
```

Input Buffer

| 1 | 0 | 1 | | U | S | A | | 1 | - | 2 | 0 | - | 1 | 9 | 9 | 9 | | 3 | 2 | 9 | 5 | . | 5 | 0 | | |

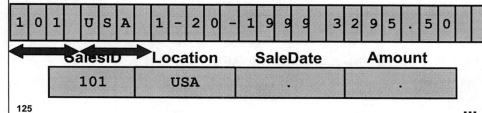

SalesID	Location	SaleDate	Amount
101	USA	.	.

125   ...

Subsetting Observations: Execution

Raw Data File

```
101 USA 1-20-1999 3295.50
3034 EUR 30JAN1999 1876,30
101 USA 1-30-1999 2938.00
128 USA 2-5-1999 2908.74
1345 EUR 6FEB1999 3145,60
109 USA 3-17-1999 2789.10
```

```
data europe;
   length SalesID $ 4
          Location $ 3;
   infile 'raw-data-file';
   input SalesID $ Location $ @;
   if Location='EUR';
   input SaleDate : date9.
         Amount : commax8.;
```

Hold record

Input Buffer

| 1 | 0 | 1 | | U | S | A | | 1 | - | 2 | 0 | - | 1 | 9 | 9 | 9 | | 3 | 2 | 9 | 5 | . | 5 | 0 | | |

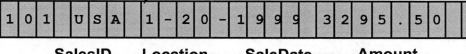

SalesID	Location	SaleDate	Amount
101	USA	.	.

126   ...

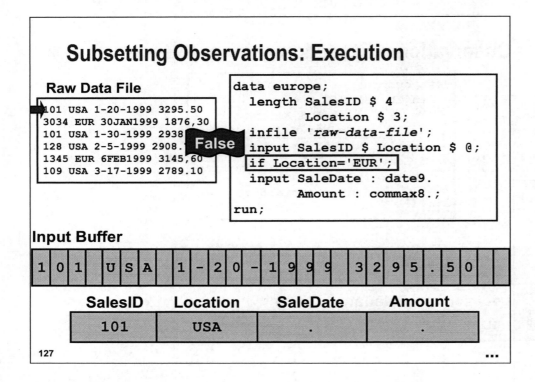

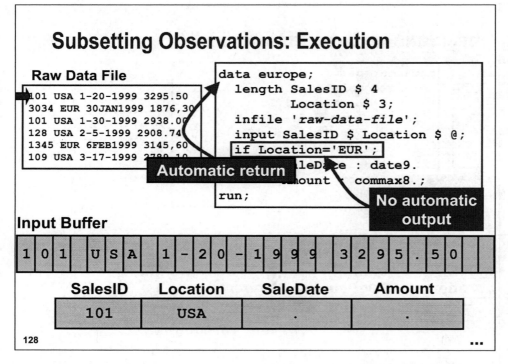

Subsetting Observations: Execution

Raw Data File

```
101 USA 1-20-1999 3295.50
3034 EUR 30JAN1999 1876,30
101 USA 1-30-1999 2938.00
128 USA 2-5-1999 2908.74
1345 EUR 6FEB1999 3145,60
109 USA 3-17-1999 2789.10
```

```
data europe;
   length SalesID $ 4
          Location $ 3;
   infile 'raw-data-file';
   input SalesID $ Location $ @;
   if Location='EUR';
   input SaleDate : date9.
         Amount : commax8.;
run;
```

Input Buffer

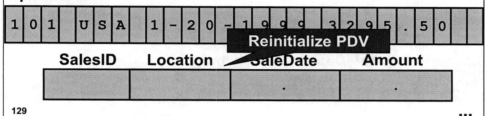

Reinitialize PDV

SalesID	Location	SaleDate	Amount
		.	.

129   ...

Subsetting Observations: Execution

Raw Data File

```
101 USA 1-20-1999 3295.50
3034 EUR 30JAN1999 1876,30
101 USA 1-30-1999 2938.00
128 USA 2-5-1999 2908.74
1345 EUR 6FEB1999 3145,60
109 USA 3-17-1999 2789.10
```

```
data europe;
   length SalesID $ 4
          Location $ 3;
   infile 'raw-data-file';
   input SalesID $ Location $ @;
   if Location='EUR';
   input SaleDate : date9.
         Amount : commax8.;
run;
```

Input Buffer

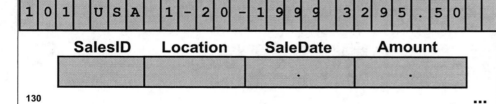

SalesID	Location	SaleDate	Amount
		.	.

130   ...

Subsetting Observations: Execution

Raw Data File

```
101 USA 1-20-1999 3295.50
3034 EUR 30JAN1999 1876,30
101 USA 1-30-1999 2938.00
128 USA 2-5-1999 2908.74
1345 EUR 6FEB1999 3145,60
109 USA 3-17-1999 2789.10
```

```
data europe;
   length SalesID $ 4
          Location $ 3;
   infile 'raw-data-file';
   input SalesID $ Location $ @;
   if Location='EUR';
   input SaleDate : date9.
         Amount : commax8.;
run;
```

Input Buffer

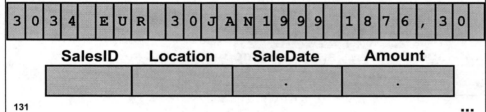

SalesID	Location	SaleDate	Amount
		.	.

131   ...

Subsetting Observations: Execution

Raw Data File

```
101 USA 1-20-1999 3295.50
3034 EUR 30JAN1999 1876,30
101 USA 1-30-1999 2938.00
128 USA 2-5-1999 2908.74
1345 EUR 6FEB1999 3145,60
109 USA 3-17-1999 2789.10
```

```
data europe;
   length SalesID $ 4
          Location $ 3;
   infile 'raw-data-file';
   input SalesID $ Location $ @;
   if Location='EUR';
   input SaleDate : date9.
         Amount : commax8.;
run;
```

Input Buffer

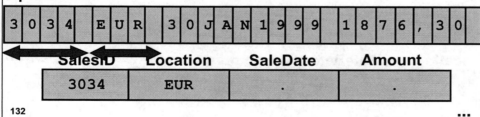

SalesID	Location	SaleDate	Amount
3034	EUR	.	.

132   ...

Subsetting Observations: Execution

Raw Data File

```
101 USA 1-20-1999 3295.50
3034 EUR 30JAN1999 1876,30
101 USA 1-30-1999 2938.00
128 USA 2-5-1999 2908.74
1345 EUR 6FEB1999 3145,60
109 USA 3-17-1999 2789.10
```

```
data europe;
  length SalesID $ 4
         Location $ 3;
  infile 'raw-data-file';
  input SalesID $ Location $ @;
  if Location='EUR';
  input SaleDate : date9.
        Amount : commax8.;
run;
```

Hold record

Input Buffer

| 3 | 0 | 3 | 4 | | E | U | R | | 3 | 0 | J | A | N | 1 | 9 | 9 | 9 | | 1 | 8 | 7 | 6 | , | 3 | 0 | |

←————→   SalesID   →————→ Location   SaleDate   Amount

| 3034 | EUR | . | . |

133   ...

Subsetting Observations: Execution

Raw Data File

```
101 USA 1-20-1999 3295.50
3034 EUR 30JAN1999 1876,30
101 USA 1-30-1999 2938.
128 USA 2-5-1999 2908.
1345 EUR 6FEB1999 3145,60
109 USA 3-17-1999 2789.10
```

```
data europe;
  length SalesID $ 4
         Location $ 3;
  infile 'raw-data-file';
  input SalesID $ Location $ @;
  if Location='EUR';
  input SaleDate : date9.
        Amount : commax8.;
run;
```

True

Input Buffer

| 3 | 0 | 3 | 4 | | E | U | R | | 3 | 0 | J | A | N | 1 | 9 | 9 | 9 | | 1 | 8 | 7 | 6 | , | 3 | 0 | |

←————→   SalesID   →————→ Location   SaleDate   Amount

| 3034 | EUR | . | . |

134   ...

Subsetting Observations: Execution

Raw Data File

```
101 USA 1-20-1999 3295.50
3034 EUR 30JAN1999 1876,30
101 USA 1-30-1999 2938.00
128 USA 2-5-1999 2908.74
1345 EUR 6FEB1999 3145,60
109 USA 3-17-1999 2789.10
```

```
data europe;
  length SalesID $ 4
         Location $ 3;
  infile 'raw-data-file';
  input SalesID $ Location $ @;
  if Location='EUR';
  input SaleDate : date9.
        Amount : commax8.;
run;
```

Input Buffer

| 3 | 0 | 3 | 4 | | E | U | R | | 3 | 0 | J | A | N | 1 | 9 | 9 | 9 | | 1 | 8 | 7 | 6 | , | 3 | 0 | |

SalesID	Location	SaleDate	Amount
3034	EUR	14274	1876.30

135   ...

Subsetting Observations: Execution

Raw Data File

```
101 USA 1-20-1999 3295.50
3034 EUR 30JAN1999 1876,30
101 USA 1-30-1999 2938.00
128 USA 2-5-1999 2908.74
1345 EUR 6FEB1999 3145,6
109 USA 3-17-1999 2789.1
```

```
data europe;
  length SalesID $ 4
         Location $ 3;
  infile 'raw-data-file';
  input SalesID $ Location $ @;
  if Location='EUR';
  input SaleDate : date9.
        Amount : commax8.;
run;
```

Automatic return

Automatic output

Input Buffer

| 3 | 0 | 3 | 4 | | E | U | R | | 3 | 0 | J | A | N | 1 | 9 | 9 | 9 | | 1 | 8 | 7 | 6 | , | 3 | 0 | |

SalesID	Location	SaleDate	Amount
3034	EUR	14274	1876.30

Write observation to **europe**.   ...

Subsetting Observations: Execution

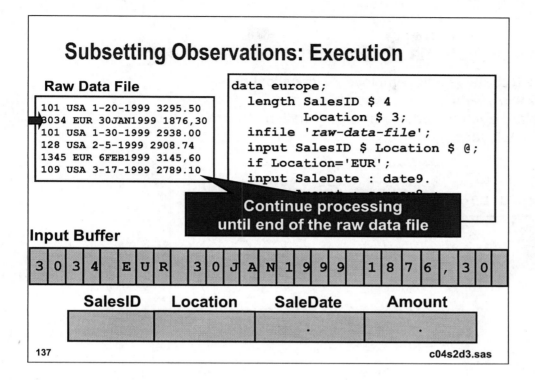

Raw Data File

```
101 USA 1-20-1999 3295.50
3034 EUR 30JAN1999 1876,30
101 USA 1-30-1999 2938.00
128 USA 2-5-1999 2908.74
1345 EUR 6FEB1999 3145,60
109 USA 3-17-1999 2789.10
```

```
data europe;
   length SalesID $ 4
          Location $ 3;
   infile 'raw-data-file';
   input SalesID $ Location $ @;
   if Location='EUR';
   input SaleDate : date9.
```

**Continue processing
until end of the raw data file**

Input Buffer

3	0	3	4		E	U	R		3	0	J	A	N	1	9	9	9		1	8	7	6	,	3	0

SalesID	Location	SaleDate	Amount
		.	.

137

c04s2d3.sas

The Subsetting IF Statement

```
proc print data=europe noobs;
run;
```

Sales ID	Location	Sale Date	Amount
3034	EUR	14274	1876.30
1345	EUR	14281	3145.60

138

c04s2d3.sas

Multiple Observations per Record

A raw data file contains each employee's identification
number and this year's contribution to his or her
retirement plan. Each record contains information
for multiple employees.

```
E00973 1400 E09872 2003 E73150 2400
E45671 4500 E34805 1980
```

139

Desired Output

The output SAS data set should have one observation
per employee.

EmpID	Contrib
E00973	1400
E09872	2003
E73150	2400
E45671	4500
E34805	1980

140

Processing: What Is Required?

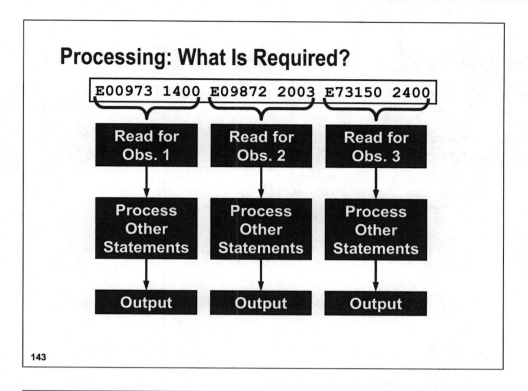

143

The Double Trailing @

The double trailing @ holds the raw data record across iterations of the DATA step until the line pointer moves past the end of the line.

> **INPUT** *var1 var2 var3 ...* @@;

Do not use "missover" and "@@" together

144

✎ The double trailing @ should only be used with list input. If used with column or formatted input, an infinite loop can result.

The Double Trailing @

```
data work.retire;
   length EmpID $ 6;
   infile 'raw-data-file';
   input EmpID $ Contrib @@;
run;
```

Hold until end
of record

145

Creating Multiple Observations per Record

Partial SAS Log

```
NOTE: 2 records were read from the
      infile 'retire.dat'.
      The minimum record length was 35.
      The maximum record length was 36.
NOTE: SAS went to a new line when INPUT
      statement reached past the end of
      a line.
NOTE: The data set WORK.RETIRE has
      5 observations and 2 variables.
```

The "SAS went to a new line" message is expected
because the double trailing @ indicates that SAS should
read until the end of each record.

146

Creating Multiple Observations per Record

```
proc print data=retire noobs;
run;
```

PROC PRINT Output

EmpID	Contrib
E00973	1400
E09872	2003
E73150	2400
E45671	4500
E34805	1980

c04s2d4.sas

147

Trailing @ versus Double Trailing @

Option	Effect
Trailing @ **INPUT** *var-1... @*;	Holds raw data record until 1) an INPUT statement with no trailing @ 2) the next iteration of the DATA step.
Double trailing @ **INPUT** *var-1 ... @@*;	Holds raw data records in the input buffer until SAS reads past the end of the line.

148

The single trailing @ and the double trailing @ are mutually exclusive; they cannot and should not be used together. If they both appear in the same INPUT statement, the last one specified is used. The MISSOVER option is also invalid with the double trailing @.

Exercises

4.   Reading Multiple Records per Observation

Medical data is stored in the raw data file **BLOODTYP**. The first record contains the patient's identification number and the patient's first and last names. The second record contains a code specifying the medical plan, the patient's blood type, a code indicating whether the patient has any allergies, and the number of dependants covered by the family's health plan.

First Record

Order	Field	Notes
1	ID Number	5-character code
2	Last Name	Longest value is 9 characters.
3	First Name	Longest value is 11 characters.

Second Record

Order	Field	Notes
1	Plan Type	1-character code
2	Blood Type	Longest value is 3 characters.
3	Allergy Code	1-character code: Y=Yes, N=No
4	Number of Dependants	Numeric field

Sample Records

```
E1009 MORGAN GEORGE
F O+ Y 1
E1017 WELCH DARIUS
F AB+ N 2
E1036 MOORE LESLIE
S AB+ Y 1
E1037 EDWARDS JENNIFER
F B- Y 1
E1038 WASHBURN GAYLE
N B+ Y 1
```

Create a SAS data set named **work.medical** that contains the patient's identification number, first name, last name, and blood type.

Partial Listing of **work.medical**

```
     Obs     ID       LName        FName         Blood

       1     E1009    MORGAN       GEORGE        O+
       2     E1017    WELCH        DARIUS        AB+
       3     E1036    MOORE        LESLIE        AB+
       4     E1037    EDWARDS      JENNIFER      B-
       5     E1038    WASHBURN     GAYLE         B+
       6     E1050    TUTTLE       THOMAS        A+
       7     E1065    CHAPMAN      NEIL          O+
```

   You do not have to read all of the fields.

5. **Reading Mixed Record Types**

Medical data is stored in the raw data file **ALLERGY**. The first six fields are always as follows:

First Part of Record

Order	Field	Notes
1	ID Number	5-character code
2	Last Name	Longest value is 9 characters
3	First Name	Longest value is 11 characters
4	Plan Type	1-character code
5	Blood Type	Longest value is 3 characters
6	Allergy Code	1-character code: Y=Yes, N=No

If the patient has an allergy (**Allergy Code = Y**), then the rest of the record is as follows:

7	Allergy Type	2-character code indicating type of allergy
8	Number of Dependants	Numeric field

If the patient does not have an allergy (**Allergy Code = N**), then the rest of the record is as follows:

7	Number of Dependants	Numeric field

Sample Records

```
E1009 MORGAN GEORGE F O+ Y DY 1
E1017 WELCH DARIUS F AB+ N 2
E1036 MOORE LESLIE S AB+ Y SM 1
E1037 EDWARDS JENNIFER F B- Y HF 1
E1038 WASHBURN GAYLE N B+ Y PA 1
E1050 TUTTLE THOMAS S A+ N 2
E1065 CHAPMAN NEIL F O+ N 2
```

Create a SAS data set named **work.allergies**.

Partial Listing of **work.allergies**

Obs	ID	LName	FName	Plan	Blood	Allergy	Algy Type	Dependants
1	E1009	MORGAN	GEORGE	F	O+	Y	DY	1
2	E1017	WELCH	DARIUS	F	AB+	N		2
3	E1036	MOORE	LESLIE	S	AB+	Y	SM	1
4	E1037	EDWARDS	JENNIFER	F	B-	Y	HF	1
5	E1038	WASHBURN	GAYLE	N	B+	Y	PA	1
6	E1050	TUTTLE	THOMAS	S	A+	N		2
7	E1065	CHAPMAN	NEIL	F	O+	N		2
8	E1076	VENTER	RANDALL	N	A+	N		1
9	E1094	STARR	ALTON	N	B+	Y	SF	1

6. Subsetting from a Raw Data File (Optional)

Modify the DATA step you wrote in the previous problem to create a SAS data set named **work.allergies2** that contains only patients with allergies. You should get 11 observations.

Partial Listing of **work.allergies2**

Obs	ID	LName	FName	Plan	Blood	Allergy	Algy Type	Dependants
1	E1009	MORGAN	GEORGE	F	O+	Y	DY	1
2	E1036	MOORE	LESLIE	S	AB+	Y	SM	1
3	E1037	EDWARDS	JENNIFER	F	B-	Y	HF	1
4	E1038	WASHBURN	GAYLE	N	B+	Y	PA	1

7. Reading Raw Data with Multiple Observations per Record

The raw data file **TRANSACT** contains daily bank transactions for a given account. For each transaction, the following information is stored:

Order	Field	Notes
1	Date of Transaction	Written in DATE9.
2	Type of Transaction	C=deposit (credit), D=withdrawal (debit)
3	Amount of Transaction	Written in COMMA9.

Sample Records

```
03JAN2001 C 9,253 04JAN2001 D 12,135 06JAN2001 C 10,562
10JAN2001 D 35,950 15JAN2001 C 951 21JAN2001 C 1,226
25JAN2001 C 86 28JAN2001 C 27,500 31JAN2001 D 75,900
```

Create a SAS data set named **work.transactions** that contains all transactions.

Listing of **work.transactions**

```
       Obs     Date     Type     Amount

        1      14978      C        9253
        2      14979      D       12135
        3      14981      C       10562
        4      14985      D       35950
        5      14990      C         951
        6      14996      C        1226
        7      15000      C          86
        8      15003      C       27500
        9      15006      D       75900
```

8. **Creating Multiple SAS Data Sets from a Single Raw Data File (Optional)**

Modify the DATA step you wrote in Exercise **7** to create two SAS data sets. Name the first data set **work.credits**; it should contain all the deposit information. Name the second data set **work.debits**; it should contain all the withdrawal information.

Hint: Create both data sets in one DATA step by listing them both in the DATA statement and using conditional logic with an OUTPUT statement (shown in Section 2.2, "Writing to Multiple Data Sets").

Listing of **work.credits**

Obs	Date	Type	Amount
1	14978	C	9253
2	14981	C	10562
3	14990	C	951
4	14996	C	1226
5	15000	C	86
6	15003	C	27500

Listing of **work.debits**

Obs	Date	Type	Amount
1	14979	D	12135
2	14985	D	35950
3	15006	D	75900

9. **Subsetting from a Fixed-Column Raw Data File (Optional)**

The READEMPS program reads a fixed-column raw data file and outputs only the salesclerks.

```
data salclrks;
   infile 'raw-data-file';
   input  @1 Division $20. @21 HireDate mmddyy10.
          @31 Salary dollar10.2 @41 LastName $15.
          @56 FirstName $15. @71 Country $15.
          @86 Location $10. @96 IdNumber $6.
          @112 JobCode $6.;
   if jobcode='SALCLK';
run;

proc print data=salclrks noobs;
   title 'Employee Information for Salesclerks';
run;
```

a. Include the READEMPS program in your Program Editor. Submit the program and verify the output.

Partial Output

```
                     Employee Information for Salesclerks

            Hire
Division    Date    Salary    LastName        FirstName

  SALES     8107    29000     DANZIN          MATHIAS
  SALES    12492    25000     HALL            DREMA A.
  SALES     9205    41000     BOOZER          KRAIG E.
  SALES     8290    27000     LIEBLE III      JAN
  SALES    12658    17000     TOUGER          ARTHUR
  SALES     7838    38000     COLE            JONI L.
  SALES    10064    31000     FINN            BETTY L.
  SALES     8620    44000     KATZ            PATRICIA B.
  SALES     9097    38000     POTTS           PAUL
  SALES    12492    44000     BENTZ           MARIE


                               Id        Job
Country            Location    Number    Code

BELGIUM            BRUSSELS     E0019     SALCLK
USA                CARY         E0044     SALCLK
USA                CARY         E0058     SALCLK
USA                ORLANDO      E0093     SALCLK
USA                CARY         E0104     SALCLK
USA                CARY         E0113     SALCLK
USA                BEDMINSTER   E0149     SALCLK
USA                KANSAS CIT   E0171     SALCLK
USA                CARY         E0199     SALCLK
FRANCE             PARIS        E0229     SALCLK
```

b. Modify the program so that it produces the output data set **as efficiently as possible**.

✎   Fixed column fields can be read in any order.

10. Using the Absolute Line Pointer Control (Optional)

The raw data file **EMPTWO** has employee information that spans two records as shown below.

Record 1

Order	Field	Notes
1	Division	Longest value is 20 characters
2	Hire Date	Written in MMDDYY10.
3	Salary	Standard numeric field

Record 2

Order	Field	Notes
1	ID Number	6 character code
2	Last Name	Longest value is 15 characters.
3	First Name	Longest value is 15 characters.

Sample Records

```
FLIGHT OPTS,03/11/1992,25000
E0001,MILLS,DOROTHY E
FINANCE,12/19/1983,27000
E0002,BOWER,EILEEN A.
HR & FACIL,03/12/1985,120000
E0003,READING,TONY R.
HR & FACIL,10/16/1989,42000
```

Read the **EMPTWO** raw data file to create the SAS data set **work.empinfo**. Use the absolute line pointer to control the default order of the fields, so that the variables in the SAS data set are in the following order:

1) Identification Number
2) Last Name
3) First Name
4) Division
5) Hire Date
6) Salary

Listing of **work.empinfo**

Obs	Id Number	LastName	FirstName	Division	Hire Date	Salary
1	E0001	MILLS	DOROTHY E	FLIGHT OPTS	11758	25000
2	E0002	BOWER	EILEEN A.	FINANCE	8753	27000
3	E0003	READING	TONY R.	HR & FACIL	9202	120000
4	E0004	JUDD	CAROL A.	HR & FACIL	10881	42000
5	E0005	WONSID	HANNA	AIRPORT OPTS	8023	19000
6	E0006	ANDERSON	CHRISTOPHER	SALES	11439	31000
7	E0007	MASSENGILL	ANNETTE M.	FLIGHT OPTS	8440	29000
8	E0008	BADINE	DAVID	CORPORATE	11733	85000
9	E0009	DEMENT	CHARLES	FINANCE	9887	34000
10	E0010	FOSKEY	JERE D.	AIRPORT OPTS	11284	29000

  For more information on the absolute line pointer control, see the note on the relative line pointer control. For help on controlling variable length while preserving their order, see the notes on using informats on the INPUT statement in Chapter 4, Section 1.

4.3   Reading Hierarchical Raw Data Files

Objectives

- Read a hierarchical file and create one observation per detail record.
- Read a hierarchical file and create one observation per header record.

151

Processing Hierarchical Files

Many files are hierarchical in structure, consisting of

- a header record
- zero or more related detail records.

Typically, each record contains a field that identifies whether it is a header record or a detail record.

152

Processing Hierarchical Files

You can read a hierarchical file into a SAS data set by creating one observation per detail record and storing the header information as part of each observation.

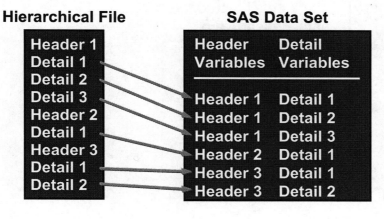

153

Processing Hierarchical Files

You can also create one observation per header record and store the information from detail records in summary variables.

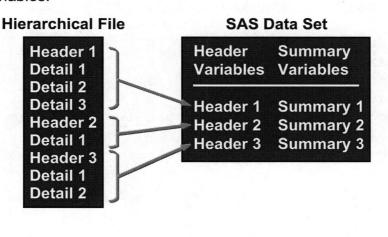

154

Creating One Observation per Detail Record

```
E:Adams:Susan
D:Michael:C
D:Lindsay:C
E:Porter:David
D:Susan:S
E:Lewis:Dorian D.
D:Richard:C
E:Dansky:Ian
E:Nicholls:James
D:Roberta:C
E:Slaydon:Marla
D:John:S
```

The raw data file has a header record containing the name of the employee and a detail record for each dependant on the employee's health insurance.

155

Desired Output

Human Resources wants a list of all the dependants and the name of the associated employee.

EmpLName	EmpFName	DepName	Relation
Adams	Susan	Michael	C
Adams	Susan	Lindsay	C
Porter	David	Susan	S
Lewis	Dorian D.	Richard	C
Nicholls	James	Roberta	C
Slaydon	Marla	John	S

156

A Hierarchical File

```
E:Adams:Susan
D:Michael:C
D:Lindsay:C
E:Porter:David
D:Susan:S
E:Lewis:Dorian D.
D:Richard:C
E:Dansky:Ian
E:Nicholls:James
D:Roberta:C
E:Slaydon:Marla
D:John:S
```

- Not all the records contain the same fields.
- The fields are separated by colons.
- There is a field indicating whether the record is a header or a detail record.

157

How to Read the Raw Data

```
input Type $ @;
if Type='E' then
    input EmpLName $ EmpFName $;
else
    input DepName $ Relation $;
```

158

How to Output Only the Dependants

```
input Type $ @;
if Type='E' then
    input EmpLName $ EmpFName $;
else do;
    input DepName $ Relation $;
    output;
end;
```

159

Creating One Obs per Detail Record: Execution

```
E:Adams:Susan
D:Michael:C
D:Lindsay:C
E:Porter:David
D:Susan:S
E:Lewis:Dorian D.
D:Richard:C
E:Dansky:Ian
E:Nicholls:James
D:Roberta:C
E:Slaydon:Marla
D:John:S
```

Input Buffer

```
data dependants(drop=Type);
    length Type $ 1 EmpLName EmpFName
           DepName $ 20 Relation $ 1;
    infile 'raw-data-file' dlm=':';
    input Type $ @;
    if Type='E' then
        input EmpLName $ EmpFName $;
    else do;
        input DepName $ Relation $;
        output;
    end;
run;
```

Type	EmpLName	EmpFName	DepName	Relation
D				

Creating One Obs per Detail Record: Execution

```
E:Adams:Susan
D:Michael:C
D:Lindsay:C
E:Porter:David
D:Susan:S
E:Lewis:Dorian D.
D:Richard:C
E:Dansky:Ian
E:Nicholls:James
D:Roberta:C
E:Slaydon:Marla
D:John:S
```

Input Buffer

```
data dependants(drop=Type);
   length Type $ 1 EmplLName EmpFName
          DepName $ 20 Relation $ 1;
   infile 'raw-data-file' dlm=':';
   input Type $ @;
   if Type='E' then
      input EmplLName $ EmpFName $;
   else do;
      input DepName $ Relation $;
      output;
   end;
run;
```

| E | : | A | d | a | m | s | : | S | u | s | a | n | | | | | | | | | |

Type	EmpLName	EmpFName	DepName	Relation

Creating One Obs per Detail Record: Execution

```
E:Adams:Susan
D:Michael:C
D:Lindsay:C
E:Porter:David
D:Susan:S
E:Lewis:Dorian D.
D:Richard:C
E:Dansky:Ian
E:Nicholls:James
D:Roberta:C
E:Slaydon:Marla
D:John:S
```

Input Buffer

```
data dependants(drop=Type);
   length Type $ 1 EmplLName EmpFName
          DepName $ 20 Relation $ 1;
   infile 'raw-data-file' dlm=':';
   input Type $ @;
   if Type='E' then
      input EmplLName $ EmpFName $;
   else do;
      input DepName $ Relation $;
      output;
   end;
run;
```

| E | : | A | d | a | m | s | : | S | u | s | a | n | | | | | | | | | |

Type	EmpLName	EmpFName	DepName	Relation
E				

Creating One Obs per Detail Record: Execution

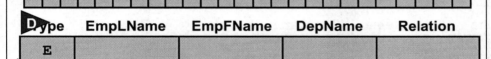

```
E:Adams:Susan
D:Michael:C
D:Lindsay:C
E:Porter:David
D:Susan:S
E:Lewis:Dorian D.
D:Richard:C
E:Dansky:Ian
E:Nicholls:James
D:Roberta:C
E:Slaydon:Marla
D:John:S
```

Hold record

```
data dependants(drop=Type);
   length Type $ 1 EmpLName EmpFName
          DepName $ 20 Relation $ 1;
   infile 'raw-data-file' dlm=':';
   input Type $ @;
   if Type='E' then
      input EmpLName $ EmpFName $;
   else do;
      input DepName $ Relation $;
      output;
   end;
run;
```

Input Buffer

| E | : | A | d | a | m | s | : | S | u | s | a | n | | | | | | | | |

D Type	EmpLName	EmpFName	DepName	Relation
E				

1

Creating One Obs per Detail Record: Execution

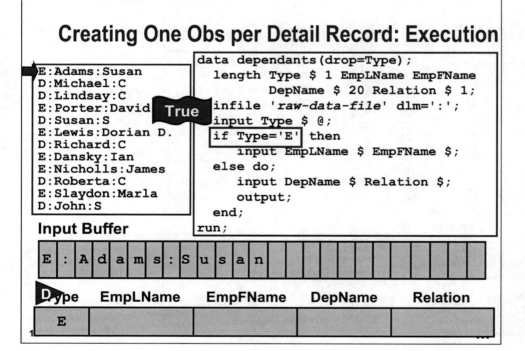

```
E:Adams:Susan
D:Michael:C
D:Lindsay:C
E:Porter:David
D:Susan:S
E:Lewis:Dorian D.
D:Richard:C
E:Dansky:Ian
E:Nicholls:James
D:Roberta:C
E:Slaydon:Marla
D:John:S
```

True

```
data dependants(drop=Type);
   length Type $ 1 EmpLName EmpFName
          DepName $ 20 Relation $ 1;
   infile 'raw-data-file' dlm=':';
   input Type $ @;
   if Type='E' then
      input EmpLName $ EmpFName $;
   else do;
      input DepName $ Relation $;
      output;
   end;
run;
```

Input Buffer

| E | : | A | d | a | m | s | : | S | u | s | a | n | | | | | | | | |

D Type	EmpLName	EmpFName	DepName	Relation
E				

1

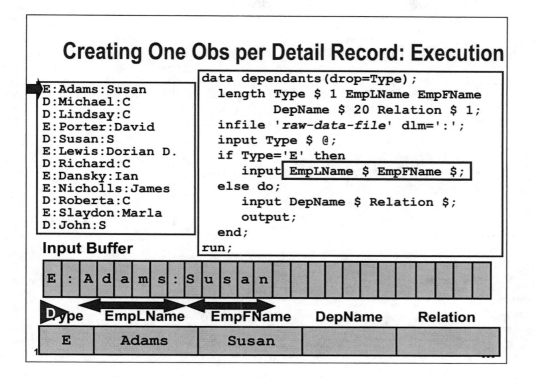

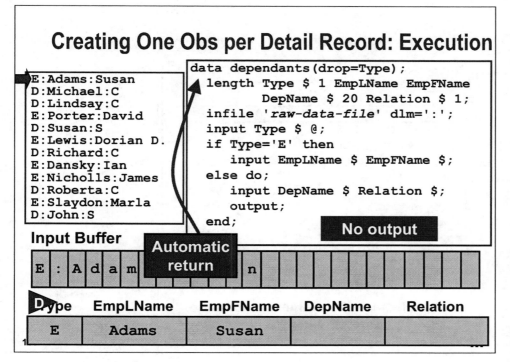

Creating One Obs per Detail Record: Execution

```
E:Adams:Susan
D:Michael:C
D:Lindsay:C
E:Porter:David
D:Susan:S
E:Lewis:Dorian D.
D:Richard:C
E:Dansky:Ian
E:Nicholls:James
D:Roberta:C
E:Slaydon:Marla
D:John:S
```

Input Buffer

```
data dependants(drop=Type);
   length Type $ 1 EmpLName EmpFName
          DepName $ 20 Relation $ 1;
   infile 'raw-data-file' dlm=':';
   input Type $ @;
   if Type='E' then
      input EmpLName $ EmpFName $;
   else do;
      input DepName $ Relation $;
      output;
   end;
run;
```

| E | : | A | d | a | m | s | : | S | u | s | a | n | | | | | **Reinitialize PDV** | | | |

Type	EmpLName	EmpFName	DepName	Relation

Creating One Obs per Detail Record: Execution

```
E:Adams:Susan
D:Michael:C
D:Lindsay:C
E:Porter:David
D:Susan:S
E:Lewis:Dorian D.
D:Richard:C
E:Dansky:Ian
E:Nicholls:James
D:Roberta:C
E:Slaydon:Marla
D:John:S
```

Input Buffer

```
data dependants(drop=Type);
   length Type $ 1 EmpLName EmpFName
          DepName $ 20 Relation $ 1;
   infile 'raw-data-file' dlm=':';
   input Type $ @;
   if Type='E' then
      input EmpLName $ EmpFName $;
   else do;
      input DepName $ Relation $;
      output;
   end;
run;
```

| E | : | A | d | a | m | s | : | S | u | s | a | n | | | | | | | | |

Type	EmpLName	EmpFName	DepName	Relation

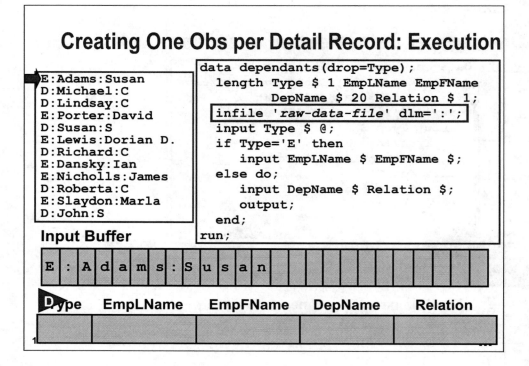

Creating One Obs per Detail Record: Execution

```
E:Adams:Susan
D:Michael:C
D:Lindsay:C
E:Porter:David
D:Susan:S
E:Lewis:Dorian D.
D:Richard:C
E:Dansky:Ian
E:Nicholls:James
D:Roberta:C
E:Slaydon:Marla
D:John:S
```
Input Buffer

```
data dependants(drop=Type);
  length Type $ 1 EmpLName EmpFName
         DepName $ 20 Relation $ 1;
  infile 'raw-data-file' dlm=':';
  input Type $ @;
  if Type='E' then
     input EmpLName $ EmpFName $;
  else do;
     input DepName $ Relation $;
     output;
  end;
run;
```

D	:	M	i	c	h	a	e	l	:	C										

Type	EmpLName	EmpFName	DepName	Relation

Creating One Obs per Detail Record: Execution

```
E:Adams:Susan
D:Michael:C
D:Lindsay:C
E:Porter:David
D:Susan:S
E:Lewis:Dorian D.
D:Richard:C
E:Dansky:Ian
E:Nicholls:James
D:Roberta:C
E:Slaydon:Marla
D:John:S
```
Input Buffer

```
data dependants(drop=Type);
  length Type $ 1 EmpLName EmpFName
         DepName $ 20 Relation $ 1;
  infile 'raw-data-file' dlm=':';
  input Type $ @;
  if Type='E' then
     input EmpLName $ EmpFName $;
  else do;
     input DepName $ Relation $;
     output;
  end;
run;
```

D	:	M	i	c	h	a	e	l	:	C										

Type	EmpLName	EmpFName	DepName	Relation
D				

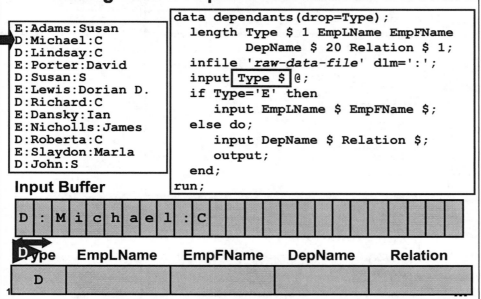

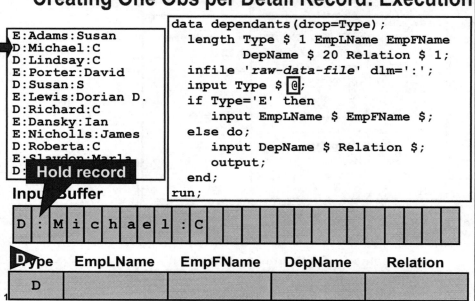

Creating One Obs per Detail Record: Execution

```
E:Adams:Susan
D:Michael:C
D:Lindsay:C
E:Porter:David
D:Susan:S
E:Lewis:Dorian D.
D:Richard:C
E:Dansky:Ian
E:Nicholls:James
D:Roberta:C
E:Slaydon:Marla
```

Hold record

```
data dependants(drop=Type);
  length Type $ 1 EmpLName EmpFName
         DepName $ 20 Relation $ 1;
  infile 'raw-data-file' dlm=':';
  input Type $ @;
  if Type='E' then
     input EmpLName $ EmpFName $;
  else do;
     input DepName $ Relation $;
     output;
  end;
run;
```

Input Buffer

| D | : | M | i | c | h | a | e | l | : | C | | | | | | | | | | |

Type	EmpLName	EmpFName	DepName	Relation
D				

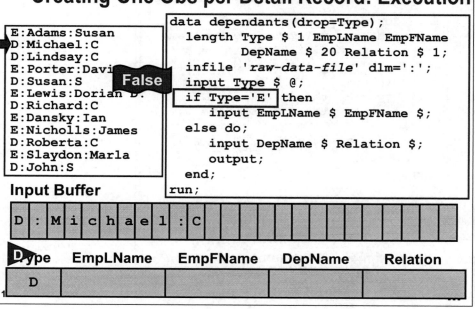

Creating One Obs per Detail Record: Execution

```
E:Adams:Susan
D:Michael:C
D:Lindsay:C
E:Porter:Davi
D:Susan:S
E:Lewis:Dorian D.
D:Richard:C
E:Dansky:Ian
E:Nicholls:James
D:Roberta:C
E:Slaydon:Marla
D:John:S
```

False

```
data dependants(drop=Type);
  length Type $ 1 EmpLName EmpFName
         DepName $ 20 Relation $ 1;
  infile 'raw-data-file' dlm=':';
  input Type $ @;
  if Type='E' then
     input EmpLName $ EmpFName $;
  else do;
     input DepName $ Relation $;
     output;
  end;
run;
```

Input Buffer

| D | : | M | i | c | h | a | e | l | : | C | | | | | | | | | | |

Type	EmpLName	EmpFName	DepName	Relation
D				

Creating One Obs per Detail Record: Execution

```
E:Adams:Susan
D:Michael:C
D:Lindsay:C
E:Porter:David
D:Susan:S
E:Lewis:Dorian D.
D:Richard:C
E:Dansky:Ian
E:Nicholls:James
D:Roberta:C
E:Slaydon:Marla
D:John:S
```

Input Buffer

```
data dependants(drop=Type);
  length Type $ 1 EmpLName EmpFName
         DepName $ 20 Relation $ 1;
  infile 'raw-data-file' dlm=':';
  input Type $ @;
  if Type='E' then
     input EmpLName $ EmpFName $;
  else do;
     input DepName $ Relation $;
     output;
  end;
run;
```

D	:	M	i	c	h	a	e	l	:	C													

Type	EmpLName	EmpFName	DepName	Relation
D				

Creating One Obs per Detail Record: Execution

```
E:Adams:Susan
D:Michael:C
D:Lindsay:C
E:Porter:David
D:Susan:S
E:Lewis:Dorian D.
D:Richard:C
E:Dansky:Ian
E:Nicholls:James
D:Roberta:C
E:Slaydon:Marla
D:John:S
```

Input Buffer

```
data dependants(drop=Type);
  length Type $ 1 EmpLName EmpFName
         DepName $ 20 Relation $ 1;
  infile 'raw-data-file' dlm=':';
  input Type $ @;
  if Type='E' then
     input EmpLName $ EmpFName $;
  else do;
     input DepName $ Relation $;
     output;
  end;
run;
```

D	:	M	i	c	h	a	e	l	:	C													

Type	EmpLName	EmpFName	DepName	Relation
D			Michael	C

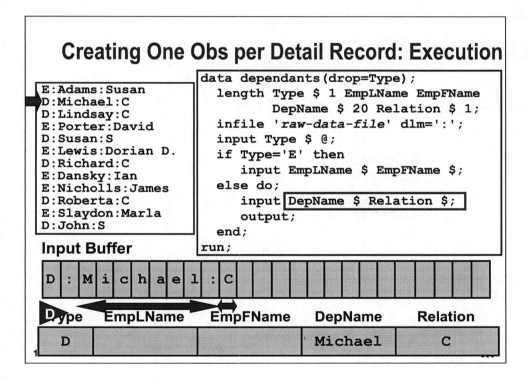

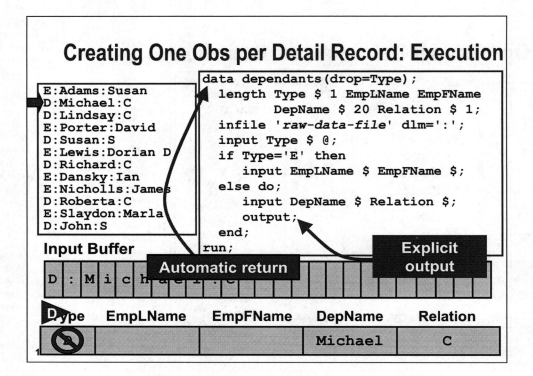

Creating One Obs per Detail Record: Execution

```
E:Adams:Susan
D:Michael:C
D:Lindsay:C
E:Porter:David
D:Susan:S
E:Lewis:Dorian D
D:Richard:C
E:Dansky:Ian
E:Nicholls:James
D:Roberta:C
E:Slaydon:Marla
D:John:S
```

Input Buffer

```
data dependants(drop=Type);
  length Type $ 1 EmpLName EmpFName
         DepName $ 20 Relation $ 1;
  infile 'raw-data-file' dlm=':';
  input Type $ @;
  if Type='E' then
     input EmpLName $ EmpFName $;
  else do;
     input DepName $ Relation $;
     output;
  end;
run;
```

| D | : | M | i | c | h | a | e | l | : | C | | | | | | | | | | | |

Automatic return

Explicit output

Type	EmpLName	EmpFName	DepName	Relation
			Michael	C

Undesirable Output

Emp LName	Emp FName	DepName	Relation
		Michael	C
		Lindsay	C
		Susan	S
		Richard	C
		Roberta	C
		John	S

176

The RETAIN Statement (Review)

General form of the RETAIN statement:

> **RETAIN** *variable-name* *<initial-value>*;

The RETAIN statement prevents SAS from reinitializing the values of new variables at the top of the DATA step. This means that values from previous records are available for processing.

177

By default, variables referenced in the RETAIN statement are set to missing before the first iteration of the DATA step. To change this, you can specify an initial value after the variable's name. For more information, see Chapter 3, "Summarizing Data," or *SAS® Language Reference: Dictionary*.

Variables referenced with the RETAIN statement are in the output data set only if they are referenced elsewhere in the DATA step or assigned initial values.

Hold EmpLName and EmpFName

```
data dependants(drop=Type);
   length Type $ 1 EmpLName EmpFName
          DepName $ 20 Relation $ 1;
   retain EmpLName EmpFName;
   infile 'raw-data-file' dlm=':';
   input Type $ @;
   if Type='E' then
      input EmpLName $ EmpFName $;
   else do;
      input DepName $ Relation $;
      output;
   end;
run;
```

178

Retaining Values: Compilation

```
data dependants(drop=Type);
   length Type $ 1 EmpLName EmpFName
          DepName $ 20 Relation $ 1;
   retain EmpLName EmpFName;
   infile 'raw-data-file' dlm=':';
   input Type $ @;
   if Type='E' then
      input EmpLName $ EmpFName $;
   else do;
      input DepName $ Relation $;
      output;
   end;
run;
```

Input Buffer

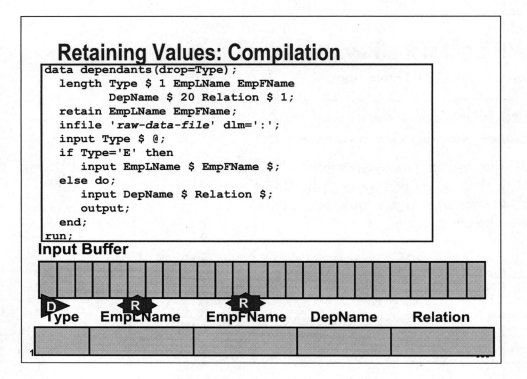

Retaining Values: Execution

```
E:Adams:Susan
D:Michael:C
D:Lindsay:C
E:Porter:David
D:Susan:S
E:Lewis:Dorian D.
D:Richard:C
E:Dansky:Ian
E:Nicholls:James
D:Roberta:C
E:Slaydon:Marla
D:John:S
```

```
data dependants(drop=Type);
   length Type $ 1 EmpLName EmpFName
          DepName $ 20 Relation $ 1;
   retain EmpLName EmpFName;
   infile 'raw-data-file' dlm=':';
   input Type $ @;
   if Type='E' then
      input EmpLName $ EmpFName $;
   else do;
      input DepName $ Relation $;
      output;
   end;
run;
```

Initialize PDV to missing

Input Buffer

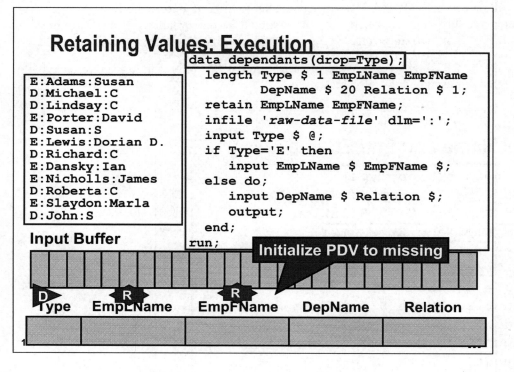

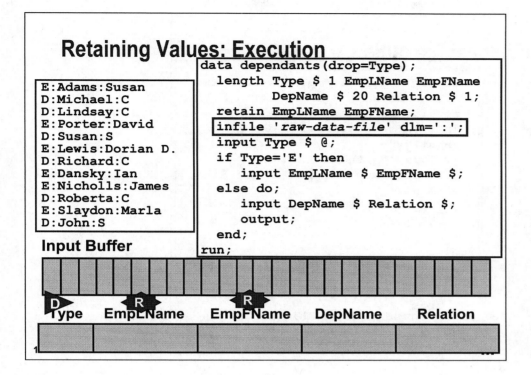

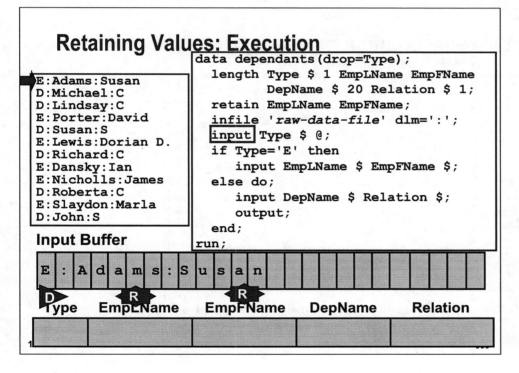

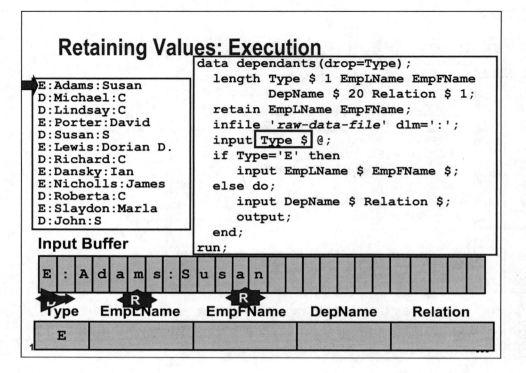

Retaining Values: Execution

```
E:Adams:Susan
D:Michael:C
D:Lindsay:C
E:Porter:David
D:Susan:S
E:Lewis:Dorian D.
D:Richard:C
E:Dansky:Ian
E:Nicholls:James
D:Roberta:C
E:Slaydon:Marla
D:John:S
```

Input Buffer

```
data dependants(drop=Type);
   length Type $ 1 EmpLName EmpFName
          DepName $ 20 Relation $ 1;
   retain EmpLName EmpFName;
   infile 'raw-data-file' dlm=':';
   input Type $ @;
   if Type='E' then
      input EmpLName $ EmpFName $;
   else do;
      input DepName $ Relation $;
      output;
   end;
run;
```

Type	EmpLName	EmpFName	DepName	Relation
E				

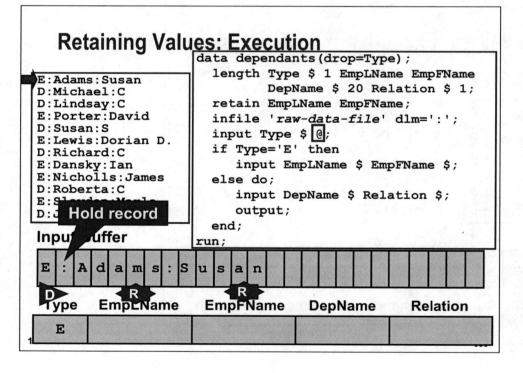

Retaining Values: Execution

```
E:Adams:Susan
D:Michael:C
D:Lindsay:C
E:Porter:David
D:Susan:S
E:Lewis:Dorian D.
D:Richard:C
E:Dansky:Ian
E:Nicholls:James
D:Roberta:C
E:Slaydon:Marla
D:John:S
```

Hold record

Input Buffer

```
data dependants(drop=Type);
   length Type $ 1 EmpLName EmpFName
          DepName $ 20 Relation $ 1;
   retain EmpLName EmpFName;
   infile 'raw-data-file' dlm=':';
   input Type $ @;
   if Type='E' then
      input EmpLName $ EmpFName $;
   else do;
      input DepName $ Relation $;
      output;
   end;
run;
```

Type	EmpLName	EmpFName	DepName	Relation
E				

Retaining Values: Execution

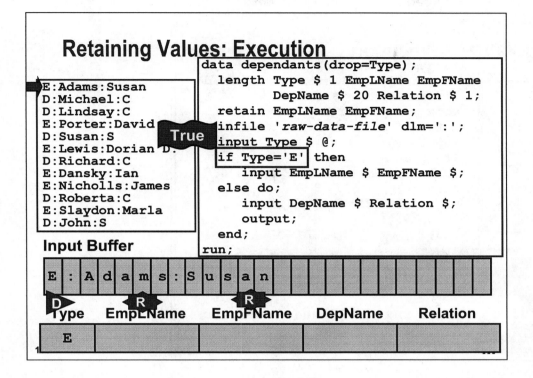

```
data dependants(drop=Type);
   length Type $ 1 EmpLName EmpFName
          DepName $ 20 Relation $ 1;
   retain EmpLName EmpFName;
   infile 'raw-data-file' dlm=':';
   input Type $ @;
   if Type='E' then
      input EmpLName $ EmpFName $;
   else do;
      input DepName $ Relation $;
      output;
   end;
run;
```

Retaining Values: Execution

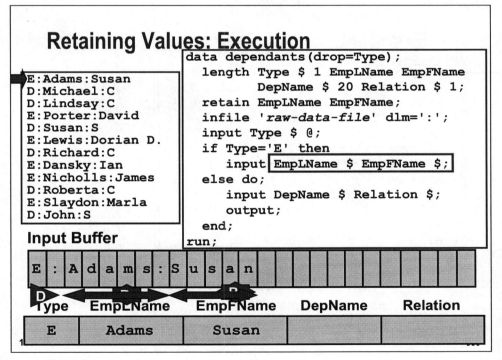

```
data dependants(drop=Type);
   length Type $ 1 EmpLName EmpFName
          DepName $ 20 Relation $ 1;
   retain EmpLName EmpFName;
   infile 'raw-data-file' dlm=':';
   input Type $ @;
   if Type='E' then
      input EmpLName $ EmpFName $;
   else do;
      input DepName $ Relation $;
      output;
   end;
run;
```

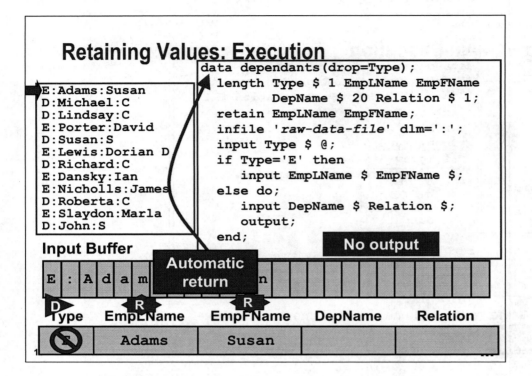

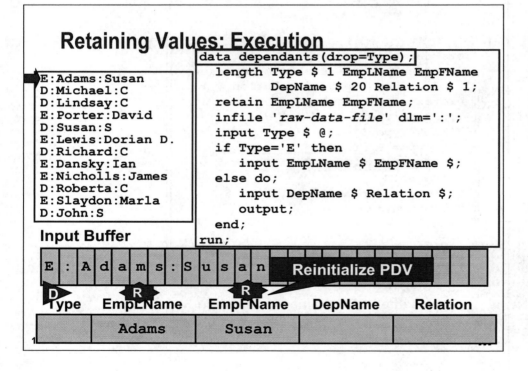

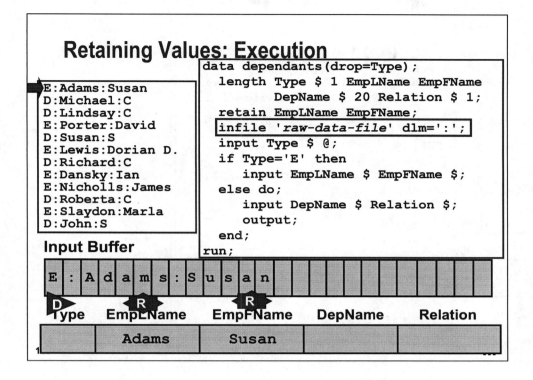

Retaining Values: Execution

Input Buffer

```
data dependants(drop=Type);
   length Type $ 1 EmpLName EmpFName
          DepName $ 20 Relation $ 1;
   retain EmpLName EmpFName;
   infile 'raw-data-file' dlm=':';
   input Type $ @;
   if Type='E' then
      input EmpLName $ EmpFName $;
   else do;
      input DepName $ Relation $;
      output;
   end;
run;
```

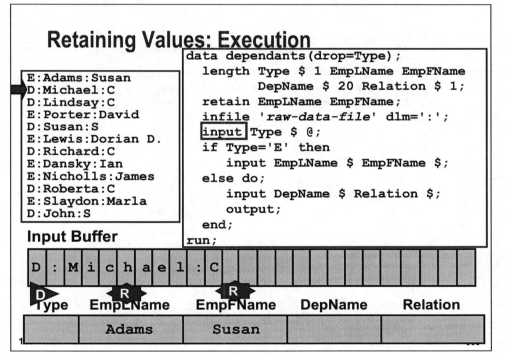

Retaining Values: Execution

Input Buffer

```
data dependants(drop=Type);
   length Type $ 1 EmpLName EmpFName
          DepName $ 20 Relation $ 1;
   retain EmpLName EmpFName;
   infile 'raw-data-file' dlm=':';
   input Type $ @;
   if Type='E' then
      input EmpLName $ EmpFName $;
   else do;
      input DepName $ Relation $;
      output;
   end;
run;
```

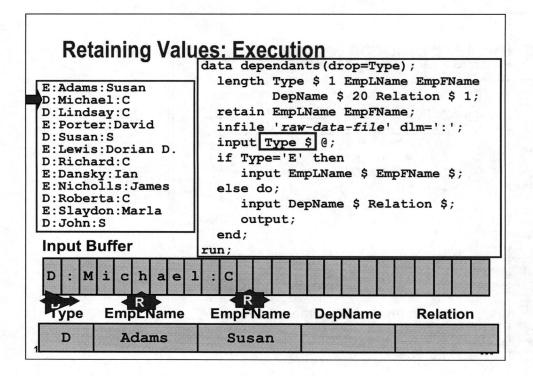

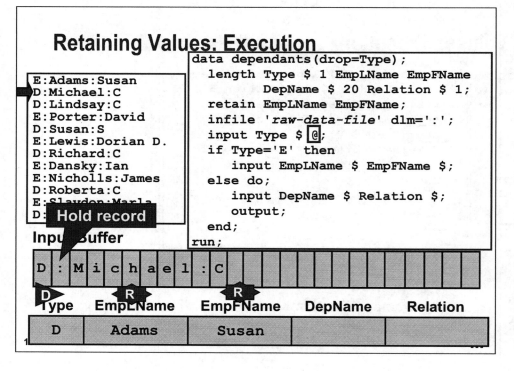

Retaining Values: Execution

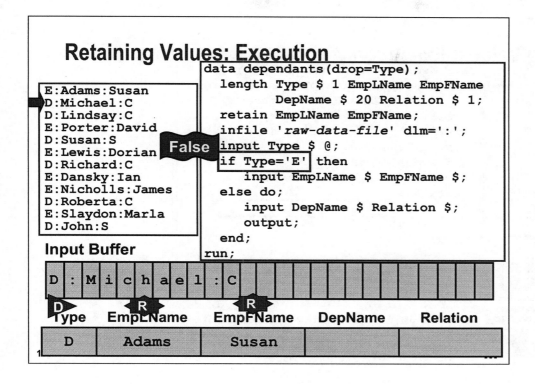

```
data dependants(drop=Type);
   length Type $ 1 EmpLName EmpFName
          DepName $ 20 Relation $ 1;
   retain EmpLName EmpFName;
   infile 'raw-data-file' dlm=':';
   input Type $ @;
   if Type='E' then
      input EmpLName $ EmpFName $;
   else do;
      input DepName $ Relation $;
      output;
   end;
run;
```

Retaining Values: Execution

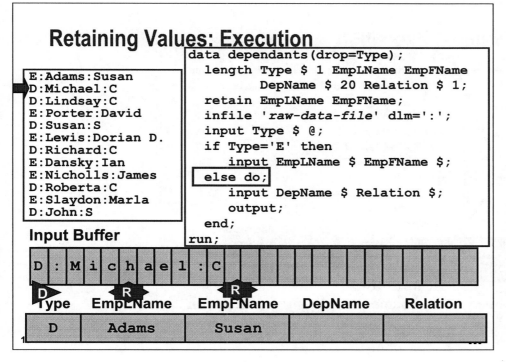

```
data dependants(drop=Type);
   length Type $ 1 EmpLName EmpFName
          DepName $ 20 Relation $ 1;
   retain EmpLName EmpFName;
   infile 'raw-data-file' dlm=':';
   input Type $ @;
   if Type='E' then
      input EmpLName $ EmpFName $;
   else do;
      input DepName $ Relation $;
      output;
   end;
run;
```

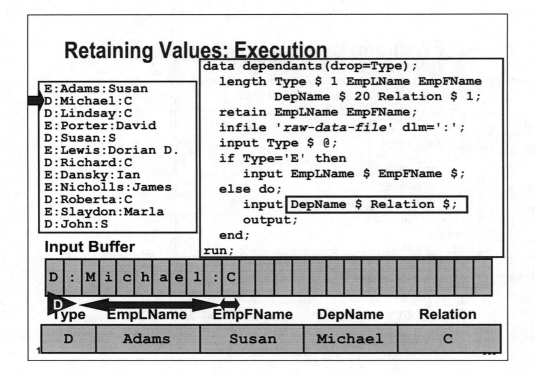

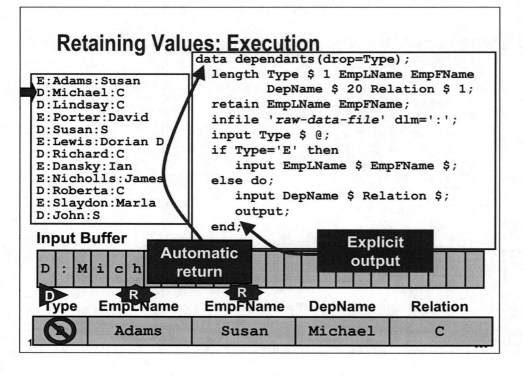

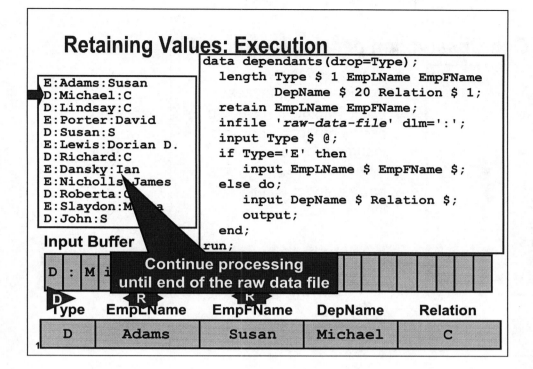

Retaining Values: Execution

```
E:Adams:Susan
D:Michael:C
D:Lindsay:C
E:Porter:David
D:Susan:S
E:Lewis:Dorian D.
D:Richard:C
E:Dansky:Ian
E:Nicholls:James
D:Roberta:C
E:Slaydon:Marla
D:John:S
```

```
data dependants(drop=Type);
   length Type $ 1 EmpLName EmpFName
          DepName $ 20 Relation $ 1;
   retain EmpLName EmpFName;
   infile 'raw-data-file' dlm=':';
   input Type $ @;
   if Type='E' then
       input EmpLName $ EmpFName $;
   else do;
       input DepName $ Relation $;
       output;
   end;
run;
```

Input Buffer

Continue processing until end of the raw data file

Type	EmpLName	EmpFName	DepName	Relation
D	Adams	Susan	Michael	C

Creating One Observation per Detail Record

```
proc print data=work.dependants noobs;
run;
```

PROC PRINT Output

EmpLName	EmpFName	DepName	Relation
Adams	Susan	Michael	C
Adams	Susan	Lindsay	C
Porter	David	Susan	S
Lewis	Dorian D.	Richard	C
Nicholls	James	Roberta	C
Slaydon	Marla	John	S

Why does Ian Dansky not appear in the output?

c04s3d1.sas

198

Creating One Observation per Header Record

```
E:E01442
D:Michael:C
D:Lindsay:C
E:E00705
D:Susan:S
E:E01577
D:Richard:C
E:E00997
E:E00955
D:Roberta:C
E:E00224
D:John:S
```

- Employee insurance is free for the employees.
- Each employee pays $50 per month for a spouse's insurance.
- Each employee pays $25 per month for a child's insurance.

199

Desired Output

Human Resources wants a list of all employees and their monthly payroll deductions for insurance.

ID	Deduct
E01442	50
E00705	50
E01577	25
E00997	0
E00955	25
E00224	50

200

Calculating the Value of Deduct

```
E:E01442
D:Michael:C
D:Lindsay:C
E:E00705
D:Susan:S
E:E01577
D:Richard:C
E:E00997
E:E00955
D:Roberta:C
E:E00224
D:John:S
```

The values of **Deduct** change according to the

- type of record read
- value of **Relation** when **Type='D'**.

201

Retaining ID

Values of **ID** and **Deduct** must be held across iterations of the DATA step.

```
retain ID;
```

- **ID** must be retained with a RETAIN statement.
- **Deduct** is created with a sum statement, so it is automatically retained.

202

When to Output?

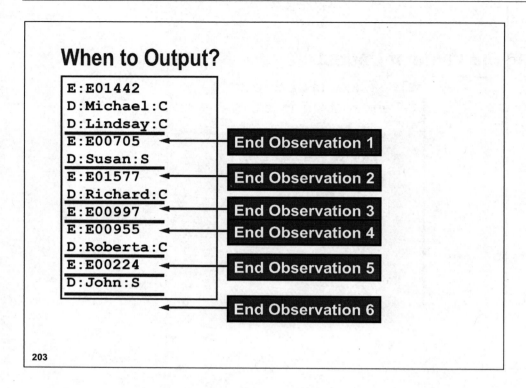

```
E:E01442
D:Michael:C
D:Lindsay:C
E:E00705          ◄──── End Observation 1
D:Susan:S
E:E01577          ◄──── End Observation 2
D:Richard:C
E:E00997          ◄──── End Observation 3
E:E00955          ◄──── End Observation 4
D:Roberta:C
E:E00224          ◄──── End Observation 5
D:John:S
                  ◄──── End Observation 6
```

203

When SAS Loads a Type E Record

1. Output what is currently in the PDV (unless this is the first time through the DATA step).

2. Read the next employee's identification number.

3. Reset **Deduct** to 0.

```
if Type='E' then do;
   if _N_ > 1 then output;
   input ID $;
   Deduct=0;
end;
```

204

When SAS Loads a Type D Record

1. Read the dependant's name and relationship.
2. Check the relationship.
3. Increment **Deduct** appropriately.

```
else do;
   input DepName $ Relation $;
   if Relation='C' then Deduct+25;
   else Deduct+50;
end;
```

Why is **DepName** read?

205

Retaining ID

```
data work.insurance(keep=ID Deduct);
   length Type $ 1 ID $ 6 DepName $ 20
          Relation $ 1;
   retain ID;
   infile 'raw-data-file' dlm=':';
   input Type $ @;
   if Type='E' then do;
      if _N_ > 1 then output;
      input ID $;
      Deduct=0;
   end;
   else do;
      input DepName $ Relation $;
      if Relation='C' then Deduct+25;
      else Deduct+50;
   end;
run;
```

206

What About the Last Record?

```
E:E01442
D:Michael:C
D:Lindsay:C
E:E00705
D:Susan:S
E:E01577
D:Richard:C
E:E00997
E:E00955
D:Roberta:C
E:E00224
D:John:S
```

No automatic output

207

The END= Option

General form of the END= option:

INFILE '*file-name*' END=*variable-name*;

where *variable-name* is any valid SAS variable name.

The END= option creates a variable that has the value

- 1 if it is the last record of the input file
- 0 otherwise.

Variables created with END= are automatically dropped.

208

The END= Option

```
data work.insurance(keep=ID Deduct);
   length Type $ 1 ID $ 6 DepName $ 20 Relation $ 1;
   retain ID;
   infile 'raw-data-file'
          dlm=':' end=LastRec;
   input Type $ @;
   if Type='E' then do;
      if _N_ > 1 then output;
      input ID $;
      Deduct=0;
   end;
   else do;
      input DepName $ Relation $;
      if Relation='C' then Deduct+25;
      else Deduct+50;
   end;
   if LastRec then output;
run;
```

209

Creating One Obs per Header: Compilation

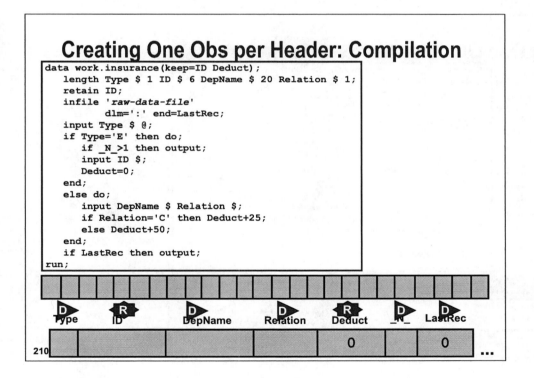

```
data work.insurance(keep=ID Deduct);
   length Type $ 1 ID $ 6 DepName $ 20 Relation $ 1;
   retain ID;
   infile 'raw-data-file'
          dlm=':' end=LastRec;
   input Type $ @;
   if Type='E' then do;
      if _N_ >1 then output;
      input ID $;
      Deduct=0;
   end;
   else do;
      input DepName $ Relation $;
      if Relation='C' then Deduct+25;
      else Deduct+50;
   end;
   if LastRec then output;
run;
```

210

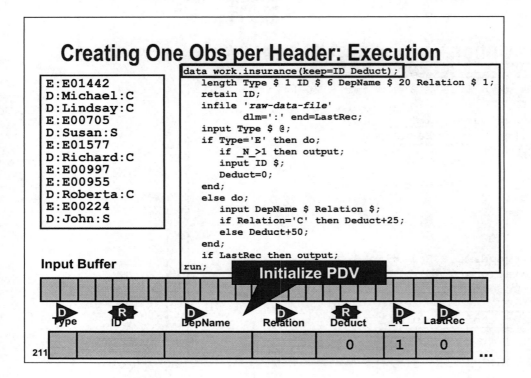

Creating One Obs per Header: Execution

```
E:E01442
D:Michael:C
D:Lindsay:C
E:E00705
D:Susan:S
E:E01577
D:Richard:C
E:E00997
E:E00955
D:Roberta:C
E:E00224
D:John:S
```

```
data work.insurance(keep=ID Deduct);
   length Type $ 1 ID $ 6 DepName $ 20 Relation $ 1;
   retain ID;
   infile 'raw-data-file'
          dlm=':' end=LastRec;
   input Type $ @;
   if Type='E' then do;
      if _N_>1 then output;
      input ID $;
      Deduct=0;
   end;
   else do;
      input DepName $ Relation $;
      if Relation='C' then Deduct+25;
      else Deduct+50;
   end;
   if LastRec then output;
run;
```

Input Buffer

Initialize PDV

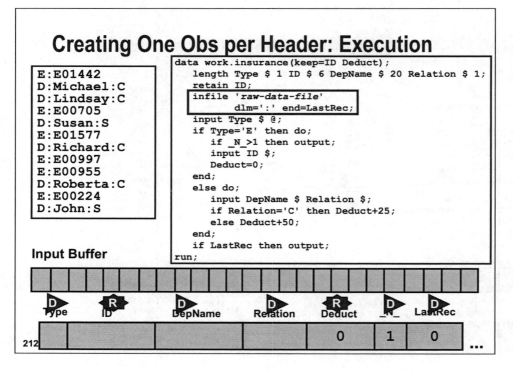

Creating One Obs per Header: Execution

```
E:E01442
D:Michael:C
D:Lindsay:C
E:E00705
D:Susan:S
E:E01577
D:Richard:C
E:E00997
E:E00955
D:Roberta:C
E:E00224
D:John:S
```

```
data work.insurance(keep=ID Deduct);
   length Type $ 1 ID $ 6 DepName $ 20 Relation $ 1;
   retain ID;
   infile 'raw-data-file'
          dlm=':' end=LastRec;
   input Type $ @;
   if Type='E' then do;
      if _N_>1 then output;
      input ID $;
      Deduct=0;
   end;
   else do;
      input DepName $ Relation $;
      if Relation='C' then Deduct+25;
      else Deduct+50;
   end;
   if LastRec then output;
run;
```

Input Buffer

Creating One Obs per Header: Execution

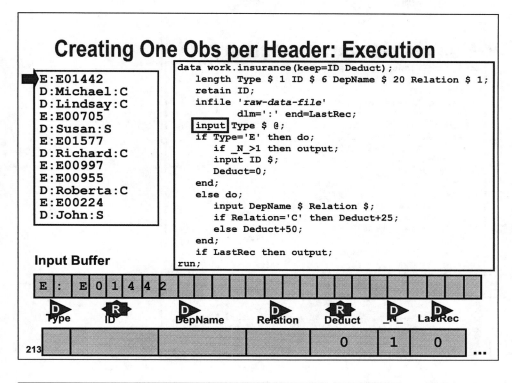

```
data work.insurance(keep=ID Deduct);
    length Type $ 1 ID $ 6 DepName $ 20 Relation $ 1;
    retain ID;
    infile 'raw-data-file'
         dlm=':' end=LastRec;
    input Type $ @;
    if Type='E' then do;
       if _N_>1 then output;
       input ID $;
       Deduct=0;
    end;
    else do;
       input DepName $ Relation $;
       if Relation='C' then Deduct+25;
       else Deduct+50;
    end;
    if LastRec then output;
run;
```

Creating One Obs per Header: Execution

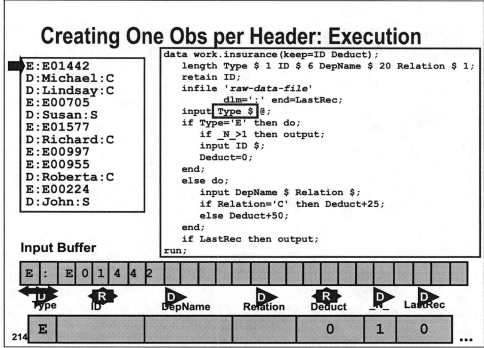

```
data work.insurance(keep=ID Deduct);
    length Type $ 1 ID $ 6 DepName $ 20 Relation $ 1;
    retain ID;
    infile 'raw-data-file'
         dlm=':' end=LastRec;
    input Type $ @;
    if Type='E' then do;
       if _N_>1 then output;
       input ID $;
       Deduct=0;
    end;
    else do;
       input DepName $ Relation $;
       if Relation='C' then Deduct+25;
       else Deduct+50;
    end;
    if LastRec then output;
run;
```

Creating One Obs per Header: Execution

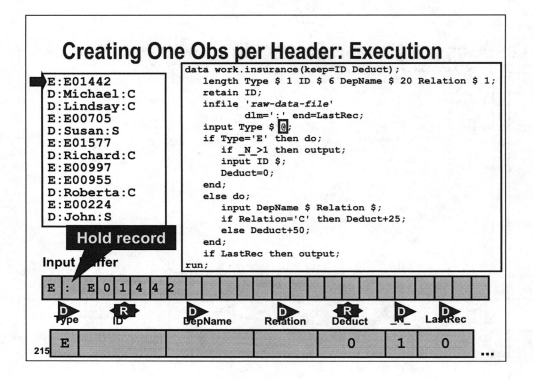

```
data work.insurance(keep=ID Deduct);
   length Type $ 1 ID $ 6 DepName $ 20 Relation $ 1;
   retain ID;
   infile 'raw-data-file'
          dlm=':' end=LastRec;
   input Type $ @;
   if Type='E' then do;
      if _N_>1 then output;
      input ID $;
      Deduct=0;
   end;
   else do;
      input DepName $ Relation $;
      if Relation='C' then Deduct+25;
      else Deduct+50;
   end;
   if LastRec then output;
run;
```

215

Creating One Obs per Header: Execution

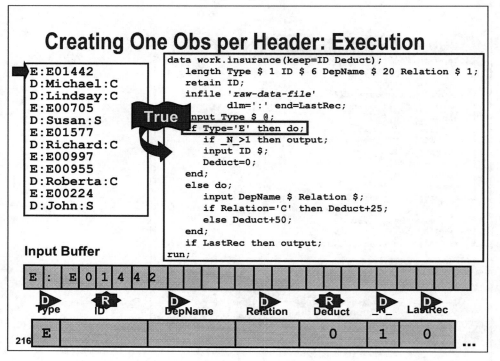

```
data work.insurance(keep=ID Deduct);
   length Type $ 1 ID $ 6 DepName $ 20 Relation $ 1;
   retain ID;
   infile 'raw-data-file'
          dlm=':' end=LastRec;
   input Type $ @;
   if Type='E' then do;
      if _N_>1 then output;
      input ID $;
      Deduct=0;
   end;
   else do;
      input DepName $ Relation $;
      if Relation='C' then Deduct+25;
      else Deduct+50;
   end;
   if LastRec then output;
run;
```

216

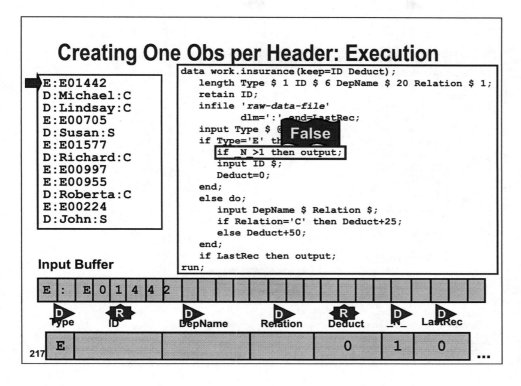

Creating One Obs per Header: Execution

```
data work.insurance(keep=ID Deduct);
   length Type $ 1 ID $ 6 DepName $ 20 Relation $ 1;
   retain ID;
   infile 'raw-data-file'
          dlm=':' end=LastRec;
   input Type $ @;
   if Type='E' then do;
      if _N_>1 then output;
      input ID $;
      Deduct=0;
   end;
   else do;
      input DepName $ Relation $;
      if Relation='C' then Deduct+25;
      else Deduct+50;
   end;
   if LastRec then output;
run;
```

E:E01442
D:Michael:C
D:Lindsay:C
E:E00705
D:Susan:S
E:E01577
D:Richard:C
E:E00997
E:E00955
D:Roberta:C
E:E00224
D:John:S

Input Buffer

217

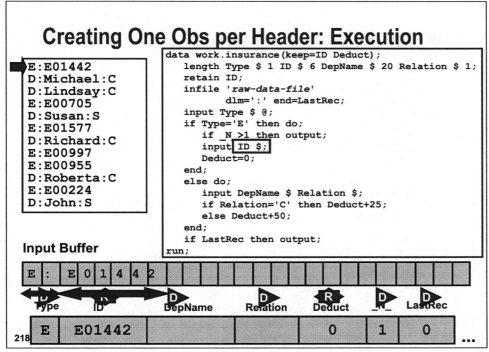

Creating One Obs per Header: Execution

```
data work.insurance(keep=ID Deduct);
   length Type $ 1 ID $ 6 DepName $ 20 Relation $ 1;
   retain ID;
   infile 'raw-data-file'
          dlm=':' end=LastRec;
   input Type $ @;
   if Type='E' then do;
      if _N_>1 then output;
      input ID $;
      Deduct=0;
   end;
   else do;
      input DepName $ Relation $;
      if Relation='C' then Deduct+25;
      else Deduct+50;
   end;
   if LastRec then output;
run;
```

E:E01442
D:Michael:C
D:Lindsay:C
E:E00705
D:Susan:S
E:E01577
D:Richard:C
E:E00997
E:E00955
D:Roberta:C
E:E00224
D:John:S

Input Buffer

218

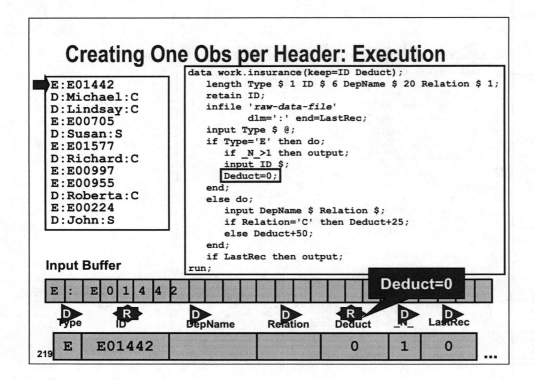

Creating One Obs per Header: Execution

```
E:E01442
D:Michael:C
D:Lindsay:C
E:E00705
D:Susan:S
E:E01577
D:Richard:C
E:E00997
E:E00955
D:Roberta:C
E:E00224
D:John:S
```

Input Buffer

```
data work.insurance(keep=ID Deduct);
   length Type $ 1 ID $ 6 DepName $ 20 Relation $ 1;
   retain ID;
   infile 'raw-data-file'
          dlm=':' end=LastRec;
   input Type $ @;
   if Type='E' then do;
      if _N_>1 then output;
      input ID $;
      Deduct=0;
   end;
   else do;
      input DepName $ Relation $;
      if Relation='C' then Deduct+25;
      else Deduct+50;
   end;
   if LastRec then output;
run;
```

Deduct=0

E	:	E	0	1	4	4	2															

Type	ID	DepName	Relation	Deduct	_N_	LastRec

E	E01442			0	1	0	...

219

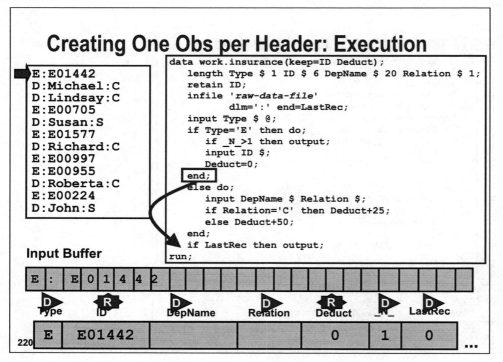

Creating One Obs per Header: Execution

```
E:E01442
D:Michael:C
D:Lindsay:C
E:E00705
D:Susan:S
E:E01577
D:Richard:C
E:E00997
E:E00955
D:Roberta:C
E:E00224
D:John:S
```

Input Buffer

```
data work.insurance(keep=ID Deduct);
   length Type $ 1 ID $ 6 DepName $ 20 Relation $ 1;
   retain ID;
   infile 'raw-data-file'
          dlm=':' end=LastRec;
   input Type $ @;
   if Type='E' then do;
      if _N_>1 then output;
      input ID $;
      Deduct=0;
   end;
   else do;
      input DepName $ Relation $;
      if Relation='C' then Deduct+25;
      else Deduct+50;
   end;
   if LastRec then output;
run;
```

E	:	E	0	1	4	4	2															

Type	ID	DepName	Relation	Deduct	_N_	LastRec

E	E01442			0	1	0	...

220

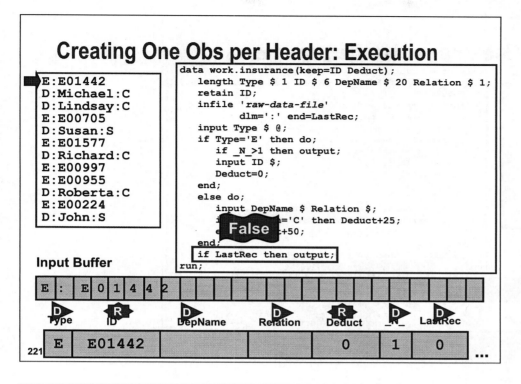

Creating One Obs per Header: Execution

E:E01442
D:Michael:C
D:Lindsay:C
E:E00705
D:Susan:S
E:E01577
D:Richard:C
E:E00997
E:E00955
D:Roberta:C
E:E00224
D:John:S

Input Buffer

```
data work.insurance(keep=ID Deduct);
   length Type $ 1 ID $ 6 DepName $ 20 Relation $ 1;
   retain ID;
   infile 'raw-data-file'
           dlm=':' end=LastRec;
   input Type $ @;
   if Type='E' then do;
      if _N_>1 then output;
      input ID $;
      Deduct=0;
   end;
   else do;
      input DepName $ Relation $;
      i        ='C' then Deduct+25;    False
      e         +50;
   end;
   if LastRec then output;
run;
```

| E | : | E | 0 | 1 | 4 | 4 | 2 | | | | | | | | | | | | | | |

Type   ID   DepName   Relation   Deduct   _N_   LastRec

| E | E01442 | | | 0 | 1 | 0 | ... |

221

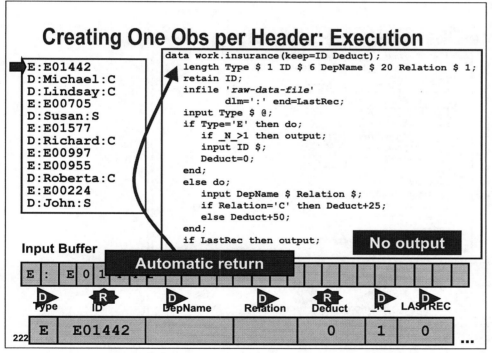

Creating One Obs per Header: Execution

E:E01442
D:Michael:C
D:Lindsay:C
E:E00705
D:Susan:S
E:E01577
D:Richard:C
E:E00997
E:E00955
D:Roberta:C
E:E00224
D:John:S

Input Buffer

```
data work.insurance(keep=ID Deduct);
   length Type $ 1 ID $ 6 DepName $ 20 Relation $ 1;
   retain ID;
   infile 'raw-data-file'
           dlm=':' end=LastRec;
   input Type $ @;
   if Type='E' then do;
      if _N_>1 then output;
      input ID $;
      Deduct=0;
   end;
   else do;
      input DepName $ Relation $;
      if Relation='C' then Deduct+25;
      else Deduct+50;
   end;
   if LastRec then output;            No output
```

Automatic return

| E | : | E | 0 | 1 | | | | | | | | | | | | | | | | | | |

Type   ID   DepName   Relation   Deduct   _N_   LASTREC

| E | E01442 | | | 0 | 1 | 0 | ... |

222

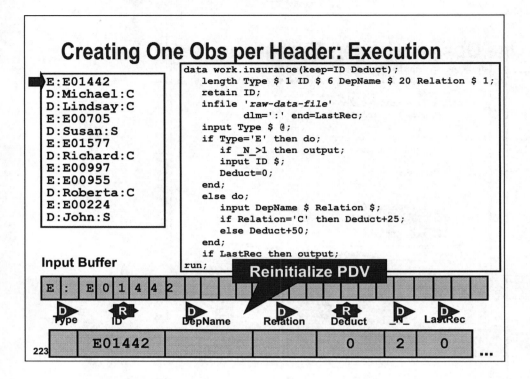

Creating One Obs per Header: Execution

```
data work.insurance(keep=ID Deduct);
   length Type $ 1 ID $ 6 DepName $ 20 Relation $ 1;
   retain ID;
   infile 'raw-data-file'
           dlm=':' end=LastRec;
   input Type $ @;
   if Type='E' then do;
      if _N_>1 then output;
      input ID $;
      Deduct=0;
   end;
   else do;
      input DepName $ Relation $;
      if Relation='C' then Deduct+25;
      else Deduct+50;
   end;
   if LastRec then output;
run;
```

E:E01442
D:Michael:C
D:Lindsay:C
E:E00705
D:Susan:S
E:E01577
D:Richard:C
E:E00997
E:E00955
D:Roberta:C
E:E00224
D:John:S

Input Buffer

Reinitialize PDV

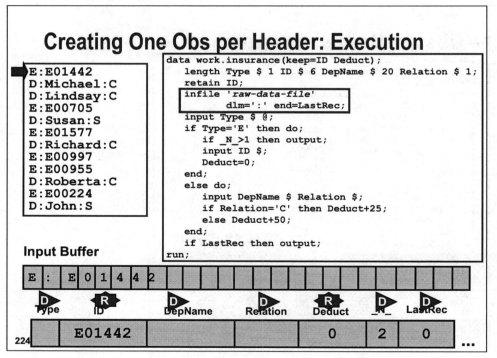

Creating One Obs per Header: Execution

```
data work.insurance(keep=ID Deduct);
   length Type $ 1 ID $ 6 DepName $ 20 Relation $ 1;
   retain ID;
   infile 'raw-data-file'
           dlm=':' end=LastRec;
   input Type $ @;
   if Type='E' then do;
      if _N_>1 then output;
      input ID $;
      Deduct=0;
   end;
   else do;
      input DepName $ Relation $;
      if Relation='C' then Deduct+25;
      else Deduct+50;
   end;
   if LastRec then output;
run;
```

E:E01442
D:Michael:C
D:Lindsay:C
E:E00705
D:Susan:S
E:E01577
D:Richard:C
E:E00997
E:E00955
D:Roberta:C
E:E00224
D:John:S

Input Buffer

Creating One Obs per Header: Execution

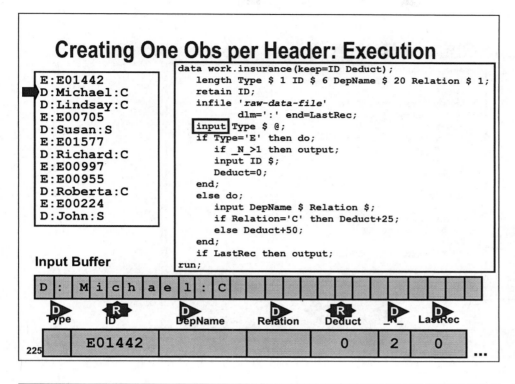

Creating One Obs per Header: Execution

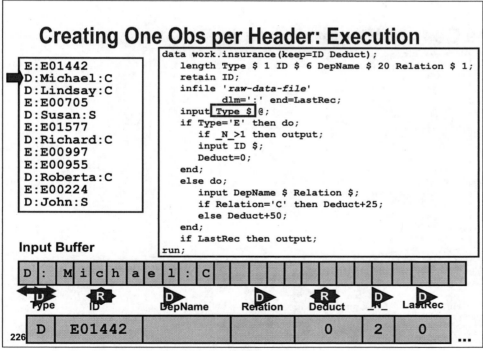

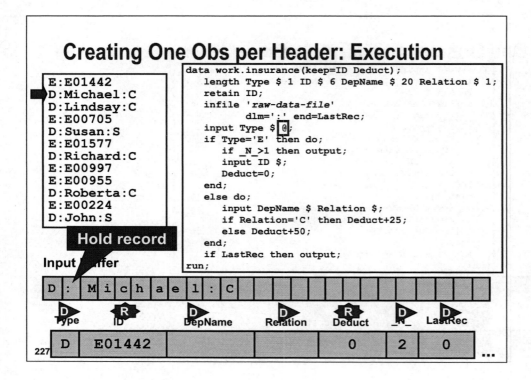

Creating One Obs per Header: Execution

```
E:E01442
D:Michael:C
D:Lindsay:C
E:E00705
D:Susan:S
E:E01577
D:Richard:C
E:E00997
E:E00955
D:Roberta:C
E:E00224
D:John:S
```

Hold record

Input Buffer

```
data work.insurance(keep=ID Deduct);
   length Type $ 1 ID $ 6 DepName $ 20 Relation $ 1;
   retain ID;
   infile 'raw-data-file'
          dlm=':' end=LastRec;
   input Type $ @;
   if Type='E' then do;
      if _N_>1 then output;
      input ID $;
      Deduct=0;
   end;
   else do;
      input DepName $ Relation $;
      if Relation='C' then Deduct+25;
      else Deduct+50;
   end;
   if LastRec then output;
run;
```

D	:	M	i	c	h	a	e	l	:	C											

Type   ID   DepName   Relation   Deduct   _N_   LastRec

D	E01442			0	2	0	...

227

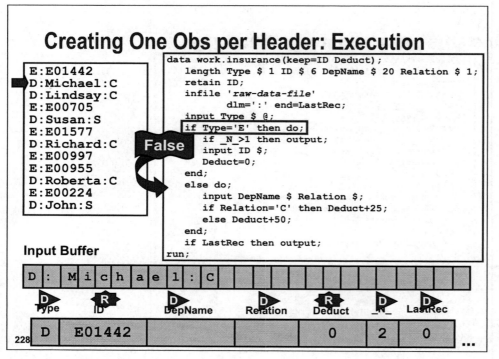

Creating One Obs per Header: Execution

```
E:E01442
D:Michael:C
D:Lindsay:C
E:E00705
D:Susan:S
E:E01577
D:Richard:C
E:E00997
E:E00955
D:Roberta:C
E:E00224
D:John:S
```

False

Input Buffer

```
data work.insurance(keep=ID Deduct);
   length Type $ 1 ID $ 6 DepName $ 20 Relation $ 1;
   retain ID;
   infile 'raw-data-file'
          dlm=':' end=LastRec;
   input Type $ @;
   if Type='E' then do;
      if _N_>1 then output;
      input ID $;
      Deduct=0;
   end;
   else do;
      input DepName $ Relation $;
      if Relation='C' then Deduct+25;
      else Deduct+50;
   end;
   if LastRec then output;
run;
```

D	:	M	i	c	h	a	e	l	:	C											

Type   ID   DepName   Relation   Deduct   _N_   LastRec

D	E01442			0	2	0	...

228

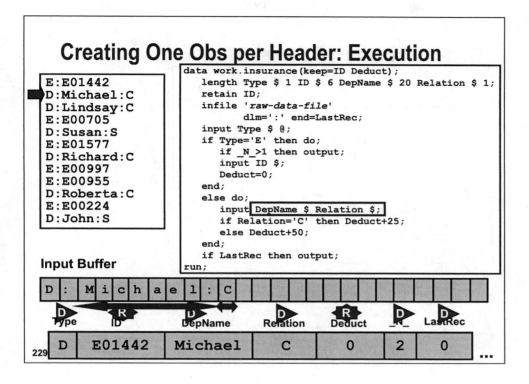

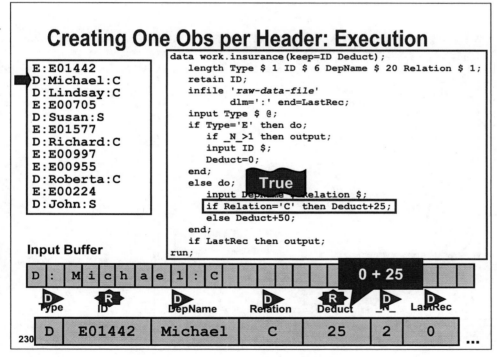

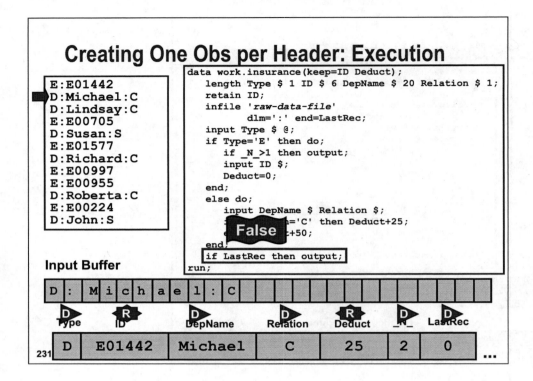

Creating One Obs per Header: Execution

```
data work.insurance(keep=ID Deduct);
   length Type $ 1 ID $ 6 DepName $ 20 Relation $ 1;
   retain ID;
   infile 'raw-data-file'
        dlm=':' end=LastRec;
   input Type $ @;
   if Type='E' then do;
      if _N_>1 then output;
      input ID $;
      Deduct=0;
   end;
   else do;
      input DepName $ Relation $;
      if  ='C' then Deduct+25;
              +50;
   end;
   if LastRec then output;
run;
```

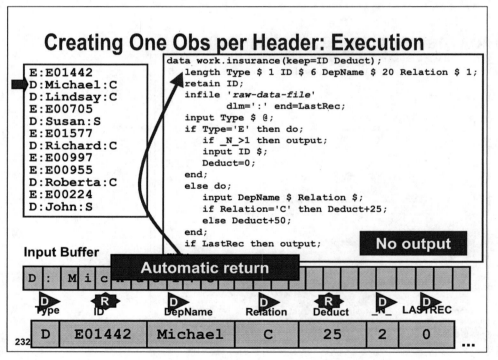

Creating One Obs per Header: Execution

```
data work.insurance(keep=ID Deduct);
   length Type $ 1 ID $ 6 DepName $ 20 Relation $ 1;
   retain ID;
   infile 'raw-data-file'
        dlm=':' end=LastRec;
   input Type $ @;
   if Type='E' then do;
      if _N_>1 then output;
      input ID $;
      Deduct=0;
   end;
   else do;
      input DepName $ Relation $;
      if Relation='C' then Deduct+25;
      else Deduct+50;
   end;
   if LastRec then output;
```

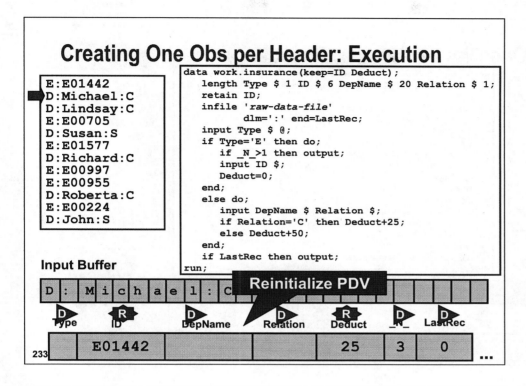

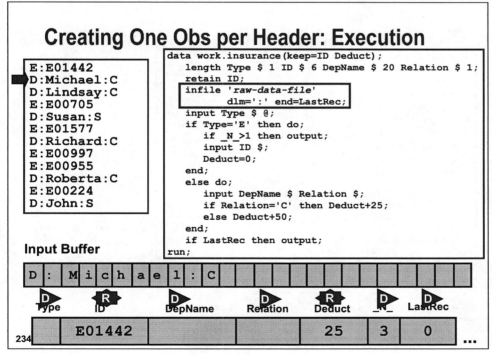

Creating One Obs per Header: Execution

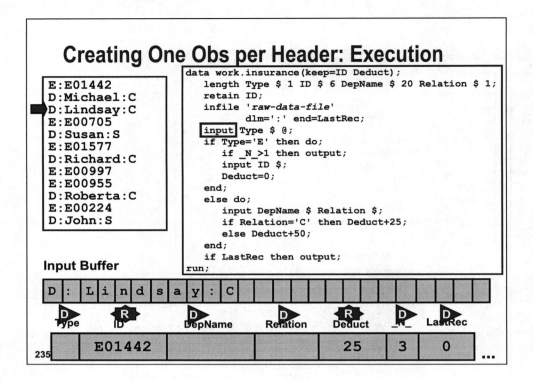

```
data work.insurance(keep=ID Deduct);
   length Type $ 1 ID $ 6 DepName $ 20 Relation $ 1;
   retain ID;
   infile 'raw-data-file'
          dlm=':' end=LastRec;
   input Type $ @;
   if Type='E' then do;
      if _N_>1 then output;
      input ID $;
      Deduct=0;
   end;
   else do;
      input DepName $ Relation $;
      if Relation='C' then Deduct+25;
      else Deduct+50;
   end;
   if LastRec then output;
run;
```

E:E01442
D:Michael:C
D:Lindsay:C
E:E00705
D:Susan:S
E:E01577
D:Richard:C
E:E00997
E:E00955
D:Roberta:C
E:E00224
D:John:S

Input Buffer

235

Creating One Obs per Header: Execution

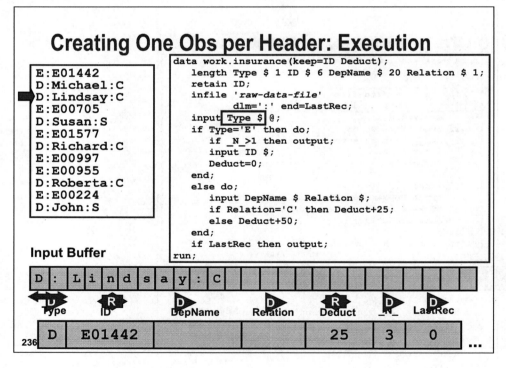

```
data work.insurance(keep=ID Deduct);
   length Type $ 1 ID $ 6 DepName $ 20 Relation $ 1;
   retain ID;
   infile 'raw-data-file'
          dlm=':' end=LastRec;
   input Type $ @;
   if Type='E' then do;
      if _N_>1 then output;
      input ID $;
      Deduct=0;
   end;
   else do;
      input DepName $ Relation $;
      if Relation='C' then Deduct+25;
      else Deduct+50;
   end;
   if LastRec then output;
run;
```

E:E01442
D:Michael:C
D:Lindsay:C
E:E00705
D:Susan:S
E:E01577
D:Richard:C
E:E00997
E:E00955
D:Roberta:C
E:E00224
D:John:S

Input Buffer

236

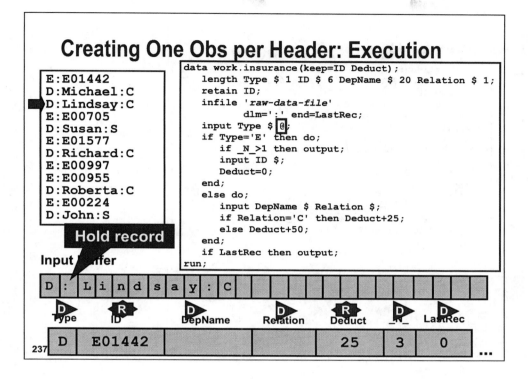

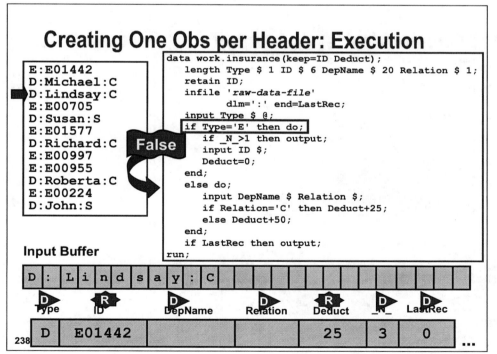

Creating One Obs per Header: Execution

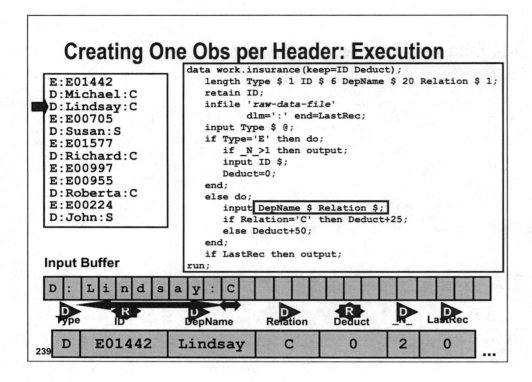

```
data work.insurance(keep=ID Deduct);
   length Type $ 1 ID $ 6 DepName $ 20 Relation $ 1;
   retain ID;
   infile 'raw-data-file'
         dlm=':' end=LastRec;
   input Type $ @;
   if Type='E' then do;
      if _N_>1 then output;
      input ID $;
      Deduct=0;
   end;
   else do;
      input DepName $ Relation $;
      if Relation='C' then Deduct+25;
      else Deduct+50;
   end;
   if LastRec then output;
run;
```

E:E01442
D:Michael:C
D:Lindsay:C
E:E00705
D:Susan:S
E:E01577
D:Richard:C
E:E00997
E:E00955
D:Roberta:C
E:E00224
D:John:S

Input Buffer

| D | : | L | i | n | d | s | a | y | : | C | | | | | | | | | | | | |

Type ID DepName Relation Deduct _N_ LastRec

239

| D | E01442 | Lindsay | C | 0 | 2 | 0 | ... |

Creating One Obs per Header: Execution

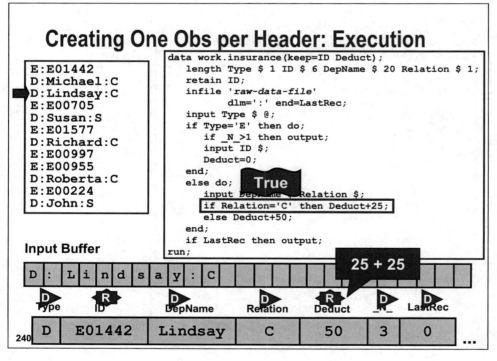

```
data work.insurance(keep=ID Deduct);
   length Type $ 1 ID $ 6 DepName $ 20 Relation $ 1;
   retain ID;
   infile 'raw-data-file'
         dlm=':' end=LastRec;
   input Type $ @;
   if Type='E' then do;
      if _N_>1 then output;
      input ID $;
      Deduct=0;
   end;
   else do;
      input DepName $ Relation $;
      if Relation='C' then Deduct+25;
      else Deduct+50;
   end;
   if LastRec then output;
run;
```

E:E01442
D:Michael:C
D:Lindsay:C
E:E00705
D:Susan:S
E:E01577
D:Richard:C
E:E00997
E:E00955
D:Roberta:C
E:E00224
D:John:S

True

25 + 25

Input Buffer

| D | : | L | i | n | d | s | a | y | : | C | | | | | | | | | | | |

Type ID DepName Relation Deduct _N_ LastRec

240

| D | E01442 | Lindsay | C | 50 | 3 | 0 | ... |

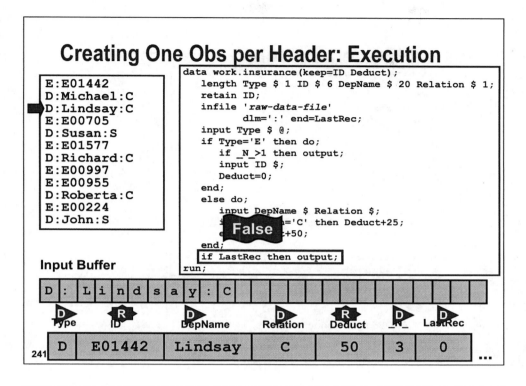

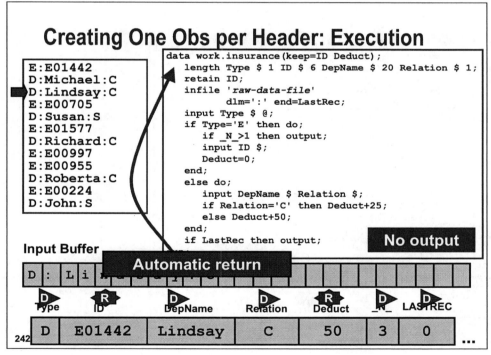

Creating One Obs per Header: Execution

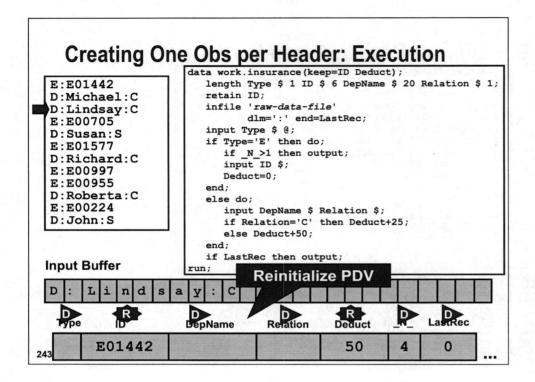

Creating One Obs per Header: Execution

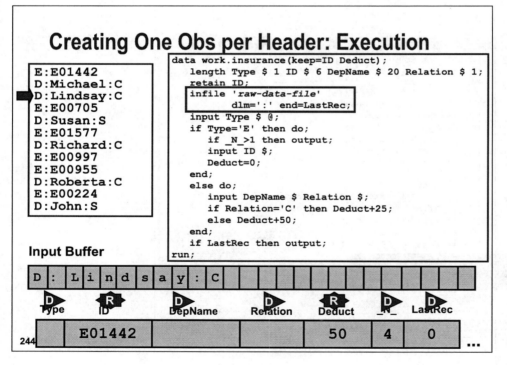

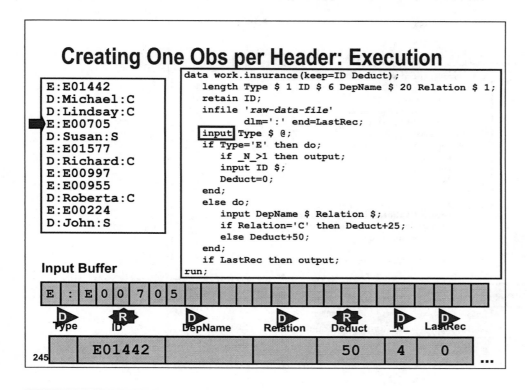

Creating One Obs per Header: Execution

```
E:E01442
D:Michael:C
D:Lindsay:C
E:E00705   ◄
D:Susan:S
E:E01577
D:Richard:C
E:E00997
E:E00955
D:Roberta:C
E:E00224
D:John:S
```

```
data work.insurance(keep=ID Deduct);
   length Type $ 1 ID $ 6 DepName $ 20 Relation $ 1;
   retain ID;
   infile 'raw-data-file'
          dlm=':' end=LastRec;
   input  Type $ @;
   if Type='E' then do;
      if _N_>1 then output;
      input ID $;
      Deduct=0;
   end;
   else do;
      input DepName $ Relation $;
      if Relation='C' then Deduct+25;
      else Deduct+50;
   end;
   if LastRec then output;
run;
```

Input Buffer

| E | : | E | 0 | 0 | 7 | 0 | 5 | | | | | | | | | | | | |

Type ID DepName Relation Deduct _N_ LastRec

| | E01442 | | | 50 | 4 | 0 | |

245

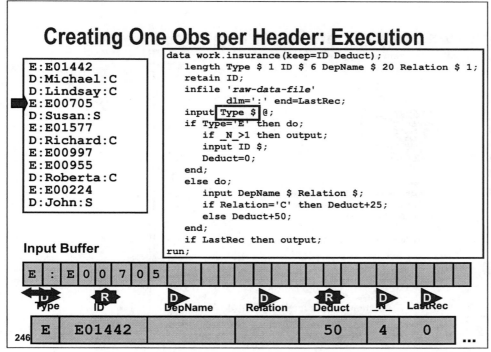

Creating One Obs per Header: Execution

```
E:E01442
D:Michael:C
D:Lindsay:C
E:E00705   ◄
D:Susan:S
E:E01577
D:Richard:C
E:E00997
E:E00955
D:Roberta:C
E:E00224
D:John:S
```

```
data work.insurance(keep=ID Deduct);
   length Type $ 1 ID $ 6 DepName $ 20 Relation $ 1;
   retain ID;
   infile 'raw-data-file'
          dlm=':' end=LastRec;
   input Type $  @;
   if Type='E' then do;
      if _N_>1 then output;
      input ID $;
      Deduct=0;
   end;
   else do;
      input DepName $ Relation $;
      if Relation='C' then Deduct+25;
      else Deduct+50;
   end;
   if LastRec then output;
run;
```

Input Buffer

| E | : | E | 0 | 0 | 7 | 0 | 5 | | | | | | | | | | | | |

Type ID DepName Relation Deduct _N_ LastRec

| E | E01442 | | | 50 | 4 | 0 | |

246

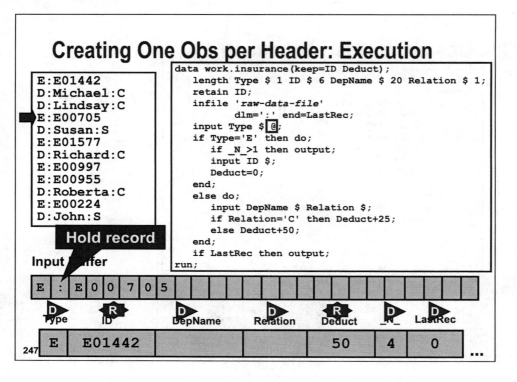

Creating One Obs per Header: Execution

```
E:E01442
D:Michael:C
D:Lindsay:C
E:E00705
D:Susan:S
E:E01577
D:Richard:C
E:E00997
E:E00955
D:Roberta:C
E:E00224
D:John:S
```

```
data work.insurance(keep=ID Deduct);
   length Type $ 1 ID $ 6 DepName $ 20 Relation $ 1;
   retain ID;
   infile 'raw-data-file'
         dlm=':' end=LastRec;
   input Type $ @;
   if Type='E' then do;
      if _N_>1 then output;
      input ID $;
      Deduct=0;
   end;
   else do;
      input DepName $ Relation $;
      if Relation='C' then Deduct+25;
      else Deduct+50;
   end;
   if LastRec then output;
run;
```

Hold record

Input Buffer

```
E : E 0 0 7 0 5
```

Type   ID   DepName   Relation   Deduct   _N_   LastRec

| E | E01442 | | | 50 | 4 | 0 | ... |

247

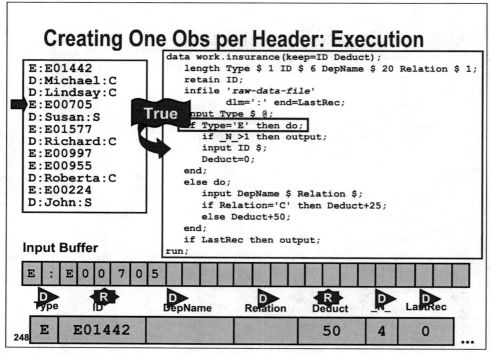

Creating One Obs per Header: Execution

```
E:E01442
D:Michael:C
D:Lindsay:C
E:E00705
D:Susan:S
E:E01577
D:Richard:C
E:E00997
E:E00955
D:Roberta:C
E:E00224
D:John:S
```

```
data work.insurance(keep=ID Deduct);
   length Type $ 1 ID $ 6 DepName $ 20 Relation $ 1;
   retain ID;
   infile 'raw-data-file'
         dlm=':' end=LastRec;
   input Type $ @;
   if Type='E' then do;
      if _N_>1 then output;
      input ID $;
      Deduct=0;
   end;
   else do;
      input DepName $ Relation $;
      if Relation='C' then Deduct+25;
      else Deduct+50;
   end;
   if LastRec then output;
run;
```

True

Input Buffer

```
E : E 0 0 7 0 5
```

Type   ID   DepName   Relation   Deduct   _N_   LastRec

| E | E01442 | | | 50 | 4 | 0 | ... |

248

Creating One Obs per Header: Execution

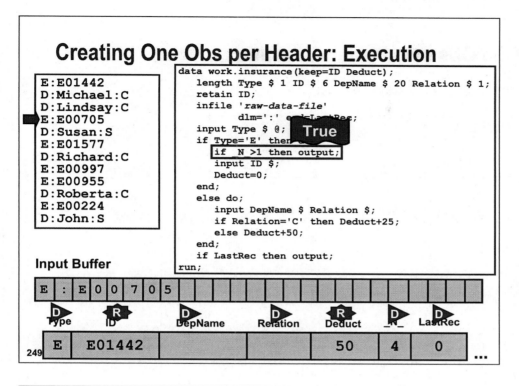

Creating One Obs per Header: Execution

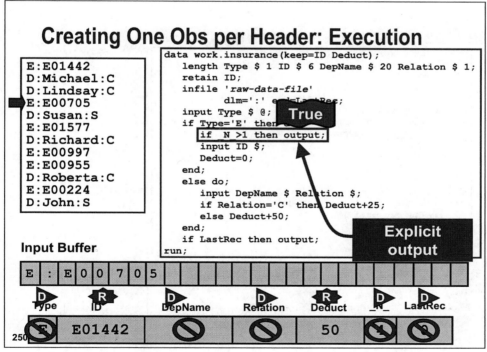

Creating One Obs per Header: Execution

Current contents of `work.insurance`

ID	Deduct
E01442	50

251   ...

Creating One Obs per Header: Execution

```
E:E01442
D:Michael:C
D:Lindsay:C
E:E00705   ◄
D:Susan:S
E:E01577
D:Richard:C
E:E00997
E:E00955
D:Roberta:C
E:E00224
D:John:S
```

```
data work.insurance(keep=ID Deduct);
   length Type $ 1 ID $ 6 DepName $ 20 Relation $ 1;
   retain ID;
   infile 'raw-data-file'
          dlm=':' end=LastRec;
   input Type $ @;
   if Type='E' then do;
      if _N_ >1 then output;
      input ID $;
      Deduct=0;
   end;
   else do;
      input DepName $ Relation $;
      if Relation='C' then Deduct+25;
      else Deduct+50;
   end;
   if LastRec then output;
run;
```

Input Buffer

| E | : | E | 0 | 0 | 7 | 0 | 5 | | | | | | | | | | | | | |

Type	ID	DepName	Relation	Deduct	_N_	LastRec
E	E00705			50	4	0

252   ...

Creating One Obs per Header: Execution

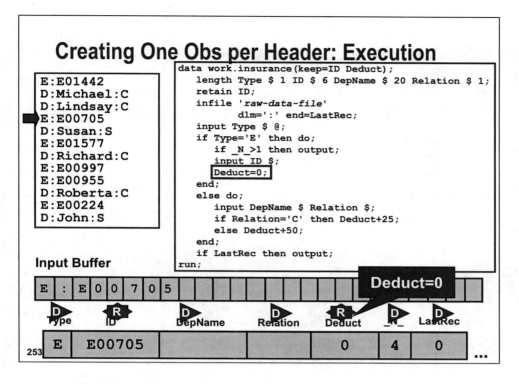

```
data work.insurance(keep=ID Deduct);
   length Type $ 1 ID $ 6 DepName $ 20 Relation $ 1;
   retain ID;
   infile 'raw-data-file'
          dlm=':' end=LastRec;
   input Type $ @;
   if Type='E' then do;
      if _N_>1 then output;
      input ID $;
      Deduct=0;
   end;
   else do;
      input DepName $ Relation $;
      if Relation='C' then Deduct+25;
      else Deduct+50;
   end;
   if LastRec then output;
run;
```

Input Buffer

253

Creating One Obs per Header: Execution

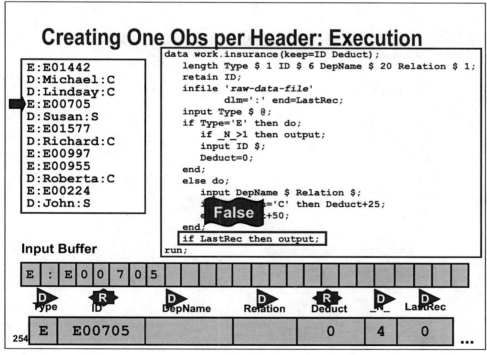

```
data work.insurance(keep=ID Deduct);
   length Type $ 1 ID $ 6 DepName $ 20 Relation $ 1;
   retain ID;
   infile 'raw-data-file'
          dlm=':' end=LastRec;
   input Type $ @;
   if Type='E' then do;
      if _N_>1 then output;
      input ID $;
      Deduct=0;
   end;
   else do;
      input DepName $ Relation $;
      if Relation='C' then Deduct+25;
      else Deduct+50;
   end;
   if LastRec then output;
run;
```

Input Buffer

254

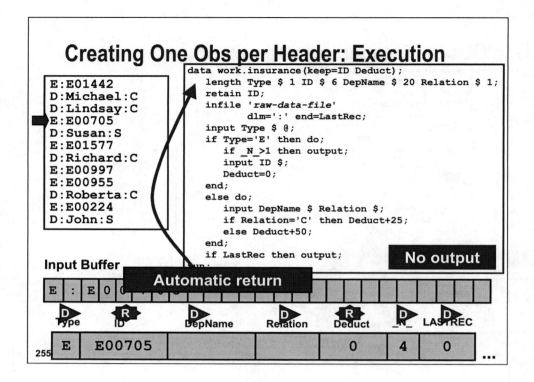

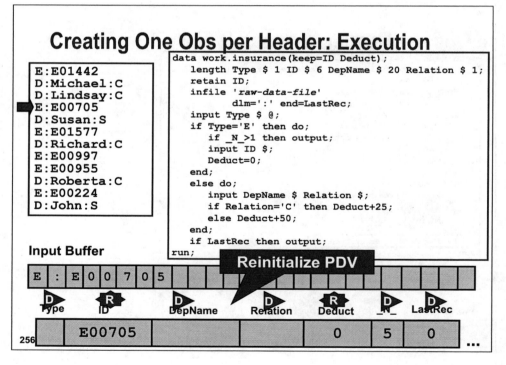

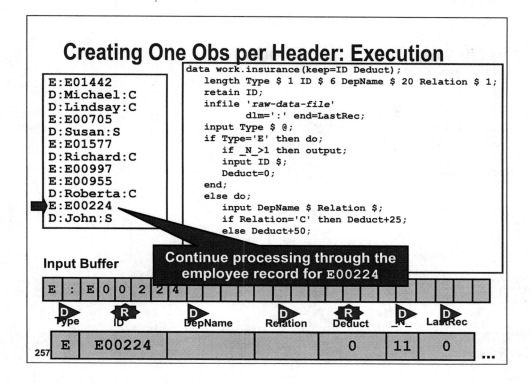

Creating One Obs per Header: Execution

```
data work.insurance(keep=ID Deduct);
   length Type $ 1 ID $ 6 DepName $ 20 Relation $ 1;
   retain ID;
   infile 'raw-data-file'
          dlm=':' end=LastRec;
   input Type $ @;
   if Type='E' then do;
      if _N_>1 then output;
      input ID $;
      Deduct=0;
   end;
   else do;
      input DepName $ Relation $;
      if Relation='C' then Deduct+25;
      else Deduct+50;
```

E:E01442
D:Michael:C
D:Lindsay:C
E:E00705
D:Susan:S
E:E01577
D:Richard:C
E:E00997
E:E00955
D:Roberta:C
► E:E00224
D:John:S

Continue processing through the
employee record for E00224

Input Buffer

| E | : | E | 0 | 0 | 2 | 2 | 4 | | | | | | | | | | | | | |

Type   ID   DepName   Relation   Deduct   _N_   LastRec

257   E   E00224   0   11   0   ...

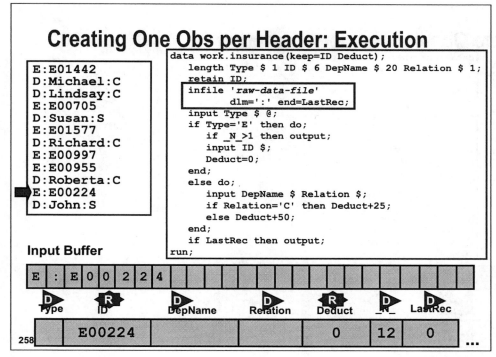

Creating One Obs per Header: Execution

```
data work.insurance(keep=ID Deduct);
   length Type $ 1 ID $ 6 DepName $ 20 Relation $ 1;
   retain ID;
   infile 'raw-data-file'
          dlm=':' end=LastRec;
   input Type $ @;
   if Type='E' then do;
      if _N_>1 then output;
      input ID $;
      Deduct=0;
   end;
   else do;
      input DepName $ Relation $;
      if Relation='C' then Deduct+25;
      else Deduct+50;
   end;
   if LastRec then output;
run;
```

E:E01442
D:Michael:C
D:Lindsay:C
E:E00705
D:Susan:S
E:E01577
D:Richard:C
E:E00997
E:E00955
D:Roberta:C
► E:E00224
D:John:S

Input Buffer

| E | : | E | 0 | 0 | 2 | 2 | 4 | | | | | | | | | | | | | |

Type   ID   DepName   Relation   Deduct   _N_   LastRec

258   E00224   0   12   0   ...

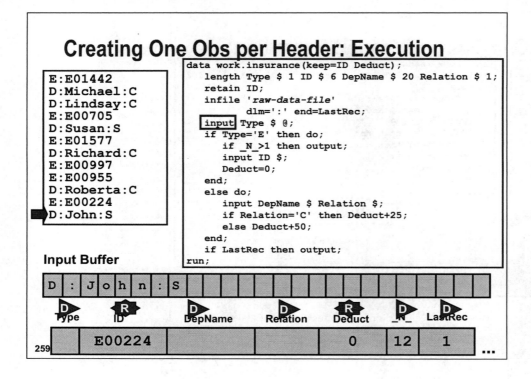

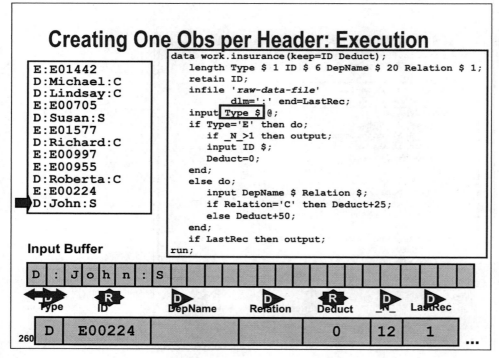

Creating One Obs per Header: Execution

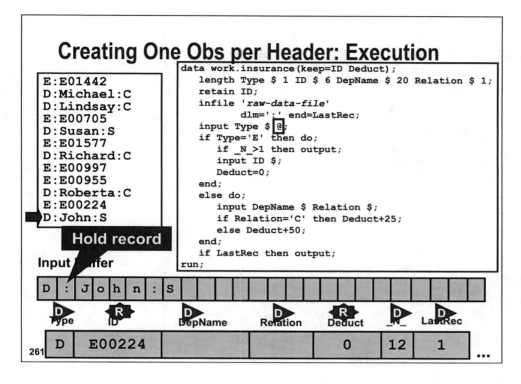

```
E:E01442
D:Michael:C
D:Lindsay:C
E:E00705
D:Susan:S
E:E01577
D:Richard:C
E:E00997
E:E00955
D:Roberta:C
E:E00224
▶ D:John:S
```

Hold record

Input Buffer

```
data work.insurance(keep=ID Deduct);
   length Type $ 1 ID $ 6 DepName $ 20 Relation $ 1;
   retain ID;
   infile 'raw-data-file'
          dlm=':' end=LastRec;
   input Type $ @;
   if Type='E' then do;
      if _N_>1 then output;
      input ID $;
      Deduct=0;
   end;
   else do;
      input DepName $ Relation $;
      if Relation='C' then Deduct+25;
      else Deduct+50;
   end;
   if LastRec then output;
run;
```

| D | : | J | o | h | n | : | S | | | | | | | | | | | | |

| D | R | D | D | R | D | D |
| Type | ID | DepName | Relation | Deduct | _N_ | LastRec |

| D | E00224 | | | 0 | 12 | 1 | ... |

261

Creating One Obs per Header: Execution

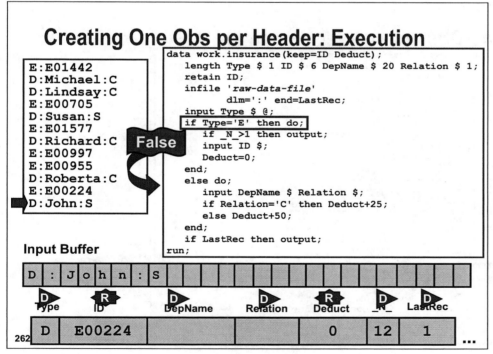

```
E:E01442
D:Michael:C
D:Lindsay:C
E:E00705
D:Susan:S
E:E01577
D:Richard:C
E:E00997
E:E00955
D:Roberta:C
E:E00224
▶ D:John:S
```

False

Input Buffer

```
data work.insurance(keep=ID Deduct);
   length Type $ 1 ID $ 6 DepName $ 20 Relation $ 1;
   retain ID;
   infile 'raw-data-file'
          dlm=':' end=LastRec;
   input Type $ @;
   if Type='E' then do;
      if _N_>1 then output;
      input ID $;
      Deduct=0;
   end;
   else do;
      input DepName $ Relation $;
      if Relation='C' then Deduct+25;
      else Deduct+50;
   end;
   if LastRec then output;
run;
```

| D | : | J | o | h | n | : | S | | | | | | | | | | | | |

| D | R | D | D | R | D | D |
| Type | ID | DepName | Relation | Deduct | _N_ | LastRec |

| D | E00224 | | | 0 | 12 | 1 | ... |

262

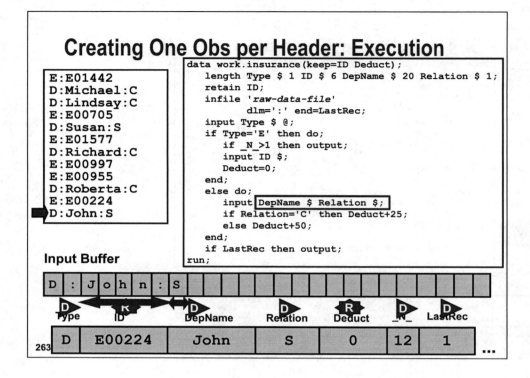

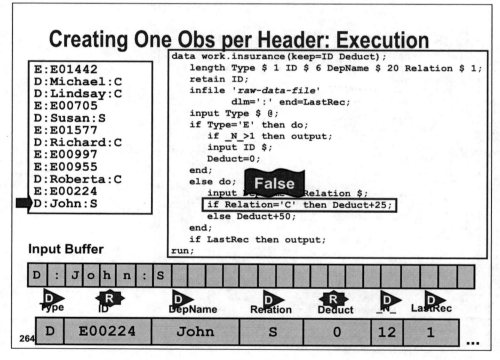

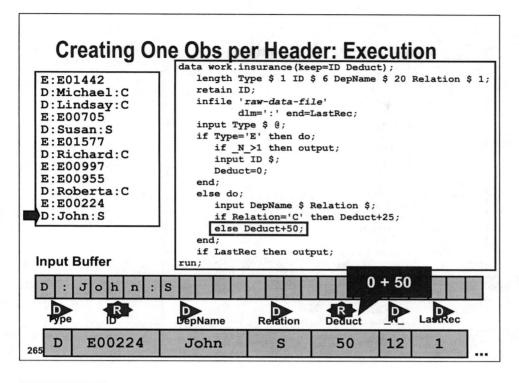

Creating One Obs per Header: Execution

```
data work.insurance(keep=ID Deduct);
    length Type $ 1 ID $ 6 DepName $ 20 Relation $ 1;
    retain ID;
    infile 'raw-data-file'
            dlm=':' end=LastRec;
    input Type $ @;
    if Type='E' then do;
        if _N_>1 then output;
        input ID $;
        Deduct=0;
    end;
    else do;
        input DepName $ Relation $;
        if Relation='C' then Deduct+25;
        else Deduct+50;
    end;
    if LastRec then output;
run;
```

E:E01442
D:Michael:C
D:Lindsay:C
E:E00705
D:Susan:S
E:E01577
D:Richard:C
E:E00997
E:E00955
D:Roberta:C
E:E00224
D:John:S

Input Buffer

| D | : | J | o | h | n | : | S |

0 + 50

Type   ID   DepName   Relation   Deduct   _N_   LastRec

265 | D | E00224 | John | S | 50 | 12 | 1 | ...

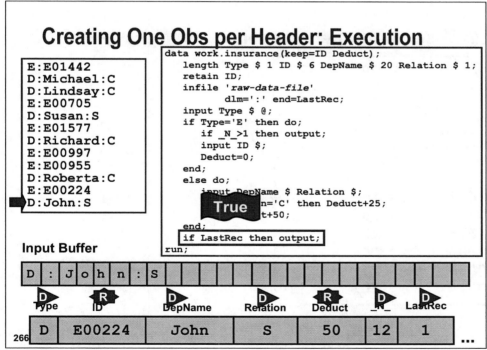

Creating One Obs per Header: Execution

```
data work.insurance(keep=ID Deduct);
    length Type $ 1 ID $ 6 DepName $ 20 Relation $ 1;
    retain ID;
    infile 'raw-data-file'
            dlm=':' end=LastRec;
    input Type $ @;
    if Type='E' then do;
        if _N_>1 then output;
        input ID $;
        Deduct=0;
    end;
    else do;
        input DepName $ Relation $;
        if Relation='C' then Deduct+25;
        else Deduct+50;
    end;
    if LastRec then output;
run;
```

E:E01442
D:Michael:C
D:Lindsay:C
E:E00705
D:Susan:S
E:E01577
D:Richard:C
E:E00997
E:E00955
D:Roberta:C
E:E00224
D:John:S

Input Buffer

| D | : | J | o | h | n | : | S |

True

Type   ID   DepName   Relation   Deduct   _N_   LastRec

266 | D | E00224 | John | S | 50 | 12 | 1 | ...

Creating One Obs per Header: Execution

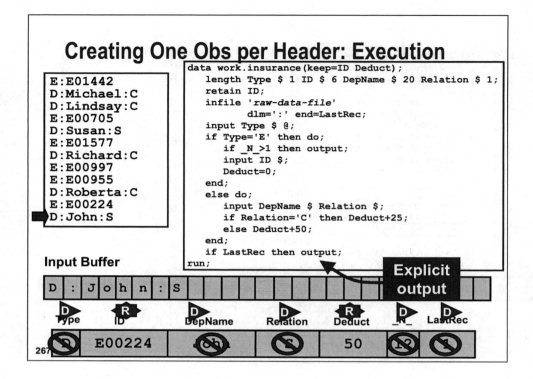

```
E:E01442
D:Michael:C
D:Lindsay:C
E:E00705
D:Susan:S
E:E01577
D:Richard:C
E:E00997
E:E00955
D:Roberta:C
E:E00224
D:John:S
```

```
data work.insurance(keep=ID Deduct);
    length Type $ 1 ID $ 6 DepName $ 20 Relation $ 1;
    retain ID;
    infile 'raw-data-file'
           dlm=':' end=LastRec;
    input Type $ @;
    if Type='E' then do;
        if _N_>1 then output;
        input ID $;
        Deduct=0;
    end;
    else do;
        input DepName $ Relation $;
        if Relation='C' then Deduct+25;
        else Deduct+50;
    end;
    if LastRec then output;
run;
```

Explicit output

Input Buffer

| D | : | J | o | h | n | : | S | | | | | | | | | | | |

Type   ID   DepName   Relation   Deduct   _N_   LastRec

| | E00224 | | | 50 | | |

267

Creating One Observation per Header

```
proc print data=insurance noobs;
run;
```

PROC PRINT Output

ID	Deduct
E01442	50
E00705	50
E01577	25
E00997	0
E00955	25
E00224	50

c04s3d2.sas

268

Summarizing a Hierarchical File with Two DATA Steps (Self-Study)

File: c04s3d3.sas

It is possible to read a hierarchical raw data file using two DATA steps instead of the method shown above. Although less efficient, this method tends to be easier to code, maintain, and debug.

Step 1: Read the hierarchical raw data file into a SAS data set and use conditional input.

```
data HierStep1;
   drop DepName;   /*We have to read DepName */
                   /* because this is list input, */
                   /*but we do not need it to summarize*/
   length Type $ 1 ID $ 6 DepName $ 20 Relation $ 1;
   retain ID;
   infile 'raw-data-file' dlm=':';
   input Type $ @;
   if Type='E' then
      input ID $;
   else input DepName $ Relation $;
run;

proc print data=hierstep1;
   title 'First Step in Summarizing a Hierarchical File';
run;
```

```
              First Step in Summarizing a Hierarchical File

              Obs    Type      ID        Relation

                1      E      E01442
                2      D      E01442         C
                3      D      E01442         C
                4      E      E00705
                5      D      E00705         S
                6      E      E01577
                7      D      E01577         C
                8      E      E00997
                9      E      E00955
               10      D      E00955         C
               11      E      E00224
               12      D      E00224         S
```

Step 2: The resulting data set is grouped by ID, though the IDs might not be in order. You can use
the techniques described in Chapter 3 and the NOTSORTED option in the BY statement
to summarize this data set by **ID**.

```
data Hierstep2;
   drop Type Relation;
   set Hierstep1;
   by ID notsorted;
     /*The NOTSORTED option indicates that the */
     /*data is grouped by the BY variable but that */
     /*the values are not necessarily*/
     /*in sort order. This creates First. and Last. */
   if First.ID then Deduct=0;
   if Relation='C' then Deduct+25;
   else if Relation='S' then Deduct+50;
     /*Must make sure Relation='S' and not missing */
   if Last.ID;
run;
```

```
                  Deductions for All Employees

              Obs      ID      Deduct

               1     E01442       50
               2     E00705       50
               3     E01577       25
               4     E00997        0
               5     E00955       25
               6     E00224       50
```

 **Exercises**

11. **Reading a Hierarchical Raw Data File and Creating One Observation per Detail Record**

    The raw data file **SALARIES** is hierarchical. The header record has the employee's identification number, first name, last name, and the date he or she was hired. The detail records have the employee's salary for each year that he or she was employed by the company.

    Header Records

Order	Field	Notes
1	Record Type	E = Header record, S = Detail record
2	Employee ID Number	6-character code
3	First Name	Longest value is 8 characters
4	Last Name	Longest value is 8 characters
5	Hire Date	Written in DATE9.

    Detail Records

Order	Field	Notes
1	Record Type	E = Header record, S = Detail record
2	Salary Year	4-digit year
3	Salary	5 digits plus embedded comma, e.g. 55,555

    Sample Records

    ```
    E E1232 JOHN SMITH 15OCT1999
    S 1999 51,684
    S 2000 56,180
    S 2001 61,065
    E E2341 ALICE JONES 01JUN1997
    S 1997 65,684
    S 1998 71,396
    S 1999 77,604
    S 2000 84,353
    S 2001 91,688
    ```

    Create the SAS data set **work.salaries** that contains the variables **ID**, **FName**, **LName**, **SalYear**, and **Salary**. There should be one observation for each year that the employee worked.

Partial Listing of **work.salaries**

```
                      Yearly Salaries Through 2001

                                        Sal
        Obs     ID      LName   FName    Year    Salary

          1    E1232    SMITH   JOHN     1999    51684
          2    E1232    SMITH   JOHN     2000    56180
          3    E1232    SMITH   JOHN     2001    61065
          4    E2341    JONES   ALICE    1997    65684
          5    E2341    JONES   ALICE    1998    71396
          6    E2341    JONES   ALICE    1999    77604
          7    E2341    JONES   ALICE    2000    84353
          8    E2341    JONES   ALICE    2001    91688
```

12. Reading a Hierarchical Raw Data File and Creating One Observation per Header Record (Optional)

Using the same raw data file as in Exercise **11**, create a SAS data set named **work.current** with the variables **ID**, **LName**, **FName**, **HireDate**, and **Salary**. There should be one observation for each employee, and the value of **Salary** should be equal to the most recent year's salary.

Listing of **work.current**

```
                        Salaries as of 2001

                                   Hire
        Obs     ID      LName      FName      Date    Salary

          1    E1232    SMITH      JOHN       14532   61065
          2    E2341    JONES      ALICE      13666   91688
          3    E3452    MOORE      LES        12352   32639
          4    E6781    LEE        JENNIFER   11947   28305
          5    E8321    LONG       GAYLE      13479   40440
          6    E1052    GREEN      THOMAS     13572   39461
          7    E1062    FOREMAN    NEIL        9991   41463
          8    E8172    THOMPSON   RANDY      14615   40650
          9    E1091    MCKINSEY   STARR      11554   40950
         10    E9992    DALTON     RICHARD    11141   40455
```

13. Reading a Hierarchical File Using Two DATA Steps (Optional)

Using the same raw data file as in Exercise **12**, create a SAS data set named **work.twostep** and use the two-step process described in the self-study section. You should get the same output as in the previous exercise.

14. Reading a Hierarchical File without an Explicit Identifying Field (Optional)

The raw data file **BSTONES** contains a header record identifying the month, plus five or more detail records that identify different birthstones associated with that month.

Header Record

Field	Notes
Month	Longest value is 9 bytes.

Detail 1

Field	Notes
Modern Birthstone	Longest value is 12 bytes.

Detail 2

Field	Notes
Traditional Birthstone	Longest value is 12 bytes.

Detail 3

Field	Notes
Mystical Birthstone	Longest value is 11 bytes.

Detail 4

Field	Notes
Ayurvedic Birthstone	Longest value is 10 bytes.

Detail 5 - 7

Field	Notes
Other Birthstone	Longest value is 15 bytes.

Sample Records

```
January
  Garnet
  Garnet
  Emerald
  Garnet
  Rose Quartz
February
  Amethyst
  Amethyst
  Bloodstone
  Amethyst
  Onyx
  Moonstone
March
  Aquamarine
  Bloodstone
  Jade
  Bloodstone
  Rock Crystal
```

✎   Not all records have more than one "Other" birthstone. For example, January has only one birthstone classified as "Other"; February has two, and October has three.

✎   Ayurvedic birthstones are the birthstones proscribed by traditional Indian medical techniques.

Use the raw data file to create **work.birthstones**, which has one observation for each month, and one variable for each type of birthstone.

Listing of **work.birthstones**

```
                     Various Birthstones for Each Month

Obs    Month         Modern         Traditional    Mystical      Ayurvedic

  1    January       Garnet         Garnet         Emerald       Garnet
  2    February      Amethyst       Amethyst       Bloodstone    Amethyst
  3    March         Aquamarine     Bloodstone     Jade          Bloodstone
  4    April         Diamond        Diamond        Opal          Diamond
  5    May           Emerald        Emerald        Sapphire      Agate
  6    June          Pearl          Alexandrite    Moonstone     Pearl
  7    July          Ruby           Ruby           Ruby          Ruby
  8    August        Peridot        Sardonyx       Diamond       Sapphire
  9    September     Sapphire       Sapphire       Agate         Moonstone
 10    October       Opal           Tourmaline     Jasper        Opal
 11    November      Yellow Topaz   Citrine        Pearl         Topaz
 12    December      Blue Topaz     Zircon         Onyx          Ruby


Obs    Other1             Other2             Other3

  1    Rose Quartz
  2    Onyx               Moonstone
  3    Rock Crystal
  4    Quartz             White Sapphire
  5    Chrysoprase        Beryl
  6    Opal               Moonstone
  7    Carnelian
  8    Jade
  9    Lapis Lazuli       Diamond            Chrsolite
 10    Pink Tourmaline    Zircon             Aquamarine
 11    Diamond
 12    Turquoise          Lapis Lazuli
```

4.4   Solutions to Exercises

1.   Reading Nonstandard Data

```
   /* z/OS: fileref='.prog2.rawdata(states)';   */
proc fslist fileref='states.dat';
run;

data states;
   /* z/OS: infile '.prog2.rawdata(states)' dlm='!'; */
   infile 'states.dat' dlm='!';
   length State $ 14;
   input State $
         Population : comma10.
         Size
         EnterDate : date9.;
run;

title1 'State Names and Facts';
proc print data=states;
   format EnterDate date9.;
run;
```

2.   Using INFILE Statement Options to Change Defaults

```
   /* z/OS: fileref='.prog2.rawdata(aromas)'; */
proc fslist fileref='aromas.dat';
run;

data aromas;
   length Condition Cure1 Cure2 Cure3 $ 11;
   /* z/OS: infile '.prog2.rawdata(aromas)'
            dsd dlm=' '; */
   infile 'aromas.dat' dsd dlm=' ' missover;
   input Condition $ Cure1 $ Cure2 $ Cure3 $;
run;

title1 'Aromatherapy Data Set';
proc print data=aromas;
run;
```

3. Reading a Fixed-Column Raw Data File with Variable Length Records (Optional)

The problem with this raw data file is that not all the records are the same length. You can verify this by looking at its properties or opening it in a text editor. Either the TRUNCOVER or the PAD option would be equally effective in this case.

```
   /* z/OS: fileref='.prog2.rawdata(aromasf)'; */
proc fslist fileref='aromasf.dat';
run;


   /* The PAD option handles the problem by adding spaces to shorter
records. */

data aromasf;
   /* z/OS: infile '.prog2.rawdata(aromasf)'; */
   infile 'aromasf.dat' pad;
   input @ 1 Condition $10.
         @11 Cure1 $11.
         @22 Cure2 $11.
         @33 Cure3 $11.;
run;

title1 'Results from PAD Option';
proc print data=aromasf;
run;


   /* The TRUNCOVER option tells SAS not to read from the
      next line when it runs out of data, but to assign
      whatever it has read to the variable. */

data aromasf;
   /* z/OS: infile '.prog2.rawdata(aromasf)' truncover; */
   infile 'aromasf.dat' truncover;
   input @ 1 Condition $10.
         @11 Cure1 $11.
         @22 Cure2 $11.
         @33 Cure3 $11.;
run;

title1 'Results from TRUNCOVER Option';
proc print data=aromasf;
run;
```

4. Reading Multiple Records per Observation

```
   /* z/OS: fileref='.prog2.rawdata(bloodtyp)'; */
proc fslist fileref='bloodtyp.dat';
run;

data medical (drop=Plan) ;
   /* z/OS: infile '.prog2.rawdata(bloodtyp)'; */
   infile 'bloodtyp.dat';
   length  ID $ 5
           LName FName $ 11
           Plan $ 1
           Blood $ 3 ;
   input   ID
           LName
           FName /
           Plan
           Blood;
run;

title1 'Patient Names and Blood Types';
proc print data=medical;
run;
```

5. Reading Mixed Record Types

```
   /* z/OS: fileref='.prog2.rawdata(allergy)'; */
proc fslist fileref='allergy.dat';
run;

data allergies;
   length ID $ 5
           LName FName $ 11
           Plan $ 1            or    allagy: $1. @;
           Blood $ 3                 If
           Allergy $ 1           If - - Algytpe: $2;
           AlgyType $ 2;
   /* z/OS: infile '.prog2.rawdata(allergy)'; */
   infile 'allergy.dat';
   input ID LName FName Plan Blood Allergy @;
   if Allergy = 'N' then
      input Dependents;
   else if Allergy = 'Y' then
      input AlgyType Dependents;
run;

title1 'Patients and Allergy Code';
proc print data=allergies;
run;
```

6. **Subsetting from a Raw Data File (Optional)**

```
data allergies2;
   length ID $ 5
          LName FName $ 11
          Plan $ 1
          Blood $ 3
          Allergy $ 1
          AlgyType $ 2;
 /* z/OS: infile '.prog2.rawdata(allergy)'; */
   infile 'allergy.dat';
   input ID
         LName
         FName
         Plan
         Blood
         Allergy @;
   if Allergy = 'Y';
   input AlgyType
         Dependents;
run;

title1 'Patients with Allergies Only';
proc print data=allergies2;
run;
```

7. **Reading Raw Data with Multiple Observations per Record**

```
 /* z/OS: fileref='.prog2.rawdata(transact)'; */
proc fslist fileref='transact.dat';
run;

data transactions;
   length Type $ 1;
 /* z/OS: infile '.prog2.rawdata(transact)'; */
   infile 'transact.dat';
   input Date: date9.
         Type
         Amount : comma9. @@;
run;

title1 'Transactions on Account';
proc print data=transactions;
   var date type amount;
run;
```

8. Creating Multiple SAS Data Sets from a Single Raw Data File (Optional)

```
   /* z/OS: fileref='.prog2.rawdata(transact)'; */
proc fslist fileref='transact.dat';
run;

data credits debits;
   length Type $ 1;
  /* z/OS: infile '.prog2.rawdata(transact)'; */
   infile 'transact.dat';
   input Date : date9.
         Type
         Amount : comma9. @@;
   if Type = 'C' then output credits;
   else if Type = 'D' then output debits;
run;

title1 'Credits to Account';
proc print data=credits;
   var date type amount;
run;

title1 'Debits to Account';
proc print data=debits;
   var date type amount;
run;
```

9. Subsetting from a Fixed-Column Raw Data File (Optional)

```
   /* z/OS: fileref='.prog2.rawdata(empfix)'; */
proc fslist fileref='empfix.dat';
run;

data salclrks;
  /* z/OS: infile '.prog2.rawdata(empfix)'; */
   infile 'empfix.dat';
   input @112 JobCode $6. @;
   if jobcode = 'SALCLK';
   input @ 1 Division $20.
         @21 HireDate mmddyy10.
         @31 Salary dollar10.2
         @41 LastName $15.
         @56 FirstName $15.
         @71 Country $15.
         @86 Location $10.
         @96 IdNumber $6.;
run;

title1 'Employee Information for Sales Clerks';
proc print data=salclrks noobs;
run;
```

10. Using the Absolute Line Pointer Control (Optional)

```
  /* z/OS: fileref='.prog2.rawdata(emptwo)'; */
proc fslist fileref='emptwo.dat';
run;

data empinfo;
  /* z/OS: infile '.prog2.rawdata(emptwo)' dlm=','; */
   infile 'emptwo.dat' dlm=',';
   input #2 IdNumber : $6.
            LastName : $15.
            FirstName : $15.
         #1 Division :$20.
            HireDate : mmddyy10.
             Salary;
run;

title1 'Employee Data';
proc print data=empinfo;
   format HireDate mmddyy10.;
run;
```

11. Reading a Hierarchical Raw Data File and Creating One Observation per Detail Record

```
  /* z/OS: fileref='.prog2.rawdata(salaries)'; */
proc fslist fileref='salaries.dat';
run;

data salaries (drop=type);
   retain ID LName FName;
   length ID $ 6;
  /* z/OS: infile '.prog2.rawdata(salaries)'; */
   infile 'salaries.dat';
   input Type $ @;
   if Type = 'E' then
      input ID
            FName $
            LName $;
   else if Type = 'S' then do;
      input SalYear
            Salary : comma6.;
      output;
   end;
run;

title1 'Yearly Salaries Through 2001';
proc print data=salaries;
run;
```

12. **Reading a Hierarchical Raw Data File and Creating One Observation per Header Record (Optional)**

```
   /* z/OS: fileref='.prog2.rawdata(salaries)'; */
proc fslist fileref='salaries.dat';
run;

data current(drop=SalYear Type);
   /* Retain all the variables in the new data set. */
   retain ID LName FName HireDate Salary;
   length ID $ 6;
   /* z/OS: infile '.prog2.rawdata(salaries)' end=LastRec; */
   infile 'salaries.dat' end=LastRec;
   input Type $ @;
   if Type = 'E' then do;
   /* Output when next employee is read. */
   if _n_ ne 1 then output;
      input ID $
            FName $
            LName $
            HireDate : date9.;
   end;
   else if Type = 'S' then do;
      input SalYear
            Salary : comma8.;
   end;
   if LastRec then output;
run;

title1 'Salaries as of 2001';
proc print data=current;
   format HireDate date9.;
run;
```

13. **Reading a Hierarchical File Using Two DATA Steps (Optional)**

```
   /* z/OS: fileref='.prog2.rawdata(salaries)'; */
proc fslist fileref='salaries.dat';
run;

data stepone(drop=SalYear Type);
   retain ID LName FName HireDate;
   length ID $ 6;
   /* z/OS: infile '.prog2.rawdata(salaries)'; */
   infile 'salaries.dat';
   input Type $ @;
   if Type = 'E' then
      input ID $
            FName $
            LName $
            HireDate : date9.;
   else if Type = 'S' then
      input SalYear
```

```
         Salary : comma8.;
   format HireDate date9.;
run;


title1 'Reading a Hierarchical File -- First Phase';
proc print data=stepone;
run;


data twostep;
   set stepone;
   by ID notsorted;
   if Last.ID then
         output;
run;


title1 'Salaries as of 2001';
proc print data=twostep;
run;
```

14. Reading a Hierarchical File without an Explicit Identifying Field (Optional)

```
   /* z/OS: fileref='.prog2.rawdata(bstones)'; */
proc fslist fileref='bstones.dat';
run;
data birthstones;
   drop Space Stone;
   retain Month Modern Traditional Mystical
         Ayurvedic Other1-Other3;
   /* z/OS: infile '.prog2.rawdata(bstones)' end=LastMonth dlm=','; */
   infile 'bstones.dat' end=LastMonth dlm=',';
   /* You can also read the birthstones with formatted input if you use
the TRUNCOVER or PAD option. */
   length  Month $ 9
           Modern Traditional $ 12
           Mystical $ 11
           Ayurvedic $ 10
           Other1-Other3 $ 15;
   input @1 Space $1. @;
   /* The leading space must be read with formatted input, or the space
will be ignored.*/
   if Space ne ' ' then do;
      if _n_ ne 1 then
           output;
      input @1 Month $;
      Stone = 1;
      other2 = '';
      other3 = '';
   end;
   /* You need to know how many detail records have been read in order
to know which variable is being read. */
   else do;
      if Stone = 1 then input Modern $;
```

```
          else if Stone = 2 then input Traditional;
          else if Stone = 3 then input Mystical ;
          else if Stone = 4 then input Ayurvedic;
          else if Stone = 5 then input Other1;
          else if Stone = 6 then input Other2;
          else if Stone = 7 then input Other3;
       Stone + 1;
    end;
    if LastMonth then output;
run;




title1 'Various Birthstones for Each Month';
proc print data=birthstones;
run;
```

Chapter 5   Data Transformations

5.1 Introduction

Objectives

- Review the syntax of SAS functions.

3

SAS Functions

The SAS System provides a large library of functions for manipulating data during DATA step execution.

A SAS function is often categorized by the type of data manipulation performed:

- truncation
- character
- date and time
- mathematical
- trigonometric

- special
- sample statistics
- financial
- random number
- state and zip code

4

See SAS documentation for a complete list of functions and their syntax.

Syntax for SAS Functions

A *SAS function* is a routine that performs a computation or system manipulation and returns a value. Functions use *arguments* supplied by the user or by the operating environment.

General form of a SAS function:

function-name(argument-1,argument-2,...,argument-n)

5

Using SAS Functions

You can use functions in executable DATA step statements anywhere that an expression can appear.

```
data contrib;
   set prog2.donate;
   Total=sum(Qtr1,Qtr2,Qtr3,Qtr4);
   if Total ge 50;
run;

proc print data=contrib noobs;
run;
```

6

Using SAS Functions

Partial PROC PRINT Output

ID	Qtr1	Qtr2	Qtr3	Qtr4	Total
E00224	12	33	22	.	67
E00367	35	48	40	30	153
E00441	.	63	89	90	242
E00587	16	19	30	29	94
E00621	10	12	15	25	62

What if you want to sum Qtr1 through Qtr400, instead of Qtr1 through Qtr4?

7

SAS Variable Lists

A *SAS variable list* is an abbreviated method of referring to a list of variable names. SAS enables you to use the following variable lists:

- numbered range lists
- name range lists
- name prefix lists
- special SAS name lists

8

Numbered range lists	`x1-x`*n*	specifies all variables from **x1** to **x***n* inclusive. You can begin with any number and end with any number as long as you do not violate the rules for user-supplied variable names and the numbers are consecutive.
Name range lists	`x--a`	specifies all variables ordered as they are in the program data vector, from **x** to **a** inclusive.
	`x-numeric-a`	specifies all numeric variables from **x** to **a** inclusive.
	`x-character-a`	specifies all character variables from **x** to **a** inclusive.
Name prefix lists	`sum(of REV:)`	tells SAS to calculate the sum of all the variables that begin with **REV**, such as **REVJAN**, **REVFEB**, and **REVMAR**.
Special SAS name lists	`_ALL_`	specifies all variables that are already defined in the current DATA step.
	`_NUMERIC_`	specifies all numeric variables that are currently defined in the current DATA step.
	`_CHARACTER_`	specifies all character variables that are currently defined in the current DATA step.

if ... in: ('Je','Jo) then--;

SAS Variable Lists

When you use a SAS variable list in a SAS function, use the keyword OF in front of the first variable name in the list.

```
data contrib;
   set prog2.donate;
   Total=sum(of Qtr1-Qtr4);
   if Total ge 50;
run;
```

If you omit the keyword OF, subtraction is performed.

9

5.2 Manipulating Character Values

Objectives

- Use SAS functions and operators to extract, edit, and search character values.

11

A Mailing Label Application

The **prog2.freqflyers** data set contains information about frequent flyers. Use this data set to create another data set suitable for mailing labels.

12

A Mailing Label Application

ID is a character variable. Its last digit represents the gender (**1** denotes female, **2** denotes male) of the frequent flyer.

prog2.freqflyers

ID	Name	Address1	Address2
F31351	Farr,Sue	15 Harvey Rd.	Macon,Bibb,GA,31298
F161	Cox,Kay B.	163 McNeil Pl.	Kern,Pond,CA,93280
F212	Mason,Ron	442 Glen Ave.	Miami,Dade,FL,33054
F25122	Ruth,G. H.	2491 Brady St.	Munger,Bay,MI,48747

13

A Mailing Label Application

labels

FullName	Address1	Address2
Ms. Sue Farr	15 Harvey Rd.	Macon, GA 31298
Ms. Kay B. Cox	163 McNeil Pl.	Kern, CA 93280
Mr. Ron Mason	442 Glen Ave.	Miami, FL 33054
Mr. G. H. Ruth	2491 Brady St.	Munger, MI 48747

The first task is to create a title of Mr. or Ms. based on the last digit of **ID**.

14

The SUBSTR Function (Right Side)

The SUBSTR function is used to extract or replace characters.

> *NewVar*=SUBSTR(*string,start<,length>*);

This form of the SUBSTR function (right side of assignment statement) extracts characters.

15

string   can be a character constant, variable, or expression.

start   specifies the starting position.

length   specifies the number of characters to extract. If omitted, the substring consists of the remainder of *string*.

✎   If the length of the created variable is not previously defined with a LENGTH statement, it is the same as the length of the first argument to SUBSTR.

The SUBSTR Function (Right Side)

Extract two characters from **Location** and start
at position 11.

```
State=substr(Location,11,2);
```

Location $ 18	State $ 18
Columbus, OH 43227	OH

16

A Mailing Label Application

```
proc print data=prog2.freqflyers noobs;
    var ID;
run;
```

PROC PRINT Output

```
                ID

            F31351
            F161
            F212
            F25122
```

In what position does the last digit of **ID** occur?

17

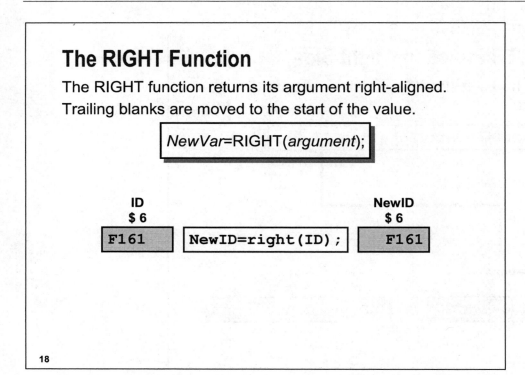

The RIGHT Function

The RIGHT function returns its argument right-aligned.
Trailing blanks are moved to the start of the value.

NewVar=RIGHT(*argument*);

ID			NewID
$ 6			$ 6
F161	NewID=right(ID);		F161

18

argument   can be a character constant, variable, or expression.

    If the length of the created variable is not previously defined with a LENGTH statement, it is the same as the length of *argument*.

The LEFT function returns its argument left-aligned. Leading blanks are moved to the end of the value. The argument's length does not change.

NewVar=LEFT(*argument*);

A Mailing Label Application

```
data labels;
   set prog2.freqflyers;
   if substr(right(ID),6)='1' then
       Title='Ms.';
   else if substr(right(ID),6)='2'
       then Title='Mr.';
run;

proc print data=labels noobs;
   var ID Title;
run;
```

The result of the RIGHT function acts as the first argument to the SUBSTR function.

19

A Mailing Label Application

PROC PRINT Output

ID	Title
F31351	Ms.
F161	Ms.
F212	Mr.
F25122	Mr.

20

A Mailing Label Application

The next task is to separate the names of the frequent flyers into two parts.

Name

Farr,Sue
Cox,Kay B.

FMName

Sue
Kay B.

LName

Farr
Cox

21

The SCAN Function

The SCAN function returns the *n*th word of a character value.

It is used to extract words from a character value when the relative order of words is known, but their starting positions are not.

> *NewVar*=SCAN(*string*,*n*<,*delimiters*>);

22

string   can be a character constant, variable, or expression.

n   specifies the *n*th word to extract from *string*.

delimiters   defines characters that delimit (separate) words.

✎   If the third argument is omitted, the default delimiters are

ASCII (PC, UNIX)	blank . < (+ | & ! $ *) ; - / , % ^
EBCDIC (z/OS)	blank . < (+ | & ! $ *) ; - / , % | ¢ ¬

The SCAN Function

When the SCAN function is used,

- the length of the created variable is 200 bytes if it is not previously defined with a LENGTH statement
- delimiters before the first word have no effect
- any character or set of characters can serve as delimiters
- two or more contiguous delimiters are treated as a single delimiter
- a missing value is returned if there are fewer than *n* words in *string*
- if *n* is negative, SCAN selects the word in the character string starting from the end of *string*.

23

The SCAN Function

Extract the second word of **Phrase**.

```
Second=scan(Phrase,2,' ');
```

Phrase
$ 21

software and services

Second
$ 200

and

1   2   3

The SCAN Function

Extract the second word of **Phrase**.

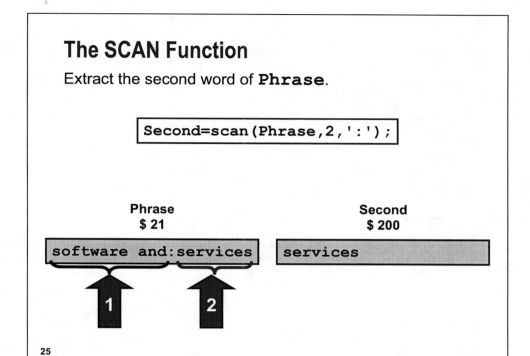

```
Second=scan(Phrase,2,':');
```

Phrase $ 21	Second $ 200
software and:services	services

1

2

25

The SCAN Function

```
data scan;
   Text='(Thursday July 4, 1776)';
   Var1=scan(Text,1);
   Var2=scan(Text,4);
   Var3=scan(Text,5);
   Var4=scan(Text,2,',');
   Var5=scan(Text,2,',)');
run;
```

26

The SCAN Function

```
data scan;
   Text='(Thursday July 4, 1776)';
   Var1=scan(Text,1);
   Var2=scan(Text,4);
   Var3=scan(Text,5);
   Var4=scan(Text,2,',');
   Var5=scan(Text,2,',)');
run;
```

Var1
$ 200

Thursday

27   ...

The SCAN Function

```
data scan;
   Text='(Thursday July 4, 1776)';
   Var1=scan(Text,1);
   Var2=scan(Text,4);
   Var3=scan(Text,5);
   Var4=scan(Text,2,',');
   Var5=scan(Text,2,',)');
run;
```

Var1   **Var2**
$ 200   **$ 200**

Thursday	1776

28   ...

The SCAN Function

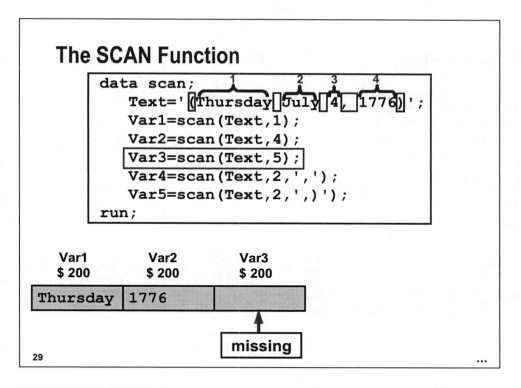

```
data scan;
   Text='(Thursday July 4, 1776)';
   Var1=scan(Text,1);
   Var2=scan(Text,4);
   Var3=scan(Text,5);
   Var4=scan(Text,2,',');
   Var5=scan(Text,2,',)');
run;
```

Var1 $ 200	Var2 $ 200	Var3 $ 200
Thursday	1776	

missing

29   ...

The SCAN Function

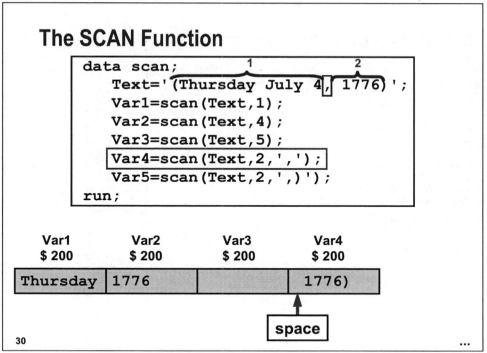

```
data scan;
   Text='(Thursday July 4, 1776)';
   Var1=scan(Text,1);
   Var2=scan(Text,4);
   Var3=scan(Text,5);
   Var4=scan(Text,2,',');
   Var5=scan(Text,2,',)');
run;
```

Var1 $ 200	Var2 $ 200	Var3 $ 200	Var4 $ 200
Thursday	1776		1776)

space

30   ...

The SCAN Function

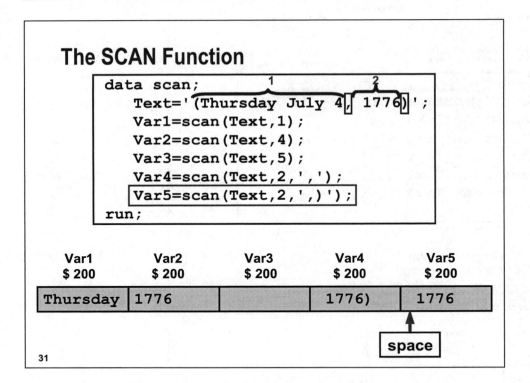

```
data scan;
   Text='(Thursday July 4, 1776)';
   Var1=scan(Text,1);
   Var2=scan(Text,4);
   Var3=scan(Text,5);
   Var4=scan(Text,2,',');
   Var5=scan(Text,2,',)');
run;
```

Var1 $ 200	Var2 $ 200	Var3 $ 200	Var4 $ 200	Var5 $ 200
Thursday	1776		1776)	1776

space

31

A Mailing Label Application

```
data labels;
   length FMName LName $ 10;
   set prog2.freqflyers;
   if substr(right(ID),6)='1' then
      Title='Ms.';
   else if substr(right(ID),6)='2' then
      Title='Mr.';
   FMName=scan(Name,2,',');
   LName=scan(Name,1,',');
run;
```

32

A Mailing Label Application

```
proc print data=labels noobs;
    var ID Name Title FMName LName;
run;
```

PROC PRINT Output

ID	Name	Title	FMName	LName
F31351	Farr,Sue	Ms.	Sue	Farr
F161	Cox,Kay B.	Ms.	Kay B.	Cox
F212	Mason,Ron	Mr.	Ron	Mason
F25122	Ruth,G. H.	Mr.	G. H.	Ruth

The next task is to join the values of **Title**, **FMName**, and **LName** into another variable.

33

Concatenation Operator

The *concatenation operator* joins character strings.

Depending on the characters available on your keyboard, the symbol to concatenate character values can be two exclamation points (!!), two vertical bars (||), or two broken vertical bars (¦¦).

```
NewVar=string1 !! string2;
```

34

Concatenation Operator

Combine **FMName** and **LName** to create **FullName**.

```
FullName=FMName !! LName;
```

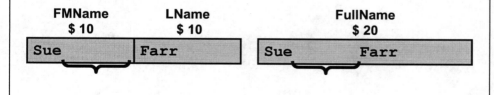

35

The TRIM Function

The TRIM function removes trailing blanks from its argument.

> *NewVar*=TRIM(*argument1*) !! *argument2*;

If the argument is blank, TRIM returns one blank.

36

argument1 and *argument2*   can be character constants, variables, or expressions.

 The TRIM and TRIMN functions are similar. TRIMN returns a null string (zero blanks) if the argument is blank.

The COMPBL function is also used to remove multiple blanks in a character string. COMPBL translates each occurrence of two or more consecutive blanks into a single blank. By default, the length of the value returned by the COMPBL function is the same as the length of the argument.

The TRIM Function

```
data trim;
   length FMName LName $ 10;
   FMName='Sue';
   LName='Farr';
   FullName1=trim(FMName);
   FullName2=trim(FMName) !! LName;
   FullName3=trim(FMName) !! ' ' !! LName;
run;
```

FullName1
  $ 10

Sue

37   ...

The TRIM Function

```
data trim;
   length FMName LName $ 10;
   FMName='Sue';
   LName='Farr';
   FullName1=trim(FMName);
   FullName2=trim(FMName) !! LName;
   FullName3=trim(FMName) !! ' ' !! LName;
run;
```

FullName1   **FullName2**
  $ 10   **$ 20**

Sue	SueFarr

38   ...

The TRIM Function

```
data trim;
   length FMName LName $ 10;
   FMName='Sue';
   LName='Farr';
   FullName1=trim(FMName);
   FullName2=trim(FMName) !! LName;
   FullName3=trim(FMName) !! ' ' !! LName;
run;
```

FullName1 $ 10	FullName2 $ 20	FullName3 $ 21
Sue	SueFarr	Sue Farr

39

The TRIM function does not remove leading blanks from a character argument. Use a combination of the TRIM and LEFT functions to remove leading and trailing blanks from a character argument.

For example, if **FMName** contained leading blanks, the following assignment statement would correctly concatenate **FMName** and **LName** into **FullName**:

```
FullName=trim(left(FMName)) !! ' ' !! LName;
```

A Mailing Label Application

```
data labels(keep=FullName Address1 Address2);
   length FMName LName $ 10;
   set prog2.freqflyers;
   if substr(right(ID),6)='1' then
      Title='Ms.';
   else if substr(right(ID),6)='2' then
      Title='Mr.';
   FMName=scan(Name,2,',');
   LName=scan(Name,1,',');
   FullName=Title !! ' ' !! trim(FMName) !!
            ' ' !! LName;
   Address2=scan(Address2,1,',') !! ', ' !!
            scan(Address2,3,',') !! ' ' !!
            scan(Address2,4,',');
run;
```

40

A Mailing Label Application

```
proc print data=labels noobs;
   var FullName Address1 Address2;
run;
```

PROC PRINT Output

FullName	Address1	Address2
Ms. Sue Farr	15 Harvey Rd.	Macon, GA 31298
Ms. Kay B. Cox	163 McNeil Pl.	Kern, CA 93280
Mr. Ron Mason	442 Glen Ave.	Miami, FL 33054
Mr. G. H. Ruth	2491 Brady St.	Munger, MI 48747

c05s2d1.sas

41

The CATX Function

The CATX function concatenates character strings, removes **leading** and **trailing** blanks, and **inserts separators**.

> **CATX**(*separator, string-1, … ,string-n*)

✎   CATX is a SAS®9 function.

42

Other SAS®9 concatenation functions are as follows:

CAT   concatenates character strings without removing leading or trailing blanks.

CATS   concatenates character strings and removes leading and trailing blanks.

CATT   concatenates character strings and removes trailing blanks only.

✎   Caution: The length returned by these functions is **up to**
  - 200 bytes in WHERE clauses and in PROC SQL
  - ~~32767~~ 200 bytes in a DATA step (except a WHERE statement)
  - 65534 bytes when the string is called from the macro processor.

A Mailing Label Application

```
data labels(keep=FullName Address1 Address2);
   length FMName LName $ 10;
   set prog2.freqflyers;
   if substr(right(ID),6)='1' then
      Title = 'Ms.';
   else if substr(right(ID),6)='2' then
      Title = 'Mr.';
   FMName = scan(Name,2,',');
   LName = scan(Name,1,',');
   FullName = catx(' ',Title,FMName,LName);
   Address2 = catx(' ',
            scan(Address2,1,',') !! ',',
            scan(Address2,3,','),
            scan(Address2,4,',')));
run;
```

43

A Mailing Label Application

```
proc print data=labels noobs;
   var FullName Address1 Address2;
run;
```

PROC PRINT Output

FullName	Address1	Address2
Ms. Sue Farr	15 Harvey Rd.	Macon, GA 31298
Ms. Kay B. Cox	163 McNeil Pl.	Kern, CA 93280
Mr. Ron Mason	442 Glen Ave.	Miami, FL 33054
Mr. G. H. Ruth	2491 Brady St.	Munger, MI 48747

c05s2d2.sas

44

 **Exercises**

1. Manipulating Character Values

All values of **Name** in **prog2.people** consist of a last name, first name, and middle initial.

Listing of **prog2.people**

```
          Name                      CityState

          DEAN, LINDSAY A.          WILMINGTON, NC
          FLORENTINO, HELEN-ASHE H. WASHINGTON, DC
          VAN ALLSBURG, JAN F.      SHORT HILLS, NJ
          LAFF, STANLEY X.          SPRINGFIELD, IL
          RIZEN, GEORGE Q.          CHICAGO, IL
          MITCHELL, MARC J.         CHICAGO, IL
          MILLS, DOROTHY E.         JOE, MT
          WEBB, JONATHAN W.         MORRISVILLE, NC
          KEENAN, MAYNARD J.        SEDONA, AZ
          LACK, PHYLLIS M.          WALTHAM, MA
          THOMPSON, KERRY L.        WINTER PARK, FL
          COX, DOROTHY E.           TIMONIUM, MD
          SEPTOFF, DONALD E.        BOSTON, MA
          PHOENIX, JANICE A.        SOMERVILLE, NJ
          HUNEYCUTT, MURRAY Y.      DIME BOX, TX
          ERICKSON, SHERRY A.       EL PASO, TX
          SCHNEIDER, CLIVE J.       CAPE MAY, NJ
          PUTNAM, KIMBERLY M.       DUNWOODY, GA
          PITTMAN, JENNIFER R.      BENNINGTON, VT
          ROLEN, STACY D.           CODY, WY
```

✎   Some names contain hyphenated first names or multiple-word last names.

Read the variables **Name** and **CityState** from **prog2.people** to create a temporary SAS data set named **separate** that contains the variables **First**, **MI**, and **Last**. Pay special attention to trailing and leading blanks, and the lengths of **First**, **MI**, and **Last**.

✎   To create **First** and **MI**, create a variable that contains each person's first name and middle initial. Do not include this variable in the **separate** data set.

Print the **separate** data set to verify your results.

Partial Listing of **separate**

```
Obs Name                        CityState        First       MI  Last

1   DEAN, LINDSAY A.            WILMINGTON, NC   LINDSAY     A.  DEAN
2   FLORENTINO, HELEN-ASHE H.   WASHINGTON, DC   HELEN-ASHE  H.  FLORENTINO
3   VAN ALLSBURG, JAN F.        SHORT HILLS, NJ  JAN         F.  VAN ALLSBURG
4   LAFF, STANLEY X.            SPRINGFIELD, IL  STANLEY     X.  LAFF
5   RIZEN, GEORGE Q.            CHICAGO, IL      GEORGE      Q.  RIZEN
```

2. Combining Character Values

Use the DATA step that creates **separate** to create a temporary SAS data set named **flname** that contains the variables **NewName** and **CityState**. The values of **NewName** should be the concatenation of each person's first name and last name with a single blank between them.

Partial Listing of **prog2.people**

```
    Name                        CityState

    DEAN, LINDSAY A.            WILMINGTON, NC
    FLORENTINO, HELEN-ASHE H.   WASHINGTON, DC
    VAN ALLSBURG, JAN F.        SHORT HILLS, NJ
    LAFF, STANLEY X.            SPRINGFIELD, IL
    RIZEN, GEORGE Q.            CHICAGO, IL
```

✏   Some names contain hyphenated first names or multiple-word last names.

Print the **flname** data set to verify your results.

Partial Listing of **flname**

```
    Obs    NewName                 CityState

     1     LINDSAY DEAN            WILMINGTON, NC
     2     HELEN-ASHE FLORENTINO   WASHINGTON, DC
     3     JAN VAN ALLSBURG        SHORT HILLS, NJ
     4     STANLEY LAFF            SPRINGFIELD, IL
     5     GEORGE RIZEN            CHICAGO, IL
```

3. Performing Additional Character Manipulations (Optional)

Use the DATA step that creates **separate** to create a temporary SAS data set named **init** that contains the variables **Name**, **Initials**, and **CityState**. The values of **Initials** should be the concatenation of the first character from each person's first name, middle name, and last name with no delimiters separating the characters.

Print the **init** data set to verify your results.

Partial Listing of **init**

```
    Obs    Name                        CityState         Initials

     1     DEAN, LINDSAY A.            WILMINGTON, NC     LAD
     2     FLORENTINO, HELEN-ASHE H.   WASHINGTON, DC     HHF
     3     VAN ALLSBURG, JAN F.        SHORT HILLS, NJ    JFV
     4     LAFF, STANLEY X.            SPRINGFIELD, IL    SXL
     5     RIZEN, GEORGE Q.            CHICAGO, IL        GQR
```

A Search Application

The **prog2.ffhistory** data set contains information about the history of each frequent flyer.

This history information consists of

- each membership level that the flyer attained (bronze, silver, or gold)
- the year that the flyer attained each level.

Create a report that shows all frequent flyers who attained silver membership status and the year each of them became silver members.

46

A Search Application

prog2.ffhistory

ID	Status	Seat Pref
F31351	Silver 1998,Gold 2000	AISLE
F161	Bronze 1999	WINDOW
F212	Bronze 1992,silver 1995	WINDOW
F25122	Bronze 1994,Gold 1996,Silver 1998	AISLE

To determine who attained silver membership status, you must search the **Status** variable for the value "Silver".

47

The FIND Function

The FIND function searches for a specific substring of characters within a character string that you specify and returns its location.

Position = FIND(*target,value<,modifiers,startpos>*);

The FIND function returns
- the starting position of the first occurrence of value within target, if value is found
- 0, if value is not found.

✎   FIND is a SAS®9 function.

48

A *modifier* can be the value I or T. I indicates that the search is case-insensitive. T indicates that the search ignores trailing blanks. These two values can be combined in either order and in either case. If this argument is omitted, the search is case-sensitive and trailing blanks are taken into consideration.

The *startpos* is an integer that specifies the position at which the search should start and the direction of the search. A positive value indicates a forward (right) search. A negative value indicates a backward (left) search. If this argument is omitted, the search starts at position 1 and moves forward.

These two optional arguments can be in either order (that is, *startpos* can precede *modifier*).

The FIND Function

Determine whether **Text** contains the string
"BULL'S-EYE".

```
Text="This target contains a BULL'S-EYE.";
Pos=find(Text,"BULL'S-EYE");
```

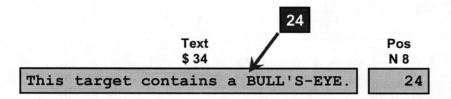

Text $ 34	Pos N 8
This target contains a BULL'S-EYE.	24

49

The FIND Function

```
data index;
    Text='DELIMIT IT WITH BLANKS.';
    Pos1=find(Text,'IT');
    Pos2=find(Text,' IT ');
    Pos3=find(Text,'it');
    Pos4=find(Text,'it','I');
run;
```

Pos1
N 8

6

50   ...

The FIND Function

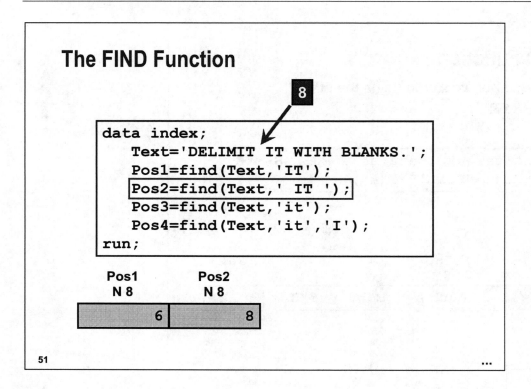

```
data index;
   Text='DELIMIT IT WITH BLANKS.';
   Pos1=find(Text,'IT');
   Pos2=find(Text,' IT ');
   Pos3=find(Text,'it');
   Pos4=find(Text,'it','I');
run;
```

Pos1 N 8	Pos2 N 8
6	8

51   ...

The FIND Function

```
data index;
   Text='DELIMIT IT WITH BLANKS.';
   Pos1=find(Text,'IT');
   Pos2=find(Text,' IT ');
   Pos3=find(Text,'it');
   Pos4=find(Text,'it','I');
run;
```

Pos1 N 8	Pos2 N 8	Pos3 N 8
6	8	0

52   ...

The FIND Function

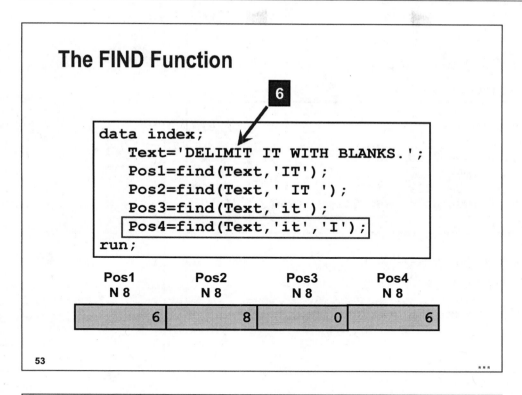

```
                              6
data index;
   Text='DELIMIT IT WITH BLANKS.';
   Pos1=find(Text,'IT');
   Pos2=find(Text,' IT ');
   Pos3=find(Text,'it');
   Pos4=find(Text,'it','I');
run;
```

Pos1 N 8	Pos2 N 8	Pos3 N 8	Pos4 N 8
6	8	0	6

53

The FIND Function

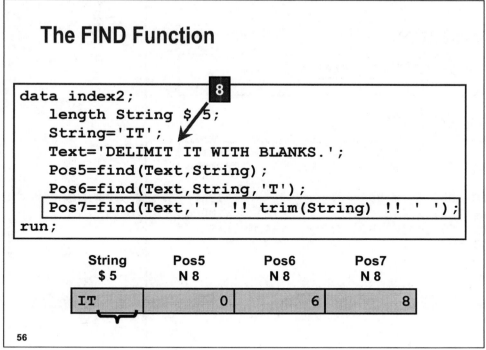

```
                      8
data index2;
   length String $ 5;
   String='IT';
   Text='DELIMIT IT WITH BLANKS.';
   Pos5=find(Text,String);
   Pos6=find(Text,String,'T');
   Pos7=find(Text,' ' !! trim(String) !! ' ');
run;
```

String $ 5	Pos5 N 8	Pos6 N 8	Pos7 N 8
IT	0	6	8

56

A Search Application

`prog2.ffhistory`

ID	Status	Seat Pref
F31351	Silver 1998,Gold 2000	AISLE
F161	Bronze 1999	WINDOW
F212	Bronze 1992,silver 1995	WINDOW
F25122	Bronze 1994,Gold 1996,Silver 1998	AISLE

```
data silver;
   set prog2.ffhistory;
   if find(Status,'silver','I') > 0;
run;
```

57

A Search Application

```
proc print data=silver noobs;
run;
```

PROC PRINT Output

ID	Status	Seat Pref
F31351	Silver 1998,Gold 2000	AISLE
F212	Bronze 1992,silver 1995	WINDOW
F25122	Bronze 1994,Gold 1996,Silver 1998	AISLE

58

The INDEX Function

The INDEX function searches a character argument for the location of a specified character value and returns its location.

> *Position*=INDEX(*target*,*value*);

The INDEX function returns
- the starting position of the first occurrence of *value* within *target*, if *value* is found
- 0, if *value* is not found.

59

target   specifies the character expression to search.

value   specifies the string of characters to search for in the character expression.

The search for *value* is literal. Capitalization and blanks (leading, embedded, and trailing) are considered.

INDEX differs from FIND in that it does not have *modifier* or *startpos* functionality.

The INDEX Function

Determine whether **Text** contains the string
"BULL'S-EYE".

```
Text="This target contains a BULL'S-EYE.";
Pos=index(Text,"BULL'S-EYE");
```

24

Text $ 34	Pos N 8
This target contains a BULL'S-EYE.	24

60

The INDEX Function

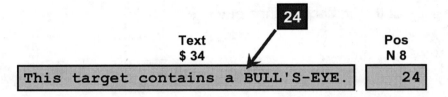

```
data index;
   Text='DELIMIT IT WITH BLANKS.';
   Pos1=index(Text,'IT');
   Pos2=index(Text,' IT ');
   Pos3=index(Text,'it');
run;
```

Pos1 N 8
6

61   ...

The INDEX Function

```
data index;
   Text='DELIMIT IT WITH BLANKS.';
   Pos1=index(Text,'IT');
   Pos2=index(Text,' IT ');
   Pos3=index(Text,'it');
run;
```

Pos1 N 8	Pos2 N 8
6	8

62   ...

The INDEX Function

```
data index;
   Text='DELIMIT IT WITH BLANKS.';
   Pos1=index(Text,'IT');
   Pos2=index(Text,' IT ');
   Pos3=index(Text,'it');
run;
```

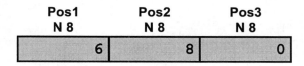

Pos1 N 8	Pos2 N 8	Pos3 N 8
6	8	0

63   ...

The INDEX Function

```
data index2;
   length String $ 5;
   String='IT';
   Text='DELIMIT IT WITH BLANKS.';
   Pos4=index(Text,String);
   Pos5=index(Text,trim(String));
   Pos6=index(Text,' ' !! trim(String) !! ' ');
run;
```

String
$ 5

64   ...

The INDEX Function

```
data index2;
   length String $ 5;
   String='IT';
   Text='DELIMIT IT WITH BLANKS.';
   Pos4=index(Text,String);
   Pos5=index(Text,trim(String));
   Pos6=index(Text,' ' !! trim(String) !! ' ');
run;
```

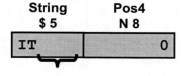

String   **Pos4**
$ 5   **N 8**

65   ...

The INDEX Function

```
data index2;              6
   length String $ 5;
   String='IT';
   Text='DELIMIT IT WITH BLANKS.';
   Pos4=index(Text,String);
   Pos5=index(Text,trim(String));
   Pos6=index(Text,' ' !! trim(String) !! ' ');
run;
```

String $ 5	Pos4 N 8	Pos5 N 8
IT	0	6

66

...

The INDEX Function

```
data index2;              8
   length String $ 5;
   String='IT';
   Text='DELIMIT IT WITH BLANKS.';
   Pos4=index(Text,String);
   Pos5=index(Text,trim(String));
   Pos6=index(Text,' ' !! trim(String) !! ' ');
run;
```

String $ 5	Pos4 N 8	Pos5 N 8	Pos6 N 8
IT	0	6	8

67

A Search Application

prog2.ffhistory

ID	Status	Seat Pref
F31351	Silver 1998,Gold 2000	AISLE
F161	Bronze 1999	WINDOW
F212	Bronze 1992,silver 1995	WINDOW
F25122	Bronze 1994,Gold 1996,Silver 1998	AISLE

```
data silver;
   set prog2.ffhistory;
   if index(Status,'Silver') > 0;
run;
```

68

A Search Application

```
proc print data=silver noobs;
run;
```

PROC PRINT Output

ID	Status	Seat Pref
F31351	Silver 1998,Gold 2000	AISLE
F25122	Bronze 1994,Gold 1996,Silver 1998	AISLE

Why was F212 not selected?

69

The UPCASE Function

The UPCASE function
- converts all letters in its argument to uppercase
- has no effect on digits and special characters.

NewVal=UPCASE(*argument*);

70

A Search Application

```
data silver(drop=Location);
   length Year $ 4;
   set prog2.ffhistory;
   Location=index(upcase(Status),'SILVER');
   if Location > 0;
   Year=substr(Status,Location+7,4);
run;

proc print data=silver noobs;
   var ID Status Year SeatPref;
run;
```

71

A Search Application

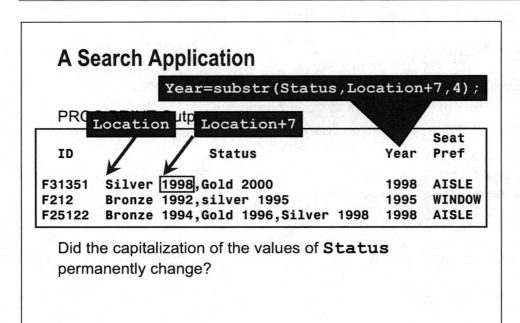

Did the capitalization of the values of **Status** permanently change?

72

The PROPCASE Function

The PROPCASE function converts all words in an argument to *proper* case, in which the first letter is uppercase and the remaining letters are lowercase.

> *NewVal*=PROPCASE(*argument <,delimiter(s)>*);

✎   PROPCASE is a SAS®9 function.

73

Delimiters are characters which separate words. The default delimiters for the PROPCASE function are the blank, forward slash, hyphen, open parenthesis, period, and tab characters.

A Search Application

```
data silver(drop=Location);
   length Year $ 4;
   set prog2.ffhistory;
   Status=propcase(Status,' ,');
   Location=find(Status,'Silver');
   if Location > 0;
   SeatPref=propcase(SeatPref);
   Year=substr(Status,Location+7,4);
run;

proc print data=silver noobs;
   var ID Status Year SeatPref;
run;
```

c05s2d3.sas

74

A Search Application

PROC PRINT Output

ID	Status	Year	Seat Pref
F31351	Silver 1998,Gold 2000	1998	Aisle
F212	Bronze 1992,Silver 1995	1995	Window
F25122	Bronze 1994,Gold 1996,Silver 1998	1998	Aisle

75

The TRANWRD Function

The TRANWRD function replaces or removes all occurrences of a given word (or a pattern of characters) within a character string.

NewVal=TRANWRD(*source,target,replacement*);

The TRANWRD function does not remove trailing blanks from *target* or *replacement*.

76

source	specifies the source string that you want to translate.
target	specifies the string searched for in *source*.
replacement	specifies the string that replaces *target*.

 If the length of the created variable is not previously defined with a LENGTH statement, it is 200 bytes.

The TRANWRD Function

Replace the first word of **Dessert**.

```
Dessert=tranwrd(Dessert,'Pumpkin','Apple');
```

Dessert $ 20	Dessert $ 20
Pumpkin pie	Apple pie

77

Using the TRANWRD function to replace an existing string with a longer string might cause truncation of the resulting value if a LENGTH statement is not used.

A Search Application

```
data silver(drop=Location);
   length Year $ 4;
   set prog2.ffhistory;
   Status=tranwrd(Status,'silver','Silver');
   Location=index(Status,'Silver');
   if Location > 0;
   Year=substr(Status,Location+7,4);
run;

proc print data=silver noobs;
   var ID Status Year SeatPref;
run;
```

c05s2d4.sas

78

A Search Application

PROC PRINT Output

```
                                          Seat
ID                  Status          Year  Pref

F31351  Silver 1998,Gold 2000       1998  AISLE
F212    Bronze 1992,Silver 1995     1995  WINDOW
F25122  Bronze 1994,Gold 1996,Silver 1998  1998  AISLE
```

79

The LOWCASE Function

The LOWCASE function
- converts all letters in its argument to lowercase
- has no effect on digits and special characters.

> *NewVal*=LOWCASE(*argument*);

80

argument   specifies any character argument.

The SUBSTR Function (Left Side)

The SUBSTR function is used to extract or replace characters.

SUBSTR(*string*,*start*<,*length*>)=*value*;

This form of the SUBSTR function (left side of assignment statement) replaces characters in a character variable.

81

string   specifies a character variable.

start   specifies a numeric expression that is the beginning character position.

length   specifies a numeric expression that is the length of the substring that will be replaced.

✎   The *length* value cannot be larger than the remaining length of *string* (including trailing blanks) after *start*.

If you omit *length*, SAS uses all of the characters on the right side of the assignment statement to replace the values of *string*, up to the limit indicated by the previous note.

The SUBSTR Function (Left Side)

Replace two characters from **Location** starting at position 11.

```
substr(Location,11,2)='OH';
```

Location
$ 18

`Columbus, GA 43227`

Location
$ 18

`Columbus, OH 43227`

82

The LOWCASE Function

```
data silver;
   set silver;
   substr(SeatPref,2)=
      lowcase(substr(SeatPref,2));
run;
```

SeatPref
$ 6

`AISLE`

c05s2d5.sas
...

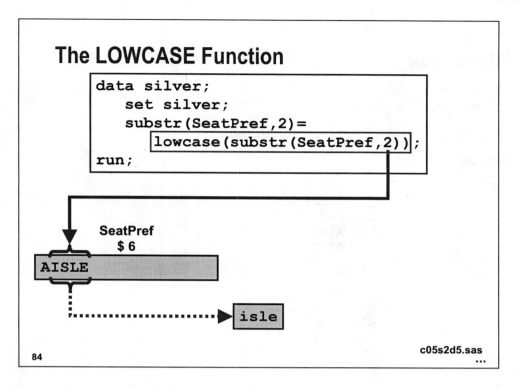

The LOWCASE Function

```
data silver;
   set silver;
   substr(SeatPref,2)=
       lowcase(substr(SeatPref,2));
run;
```

SeatPref
$ 6

AISLE

isle

c05s2d5.sas

84   ...

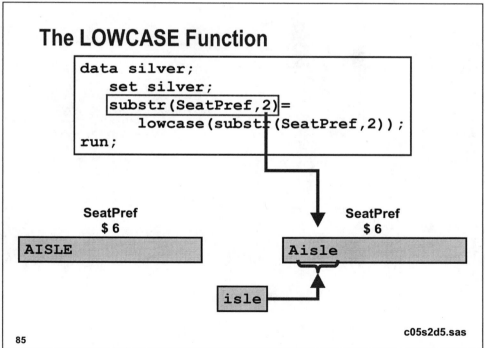

The LOWCASE Function

```
data silver;
   set silver;
   substr(SeatPref,2)=
       lowcase(substr(SeatPref,2));
run;
```

SeatPref
$ 6

AISLE

SeatPref
$ 6

Aisle

isle

c05s2d5.sas

85

A Search Application

```
proc print data=silver noobs;
   var ID Year SeatPref;
run;
```

PROC PRINT Output

```
                             Seat
            ID      Year     Pref

            F31351  1998     Aisle
            F212    1995     Window
            F25122  1998     Aisle
```

 **Exercises**

4. Searching for a Character Value

Read the variables **Name** and **CityState** from **prog2.people** to create a temporary SAS data set named **prairie** that contains only those people who live in the state of Illinois (IL). Use an appropriate function to search through the values of **CityState**.

Partial Listing of **prog2.people**

```
Name                          CityState

DEAN, LINDSAY A.              WILMINGTON, NC
FLORENTINO, HELEN-ASHE H.     WASHINGTON, DC
VAN ALLSBURG, JAN F.          SHORT HILLS, NJ
LAFF, STANLEY X.              SPRINGFIELD, IL
RIZEN, GEORGE Q.              CHICAGO, IL
```

Print the **prairie** data set to verify your results. There should be three observations.

Listing of **prairie**

```
Obs        Name              CityState

 1     LAFF, STANLEY X.      SPRINGFIELD, IL
 2     RIZEN, GEORGE Q.      CHICAGO, IL
 3     MITCHELL, MARC J.     CHICAGO, IL
```

 Illinois is unofficially known as the Prairie State. This nickname originates from the practice of declaring the third full week in September each year as Illinois Prairie Week to demonstrate the value of preserving and re-establishing native Illinois prairies.

5. Performing Additional Character Manipulations

Read the variables **Name** and **CityState** from **prairie** to create a temporary SAS data set named **mixedprairie** that contains the values of **Name** converted from all uppercase to mixed case as shown below.

Print the **mixedprairie** data set to verify your results.

Listing of **mixedprairie**

```
Obs        Name              CityState

 1     Laff, Stanley X.      SPRINGFIELD, IL
 2     Rizen, George Q.      CHICAGO, IL
 3     Mitchell, Marc J.     CHICAGO, IL
```

6. Using Additional Character Functions

Read the variables **Name** and **CityState** from **prog2.people** to create a temporary
SAS data set named **statelong**. Use the STNAMEL function to convert the state postal code
in **CityState** to the corresponding state name. Store these state names in a variable named
StateName.

The STNAMEL function converts a two-character state postal code (or world-wide GSA geographic
code for U.S. territories), such as IL for Illinois, to the corresponding state name in mixed case.
Returned values can contain up to 20 characters.

> NewState=STNAMEL(*postal-code*);

postal-code   specifies a character expression that contains the two-character standard state postal
code. Characters can be mixed case.

✎   STNAMEL ignores trailing blanks but generates an error if the expression contains leading
blanks.

Partial Listing of **statelong**

Obs	Name	StateName
1	DEAN, LINDSAY A.	North Carolina
2	FLORENTINO, HELEN-ASHE H.	District of Columbia
3	VAN ALLSBURG, JAN F.	New Jersey
4	LAFF, STANLEY X.	Illinois
5	RIZEN, GEORGE Q.	Illinois

7. Performing Additional Character Manipulations (Optional)

Read the variables **Name** and **CityState** from **prog2.people** to create a temporary SAS data
set named **mixedall** that contains the values of **Name** converted from all uppercase to mixed case
as shown below.

Print the **mixedall** data set to verify your results.

Partial Listing of **mixedall**

Obs	Name	CityState
1	Dean, Lindsay A.	WILMINGTON, NC
2	Florentino, Helen-Ashe H.	WASHINGTON, DC
3	Van Allsburg, Jan F.	SHORT HILLS, NJ
4	Laff, Stanley X.	SPRINGFIELD, IL
5	Rizen, George Q.	CHICAGO, IL

✎   Some names contain hyphenated first names or multiple-word last names.

5.3   Manipulating Numeric Values

Objectives

- Use SAS functions to truncate numeric values.
- Use SAS functions to compute sample statistics of numeric values.

89

Truncation Functions

Selected functions that truncate numeric values include

- ROUND function
- CEIL function
- FLOOR function
- INT function.

90

The ROUND Function

The ROUND function returns a value rounded to the nearest round-off unit.

> *NewVar*=ROUND(*argument*<,*round-off-unit*>);

If *round-off-unit* is not provided, *argument* is rounded to the nearest integer.

91

argument   is numeric.

round-off-unit   is numeric and positive.

The ROUND Function

```
data truncate;
   NewVar1=round(12.12);
   NewVar2=round(42.65,.1);
   NewVar3=round(6.478,.01);
   NewVar4=round(96.47,10);
run;
```

NewVar1	NewVar2	NewVar3	NewVar4
12	42.7	6.48	100

95

The CEIL Function

The CEIL function returns the smallest integer greater than or equal to the argument.

NewVar=CEIL(*argument*);

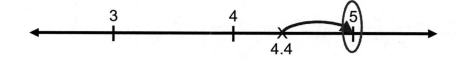

x=ceil(4.4);

96

argument   is numeric.

The FLOOR Function

The FLOOR function returns the greatest integer less than or equal to the argument.

NewVar=FLOOR(*argument*);

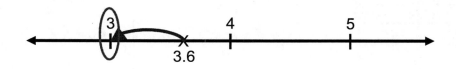

y=floor(3.6);

97

argument   is numeric.

The INT Function

The INT function returns the integer portion of the argument.

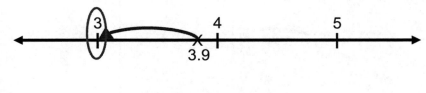

$$NewVar=\text{INT}(argument);$$

```
z=int(3.9);
```

98

argument   is numeric.

Truncation Functions

```
data truncate;
   Var1=6.478;
   NewVar1=ceil(Var1);
   NewVar2=floor(Var1);
   NewVar3=int(Var1);
run;
```

Var1	NewVar1	NewVar2	NewVar3
6.478	7	6	6

101

Truncation Functions

Use the same functions with a negative value for the variable Var1.

```
data truncate;
   Var1=-6.478;
   NewVar1=ceil(Var1);
   NewVar2=floor(Var1);
   NewVar3=int(Var1);
run;
```

Var1	NewVar1	NewVar2	NewVar3
-6.478	-6	-7	-6

104

For values greater than 0, FLOOR and INT return the same value. For values less than 0, CEIL and INT return the same value.

Functions That Compute Statistics

Selected functions that compute sample statistics based on a group of values:

- SUM function (total of values)
- MEAN function (average of values)
- MIN function (lowest value)
- MAX function (highest value)

105

These functions

- accept multiple arguments in any order
- use the same algorithm as SAS statistical procedures
- ignore missing values.

The MIN function returns the smallest non-missing value:

> **MIN**(*argument-1*,*argument-2*,…,*argument-n*)

The MAX function returns the largest value:

> **MAX**(*argument-1*,*argument-2*,…,*argument-n*)

argument-1 through *argument-n*   are numeric. At least two arguments are required. The argument list might consist of a variable list, which is preceded by OF.

The SUM Function

The SUM function adds values together and ignores missing values.

NewVar=SUM(*argument-1,argument-2,...,argument-n*);

106

argument-1 through *argument-n*   are numeric.

The SUM Function

```
data summary;
   Var1=12;
   Var2=.;
   Var3=6;
   NewVar=sum(Var1,Var2,Var3);
run;
```

Var1	Var2	Var3	NewVar
12	.	6	18

107   ...

The SUM Function

```
data summary;
   Var1=12;
   Var2=.;
   Var3=6;
   NewVar=sum(Var1,Var2,Var3);
run;
```

Var1	Var2	Var3	NewVar
12	.	6	18

What would be the value of **NewVar** if an arithmetic operator was used instead of the SUM function?

108

The assignment statement can be rewritten to take advantage of SAS variable lists:

```
NewVar=sum(of Var1-Var3);
```

The SUM Function

```
data summary;
   Var1=12;
   Var2=.;
   Var3=6;
   NewVar=Var1+Var2+Var3;
run;
```

Var1	Var2	Var3	NewVar
12	.	6	.

109

The MEAN Function

The MEAN function calculates the arithmetic mean (average) of values and ignores missing values.

> *NewVar*=MEAN(*argument-1*,*argument-2*,...,*argument-n*);

110

argument-1 through *argument-n*   are numeric.

The MEAN Function

```
data summary;
    Var1=12;
    Var2=.;
    Var3=6;
    NewVar=mean(Var1,Var2,Var3);
run;
```

Var1	Var2	Var3	NewVar
12	.	6	9

111

The assignment statement can be rewritten to take advantage of SAS variable lists:

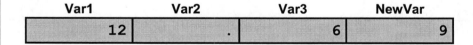

```
NewVar=mean(of Var1-Var3);
```

 **Exercises**

8. Manipulating Numeric Values

Create a data set named **final** from **prog2.grade**. The **final** data set should contain a new variable **Overall** that is the semester average grade. Calculate **Overall** by averaging all the tests plus the final. The final is weighted twice as much as any of the other tests, so count the final twice when calculating **Overall**. Store **Overall** rounded to the nearest integer. Print the **final** data set.

Partial Listing of **prog2.grade**

SSN	Course	Test1	Test2	Test3	Final
012-40-4928	BUS450	80	70	80	80
012-83-3816	BUS450	90	90	60	80
341-44-0781	MATH400	78	87	90	91
423-01-7721	BUS450	80	70	75	95
448-23-8111	MATH400	88	91	100	95

Partial Listing of **final**

Obs	SSN	Course	Test1	Test2	Test3	Final	Overall
1	012-40-4928	BUS450	80	70	80	80	78
2	012-83-3816	BUS450	90	90	60	80	80
3	341-44-0781	MATH400	78	87	90	91	87
4	423-01-7721	BUS450	80	70	75	95	83
5	448-23-8111	MATH400	88	91	100	95	94

9. Performing Additional Numeric Manipulations (Optional)

Modify the DATA step created in the previous exercise so that the value of **Overall** is the average of the two highest test scores and the final. (The lowest test score should not be used to calculate **Overall**.) As before, the final should be counted twice. Store **Overall** rounded to the nearest integer. Print the **final** data set.

Partial Listing of **final**

Obs	SSN	Course	Test1	Test2	Test3	Final	Overall
1	012-40-4928	BUS450	80	70	80	80	80
2	012-83-3816	BUS450	90	90	60	80	85
3	341-44-0781	MATH400	78	87	90	91	90
4	423-01-7721	BUS450	80	70	75	95	86
5	448-23-8111	MATH400	88	91	100	95	95

5.4 Manipulating Numeric Values Based on Dates

Objectives

- Review SAS functions used to create SAS date values.
- Review SAS functions to extract information from SAS date values.
- Use SAS functions to determine intervals between two SAS date values.

114

Creating SAS Date Values

You can use the MDY or TODAY functions to create SAS date values.

The MDY function creates a SAS date value from month, day, and year values.

> *NewDate*=MDY(*month,day,year*);

The TODAY function returns the current date as a SAS date value.

> *NewDate*=TODAY();

115

month   specifies a numeric expression representing an integer from 1 to 12.

day   specifies a numeric expression representing an integer from 1 to 31.

year   specifies a numeric expression representing an integer that identifies a specific two- or four-digit year.

✎   The DATE function is synonymous with the TODAY function.

Extracting Information

You can use the MONTH, DAY, and YEAR functions to extract information from SAS date values.

The MONTH function creates a numeric value (1-12) that represents the month of a SAS date value.

NewMonth=MONTH(*SAS-date-value*);

116   *continued...*

Extracting Information

The DAY function creates a numeric value (1-31) that represents the day of a SAS date value.

NewDay=DAY(*SAS-date-value*);

The YEAR function creates a four-digit numeric value that represents the year.

NewYear=YEAR(*SAS-date-value*);

117

Other similar functions include the following:

QTR	returns the quarter of the SAS date value (1-4; 1 represents January through March, 2 represents April through June, and so on).
WEEKDAY	returns the day of the week of a SAS date value (1-7; 1 represents Sunday, 7 represents Saturday).

 **Exercises**

10. Manipulating Numeric Values Based on Dates

The **prog2.noday** data set contains information about employees. Use **prog2.noday** to create a new data set named **emphire**.

Use the existing **HiredMonth** and **HiredYear** variables to create a new variable, **Hired**, that stores the SAS date value for each employee's date of hire. Assume each employee was hired on the 15th day of the month.

The values of **Hired** should be displayed using a DATE9. format.

The **emphire** data set should contain three variables: **ID** and **Hired**. Print the data set to verify your results.

Listing of **prog2.noday**

ID	Hired Month	Hired Year
E03464	3	1994
E06523	8	1996
E07346	1	1997
E09965	10	1999
E13467	2	2000

Listing of **emphire**

Obs	ID	Hired	Years
1	E03464	15MAR1994	12
2	E06523	15AUG1996	10
3	E07346	15JAN1997	9
4	E09965	15OCT1999	7
5	E13467	15FEB2000	6

✎ The results above were generated on January 9, 2007. Your values for **Years** might differ.

5.5 Converting Variable Type

Objectives

- Understand automatic conversion of character data into numeric data.
- Explicitly convert character data into numeric data.
- Understand automatic conversion of numeric data into character data.
- Explicitly convert numeric data into character data.

120

Data Conversion

In many applications, you might need to convert one data type to another.

- You might need to read digits in character form into a numeric value.
- You might need to write a numeric value to a character string.

121

Data Conversion

You can convert data types

- implicitly by allowing the SAS System to do it for you
- explicitly with these functions:
  - INPUT   character-to-numeric conversion
  - PUT   numeric-to-character conversion.

122

The INPUT statement uses an informat to read a data value and then optionally stores that value in a variable. The INPUT function returns the value produced when a SAS expression is read using a specified informat.

The PUT statement writes a value to an external destination (either the log or a destination you specify). The PUT function returns a value using a specified format.

Automatic Character-to-Numeric Conversion

The `prog2.salary1` data set contains a character variable `GrossPay`. Compute a ten percent bonus for each employee.

What will happen when the character values of `GrossPay` are used in an arithmetic expression?

123

Automatic Character-to-Numeric Conversion

`prog2.salary1`

ID	GrossPay
$11	$5
201-92-2498	52000
482-87-7945	32000
330-40-7172	49000

```
data bonuses;
   set prog2.salary1;
   Bonus=.10*GrossPay;
run;
```

c05s5d1.sas

124

Automatic Character-to-Numeric Conversion

Partial Log

```
2      data bonuses;
3         set prog2.salary1;
4         Bonus=.10*GrossPay;
5      run;

NOTE: Character values have been
      converted to numeric values at the
      places given by: (Line):(Column).
      4:14
NOTE: The data set WORK.BONUSES has 3
      observations and 3 variables.
```

125

Automatic Character-to-Numeric Conversion

```
proc print data=bonuses noobs;
run;
```

PROC PRINT Output

ID	GrossPay	Bonus
201-92-2498	52000	5200
482-87-7945	32000	3200
330-40-7172	49000	4900

126

Automatic Character-to-Numeric Conversion

SAS automatically converts a character value to a numeric value when the character value is used in a numeric context, such as

- assignment to a numeric variable
- an arithmetic operation
- logical comparison with a numeric value
- a function that takes numeric arguments.

127

The WHERE statement and WHERE= data set option do not perform any automatic conversion in comparisons.

Automatic Character-to-Numeric Conversion

The automatic conversion

- uses the *w.* informat
- produces a numeric missing value from a character value that does not conform to standard numeric notation (digits with optional decimal point and/or leading sign and/or E-notation).

128

Automatic Character-to-Numeric Conversion

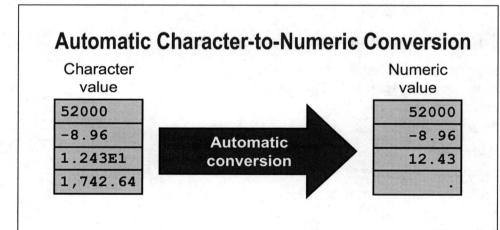

Character value		Numeric value
52000		52000
-8.96	Automatic conversion	-8.96
1.243E1		12.43
1,742.64		.

129

The INPUT Function

The INPUT function is used primarily for converting character values to numeric values.

NumVar=INPUT(*source*,*informat*);

The INPUT function returns the value produced when *source* is read with *informat*.

130

source   contains the SAS character expression to which you want to apply a specific informat.

informat is the SAS informat that you want to apply to the source.

If you use the INPUT function to create a variable not previously defined, the type and length of the variable is defined by the informat.

    No conversion messages are written to the log by the INPUT function.

The INPUT Function

```
data conversion;
   CVar1='32000';
   CVar2='32,000';
   CVar3='03may2008';
   CVar4='050308';
   NVar1=input(CVar1,5.);
   NVar2=input(CVar2,comma6.);
   NVar3=input(CVar3,date9.);
   NVar4=input(CVar4,mmddyy6.);
run;
```

131

The INPUT Function

```
proc contents data=conversion;
run;
```

Partial PROC CONTENTS Output

```
----Alphabetic List of Variables and Attributes----

        #     Variable    Type    Len

        1     CVar1       Char     5
        2     CVar2       Char     6
        3     CVar3       Char     9
        4     CVar4       Char     6
        5     NVar1       Num      8
        6     NVar2       Num      8
        7     NVar3       Num      8
        8     NVar4       Num      8
```

132

The INPUT Function

```
proc print data=conversion noobs;
run;
```

PROC PRINT Output

CVar1	CVar2	CVar3	CVar4	NVar1
32000	32,000	03may2008	050308	32000

NVar2	NVar3	NVar4		
32000	17655	17655		

133

Explicit Character-to-Numeric Conversion

The values of the variable **GrossPay** in the SAS data set **prog2.salary2** contain commas. Attempt to use automatic conversion to compute a 10 percent bonus.

prog2.salary2

ID $11	GrossPay $6
201-92-2498	52,000
482-87-7945	32,000
330-40-7172	49,000

134

Explicit Character-to-Numeric Conversion

```
data bonuses;
   set prog2.salary2;
   Bonus=.10*GrossPay;
run;

proc print data=bonuses;
run;
```

PROC PRINT Output

ID	GrossPay	Bonus
201-92-2498	52,000	.
482-87-7945	32,000	.
330-40-7172	49,000	.

135

Explicit Character-to-Numeric Conversion

```
data bonuses;
   set prog2.salary2;
   Bonus=.10*input(GrossPay,comma6.);
run;

proc print data=bonuses;
run;
```

PROC PRINT Output

ID	GrossPay	Bonus
201-92-2498	52,000	5200
482-87-7945	32,000	3200
330-40-7172	49,000	4900

136   c05s5d2.sas

Data Conversion

```
proc contents data=bonuses;
run;
```

Partial PROC CONTENTS Output

```
----Alphabetic List of Variables and Attributes----

     #     Variable     Type     Len
    _____
     3     Bonus        Num        8
     2     GrossPay     Char       6
     1     ID           Char      11
```

How can you convert **GrossPay** to a numeric variable
with the same name?

137

Data Conversion

You cannot convert data by assigning the converted
variable value to a variable with the same name.

```
GrossPay=input(GrossPay,comma6.);
```

  This assignment statement
does **not** change **GrossPay**
from a character variable
to a numeric variable.

138

Data Conversion

On the left side of the assignment statement, you want **GrossPay** to be numeric. However, on the right side of the assignment statement, **GrossPay** is character.

```
GrossPay=input(GrossPay,comma6.);
```

A variable is character
or numeric. After the
variable type is established,
it cannot be changed.

139

Data Conversion

First, use the RENAME= data set option to rename the variable you want to convert.

> *SAS-data-set*(RENAME=(*old-name*=*new-name*))

```
data bonuses;
   set prog2.salary2(rename=(GrossPay=
                       CharGross));
   additional SAS statements
run;
```

140

old-name   specifies the variable you want to rename.

new-name   specifies the new name of the variable. It must be a valid SAS name.

The new name of the variable you want to convert is arbitrary. In this example, the existing variable is renamed **CharGross** to emphasize that a character variable is being converted.

To rename more than one variable from the same data set, separate the variables you want to rename with a space. For example, to rename not only **GrossPay**, but also **ID**, use the following statement.

```
set prog2.salary2(rename=(GrossPay=CharGross  ID=IDNum));
```

Data Conversion

Second, use the INPUT function in an assignment
statement to create a new variable whose name is the
original name of the variable you renamed previously.

```
data bonuses;
   set prog2.salary2(rename=(GrossPay=
                            CharGross));
   GrossPay=input(CharGross,comma6.);
   additional SAS statements
run;
```

141

Data Conversion

Third, use a DROP= data set option in the DATA
statement to exclude the original variable from the
output SAS data set.

```
data bonuses(drop=CharGross);
   set prog2.salary2(rename=(GrossPay=
                            CharGross));
   GrossPay=input(CharGross,comma6.);
   Bonus=.10*GrossPay;
run;
```

c05s5d3.sas

142

Data Conversion: Compilation

```
data bonuses(drop=CharGross);
    set prog2.salary2(rename=(GrossPay=
                      CharGross));
    GrossPay=input(CharGross,comma6.);
    Bonus=.10*GrossPay;
run;
```

PDV

ID $ 4	CharGross $ 6

143   ...

Data Conversion: Compilation

```
data bonuses(drop=CharGross);
    set prog2.salary2(rename=(GrossPay=
                      CharGross));
    GrossPay=input(CharGross,comma6.);
    Bonus=.10*GrossPay;
run;
```

PDV

ID $ 4	CharGross $ 6	GrossPay N 8

144   ...

Data Conversion: Compilation

```
data bonuses(drop=CharGross);
   set prog2.salary2(rename=(GrossPay=
                            CharGross));
   GrossPay=input(CharGross,comma6.);
   Bonus=.10*GrossPay;
run;
```

PDV

ID	CharGross	GrossPay	Bonus
$ 4	$ 6	N 8	N 8

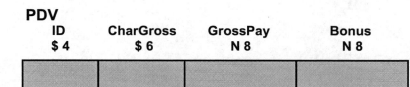

145   ...

Data Conversion: Compilation

```
data bonuses(drop=CharGross);
   set prog2.salary2(rename=(GrossPay=
                            CharGross));
   GrossPay=input(CharGross,comma6.);
   Bonus=.10*GrossPay;
run;
```

PDV

ID	CharGross	GrossPay	Bonus
$ 4	$ 6	N 8	N 8

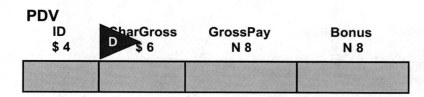

146

Converting Character Dates to SAS Dates

`prog2.born`

Name $12	Date $7
Ruth, G. H.	13apr72
Delgado, Ed	25aug68
Overby, Phil	08jun71

```
data birth(drop=Date);
   set prog2.born;
   Birthday=input(Date,date7.);
run;
```

c05s5d4.sas

147

Converting Character Dates to SAS Dates

```
proc print data=birth noobs;
run;
```

PROC PRINT Output

Name	Birthday
Ruth, G. H.	4486
Delgado, Ed	3159
Overby, Phil	4176

148

Automatic Numeric-to-Character Conversion

The **prog2.phones** data set contains a numeric
variable **Code** (area code) and a character variable
Telephone (telephone number). Create a character
variable that contains the area code in parentheses
followed by the telephone number.

149

Automatic Numeric-to-Character Conversion

prog2.phones

Code	Telephone
N8	$8
303	393-0956
919	770-8292
301	449-5239

```
data phonenumbers;
   set prog2.phones;
   Phone='(' !! Code !! ') ' !! Telephone;
run;
```

c05s5d5.sas

150

Automatic Numeric-to-Character Conversion

Partial Log

```
13    data phonenumbers;
14       set prog2.phones;
15       Phone='(' !! Code !! ') ' !! Telephone;
16    run;

NOTE: Numeric values have been converted to
      character values at the places given by:
      (Line):(Column).
      15:17
NOTE: The data set WORK.PHONENUMBERS has 3
      observations and 3 variables.
```

151

Automatic Numeric-to-Character Conversion

```
proc print data=phonenumbers noobs;
run;
```

PROC PRINT Output

Code	Telephone		Phone	
303	393-0956	(	303)	393-0956
919	770-8292	(	919)	770-8292
301	449-5239	(	301)	449-5239

152

Automatic Numeric-to-Character Conversion

SAS automatically converts a numeric value to a character value when the numeric value is used in a character context, such as

- assignment to a character variable
- a concatenation operation
- a function that accepts character arguments.

153

The WHERE statement and WHERE= data set option do not perform any automatic conversion in comparisons.

Automatic Numeric-to-Character Conversion

The automatic conversion

- uses the BEST12. format
- right-aligns the resulting character value.

Numeric value: 8 bytes

303   Automatic conversion →

Character value: 12 bytes

303

9 leading blanks

154

Automatic Numeric-to-Character Conversion

```
data phonenumbers;
   set prog2.phones;
   Phone='(' !! Code !! ') ' !! Telephone;
run;
```

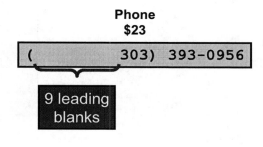

**Phone
$23**

9 leading
blanks

155

The PUT Function

The PUT function writes values with a specific format.

> *CharVar*=PUT(*source,format*);

The PUT function returns the value produced when
source is written with *format*.

156

source   identifies the SAS variable or constant whose value you want to reformat. This argument
can be character or numeric.

format   contains the SAS format that you want applied to the variable or constant that is specified
in the source. It must agree with the source in type.

The PUT function always returns a character string.

Numeric formats right-align the results. Character formats left-align the results.

If you use the PUT function to create a variable not previously defined, it creates a character variable
with a length equal to the format width.

    No conversion messages are written to the log by the PUT function.

The PUT Function

```
data conversion;
   NVar1=614;
   NVar2=55000;
   NVar3=366;
   CVar1=put(NVar1,3.);
   CVar2=put(NVar2,dollar7.);
   CVar3=put(NVar3,date9.);
run;
```

157

The PUT Function

```
proc contents data=conversion varnum;
run;
```

The VARNUM option in the PROC CONTENTS statement prints
a list of the variables by their logical position in the data set.

Partial PROC CONTENTS Output

```
-----Variables Ordered by Position-----

    #     Variable     Type     Len

    1     NVar1        Num        8
    2     NVar2        Num        8
    3     NVar3        Num        8
    4     CVar1        Char       3
    5     CVar2        Char       7
    6     CVar3        Char       9
```

158

The PUT Function

```
proc print data=conversion noobs;
run;
```

PROC PRINT Output

NVar1	NVar2	NVar3	CVar1	CVar2	CVar3
614	55000	366	614	$55,000	01JAN1961

159

Explicit Numeric-to-Character Conversion

```
data phonenumbers;
   set prog2.phones;
   Phone='(' !! put(Code,3.) !! ') ' !!
         Telephone;
run;
```

Partial Log

```
20    data phonenumbers;
21       set prog2.phone;
22       Phone='(' !! put(Code,3.) !! ') ' !! Telephone;
23    run;

NOTE: The data set WORK.PHONENUMBERS has 3 observations
      and 3 variables.
```

c05s5d6.sas

160

Automatic Numeric-to-Character Conversion

```
proc print data=phonenumbers noobs;
run;
```

PROC PRINT Output

Code	Telephone	Phone
303	393-0956	(303) 393-0956
919	770-8292	(919) 770-8292
301	449-5239	(301) 449-5239

161

 **Exercises**

11. Converting Variable Type

The data set **prog2.students** contains information about students.

Partial PROC CONTENTS Output of **prog2.students**

```
-----Alphabetic List of Variables and Attributes-----

       #    Variable    Type    Len

       3    DOB         Char      9
       2    Number      Num       8
       1    SSN         Char     11
```

Partial Listing of **prog2.students**

```
            SSN          Number       DOB

        012-40-4928     5467887     05DEC1968
        012-83-3816     6888321     03MAY1965
        341-44-0781     9418123     23NOV1972
        423-01-7721     7839191     28JUN1967
        448-23-8111     9428122     30NOV1960
```

Create a new data set named **students** from **prog2.students**. Create a new character variable **Telephone** that has this pattern: XXX-XXXX, where XXXXXXX is the value of **Number**. Print the **students** data set and list all the variables to verify the data conversion.

Recall the previous program and alter it to create a new numeric variable **Birthday** from the **DOB** variable. **Birthday** should contain SAS date values and have a format of MMDDYY10. Print the **students** data set and list all the variables to verify the data conversion.

When you are confident that both variables were converted correctly, use a DROP= or KEEP= data set option to ensure that the only variables in the **students** data set are **SSN**, **Telephone**, and **Birthday**.

Print your data set to verify your results.

Partial Listing of **students**

```
        Obs        SSN        Telephone     Birthday

         1     012-40-4928     546-7887     12/05/1968
         2     012-83-3816     688-8321     05/03/1965
         3     341-44-0781     941-8123     11/23/1972
         4     423-01-7721     783-9191     06/28/1967
         5     448-23-8111     942-8122     11/30/1960
```

5.6   Solutions to Exercises

1. **Manipulating Character Values**

```
data separate(drop=FMnames);
   length      FMnames
        First $ 30
        MI    $  2
        Last  $ 30;
   set prog2.people;
   FMnames = left(scan(Name,2,','));
   First = scan(FMnames,1,' ');
   MI = left(scan(FMnames,2,' '));
   Last = scan(Name,1,',');
run;

proc print data=separate;
   var Name CityState First MI Last;
run;
```

2. **Combining Character Values**

```
data flname(keep=NewName CityState);
   length FMnames First MI Last $ 30;
   set prog2.people;
   FMnames=left(scan(Name,2,','));
   First=scan(FMnames,1,' ');
   MI=left(scan(FMnames,2,' '));
   Last=left(scan(Name,1,','));

   /* Put together just the first name and the last
      name. */

   NewName=trim(First) !! ' ' !! Last;
run;

proc print data=flname;
   var NewName CityState;
run;
```

Alternate solution (SAS®9):

```
data flname(keep=NewName CityState);
   length FMnames First MI Last $ 30;
   set prog2.people;
   FMnames=left(scan(Name,2,','));
   First=scan(FMnames,1,' ');
   MI=left(scan(FMnames,2,' '));
   Last=left(scan(Name,1,','));
   NewName=catx(' ',First,Last);
run;

proc print data=flname;
   var NewName CityState;
run;
```

3. Performing Additional Character Manipulations (Optional)

```
data init(drop=First MI Last FMNames);
   length Initials $ 3 Last FMNames First MI $ 30;
   set prog2.people;
   FMNames=scan(Name,2,',');
   First=scan(FMNames,1,' ');
   MI=scan(FMNames,2,' ');
   Last=scan(Name,1,',');

   /* Put together just the first letters */

   Initials=substr(First,1,1) !!
            substr(MI,1,1) !!
            substr(Last,1,1);
run;

proc print data=init;
   var Name CityState initials;
run;
```

The TRIMN function returns a null string (zero blanks) for a blank string. The TRIM function returns a single blank.

Alternate solution (SAS®9):

```
data init(drop=First MI Last FMNames);
   length Initials      $  3
          Last First MI $  1
          FMNames       $ 30;
   set prog2.people;
   FMNames = scan(Name,2,',');
   /* By assigning entire names into 1-byte
      character variables, everything is truncated
      except the first letter. */
   First = left(FMNames);
   MI = scan(FMNames,2,' ');
   Last = Name;
   /* The CAT function concatenates without
      trimming or inserting separators. */
   Initials = cat(First,MI,Last);
run;

proc print data=init;
   var Name CityState initials;
run;
```

4. **Searching for a Character Value**

```
data prairie;
   set prog2.people;

/* Second argument to INDEX function must include a leading blank to
avoid extraneous results. The SAS®9 FIND function can also be used
here. */

   if index(CityState,' IL') > 0;
run;

proc print data=prairie;
run;
```

5. Performing Additional Character Manipulations

```
data mixedprairie(drop=First MI Last FMNames);
   length Last FMNames First MI $ 30;
   set prairie;
   Last=scan(Name,1,',');
   FMnames=scan(Name,2,',');
   First=scan(FMnames,1,' ');
   MI=scan(FMnames,2,' ');
   substr(First,2)=lowcase(substr(First,2));
   substr(Last,2)=lowcase(substr(Last,2));
   Name=trim(Last) !! ', ' !! trim(First) !! ' ' !! MI;
run;

proc print data=mixedprairie;
run;
```

Alternate solution (SAS®9):

```
data mixedprairie;
   set prairie;
   Name = propcase(Name);
run;

proc print data=mixedprairie;
run;
```

6. Using Additional Character Functions

```
data statelong(keep=Name StateName);
   length StateName State $20;
   set prog2.people;

   /* Second word of CITYSTATE is extracted.
      Resulting second word of CITYSTATE is left-
      aligned to eliminate leading blank.

      Once the leading blank is removed, STNAMEL
      can be used to determine state name. */

   State=left(scan(CityState,2,','));
   StateName=stnamel(State);
run;

proc print data=statelong;
   var Name StateName;
run;
```

7. Performing Additional Character Manipulations (Optional)

```
data mixedall(keep=Name CityState);
   length FMNames MName FName LName $ 30;
   set prog2.people;

   /* The entire value of Name is transformed into
      lowercase letters because, in your final
      results, most of the letters in the value of
      Name are lowercase. */

Name=lowcase(Name);

   /* Extract the last name, and place its first
      character back into uppercase. */

LName=scan(Name,1,',');
substr(LName,1,1)=upcase(substr(LName,1,1));

   /* Use the INDEX function to search for a blank
      within the value of LName. If a blank is found,
      uppercase the character one position to its
      right. This is the first character of the second
      word of a multiple-word last name. */

BlankPos=index(LName,' ');
if BlankPos gt 0 then
   substr(LName,BlankPos+1,1)=
         upcase(substr(LName,BlankPos+1,1));

   /* Extract the first and middle names, and place
      their first characters back into uppercase. */

FMNames=left(scan(Name,2,','));
FName=scan(FMNames,1,' ');
MName=scan(FMNames,2,' ');
substr(FName,1,1)=upcase(substr(FName,1,1));
substr(MName,1,1)=upcase(substr(MName,1,1));
   /* Use the INDEX function to search for a hyphen
      within the value of LName. If a hyphen is found,
      uppercase the character one position to its
      right.
      This is the first character of the second word
      of a multiple-word last name. */

DashPos=index(FName,'-');
if DashPos gt 0 then
   substr(FName,DashPos+1,1)=
         upcase(substr(FName,DashPos+1,1));
Name=trim(LName) !! ', ' !! trim(FName) !!
     ' ' !! MName;
run;

proc print data=mixedall;
run;
```

Alternate solution (SAS®9):

```
data mixedall;
    set prog2.people;
    Name = propcase(Name);
run;


proc print data=mixedall;
run;
```

8. Manipulating Numeric Values

```
data final;
   set prog2.grade;
   Overall=round(mean(Test1,Test2,Test3,Final,Final));
run;

  /* The assignment statement above could be replaced
     with Overall=round(mean(of Test1-Test3,Final,Final)); */

proc print data=final;
run;
```

9. Performing Additional Numeric Manipulations (Optional)

```
data final (drop=OverallTotal);
   set prog2.grade;
   OverallTotal=sum(Test1,Test2,Test3,Final,Final)-
                min(Test1,Test2,Test3);
   Overall=round(OverallTotal/4);
run;

    /* The first assignment statement above could be
       replaced with
       OverallTotal=sum(of Test1-Test3,Final,Final)-
                    min(of Test1-Test3); */

proc print data=final;
run;
```

10. Manipulating Numeric Values Based on Dates

```
data emphire (keep=ID Hired);
   set prog2.noday;
   Hired=mdy(HiredMonth,15,HiredYear);

   /* The FLOOR function could be used in the
      following assignment statement: */

   format Hired date9.;
run;

proc print data=emphire;
run;
```

11. Converting Variable Type

```
data students(drop=Number DOB);
   set prog2.students;

   /* The PUT function is used to convert NUMBER from
      numeric to character, and then the resulting
      character value is manipulated with the SUBSTR
      function to extract the first three characters,
      and the last four characters. */

   Telephone=substr(put(Number,7.),1,3) !! '-' !!
             substr(put(Number,7.),4);

   /* The INPUT function is used to convert DOB
      from character to numeric. Because the
      character values are in the form ddMMMyyyy,
      the DATE9. format is used in the conversion. */

   Birthday=input(DOB,date9.);
   format Birthday mmddyy10.;
run;

proc print data=students;
run;
```

Chapter 6   Debugging Techniques (Self-Study)

6.1 Using the PUT Statement

Objectives

- Use the PUT statement in the DATA step to help identify logic problems.

3

Scenario

You took a new position in the company. Your predecessor wrote some code that is not working. Identify what the program code is currently doing and determine the problem.

4

Input Data

```
CityCountry                     State

Auckland, New Zealand
Kansas City, USA                Missouri
Canberra, Australia             Australian Capital
Athens (Athinai), Greece
Amsterdam, Netherlands
Anchorage, USA                  Alaska
Birmingham, USA                 Alabama
Bangkok, Thailand
Nashville, USA                  Tennessee
Boston, USA                     Massachusetts
```

5

Expected Results

```
                TrueLocation

Auckland, New Zealand
Kansas City, Missouri
Canberra, Australia
Athens (Athinai), Greece
Amsterdam, Netherlands
Anchorage, Alaska
Birmingham, Alabama
Bangkok, Thailand
Nashville, Tennessee
Boston, Massachusetts
```

6

Current Program

```
data work.agents2;
   set prog2.agents;
   length Country $ 20;
   Country=scan(CityCountry,2,',');
   if Country='USA'
      then TrueLocation
              = scan(CityCountry,1,',')
              !! ', ' !! State;
   else /* not USA */
      TrueLocation = CityCountry;
run;
```

7

Current Results

```
           TrueLocation

Auckland, New Zealand
Kansas City, USA
Canberra, Australia
Athens (Athinai), Greece
Amsterdam, Netherlands
Anchorage, USA
Birmingham, USA
Bangkok, Thailand
Nashville, USA
Boston, USA
```

8

Syntax Errors Versus Logic Errors

- A *syntax error* occurs when program statements do not conform to the rules of the SAS language. An error message is produced by the SAS System and written to the log.
- A *logic error* occurs when the program statements follow the rules, but the results are not correct.

This section focuses on logic errors.

9

Because logic errors do not produce notes in the log, they are often difficult to detect and correct. The PUT statement and the DATA step debugger (discussed in the next section) are two methods for detecting logic errors.

The PUT Statement

If you do not specify a FILE statement, the PUT statement writes information to the log. This is useful to determine

- which piece of code is executing
- which piece of code is not executing
- the current value of a particular variable
- the current values of all variables.

10

General Forms of the PUT Statement

PUT '*text*';

writes the literal text string.

Example:

```
put 'I am here.';
```

writes I am here. to the log.

11

General Forms of the PUT Statement

PUT *variable-name*=;

writes the name of the variable followed by an equal sign and the value.

Example:

If the value of the variable **Var** is 5, the statement

```
put Var=;
```

writes Var=5 to the log.

12

General Forms of the PUT Statement

PUT *variable-name format-name.***;**

writes the variable value with the indicated format.

Example:

If the value of the variable **ChVar** is THIS with a leading space, the statement

```
put ChVar $quote20.;
```

writes   **" THIS"**   to the log.

13

    The format $QUOTE*w*. writes a character value with quotes around it and preserves any leading spaces.

General Forms of the PUT Statement

PUT _ALL_;

writes the name of each variable in the PDV followed by an equal sign and the value of the variable.

14

    The PUT statement can be used in SAS in both the batch and interactive modes.

The PUTLOG Statement

The PUTLOG statement is similar to the PUT statement, except that it writes only to the log. It is unaffected by the FILE statement.

PUTLOG *message*;

where *message* can include character literals (enclosed in quotation marks), variable names, formats, and pointer controls.

✎ PUTLOG is a SAS®9 statement.

15

The advantage of the PUTLOG statement is that it can be inserted in a DATA step which has PUT and FILE statements writing to a non-log destination (such as a disk file) without affecting that logic.

Determining Logic Errors

c06s1d1.sas, c06s1d2.sas

This demonstration shows how to detect and correct logic errors using the PUT statement.

```
data work.agents2;
   set prog2.agents;
   length Country $ 20 TrueLocation $ 40;
   Country = scan(CityCountry,2,',');
   if country = 'USA'
      then TrueLocation = scan(CityCountry,1,',')
           !! ', ' !! State;
   else /* not USA */
      TrueLocation = CityCountry;
run;

proc print data=work.agents2 noobs;
   var TrueLocation CityCountry State;
   title 'Current Output from Program';
run;
```

PROC PRINT Output

	Current Output from Program	
CityCountry	TrueLocation	State
Auckland, New Zealand	Auckland, New Zealand	
Kansas City, USA	Kansas City, USA	Missouri
Canberra, Australia	Canberra, Australia	Australian Capital
Athens (Athinai), Greece	Athens (Athinai), Greece	
Amsterdam, Netherlands	Amsterdam, Netherlands	
Anchorage, USA	Anchorage, USA	Alaska
Birmingham, USA	Birmingham, USA	Alabama
Bangkok, Thailand	Bangkok, Thailand	
Nashville, USA	Nashville, USA	Tennessee
Boston, USA	Boston, USA	Massachusetts

Bring the code into the Editor window.

1. Determine what code is executing.

   Convert the IF-THEN statement that creates **TrueLocation** for USA branches into a DO group, and insert a PUT (or PUTLOG – SAS®9) statement to determine whether the code is executing.

```
data work.agents2;
   set prog2.agents;
   length Country $ 20 TrueLocation $ 40;
   Country=scan(CityCountry,2,',');
   if Country='USA' then do;
      TrueLocation = scan(CityCountry,1,',')
                     !! ', ' !! State;
      put 'Country is USA';
   end;
   else /* not USA */
      TrueLocation = CityCountry;
run;
```

   Submit the code. The text string in the PUT statement does not appear in the log.

2. Determine the value of **Country** before the IF-THEN statement.

   Insert a PUT statement between the assignment statement for **Country** and the IF-THEN statement that creates **TrueLocation** for USA branches.

```
data work.agents2;
   set prog2.agents;
   length Country $ 20 TrueLocation $ 40;
   Country=scan(CityCountry,2,',');
   put Country=;
   if Country='USA' then do;
      TrueLocation = scan(CityCountry,1,',')
                     !! ', ' !! State;
      put 'Country is USA';
   end;
else /* not USA */
   TrueLocation = CityCountry;
run;
```

   Submit the code. The values of **Country** seem to be created appropriately.

   Partial Log

```
Country=New Zealand
Country=USA
Country=Australia
Country=Greece
Country=Netherlands
Country=USA
```

3. Use the $QUOTE*w.* format to check for leading blanks.

By default, character values are written with the standard character format $*w.*, where *w* is the length of the character variable. The standard character format left-justifies the value and removes leading blanks.

To check for leading blanks in the value for **Country**, change the PUT statement as shown below:

```
data work.agents2;
   set prog2.agents;
   length Country $ 20 TrueLocation $ 40;
   Country=scan(CityCountry,2,',');
   put Country $quote20.;
   if Country='USA' then do;
      TrueLocation = scan(CityCountry,1,',')
                        !! ', ' !! State;
      put 'Country is USA';
   end;
   else /* not USA */
      TrueLocation = CityCountry;
run;
```

Submit the code and check the log. Notice that each value shows one leading blank.

Partial Log

```
" New Zealand"
" USA"
" Australia"
" Greece"
" Netherlands"
" USA"
```

4. Use the LEFT function to remove leading blanks from the values of **Country**.

```
data work.agents2;
   set prog2.agents;
   length Country $ 20 TrueLocation $ 40;
   Country=left(scan(CityCountry,2,','));
   put Country $quote20.;
   if Country='USA' then do;
      TrueLocation = scan(CityCountry,1,',')
                        !! ', ' !! State;
      put 'Country is USA';
   end;
   else /* not USA */
      TrueLocation = CityCountry;
run;
```

Submit the code and check the log. The PUT statement in the DO group writes to the log at the appropriate time.

Partial Log

```
"New Zealand"
"USA"
Country is USA
"Australia"
"Greece"
"Netherlands"
"USA"
Country is USA
```

```
proc print data=work.agents2 noobs;
   var TrueLocation CityCountry State;
   title 'Output with Leading Spaces Removed';
run;
```

PROC PRINT Output

```
                    Output with Leading Spaces Removed

       TrueLocation              CityCountry              State

Auckland, New Zealand        Auckland, New Zealand
Kansas City, Missouri        Kansas City, USA           Missouri
Canberra, Australia          Canberra, Australia        Australian Capital
Athens (Athinai), Greece     Athens (Athinai), Greece
Amsterdam, Netherlands       Amsterdam, Netherlands
Anchorage, Alaska            Anchorage, USA             Alaska
Birmingham, Alabama          Birmingham, USA            Alabama
Bangkok, Thailand            Bangkok, Thailand
Nashville, Tennessee         Nashville, USA             Tennessee
Boston, Massachusetts        Boston, USA                Massachusetts
```

break * 1431 when (citycountry= "Anchorage, USA"); go

5. Remove the PUT statements and the DO group from the DATA step.

```
data work.agents2 (drop=Country);
   set prog2.agents;
   length Country $ 20 TrueLocation $ 40;
   Country=left(scan(CityCountry,2,','));
   if Country='USA' then
      TrueLocation = scan(CityCountry,1,',')
                     !! ', ' !! State;
   else /* not USA */
      TrueLocation = CityCountry;
run;

proc print data=work.agents2 noobs;
   var TrueLocation CityCountry State;
   title 'Corrected Output';
run;
```

Submit the code and check the log and output.

PROC PRINT Output

```
                            Corrected Output


       TrueLocation            CityCountry              State

Auckland, New Zealand     Auckland, New Zealand
Kansas City, Missouri     Kansas City, USA           Missouri
Canberra, Australia       Canberra, Australia        Australian Capital
Athens (Athinai), Greece  Athens (Athinai), Greece
Amsterdam, Netherlands    Amsterdam, Netherlands
Anchorage, Alaska         Anchorage, USA             Alaska
Birmingham, Alabama       Birmingham, USA            Alabama
Bangkok, Thailand         Bangkok, Thailand
Nashville, Tennessee      Nashville, USA             Tennessee
Boston, Massachusetts     Boston, USA                Massachusetts
```

6.2 Using the DEBUG Option

Objectives

- Use the DEBUG option in the DATA statement to help identify logic problems.

18

Scenario

You took a new position in the company. Your predecessor wrote some code that is not working. Identify what the program code is currently doing and determine the problem.

19

Input Data

```
CityCountry                State

Auckland, New Zealand
Kansas City, USA           Missouri
Canberra, Australia        Australian Capital
Athens (Athinai), Greece
Amsterdam, Netherlands
Anchorage, USA             Alaska
Birmingham, USA            Alabama
Bangkok, Thailand
Nashville, USA             Tennessee
Boston, USA                Massachusetts
```

20

Expected Results

```
         TrueLocation

Auckland, New Zealand
Kansas City, Missouri
Canberra, Australia
Athens (Athinai), Greece
Amsterdam, Netherlands
Anchorage, Alaska
Birmingham, Alabama
Bangkok, Thailand
Nashville, Tennessee
Boston, Massachusetts
```

21

Current Program

```
data work.agents2;
   set prog2.agents;
   length Country $ 20;
   Country=scan(CityCountry,2,',');
   if Country='USA'
      then TrueLocation
              = scan(CityCountry,1,',')
                !! ', ' !! State;
   else /* not USA */
      TrueLocation = CityCountry;
run;
```

22

Current Results

```
        TrueLocation

Auckland, New Zealand
Kansas City, USA
Canberra, Australia
Athens (Athinai), Greece
Amsterdam, Netherlands
Anchorage, USA
Birmingham, USA
Bangkok, Thailand
Nashville, USA
Boston, USA
```

23

The DEBUG Option

The DEBUG option is an interactive interface to the DATA step during DATA step execution. This option is useful for determining the following:

- the code that is executing
- the code that is **not** executing
- the current value of a particular variable
- when the value of a variable changes

24

 The DEBUG option can be used only in the SAS System's interactive mode.

The DEBUG Option

General form of the DEBUG option:

> **DATA** *data-set-name* / DEBUG;

25

DEBUG Commands

Common commands used with the DEBUG option:

Command	Abbreviation	Action
STEP	ENTER key	Steps through a program one statement at a time.
EXAMINE	E *variable(s)*	Displays the value of the variable.
WATCH	W *variable(s)*	Suspends execution when the value of the variable changes.
LIST WATCH	L W	Lists variables that are watched.
QUIT	Q	Halts execution of the DATA step.

26

The W and E commands precede the name of the variable, for example:

```
W Country
```

To view the values of all variables, use the command

```
e _all_
```

You can also select these commands from the drop-down menu if it is turned on.

Determining Logic Errors

c06s2d1.sas

Use the DEBUG option to detect the logic error in the following program:

```
data work.agents2;
   set prog2.agents;
   length Country $ 20 TrueLocation $ 40;
   Country=scan(CityCountry,2,',');
   if Country='USA'
      then TrueLocation = scan(CityCountry,1,',')
                          !! ', ' !! State;
   else /* not USA */
      TrueLocation = CityCountry;
run;

proc print data=work.agents2 noobs;
   var TrueLocation State;
   title 'Locations of Ticket Agents';
run;
```

PROC PRINT Output

Locations of Ticket Agents		
TrueLocation	CityCountry	State
Auckland, New Zealand	Auckland, New Zealand	
Kansas City, USA	Kansas City, USA	Missouri
Canberra, Australia	Canberra, Australia	Australian Capital
Athens (Athinai), Greece	Athens (Athinai), Greece	
Amsterdam, Netherlands	Amsterdam, Netherlands	
Anchorage, USA	Anchorage, USA	Alaska
Birmingham, USA	Birmingham, USA	Alabama
Bangkok, Thailand	Bangkok, Thailand	
Nashville, USA	Nashville, USA	Tennessee
Boston, USA	Boston, USA	Massachusetts

The correct output is shown below:

Locations of Ticket Agents		
TrueLocation	CityCountry	State
Auckland, New Zealand	Auckland, New Zealand	
Kansas City, Missouri	Kansas City, USA	Missouri
Canberra, Australia	Canberra, Australia	Australian Capital
Athens (Athinai), Greece	Athens (Athinai), Greece	
Amsterdam, Netherlands	Amsterdam, Netherlands	
Anchorage, Alaska	Anchorage, USA	Alaska
Birmingham, Alabama	Birmingham, USA	Alabama
Bangkok, Thailand	Bangkok, Thailand	
Nashville, Tennessee	Nashville, USA	Tennessee
Boston, Massachusetts	Boston, USA	Massachusetts

1. Add the DEBUG option to the end of the DATA statement.

```
data work.agents2 / debug;
   set prog2.agents;
   length Country $ 20 TrueLocation $ 40;
   Country=scan(CityCountry,2,',');
   if Country='USA'
      then TrueLocation = scan(CityCountry,1,',')
                          !! ', ' !! State;
   else /* not USA */
      TrueLocation = CityCountry;
run;
```

2. Submit the DATA step.

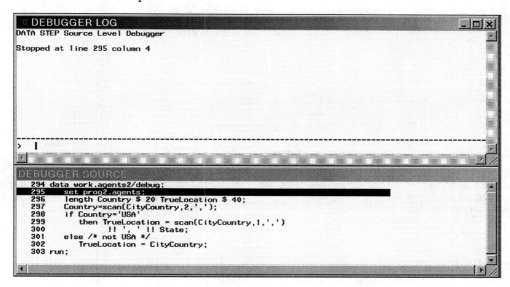

/   The debugger source highlights the next statement to be executed.

3. Press the ENTER key to execute the SET statement.

4. Use the Examine command to examine the value of **CityCountry**:

```
e citycountry
```

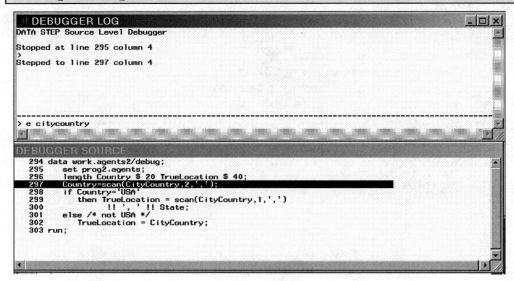

5. Press ENTER to execute the assignment statement for **Country**.

6. Use the Examine command to examine the value of **Country**:

```
e country
```

7. Press ENTER to check the conditional statement.

8. Press ENTER to execute the ELSE statement.

9. Use the Examine command to examine the value of **TrueLocation**:

```
e truelocation
```

10. Use the Watch command to monitor the values of **TrueLocation**, **Country**, and **CityCountry**:

```
w truelocation country citycountry
```

11. Press ENTER until you execute the SET statement and the assignment statement for **Country**. The value of **Country** is now USA.

```
DEBUGGER LOG                                              _ □ ×
Stepped to line 297 column 4
>
Country =  USA
Old value =
Value changed at line 297 column 4
Stepped to line 298 column 4



>
DEBUGGER SOURCE
   294 data work.agents2/debug;
   295    set prog2.agents;
   296    length Country $ 20 TrueLocation $ 40;
   297    Country=scan(CityCountry,2,',');
   298    if Country='USA'
   299       then TrueLocation = scan(CityCountry,1,',')
   300          !! ', ' !! State;
   301    else /* not USA */
   302       TrueLocation = CityCountry;
   303 run;
```

12. Press ENTER to check the IF-THEN statements.

13. Notice the changes in the values of the watched variables from step 10.

```
DEBUGGER LOG                                              _ □ ×
Stepped to line 297 column 4
>
Country =  USA
Old value =
Value changed at line 297 column 4
Stepped to line 298 column 4
>
Stepped to line 302 column 7
>
TrueLocation = Kansas City, USA
Old value =
Value changed at line 302 column 7
Stepped to line 303 column 1
-------------------------------------------------------
> |
DEBUGGER SOURCE
   294 data work.agents2/debug;
   295    set prog2.agents;
   296    length Country $ 20 TrueLocation $ 40;
   297    Country=scan(CityCountry,2,',');
   298    if Country='USA'
   299       then TrueLocation = scan(CityCountry,1,',')
   300          !! ', ' !! State;
   301    else /* not USA */
   302       TrueLocation = CityCountry;
   303 run;
```

14. Use the Examine command to check the value of **Country** for leading spaces:

```
e country $quote20.
```

```
DEBUGGER LOG                                                    _ □ x
Value changed at line 302 column 7
Stepped to line 303 column 1
> e country $quote20.
Country = " USA"



-----------------------------------------------------------------
> |
```

```
DEBUGGER SOURCE
    294 data work.agents2/debug;
    295    set prog2.agents;
    296    length Country $ 20 TrueLocation $ 40;
    297    Country=scan(CityCountry,2,',');
    298    if Country='USA'
    299       then TrueLocation = scan(CityCountry,1,',')
    300             !! ', ' !! State;
    301    else /* not USA */
    302       TrueLocation = CityCountry;
    303 run;
```

15. Press ENTER until SAS reaches the bottom of the DATA step.

16. Use the Quit command to halt the DATA step.

17. Remove the DEBUG option from the DATA step and use the LEFT function to remove the leading space.

```
data work.agents2(drop=CityCountry Country);
   set prog2.agents;
   length Country $ 20 TrueLocation $ 40;
   Country=left(scan(CityCountry,2,','));
   if Country='USA'
      then TrueLocation = scan(CityCountry,1,',')
                           !! ', ' !! State;
   else /* not USA */
      TrueLocation = CityCountry;
run;

proc print data=work.agents2 noobs;
   var TrueLocation CityCountry State;
   title 'Locations of Ticket Agents';
run;
```

PROC PRINT Output

```
                        Locations of Ticket Agents

      TrueLocation              CityCountry                State

Auckland, New Zealand      Auckland, New Zealand
Kansas City, Missouri      Kansas City, USA           Missouri
Canberra, Australia        Canberra, Australia        Australian Capital
Athens (Athinai), Greece   Athens (Athinai), Greece
Amsterdam, Netherlands     Amsterdam, Netherlands
Anchorage, Alaska          Anchorage, USA             Alaska
Birmingham, Alabama        Birmingham, USA            Alabama
Bangkok, Thailand          Bangkok, Thailand
Nashville, Tennessee       Nashville, USA             Tennessee
Boston, Massachusetts      Boston, USA                Massachusetts
```

Chapter 7   Processing Data Iteratively

7.1 DO Loop Processing

Objectives

- Understand iterative DO loops.
- Use DO loops to generate data.
- Use DO loops to eliminate redundant code.
- Use DO loop processing to conditionally execute code.

3

DO Loop Processing

Statements within a DO loop execute for a specific number of iterations or until a specific condition stops the loop.

```
DATA statement
    <additional SAS statements>
    DO statement
        iterated SAS statements
    END statement
    <additional SAS statements>
RUN statement
```

4

DO Loop Processing

You can use DO loops to

- perform repetitive calculations
- generate data
- eliminate redundant code
- execute SAS code conditionally.

5

Repetitive Coding

Compare the interest for yearly versus quarterly compounding on a $50,000 investment made for one year at 7.5 percent interest.

How much money will a person accrue in each situation?

6

Repetitive Coding

```
data compound;
   Amount=50000;
   Rate=.075;
   Yearly=Amount*Rate;
   Quarterly+((Quarterly+Amount)*Rate/4);
   Quarterly+((Quarterly+Amount)*Rate/4);
   Quarterly+((Quarterly+Amount)*Rate/4);
   Quarterly+((Quarterly+Amount)*Rate/4);
run;
```

7

Repetitive Coding

```
proc print data=compound noobs;
run;
```

PROC PRINT Output

Amount	Rate	Yearly	Quarterly
50000	0.075	3750	3856.79

What if you wanted to determine the quarterly compounded interest after a period of 20 years (80 quarters)?

8

DO Loop Processing

```
data compound(drop=i);
   Amount=50000;
   Rate=.075;
   Yearly=Amount*Rate;
   do i=1 to 4;
      Quarterly+((Quarterly+Amount)*Rate/4);
   end;
run;
```

9

The Iterative DO Statement

The iterative DO statement executes statements between DO and END statements repetitively, based on the value of an index variable.

```
DO index-variable=specification-1 <,...specification-n>;
    iterated SAS statements
END;
```

specification-1...specification-n can represent a range of values or a list of specific values.

10

index-variable	names a variable whose value governs execution of the DO loop. The *index-variable* argument is required.
specification	denotes an expression or a series of expressions. The iterative DO statement requires at least one *specification* argument.

The index variable, unless dropped, is included in the data set that is being created.

Avoid changing the value of the index variable within the DO loop. If you modify the value of the index variable within the DO loop, you could cause infinite looping.

The Iterative DO Statement

DO *index-variable=start* TO *stop* <BY *increment*>;

The values of *start*, *stop*, and *increment*
- must be numbers or expressions that yield numbers
- are established before executing the loop.

Any changes to the values of *stop* or *increment* made
within the DO loop do not affect the number of iterations.

11

start	specifies the initial value of the index variable.
stop	specifies the ending value of the index variable.
increment	optionally specifies a positive or negative number to control the incrementing of *index-variable*. If *increment* is not specified, the index variable is increased by 1.

When *increment* is positive, *start* must be the lower bound and *stop*, if present, must be the upper bound for the loop. If *increment* is negative, *start* must be the upper bound and *stop*, if present, must be the lower bound for the loop.

The Iterative DO Statement

What are the values of each of the four index variables?

```
do i=1 to 12;
     1 2 3 4 5 6 7 8 9 10 11 12  13    Out of range
do j=2 to 10 by 2;    Out of range
     2 4 6 8 10  12
do k=14 to 2 by -2;          Out of range
     14 12 10 8 6 4 2  0
do m=3.6 to 3.8 by .05;            Out of range
     3.60 3.65 3.70 3.75 3.80  3.85
```

16

The Iterative DO Statement

> **DO** *index-variable=item-1 <,...item-n>;*

item-1 through *item-n* can be either all numeric or all character constants, or they can be variables.

The DO loop is executed once for each value in the list.

17

Enclose character constants in quotation marks.

The Iterative DO Statement

How many times will each DO loop execute?

```
do Month='JAN','FEB','MAR';
     Three times.
do Fib=1,2,3,5,8,13,21;
     Seven times.
do i=Var1,Var2,Var3;
     Three times.
do j=BeginDate to Today() by 7;
     Unknown. The number of iterations depends
     on the values of BeginDate and Today().
do k=Test1-Test50;
     One time. A single value of k is determined
     by subtracting Test50 from Test1.
```

23   ***

DO Loop Logic

24

DO Loop Logic

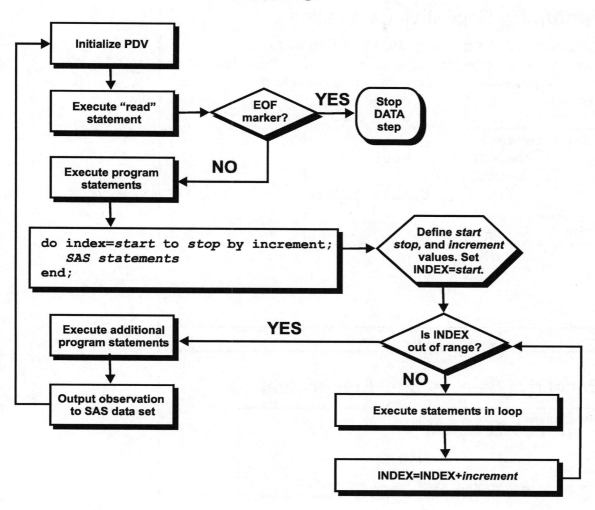

Performing Repetitive Calculations

On January 1 of each year, $5,000 is invested in an account. Determine the value of the account after three years based on a constant annual interest rate of 7.5 percent.

```
data invest;
   do Year=2001 to 2003;
      Capital+5000;
      Capital+(Capital*.075);
   end;
run;
```

25

Repetitive Calculations: Compilation

```
data invest;
   do Year=2001 to 2003;
      Capital+5000;
      Capital+(Capital*.075);
   end;
run;
```

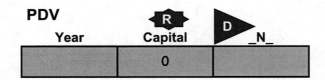

PDV

Year	Capital	_N_
	0	

26

...

Repetitive Calculations: Execution

```
data invest;
   do Year=2001 to 2003;
      Capital+5000;
      Capital+(Capital*.075);
   end;
run;
```

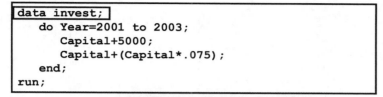

Initialize PDV to missing

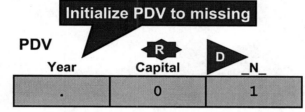

PDV

Year	Capital	_N_
.	0	1

27

...

Repetitive Calculations: Execution

```
data invest;
   do Year=2001 to 2003;
      Capital+5000;
      Capital+(Capital*.075);
   end;
run;
```

Is Year out of range?

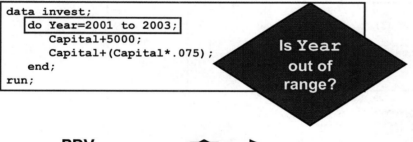

PDV

Year	Capital	_N_
2001	0	1

28

...

Repetitive Calculations: Execution

```
data invest;
   do Year=2001 to 2003;
      Capital+5000;
      Capital+(Capital*.075);
   end;
run;
```

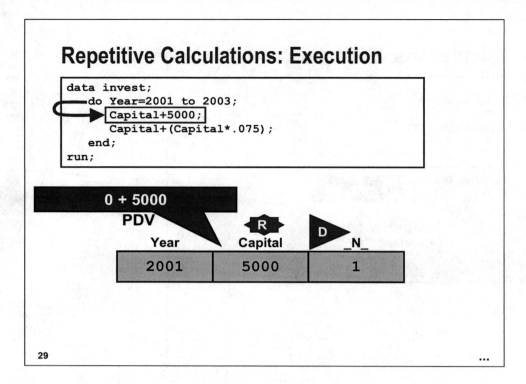

0 + 5000

PDV

Year	Capital	_N_
2001	5000	1

29

...

Repetitive Calculations: Execution

```
data invest;
   do Year=2001 to 2003;
      Capital+5000;
      Capital+(Capital*.075);
   end;
run;
```

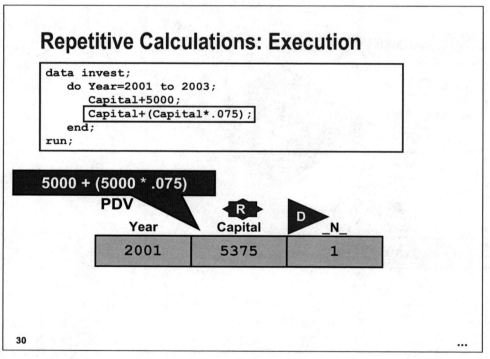

5000 + (5000 * .075)

PDV

Year	Capital	_N_
2001	5375	1

30

...

Repetitive Calculations: Execution

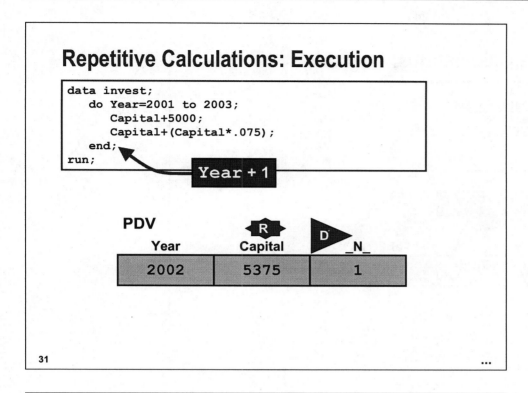

Repetitive Calculations: Execution

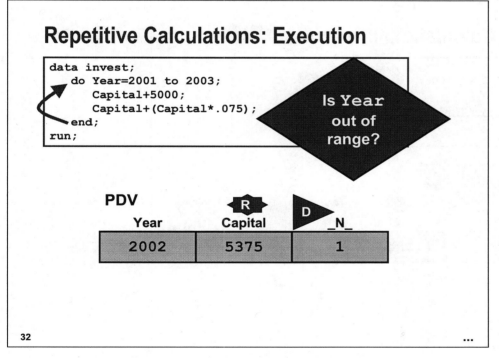

31

32

Repetitive Calculations: Execution

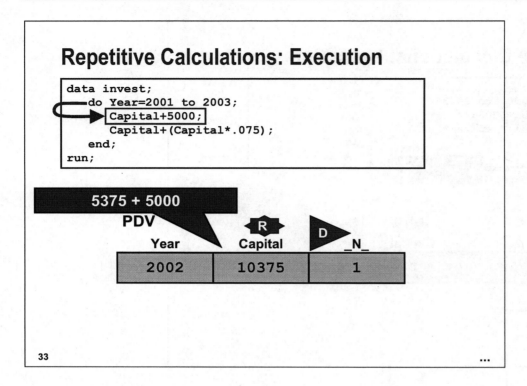

```
data invest;
   do Year=2001 to 2003;
      Capital+5000;
      Capital+(Capital*.075);
   end;
run;
```

5375 + 5000

PDV

Year	Capital	_N_
2002	10375	1

33

Repetitive Calculations: Execution

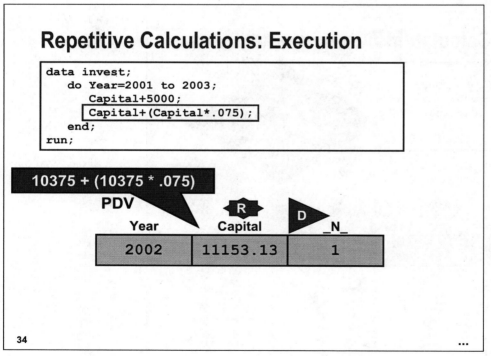

```
data invest;
   do Year=2001 to 2003;
      Capital+5000;
      Capital+(Capital*.075);
   end;
run;
```

10375 + (10375 * .075)

PDV

Year	Capital	_N_
2002	11153.13	1

34

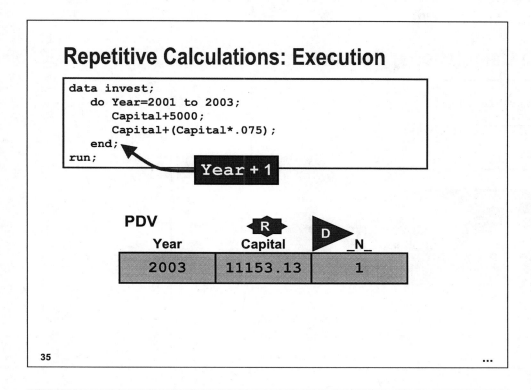

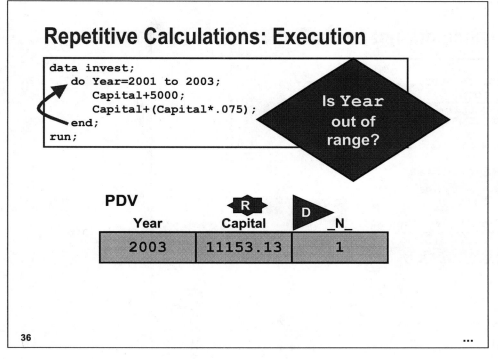

Repetitive Calculations: Execution

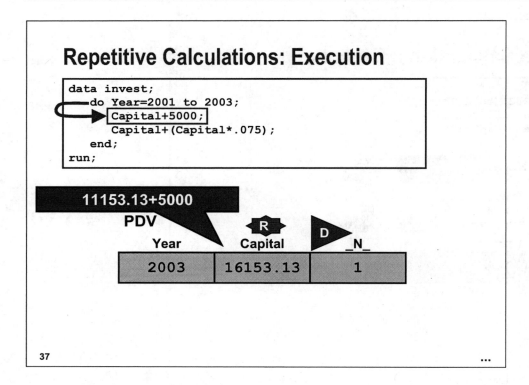

```
data invest;
   do Year=2001 to 2003;
      Capital+5000;
      Capital+(Capital*.075);
   end;
run;
```

11153.13+5000

PDV

Year	Capital	_N_
2003	16153.13	1

37   ...

Repetitive Calculations: Execution

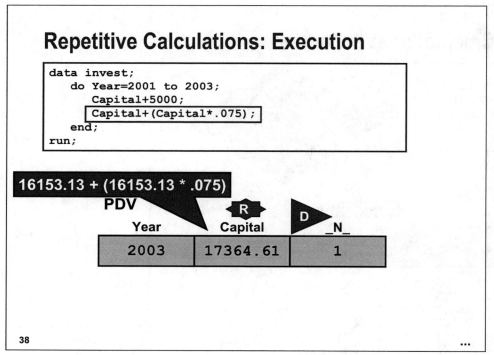

```
data invest;
   do Year=2001 to 2003;
      Capital+5000;
      Capital+(Capital*.075);
   end;
run;
```

16153.13 + (16153.13 * .075)

PDV

Year	Capital	_N_
2003	17364.61	1

38   ...

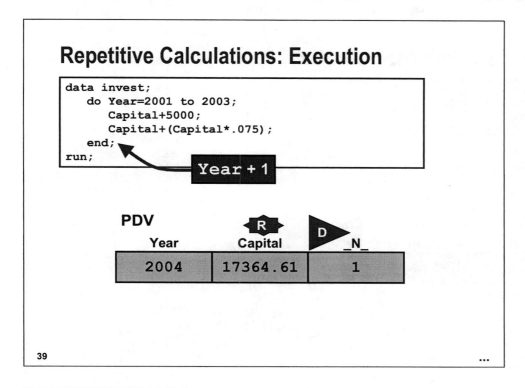

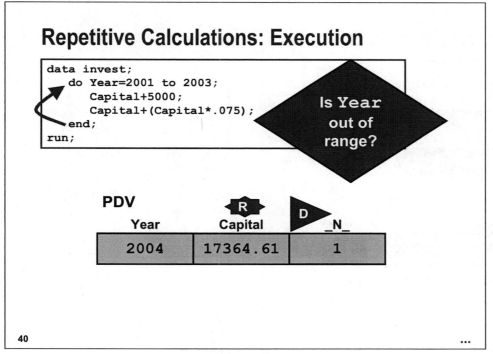

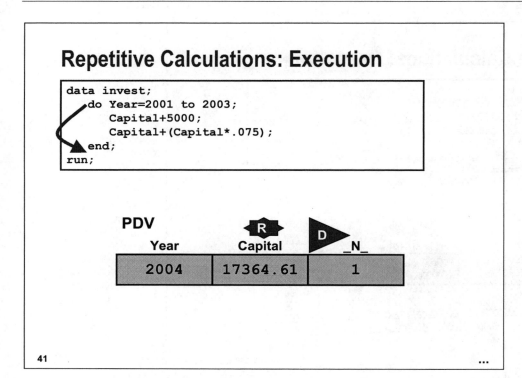

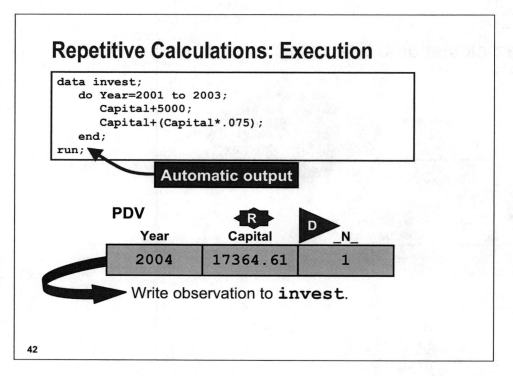

Performing Repetitive Calculations

```
proc print data=invest noobs;
run;
```

PROC PRINT Output

Year	Capital
2004	17364.61

43

Performing Repetitive Calculations

Generate a separate observation for each year.

```
data invest;
   do Year=2001 to 2003;
      Capital+5000;
      Capital+(Capital*.075);
      output;
   end;
run;

proc print data=invest noobs;
run;
```

c07s1d1.sas

44

Performing Repetitive Calculations

PROC PRINT Output

Year	Capital
2001	5375.00
2002	11153.13
2003	17364.61

Why is the value of **Year** not equal to 2004 in the last observation?

45

Reducing Redundant Code

Recall the example that forecasts the growth of each division of an airline.

Partial Listing of **prog2.growth**

Division	Num Emps	Increase
APTOPS	205	0.075
FINACE	198	0.040
FLTOPS	187	0.080

46

A Forecasting Application (Review)

```
data forecast;
   set prog2.growth(rename=(NumEmps=NewTotal));
   Year=1;
   NewTotal=NewTotal*(1+Increase);
   output;
   Year=2;
   NewTotal=NewTotal*(1+Increase);
   output;
   Year=3;
   NewTotal=NewTotal*(1+Increase);
   output;
run;
```

What if you want to forecast growth over the next 30 years?

47

Reducing Redundant Code

Use a DO loop to eliminate the redundant code
in the previous example.

```
data forecast;
   set prog2.growth(rename=(NumEmps=NewTotal));
   do Year=1 to 3;
      NewTotal=NewTotal*(1+Increase);
      output;
   end;
run;
```

c07s1d2.sas

48

Reducing Redundant Code

```
proc print data=forecast noobs;
run;
```

Partial PROC PRINT Output

Division	New Total	Increase	Year
APTOPS	220.38	0.075	1
APTOPS	236.90	0.075	2
APTOPS	254.67	0.075	3
FINACE	205.92	0.040	1

What if you want to forecast the number of years it would take for the size of the Airport Operations Division to exceed 300 people?

49

Conditional Iterative Processing

You can use DO WHILE and DO UNTIL statements to stop the loop when a condition is met rather than when the index variable exceeds a specific value.

To avoid infinite loops, be sure that the condition specified will be met.

50

The DO WHILE Statement

The DO WHILE statement executes statements
in a DO loop while a condition is true.

```
DO WHILE (expression);
    additional SAS statements
END;
```

expression is evaluated at the **top** of the loop.

The statements in the loop never execute if *expression*
is initially false.

51

The DO UNTIL Statement

The DO UNTIL statement executes statements
in a DO loop until a condition is true.

```
DO UNTIL (expression);
    additional SAS statements
END;
```

expression is evaluated at the **bottom** of the loop.

The statements in the loop are executed at least once.

52

Conditional Iterative Processing

Determine the number of years it would take for an account to exceed $1,000,000 if $5,000 is invested annually at 7.5 percent.

53

Conditional Iterative Processing

```
data invest;
   do until(Capital>1000000);
      Year+1;
      Capital+5000;
      Capital+(Capital*.075);
   end;
run;

proc print data=invest noobs;
run;
```

54

Conditional Iterative Processing

PROC PRINT Output

Capital	Year
1047355.91	38

How could you generate the same result with
a DO WHILE statement?

55

Conditional Iterative Processing

```
data invest;
   do while (Capital le 1000000);
      Year+1;
      Capital+5000;
      Capital+(Capital*.075);
   end;
run;

proc print data=invest noobs;
run;
```

56

The Iterative DO Statement with a Conditional Clause

You can combine DO WHILE and DO UNTIL statements with the iterative DO statement.

```
DO index-variable=start TO stop <BY increment>
    WHILE | UNTIL (expression);
    additional SAS statements
END;
```

This is one method of avoiding an infinite loop in DO WHILE or DO UNTIL statements.

57

In a DO WHILE statement, the conditional clause is checked **after** the index variable is incremented.

In a DO UNTIL statement, the conditional clause is checked **before** the index variable is incremented.

The Iterative DO Statement with a Conditional Clause

Determine the return of the account again.

Stop the loop if 25 years is reached or more than $250,000 is accumulated.

58

The Iterative DO Statement with a Conditional Clause

```
data invest;
   do Year=1 to 25 until(Capital>250000);
      Capital+5000;
      Capital+(Capital*.075);
   end;
run;

proc print data=invest noobs;
run;
```

59

The Iterative DO Statement with a Conditional Clause

PROC PRINT Output

Year	Capital
21	255594.86

60

Nested DO Loops

Nested DO loops are loops within loops.

When you nest DO loops,

- use different index variables for each loop
- be certain that each DO statement has a corresponding END statement.

61

Nested DO Loops

Create one observation per year for five years, and show the earnings if you invest $5,000 per year with 7.5 percent annual interest compounded quarterly.

62

Nested DO Loops

```
data invest(drop=Quarter);
  do Year=1 to 5;
    Capital+5000;
    do Quarter=1 to 4;
      Capital+(Capital*(.075/4));
    end;
    output;
  end;
run;

proc print data=invest noobs;
run;
```

5x 4x

63

Nested DO Loops

PROC PRINT Output

Year	Capital
1	5385.68
2	11186.79
3	17435.37
4	24165.94
5	31415.68

How could you generate one observation for each quarterly amount?

64

Nested DO Loops

Compare the final results of investing $5,000 a year for five years in three different banks that compound quarterly. Assume each bank has a fixed interest rate.

prog2.banks

Name	Rate
Calhoun Bank and Trust	0.0718
State Savings Bank	0.0721
National Savings and Trust	0.0728

65

Nested DO Loops

```
data invest(drop=Quarter Year);
   set prog2.banks;
   Capital=0;
   do Year=1 to 5;
      Capital+5000;
      do Quarter=1 to 4;
         Capital+(Capital*(Rate/4));
      end;
   end;
run;
```

3x
5x
4x

This program is similar to the previous program. The changes are noted.

66

c07s1d3.sas

Nested DO Loops: Execution

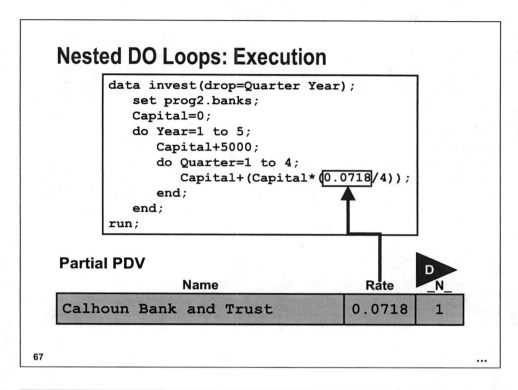

```
data invest(drop=Quarter Year);
   set prog2.banks;
   Capital=0;
   do Year=1 to 5;
      Capital+5000;
      do Quarter=1 to 4;
         Capital+(Capital*(0.0718/4));
      end;
   end;
run;
```

Partial PDV

Name	Rate	_N_
Calhoun Bank and Trust	0.0718	1

67 ...

Nested DO Loops: Execution

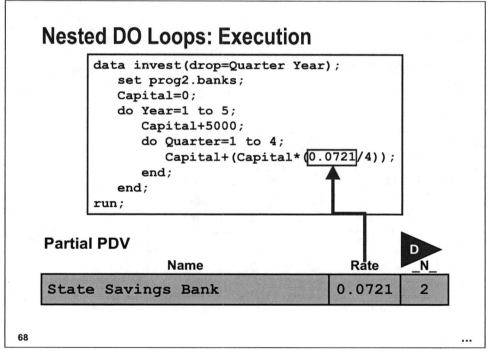

```
data invest(drop=Quarter Year);
   set prog2.banks;
   Capital=0;
   do Year=1 to 5;
      Capital+5000;
      do Quarter=1 to 4;
         Capital+(Capital*(0.0721/4));
      end;
   end;
run;
```

Partial PDV

Name	Rate	_N_
State Savings Bank	0.0721	2

68 ...

Nested DO Loops: Execution

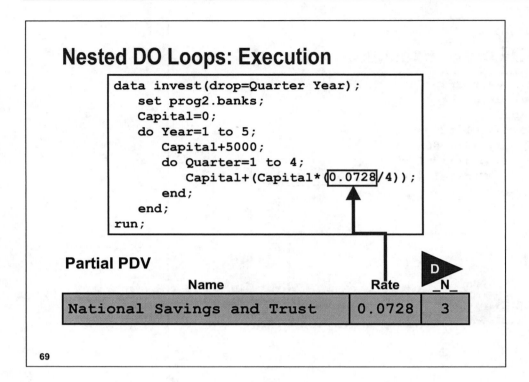

```
data invest(drop=Quarter Year);
   set prog2.banks;
   Capital=0;
   do Year=1 to 5;
      Capital+5000;
      do Quarter=1 to 4;
         Capital+(Capital*(0.0728/4));
      end;
   end;
run;
```

Partial PDV

Name	Rate	_N_
National Savings and Trust	0.0728	3

69

Nested DO Loops

```
proc print data=invest noobs;
run;
```

PROC PRINT Output

Name	Rate	Capital
Calhoun Bank and Trust	0.0718	31106.73
State Savings Bank	0.0721	31135.55
National Savings and Trust	0.0728	31202.91

70

 **Exercises**

1. Performing Computations with DO Loops

The payroll department must project total employee costs (wages, retirement, benefits, and medical benefits) through future years based on assumed increases.

a. Create a SAS data set named **future** with four variables: **Year** and the three variables shown below.

Initialize each of the variables below to their current values, and use a DO loop to calculate their estimated values for the next ten years. For example, next year's wage expense will be this year's wage expense plus 6 percent of this year's amount; in two years, the wage expense will be next year's amount plus 6 percent; and so on. Create one observation for each year.

Variable	Current value	Estimated annual increase
Wages	$12,874,000	6.0%
Retire	1,765,000	1.4%
Medical	649,000	9.5%

Use SAS date functions to guarantee that the value of **Year** in the first observation is the upcoming year, regardless of the current year. (If the current year is 2001, the value of **Year** in the first observation will be 2002. If the program is run in 2006 without any modifications, the value of **Year** in the first observation will be 2007.)

Print the data set to verify your results.

Obs	Year	Wages	Retire	Medical
1	2008	13646440.00	1789710.00	710655.00
2	2009	14465226.40	1814765.94	778167.23
3	2010	15333139.98	1840172.66	852093.11
4	2011	16253128.38	1865935.08	933041.96
5	2012	17228316.09	1892058.17	1021680.94
6	2013	18262015.05	1918546.99	1118740.63
7	2014	19357735.95	1945406.64	1225020.99
8	2015	20519200.11	1972642.34	1341397.99
9	2016	21750352.12	2000259.33	1468830.80
10	2017	23055373.25	2028262.96	1608369.72

   The results above were generated on January 10, 2007. Your values for **Year** might differ.

b. Modify the previous program to create a new variable named **TotCost** that is the sum of the wage, retirement, and medical costs for each year.

Print the data set.

Obs	Year	Wages	Retire	Medical	TotCost
1	2008	13646440.00	1789710.00	710655.00	16146805.00
2	2009	14465226.40	1814765.94	778167.23	17058159.57
3	2010	15333139.98	1840172.66	852093.11	18025405.76
4	2011	16253128.38	1865935.08	933041.96	19052105.42
5	2012	17228316.09	1892058.17	1021680.94	20142055.20
6	2013	18262015.05	1918546.99	1118740.63	21299302.67
7	2014	19357735.95	1945406.64	1225020.99	22528163.59
8	2015	20519200.11	1972642.34	1341397.99	23833240.44
9	2016	21750352.12	2000259.33	1468830.80	25219442.24
10	2017	23055373.25	2028262.96	1608369.72	26692005.93

The results above were generated on January 10, 2007. Your values for **Year** might differ.

c. Corporate income for last year was $50,000,000. Income is projected to increase at 1 percent per year. Modify the previous program so that the DO loop stops when the year's total costs exceed the year's income.

Print the data set to verify that total costs exceed income after 26 observations.

Obs	Year	Income	TotCost
1	2008	50500000.00	16146805.00
2	2009	51005000.00	17058159.57
3	2010	51515050.00	18025405.76
4	2011	52030200.50	19052105.42
5	2012	52550502.51	20142055.20
6	2013	53076007.53	21299302.67
7	2014	53606767.61	22528163.59
8	2015	54142835.28	23833240.44
9	2016	54684263.63	25219442.24
10	2017	55231106.27	26692005.93
11	2018	55783417.33	28256519.13
12	2019	56341251.51	29918944.75
13	2020	56904664.02	31685647.29
14	2021	57473710.66	33563421.13
15	2022	58048447.77	35559520.91
16	2023	58628932.25	37681694.14
17	2024	59215221.57	39938216.30
18	2025	59807373.78	42337928.49
19	2026	60405447.52	44890278.01
20	2027	61009502.00	47605361.89
21	2028	61619597.02	50493973.81
22	2029	62235792.99	53567654.57
23	2030	62858150.92	56838746.30
24	2031	63486732.43	60320451.03
25	2032	64121599.75	64026893.56
26	2033	64762815.75	67973189.29

The results above were generated on January 10, 2007. Your values for **Year** might differ.

7.2 SAS Array Processing

Objectives

- Understand the concepts of SAS arrays.
- Use SAS arrays to perform repetitive calculations.

73

Performing Repetitive Calculations

Employees contribute an amount to charity every quarter. The SAS data set `prog2.donate` contains contribution data for each employee. The employer supplements each contribution by 25 percent.

Calculate each employee's quarterly contribution including the company supplement.

Partial Listing of `prog2.donate`

ID	Qtr1	Qtr2	Qtr3	Qtr4
E00224	12	33	22	.
E00367	35	48	40	30

74

Performing Repetitive Calculations

```
data charity;
    set prog2.donate;
    Qtr1=Qtr1*1.25;
    Qtr2=Qtr2*1.25;
    Qtr3=Qtr3*1.25;
    Qtr4=Qtr4*1.25;
run;

proc print data=charity noobs;
run;
```

75

Performing Repetitive Calculations

Partial PROC PRINT Output

ID	Qtr1	Qtr2	Qtr3	Qtr4
E00224	15.00	41.25	27.50	.
E00367	43.75	60.00	50.00	37.50
E00441	.	78.75	111.25	112.50
E00587	20.00	23.75	37.50	36.25
E00598	5.00	10.00	7.50	1.25

What if you want to similarly modify 52 weeks of data
stored in **Week1** through **Week52**?

76

Array Processing

You can use arrays to simplify programs that

- perform repetitive calculations
- create many variables with the same attributes
- read data
- rotate SAS data sets by making variables into observations or observations into variables
- compare variables
- perform a table lookup.

77

What Is a SAS Array?

A *SAS array*

- is a temporary grouping of SAS variables that are arranged in a particular order
- is identified by an *array name*
- exists only for the duration of the current DATA step
- is **not** a variable.

78

SAS arrays are different from arrays in many other programming languages. In the SAS System, an array is **not** a data structure. It is simply a convenient way of temporarily identifying a group of variables.

What Is a SAS Array?

Each value in an array is

- called an *element*
- identified by a *subscript* that represents the position of the element in the array.

When you use an *array reference*, the corresponding value is substituted for the reference.

79

What Is a SAS Array?

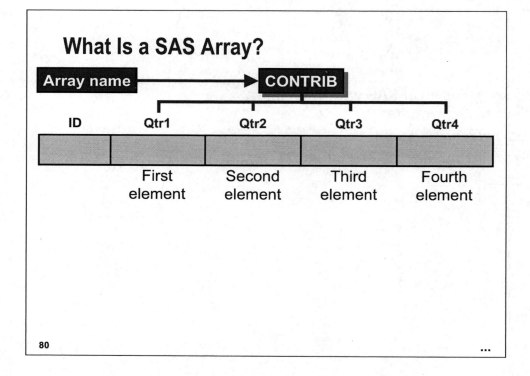

80

...

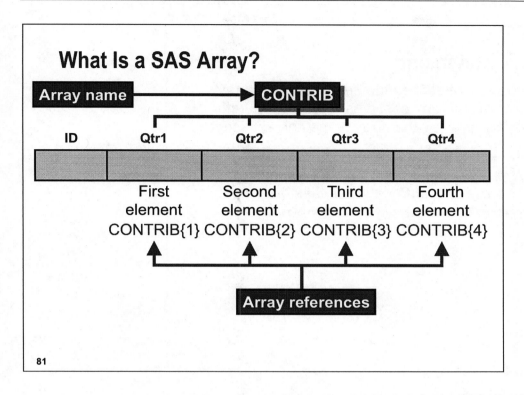

What Is a SAS Array?

Array name → CONTRIB

| ID | Qtr1 | Qtr2 | Qtr3 | Qtr4 |

First element CONTRIB{1}
Second element CONTRIB{2}
Third element CONTRIB{3}
Fourth element CONTRIB{4}

Array references

81

The ARRAY Statement

The ARRAY statement defines the elements in an array. These elements can be processed as a group. You refer to elements of the array by the array name and subscript.

> **ARRAY** *array-name* {*subscript*} <$> <*length*>
> <*array-elements*> <(*initial-value-list*)>;

82

array-name	specifies the name of the array.
{*subscript*}	describes the number and arrangement of elements in the array by using an asterisk, a number, or a range of numbers. *subscript* is enclosed in braces (**{ }**). Brackets (**[ ]**) and parentheses (**( )**) are also allowed. *subscript* often has the form {*dimension-size(s)*}. {*dimension-size(s)*} is used to indicate a numeric representation of either the number of elements in a one-dimensional array or the number of elements in each dimension of a multidimensional array.
$	indicates that the elements in the array are character elements. The dollar sign is not necessary if the elements in the array were previously defined as character elements.
length	specifies the length of elements in the array that were not previously assigned a length.
array-elements	names the elements that make up the array. Array elements can be listed in any order.
(*initial-value-list*)	gives initial values for the corresponding elements in the array. The values for elements can be numbers or character strings. You must enclose all character strings in quotation marks.

✎ Array names cannot be used in LABEL, FORMAT, DROP, KEEP, or LENGTH statements.

If you use a function name as the name of the array, SAS treats parenthetical references that involve the name as array references, not function references, for the duration of the DATA step.

The ARRAY Statement

The ARRAY statement

- must contain all numeric or all character elements
- must be used to define an array before the array name can be referenced
- creates variables if they do not already exist in the PDV
- is a compile-time statement.

83

You can use special SAS name lists to reference variables that were previously defined in the same DATA step. The _CHARACTER_ variable lists character values only. The _NUMERIC_ variable lists numeric values only.

Avoid using the _ALL_ special SAS name list to reference variables, because the elements in an array must be either all character or all numeric values.

Good Selection of arrays on:

SAS Procedures

Base SAS

SAS Language Reference: Concepts

Defining an Array

Write an ARRAY statement that defines the four quarterly contribution variables as elements of an array.

```
array Contrib{4} Qtr1 Qtr2 Qtr3 Qtr4;
```

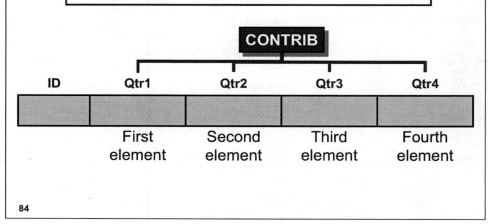

84

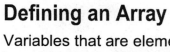 The four variables, **Qtr1**, **Qtr2**, **Qtr3**, and **Qtr4**, can now be referenced via the array name **Contrib**.

Defining an Array

Variables that are elements of an array do **not** need to have similar, related, or numbered names.

```
array Contrib2{4} Q1 Qrtr2 ThrdQ Qtr4;
```

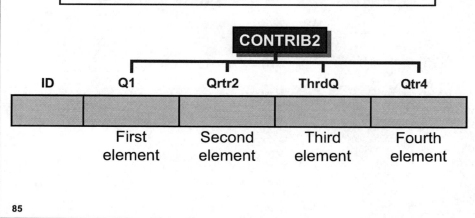

85

Processing an Array

Array processing often occurs within DO loops. An iterative DO loop that processes an array typically has the following form:

```
DO index-variable=1 TO number-of-elements-in-array;
    additional SAS statements
        using array-name{index-variable}...
END;
```

To execute the loop as many times as there are elements in the array, specify that the values of *index-variable* range from 1 to *number-of-elements-in-array*.

86

You must tell SAS which variable in the array to use in each iteration of the loop. You can write programming statements so that the index variable of the DO loop is the subscript of the array reference (for example, *array-name{index-variable}*). When the value of the index variable changes, the subscript of the array reference (and therefore the variable that is referenced) also changes.

To process particular elements of an array, specify those elements as the range of the iterative DO statement.

By default, SAS includes *index-variable* in the output data set. Use a DROP statement or the DROP= data set option to prevent the index variable from being written to your output data set.

Processing an Array

```
array Contrib{4} Qtr1 Qtr2 Qtr3 Qtr4;
do i=1 to 4;
   Contrib{i}=Contrib{i}*1.25;
end;
```

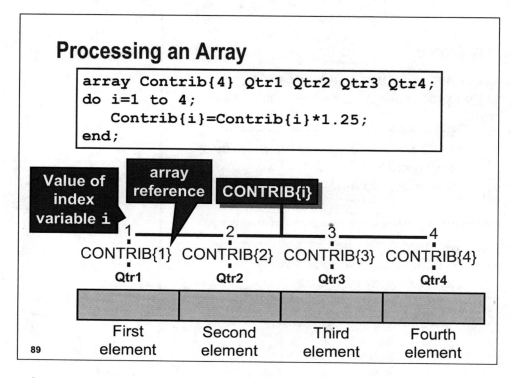

The name **i** is used here for the index variable. Any valid SAS variable name can be used.

Performing Repetitive Calculations

```
data charity(drop=i);
   set prog2.donate;
   array Contrib{4} Qtr1 Qtr2 Qtr3 Qtr4;
   do i=1 to 4;
      Contrib{i}=Contrib{i}*1.25;
   end;
run;
```

90   c07s2d1.sas

Performing Repetitive Calculations

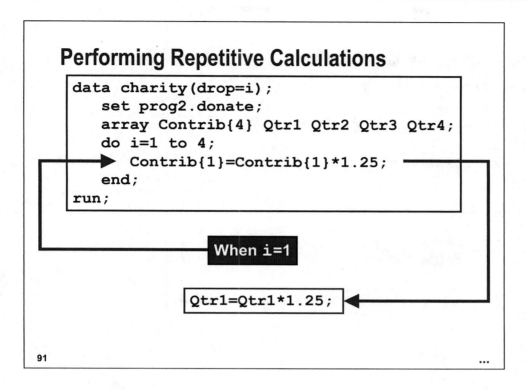

```
data charity(drop=i);
   set prog2.donate;
   array Contrib{4} Qtr1 Qtr2 Qtr3 Qtr4;
   do i=1 to 4;
      Contrib{1}=Contrib{1}*1.25;
   end;
run;
```

When i=1

Qtr1=Qtr1*1.25;

91

...

Performing Repetitive Calculations

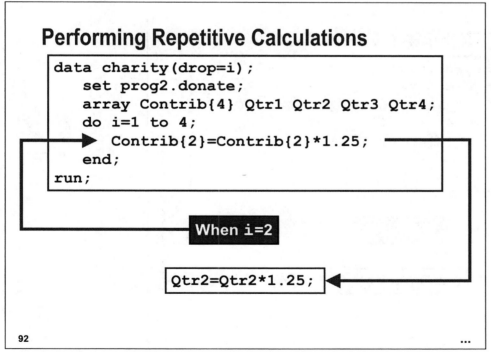

```
data charity(drop=i);
   set prog2.donate;
   array Contrib{4} Qtr1 Qtr2 Qtr3 Qtr4;
   do i=1 to 4;
      Contrib{2}=Contrib{2}*1.25;
   end;
run;
```

When i=2

Qtr2=Qtr2*1.25;

92

...

Performing Repetitive Calculations

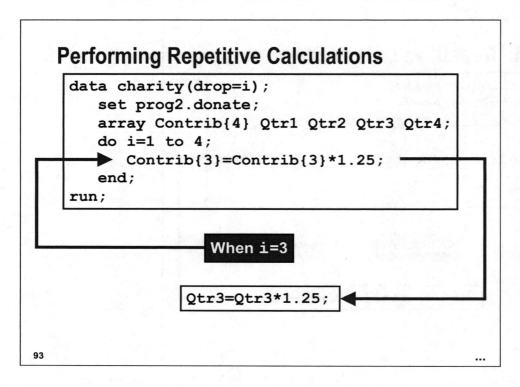

```
data charity(drop=i);
   set prog2.donate;
   array Contrib{4} Qtr1 Qtr2 Qtr3 Qtr4;
   do i=1 to 4;
      Contrib{3}=Contrib{3}*1.25;
   end;
run;
```

When i=3

```
Qtr3=Qtr3*1.25;
```

93   ...

Performing Repetitive Calculations

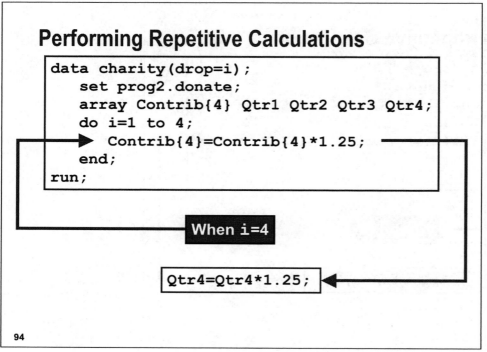

```
data charity(drop=i);
   set prog2.donate;
   array Contrib{4} Qtr1 Qtr2 Qtr3 Qtr4;
   do i=1 to 4;
      Contrib{4}=Contrib{4}*1.25;
   end;
run;
```

When i=4

```
Qtr4=Qtr4*1.25;
```

94

Performing Repetitive Calculations

```
proc print data=charity noobs;
run;
```

Partial PROC PRINT Output

ID	Qtr1	Qtr2	Qtr3	Qtr4
E00224	15.00	41.25	27.50	.
E00367	43.75	60.00	50.00	37.50
E00441	.	78.75	111.25	112.50
E00587	20.00	23.75	37.50	36.25
E00598	5.00	10.00	7.50	1.25

95

Exercises

2. Using Arrays for Repetitive Computations

A ski resort has a weather-recording device that writes an observation to a SAS data set every day. Each observation in the data set **prog2.ski** contains the date and 24 hourly readings of the temperature in degrees Fahrenheit starting at 1:00 a.m.

Partial Listing of **prog2.ski**

Date	T1	T2	T3	T4	T5	T6	T7	T8	T9	T10	T11	T12
18FEB2000	23	22	20	20	21	24	26	28	28	29	31	31
19FEB2000	25	25	26	30	31	33	33	35	36	37	39	40
20FEB2000	31	31	30	29	29	28	29	30	30	31	30	30
21FEB2000	13	15	16	17	19	20	20	21	23	24	26	27
22FEB2000	20	22	23	25	26	27	29	31	33	35	36	36

T13	T14	T15	T16	T17	T18	T19	T20	T21	T22	T23	T24
32	32	31	32	31	33	32	31	29	27	26	25
40	41	42	42	43	42	41	40	38	36	34	32
30	29	28	26	25	23	22	21	19	17	15	13
29	30	31	30	30	31	30	27	23	22	21	20
37	38	37	34	32	31	30	26	24	25	21	20

Create a data set named **celsius** by reading the **prog2.ski** data set. Convert all of the temperatures stored in T1 through T24 to Celsius by using this formula:

$$\text{Celsius temperature} = 5*(\text{Fahrenheit temperature} - 32)/9$$

These Celsius temperatures will be stored in T1 through T24. (You do not need to create 24 new variables for the Celsius temperatures.)

Create a variable **Cost** that contains the daily cost of running a snowmaking machine if the machine automatically runs for one hour when the detected temperature is lower than 2 degrees Celsius. It costs $125.00 per hour to run the machine.

Print the data set. Round the temperature values to the first decimal place.

Partial PROC PRINT Output

Obs	Date	T1	T2	T3	T4	T5	T6	T7
1	18FEB2000	-5.0	-5.6	-6.7	-6.7	-6.1	-4.4	-3.3
2	19FEB2000	-3.9	-3.9	-3.3	-1.1	-0.6	0.6	0.6
3	20FEB2000	-0.6	-0.6	-1.1	-1.7	-1.7	-2.2	-1.7
4	21FEB2000	-10.6	-9.4	-8.9	-8.3	-7.2	-6.7	-6.7
5	22FEB2000	-6.7	-5.6	-5.0	-3.9	-3.3	-2.8	-1.7

Obs	T8	T9	T10	T11	T12	T13	T14	T15	T16	T17
1	-2.2	-2.2	-1.7	-0.6	-0.6	0.0	0.0	-0.6	0.0	-0.6
2	1.7	2.2	2.8	3.9	4.4	4.4	5.0	5.6	5.6	6.1
3	-1.1	-1.1	-0.6	-1.1	-1.1	-1.1	-1.7	-2.2	-3.3	-3.9
4	-6.1	-5.0	-4.4	-3.3	-2.8	-1.7	-1.1	-0.6	-1.1	-1.1
5	-0.6	0.6	1.7	2.2	2.2	2.8	3.3	2.8	1.1	0.0

Obs	T18	T19	T20	T21	T22	T23	T24	Cost
1	0.6	0.0	-0.6	-1.7	-2.8	-3.3	-3.9	3000
2	5.6	5.0	4.4	3.3	2.2	1.1	0.0	1250
3	-5.0	-5.6	-6.1	-7.2	-8.3	-9.4	-10.6	3000
4	-0.6	-1.1	-2.8	-5.0	-5.6	-6.1	-6.7	3000
5	-0.6	-1.1	-3.3	-4.4	-3.9	-6.1	-6.7	2375

7.3   Using SAS Arrays

Objectives

- Use SAS arrays to create new variables.
- Use SAS arrays to perform a table lookup.
- Use SAS arrays to rotate a SAS data set.

98

Creating Variables with Arrays

Calculate the percentage that each quarter's contribution represents of the employee's total annual contribution. Base the percentage only on the employee's actual contribution and ignore the company contributions.

Partial Listing of `prog2.donate`

ID	Qtr1	Qtr2	Qtr3	Qtr4
E00224	12	33	22	.
E00367	35	48	40	30

99

Creating Variables with Arrays

```
data percent(drop=i);
    set prog2.donate;
    Total=sum(of Qtr1-Qtr4);
    array Contrib{4} Qtr1-Qtr4;
    array Percent{4};
    do i=1 to 4;
        Percent{i}=Contrib{i}/Total;
    end;
run;
```

The second ARRAY statement creates four numeric variables: **Percent1**, **Percent2**, **Percent3**, and **Percent4**.

c07s3d1.sas

100

The first ARRAY statement uses the existing variables **Qtr1**, **Qtr2**, **Qtr3**, and **Qtr4**. In that ARRAY statement, a numbered range SAS variable list is used.

Creating Variables with Arrays

```
proc print data=percent noobs;
   var ID Percent1-Percent4;
   format Percent1-Percent4 percent6.;
run;
```

Partial PROC PRINT Output

ID	Percent1	Percent2	Percent3	Percent4
E00224	18%	49%	33%	.
E00367	23%	31%	26%	20%
E00441	.	26%	37%	37%
E00587	17%	20%	32%	31%
E00598	21%	42%	32%	5%

101

The PERCENT*w.d* format multiplies values by 100, formats them in the same way as the BEST*w.d* format, and adds a percent sign (%) to the end of the formatted value. Negative values are enclosed in parentheses. The PERCENT*w.d* format allows room for a percent sign and parentheses, even if the value is not negative.

Creating Variables with Arrays

Calculate the difference in each employee's actual contribution from one quarter to the next.

Partial Listing of
prog2.donate

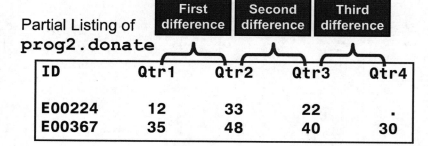

	First difference	Second difference	Third difference	
ID	Qtr1	Qtr2	Qtr3	Qtr4
E00224	12	33	22	.
E00367	35	48	40	30

104

Creating Variables with Arrays

```
data change(drop=i);
   set prog2.donate;
   array Contrib{4} Qtr1-Qtr4;
   array Diff{3};
   do i=1 to 3;
      Diff{i}=Contrib{i+1}-Contrib{i};
   end;
run;
```

c07s3d2.sas

105

Creating Variables with Arrays

```
data change(drop=i);
   set prog2.donate;
   array Contrib{4} Qtr1-Qtr4;
   array Diff{3};                {i+1}
   do i=1 to 3;
      Diff{1}=Contrib{2}-Contrib{1};
   end;
run;
```

When i=1

```
Diff1=Qtr2-Qtr1;
```

106   ...

Creating Variables with Arrays

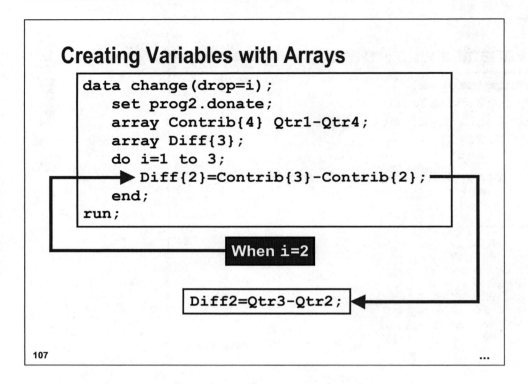

```
data change(drop=i);
   set prog2.donate;
   array Contrib{4} Qtr1-Qtr4;
   array Diff{3};
   do i=1 to 3;
      Diff{2}=Contrib{3}-Contrib{2};
   end;
run;
```

When i=2

```
Diff2=Qtr3-Qtr2;
```

107   ...

Creating Variables with Arrays

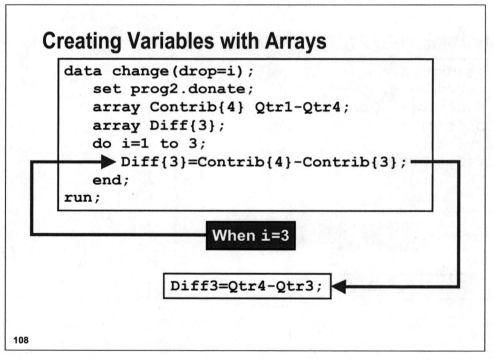

```
data change(drop=i);
   set prog2.donate;
   array Contrib{4} Qtr1-Qtr4;
   array Diff{3};
   do i=1 to 3;
      Diff{3}=Contrib{4}-Contrib{3};
   end;
run;
```

When i=3

```
Diff3=Qtr4-Qtr3;
```

108

Creating Variables with Arrays

```
proc print data=change noobs;
   var ID Diff1-Diff3;
run;
```

Partial PROC PRINT Output

ID	Diff1	Diff2	Diff3
E00224	21	-11	.
E00367	13	-8	-10
E00441	.	26	1
E00587	3	11	-1
E00598	4	-2	-5

109

Assigning Initial Values

Determine the difference between employee contributions and last year's average quarterly goals of $10, $15, $5, and $10 per employee.

```
data compare(drop=i Goal1-Goal4);
   set prog2.donate;
   array Contrib{4} Qtr1-Qtr4;
   array Diff{4};
   array Goal{4} Goal1-Goal4 (10,15,5,10);
   do i=1 to 4;
      Diff{i}=Contrib{i}-Goal{i};
   end;
run;
```

110

Elements and values are matched by position. If there are more array elements than initial values, the remaining array elements are assigned missing values and SAS issues a warning.

You can separate the values in the initial value list with either a comma or a blank space.

    Initial values are retained until a new value is assigned to the array element.

This is an example of a simple *table lookup* program.

Assigning Initial Values

```
proc print data=compare noobs;
   var ID Diff1 Diff2 Diff3 Diff4;
run;
```

Partial PROC PRINT Output

ID	Diff1	Diff2	Diff3	Diff4
E00224	2	18	17	.
E00367	25	33	35	20
E00441	.	48	84	80
E00587	6	4	25	19
E00598	-6	-7	1	-9

111

Creating Variables with Arrays: Compilation

Partial Listing of **prog2.donate**

ID	Qtr1	Qtr2	Qtr3	Qtr4
E00224	12	33	22	.
E00367	35	48	40	30

```
data compare(drop=i Goal1-Goal4);
   set prog2.donate;
   array Contrib{4} Qtr1-Qtr4;
   array Diff{4};
   array Goal{4} Goal1-Goal4
      (10,15,5,10);
   do i=1 to 4;
      Diff{i}=Contrib{i}-
         Goal{i};
   end;
run;
```

PDV

ID	Qtr1	Qtr2	Qtr3	Qtr4

112   ...

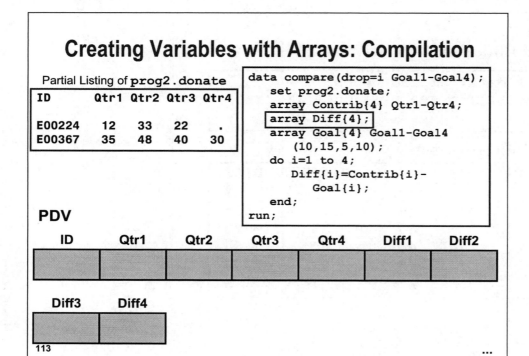

Creating Variables with Arrays: Compilation

Partial Listing of `prog2.donate`

ID	Qtr1	Qtr2	Qtr3	Qtr4
E00224	12	33	22	.
E00367	35	48	40	30

```
data compare(drop=i Goal1-Goal4);
   set prog2.donate;
   array Contrib{4} Qtr1-Qtr4;
   array Diff{4};
   array Goal{4} Goal1-Goal4
      (10,15,5,10);
   do i=1 to 4;
      Diff{i}=Contrib{i}-
         Goal{i};
   end;
run;
```

PDV

ID	Qtr1	Qtr2	Qtr3	Qtr4	Diff1	Diff2

Diff3	Diff4

113   ...

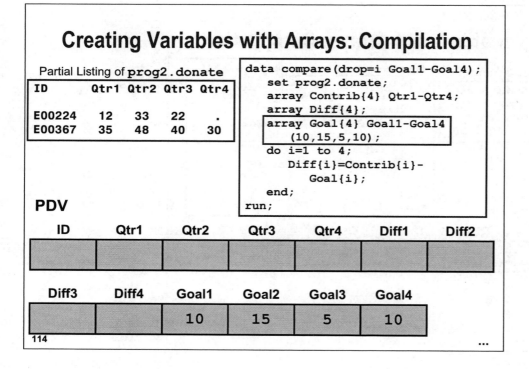

Creating Variables with Arrays: Compilation

Partial Listing of `prog2.donate`

ID	Qtr1	Qtr2	Qtr3	Qtr4
E00224	12	33	22	.
E00367	35	48	40	30

```
data compare(drop=i Goal1-Goal4);
   set prog2.donate;
   array Contrib{4} Qtr1-Qtr4;
   array Diff{4};
   array Goal{4} Goal1-Goal4
      (10,15,5,10);
   do i=1 to 4;
      Diff{i}=Contrib{i}-
         Goal{i};
   end;
run;
```

PDV

ID	Qtr1	Qtr2	Qtr3	Qtr4	Diff1	Diff2

Diff3	Diff4	Goal1	Goal2	Goal3	Goal4
		10	15	5	10

114   ...

Creating Variables with Arrays: Compilation

Partial Listing of `prog2.donate`

ID	Qtr1	Qtr2	Qtr3	Qtr4
E00224	12	33	22	.
E00367	35	48	40	30

```
data compare(drop=i Goal1-Goal4);
   set prog2.donate;
   array Contrib{4} Qtr1-Qtr4;
   array Diff{4};
   array Goal{4} Goal1-Goal4
       (10,15,5,10);
   do i=1 to 4;
       Diff{i}=Contrib{i}-
           Goal{i};
   end;
run;
```

PDV

ID	Qtr1	Qtr2	Qtr3	Qtr4	Diff1	Diff2

Diff3	Diff4	Goal1	Goal2	Goal3	Goal4	i
		10	15	5	10	

115   ...

Creating Variables with Arrays: Compilation

Partial Listing of `prog2.donate`

ID	Qtr1	Qtr2	Qtr3	Qtr4
E00224	12	33	22	.
E00367	35	48	40	30

```
data compare(drop=i Goal1-Goal4);
   set prog2.donate;
   array Contrib{4} Qtr1-Qtr4;
   array Diff{4};
   array Goal{4} Goal1-Goal4
       (10,15,5,10);
   do i=1 to 4;
       Diff{i}=Contrib{i}-
           Goal{i};
   end;
run;
```

PDV

ID	Qtr1	Qtr2	Qtr3	Qtr4	Diff1	Diff2

Diff3	Diff4	Goal1	Goal2	Goal3	Goal4	i
		10	15	5	10	

116

Performing a Table Lookup

You can use the keyword _TEMPORARY_ instead of
specifying variable names when you create an array
to define temporary array elements.

```
data compare(drop=i);
   set prog2.donate;
   array Contrib{4} Qtr1-Qtr4;
   array Diff{4};
   array Goal{4} _temporary_ (10,15,5,10);
   do i=1 to 4;
      Diff{i}=Contrib{i}-Goal{i};
   end;
run;
```

117   c07s3d3.sas

Arrays of temporary elements are useful when the only purpose for creating an array is to perform
a calculation. To preserve the result of the calculation, assign it to a variable.

    Temporary data elements do not appear in the output data set.

Temporary data element values are always automatically retained.

Performing a Table Lookup

```
proc print data=compare noobs;
   var ID Diff1 Diff2 Diff3 Diff4;
run;
```

Partial PROC PRINT Output

ID	Diff1	Diff2	Diff3	Diff4
E00224	2	18	17	.
E00367	25	33	35	20
E00441	.	48	84	80
E00587	6	4	25	19
E00598	-6	-7	1	-9

118

Rotating a SAS Data Set

Rotating, or transposing, a SAS data set can be accomplished by using array processing. When a data set is rotated, the values of an observation in the input data set become values of a variable in the output data set.

Partial Listing of `prog2.donate`

ID	Qtr1	Qtr2	Qtr3	Qtr4
E00224	12	33	22	.
E00367	35	48	40	30

119

The TRANSPOSE procedure is also used to create an output data set by restructuring the values in a SAS data set, transposing selected variables into observations.

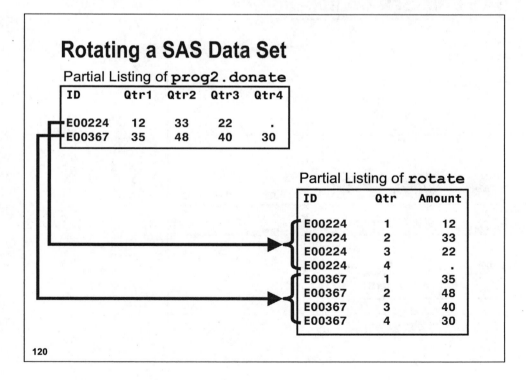

Rotating a SAS Data Set

Partial Listing of `prog2.donate`

ID	Qtr1	Qtr2	Qtr3	Qtr4
E00224	12	33	22	.
E00367	35	48	40	30

Partial Listing of `rotate`

ID	Qtr	Amount
E00224	1	12
E00224	2	33
E00224	3	22
E00224	4	.
E00367	1	35
E00367	2	48
E00367	3	40
E00367	4	30

120

Rotating a SAS Data Set

```
data rotate(drop=Qtr1-Qtr4);
    set prog2.donate;
    array Contrib{4} Qtr1-Qtr4;
    do Qtr=1 to 4;
        Amount=Contrib{Qtr};
        output;
    end;
run;
```

c07s3d4.sas

121

Rotating a SAS Data Set: Compilation

```
data rotate(drop=Qtr1-Qtr4);
    set prog2.donate;
    array Contrib{4} Qtr1-Qtr4;
    do Qtr=1 to 4;
        Amount=Contrib{Qtr};
        output;
    end;
run;
```

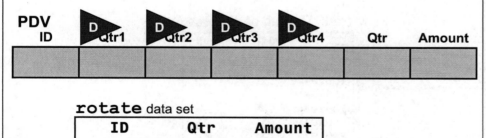

PDV

ID	D Qtr1	D Qtr2	D Qtr3	D Qtr4	Qtr	Amount

rotate data set

ID	Qtr	Amount

122

...

Rotating a SAS Data Set: Execution

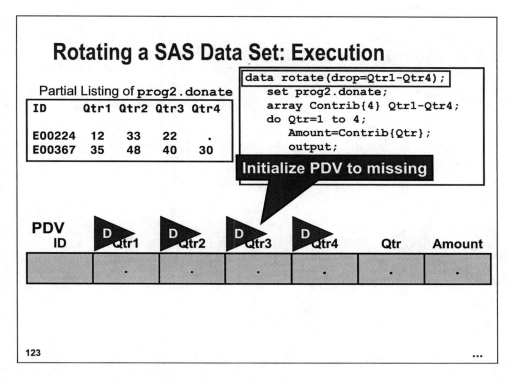

Partial Listing of `prog2.donate`

ID	Qtr1	Qtr2	Qtr3	Qtr4
E00224	12	33	22	.
E00367	35	48	40	30

```
data rotate(drop=Qtr1-Qtr4);
   set prog2.donate;
   array Contrib{4} Qtr1-Qtr4;
   do Qtr=1 to 4;
      Amount=Contrib{Qtr};
      output;
```

Initialize PDV to missing

PDV ID	D Qtr1	D Qtr2	D Qtr3	D Qtr4	Qtr	Amount
	.	.	.	.	.	.

123

...

Rotating a SAS Data Set: Execution

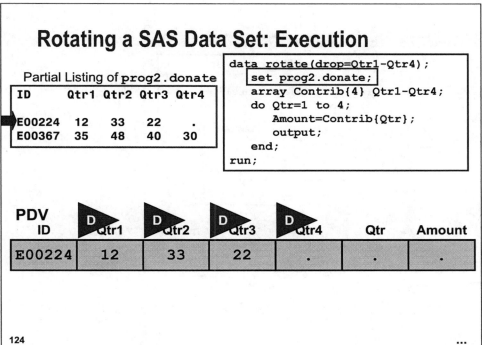

Partial Listing of `prog2.donate`

ID	Qtr1	Qtr2	Qtr3	Qtr4
E00224	12	33	22	.
E00367	35	48	40	30

```
data rotate(drop=Qtr1-Qtr4);
   set prog2.donate;
   array Contrib{4} Qtr1-Qtr4;
   do Qtr=1 to 4;
      Amount=Contrib{Qtr};
      output;
   end;
run;
```

PDV ID	D Qtr1	D Qtr2	D Qtr3	D Qtr4	Qtr	Amount
E00224	12	33	22	.	.	.

124

...

Rotating a SAS Data Set: Execution

Partial Listing of `prog2.donate`

ID	Qtr1	Qtr2	Qtr3	Qtr4
E00224	12	33	22	.
E00367	35	48	40	30

```
data rotate(drop=Qtr1-Qtr4);
  set prog2.donate;
  array Contrib{4} Qtr1-Qtr4;
  do Qtr=1 to 4;
    Amount=Contrib{Qtr};
    output;
  end;
run;
```

PDV

ID	D Qtr1	D Qtr2	D Qtr3	D Qtr4	Qtr	Amount
E00224	12	33	22	.	1	.

125   ...

Rotating a SAS Data Set: Execution

Partial Listing of `prog2.donate`

ID	Qtr1	Qtr2	Qtr3	Qtr4
E00224	12	33	22	.
E00367	35	48	40	30

```
data rotate(drop=Qtr1-Qtr4);
  set prog2.donate;
  array Contrib{4} Qtr1-Qtr4;
  do Qtr=1 to 4;
    Amount=Contrib{Qtr};
    output;
  end;
run;
```

`Amount=Contrib{1};`

PDV

ID	D Qtr1	D Qtr2	D Qtr3	D Qtr4	Qtr	Amount
E00224	12	33	22	.	1	12

126   ...

Rotating a SAS Data Set: Execution

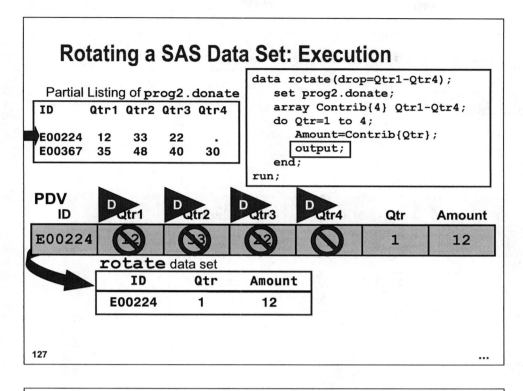

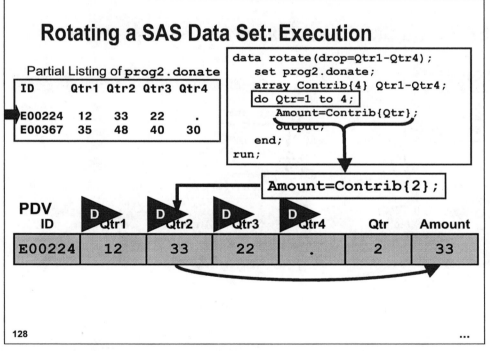

127

128

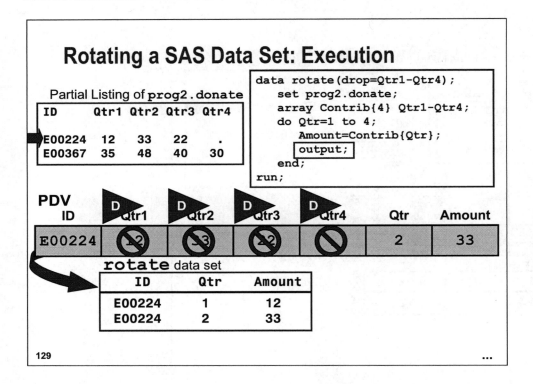

Rotating a SAS Data Set: Execution

Partial Listing of `prog2.donate`

ID	Qtr1	Qtr2	Qtr3	Qtr4
E00224	12	33	22	.
E00367	35	48	40	30

```
data rotate(drop=Qtr1-Qtr4);
   set prog2.donate;
   array Contrib{4} Qtr1-Qtr4;
   do Qtr=1 to 4;
      Amount=Contrib{Qtr};
      output;
   end;
run;
```

PDV

ID	Qtr1	Qtr2	Qtr3	Qtr4	Qtr	Amount
E00224	12	33	22		2	33

`rotate` data set

ID	Qtr	Amount
E00224	1	12
E00224	2	33

129   ...

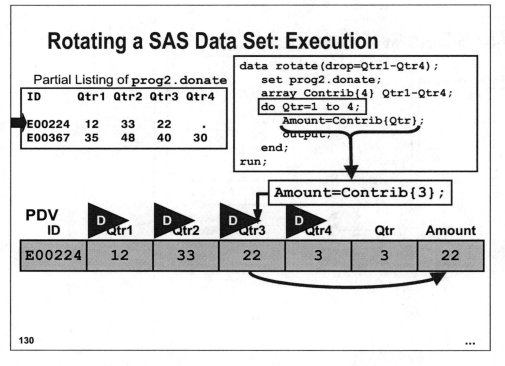

Rotating a SAS Data Set: Execution

Partial Listing of `prog2.donate`

ID	Qtr1	Qtr2	Qtr3	Qtr4
E00224	12	33	22	.
E00367	35	48	40	30

```
data rotate(drop=Qtr1-Qtr4);
   set prog2.donate;
   array Contrib{4} Qtr1-Qtr4;
   do Qtr=1 to 4;
      Amount=Contrib{Qtr};
      output;
   end;
run;
```

`Amount=Contrib{3};`

PDV

ID	Qtr1	Qtr2	Qtr3	Qtr4	Qtr	Amount
E00224	12	33	22	3	3	22

130   ...

Rotating a SAS Data Set: Execution

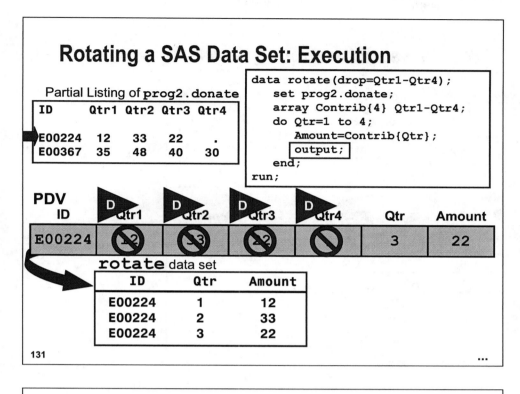

Partial Listing of `prog2.donate`

ID	Qtr1	Qtr2	Qtr3	Qtr4
E00224	12	33	22	.
E00367	35	48	40	30

```
data rotate(drop=Qtr1-Qtr4);
   set prog2.donate;
   array Contrib{4} Qtr1-Qtr4;
   do Qtr=1 to 4;
      Amount=Contrib{Qtr};
      output;
   end;
run;
```

PDV

ID	D Qtr1	D Qtr2	D Qtr3	D Qtr4	Qtr	Amount
E00224	12	33	22		3	22

rotate data set

ID	Qtr	Amount
E00224	1	12
E00224	2	33
E00224	3	22

131

Rotating a SAS Data Set: Execution

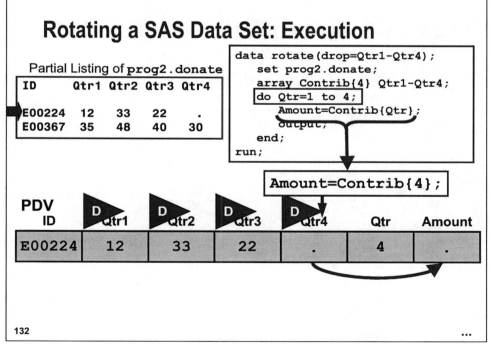

Partial Listing of `prog2.donate`

ID	Qtr1	Qtr2	Qtr3	Qtr4
E00224	12	33	22	.
E00367	35	48	40	30

```
data rotate(drop=Qtr1-Qtr4);
   set prog2.donate;
   array Contrib{4} Qtr1-Qtr4;
   do Qtr=1 to 4;
      Amount=Contrib{Qtr};
      output;
   end;
run;
```

`Amount=Contrib{4};`

PDV

ID	D Qtr1	D Qtr2	D Qtr3	D Qtr4	Qtr	Amount
E00224	12	33	22	.	4	.

132

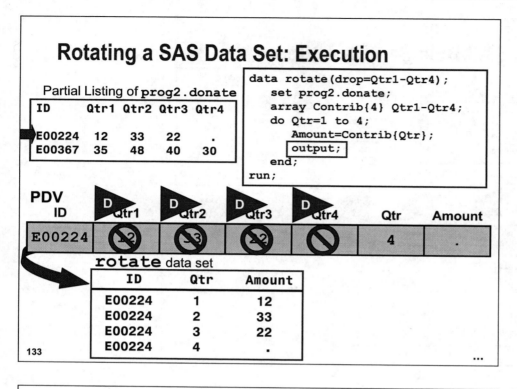

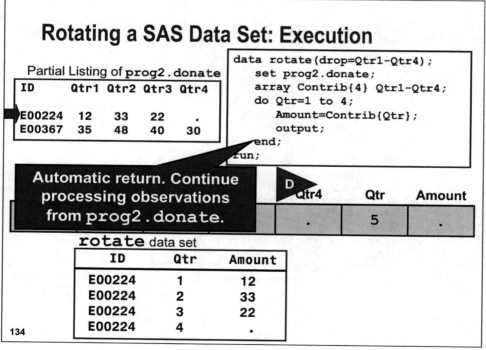

Rotating a SAS Data Set

```
proc print data=rotate noobs;
run;
```

Partial PROC PRINT Output

ID	Qtr	Amount
E00224	1	12
E00224	2	33
E00224	3	22
E00224	4	.
E00367	1	35
E00367	2	48
E00367	3	40
E00367	4	30

135

Exercises

3. Using Arrays to Create Variables

Write a DATA step that reads the SAS data set **prog2.donate** and creates a SAS data set named **quarter**. Calculate the average contribution for an employee across all four quarters, and then calculate the difference between each quarterly contribution and the average. Use arrays to help perform the calculation.

Partial Listing of **prog2.donate**

ID	Qtr1	Qtr2	Qtr3	Qtr4
E00224	12	33	22	.
E00367	35	48	40	30
E00441	.	63	89	90
E00587	16	19	30	29
E00598	4	8	6	1

Print the data set. The desired report is shown below.

Partial PROC PRINT Output

Obs	ID	Average	Diff1	Diff2	Diff3	Diff4
1	E00224	22.3333	-10.3333	10.6667	-0.3333	.
2	E00367	38.2500	-3.2500	9.7500	1.7500	-8.2500
3	E00441	80.6667	.	-17.6667	8.3333	9.3333
4	E00587	23.5000	-7.5000	-4.5000	6.5000	5.5000
5	E00598	4.7500	-0.7500	3.2500	1.2500	-3.7500

4. Using Arrays for Table Lookup (Optional)

A driver's license renewal test consists of ten multiple-choice questions. Each question has five choices (A-E). Each day, all test results are entered into the SAS data set **prog2.testans** shown below. Each observation in **prog2.testans** contains a single person's answers.

Listing of **prog2.testans**

ID	Q1	Q2	Q3	Q4	Q5	Q6	Q7	Q8	Q9	Q10
291192	A	C	C	B	D	E	D	B	B	A
593137	B	C	C		E	E	D	B	A	A
721311	A	C	C	B	D	D	E	B	B	C
345221	B	C	C	A	D	B	B	C	A	D
193920	A	C	C	B	E	E	D	B	B	A
257672	B	C	C	B	D	D	D	B	B	A
357899	C	C	C	B	E	E	E	B	B	A
564332	A	C	C	B	E	E	D	B	B	A
111033		A	C	B	D	D	D	B	B	A
445732	C	C	C	C	E	E	D	B	B	B
824610	B	B	E	B	E	E	D	B	B	A
774235	A	C	C	B	E	E	D	B	B	A
943244	C	C	C	B	E	E	D	B	B	A
647893	A	C	C	B	E	E	E	B	B	A
432118	A	C	C	B	E	E	D	B	B	A

The correct answers for the questions are shown below:

Question:	1	2	3	4	5	6	7	8	9	10
Answer:	A	C	C	B	E	E	D	B	B	A

Read **prog2.testans** and determine whether each person passed or failed the test. Compute a variable **score** that contains the total correct answers for each person.

 Create a temporary array for the answer key.

If a person scores 7 or higher, write the observation to a data set named **passed**. Print the data set to verify that there are 12 observations in **passed**.

PROC PRINT Output

Obs	ID	Q1	Q2	Q3	Q4	Q5	Q6	Q7	Q8	Q9	Q10	Score
1	291192	A	C	C	B	D	E	D	B	B	A	9
2	593137	B	C	C		E	E	D	B	A	A	7
3	193920	A	C	C	B	E	E	D	B	B	A	10
4	257672	B	C	C	B	D	D	D	B	B	A	7
5	357899	C	C	C	B	E	E	E	B	B	A	8
6	564332	A	C	C	B	E	E	D	B	B	A	10
7	445732	C	C	C	C	E	E	D	B	B	B	7
8	824610	B	B	E	B	E	E	D	B	B	A	7
9	774235	A	C	C	B	E	E	D	B	B	A	10
10	943244	C	C	C	B	E	E	D	B	B	A	9
11	647893	A	C	C	B	E	E	E	B	B	A	9
12	432118	A	C	C	B	E	E	D	B	B	A	10

If a person scores less than 7, write the observation to a data set named **failed**. Print the data set to verify that there are three observations in **failed**.

PROC PRINT Output

Obs	ID	Q1	Q2	Q3	Q4	Q5	Q6	Q7	Q8	Q9	Q10	Score
1	721311	A	C	C	B	D	D	E	B	B	C	6
2	345221	B	C	C	A	D	B	B	C	A	D	2
3	111033		A	C	B	D	D	D	B	B	A	6

7.4 Solutions to Exercises

1. Performing Computations with DO Loops

a.

```
data future;
   Wages=12874000;
   Retire=1765000;
   Medical=649000;
   Year=year(today());
   do until(Year=year(today())+10);
      Year+1;

   /* If a DO UNTIL statement is used, you must
      remember to increment the value of Year. */

      Wages+(Wages*.06);
      Retire+(Retire*.014);
      Medical+(Medical*.095);
      output;
   end;
run;

proc print data=future;
   var Year Wages Retire Medical;
run;
```

Alternate solution:

```
data future;
   Wages=12874000;
   Retire=1765000;
   Medical=649000;
   do Year=year(today())+1 to year(today())+10;
      Wages+(Wages*.06);
      Retire+(Retire*.014);
      Medical+(Medical*.095);
      output;
   end;
run;

proc print data=future;
   var Year Wages Retire Medical;
run;
```

b.

```
data future;
   Wages=12874000;
   Retire=1765000;
   Medical=649000;
   Year=year(today());
   do until(Year=year(today())+10);
      Year+1;

   /* If a DO UNTIL statement is used, you must
      remember to increment the value of Year. */

      Wages+(Wages*.06);
      Retire+(Retire*.014);
      Medical+(Medical*.095);
      TotCost=sum(Wages,Retire,Medical);
      output;
   end;
run;

proc print data=future;
   var Year Wages Retire Medical TotCost;
run;
```

Alternate solution:

```
data future;
   Wages=12874000;
   Retire=1765000;
   Medical=649000;
   do Year=year(today())+1 to year(today())+10;
      Wages+(Wages*.06);
      Retire+(Retire*.014);
      Medical+(Medical*.095);
      TotCost=sum(Wages,Retire,Medical);
      output;
   end;
run;

proc print data=future;
   var Year Wages Retire Medical TotCost;
run;
```

c.

```
data future;
   Year=year(today());
   Wages=12874000;
   Retire=1765000;
   Medical=649000;
   Income=50000000;
   do until(TotCost gt Income);
      Wages+(Wages*.06);
      Retire+(Retire*.014);
      Medical+(Medical*.095);
      TotCost=sum(Wages,Retire,Medical);
      Income+(Income*.01);
      Year+1;
      output;
   end;
run;

proc print data=future;
   var Year Income TotCost;
run;
```

2. **Using Arrays for Repetitive Computations**

```
data celsius(drop=i);
   set prog2.ski;

   /* You must reset cost to zero every time an
      observation from prog2.ski is read. */

   Cost=0;
   array Temps{24} T1-T24;
   do i=1 to 24;
      Temps{i}=round(5*(Temps{i}-32)/9,.1);
      if Temps{i} lt 2 then
         Cost+125;
   end;
run;

proc print data=celsius;
run;
```

3. Using Arrays to Create Variables

```
data quarter(drop=Qtr);
   set prog2.donate;

   /* Two ARRAY statements are necessary. The first
      ARRAY statement creates a SAS array that
      contains the four quarterly contributions.
      The second ARRAY statement creates a SAS array
      that contains the four differences that will be
      calculated during the DATA step. */

   array Contrib{4} Qtr1-Qtr4;
   array Diff{4};

   Average=mean(of Qtr1-Qtr4);
   do Qtr=1 to 4;
      Diff{Qtr}=Contrib{Qtr}-Average;
   end;
run;

proc print data=quarter;
   var ID Average Diff1-Diff4;
run;
```

4. **Using Arrays for Table Lookup (Optional)**

```
data passed(drop=i) failed(drop=i);
   set prog2.testans;

   /* Two ARRAY statements are necessary. The first
      ARRAY statement creates a SAS array that
      contains the ten responses each test-taker
      selected. The second ARRAY statement creates a
      SAS array that contains the ten correct answers
      for each of the ten questions. */

   array Response{10} Q1-Q10;
   array Answer{10} $ 1 _temporary_ ('A','C','C','B','E',
                                     'E','D','B','B','A');
   Score=0;
   do i=1 to 10;
      if Answer{i}=Response{i} then Score+1;
   end;
   if Score ge 7 then output passed;
   else output failed;
run;

proc print data=passed;
run;

proc print data=failed;
run;
```

Chapter 8 Combining SAS® Data Sets

8.1 Match-Merging Two or More SAS Data Sets

Objectives

- Perform a match-merge.
- Perform explicit output for matching and non-matching observations.

3

Merging Data Sets

A merge combines two or more existing data sets by joining observations side-by-side.

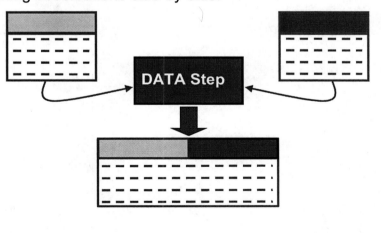

4

Match-Merge

The most common type of merge is a match-merge, which uses a common variable to join observations.

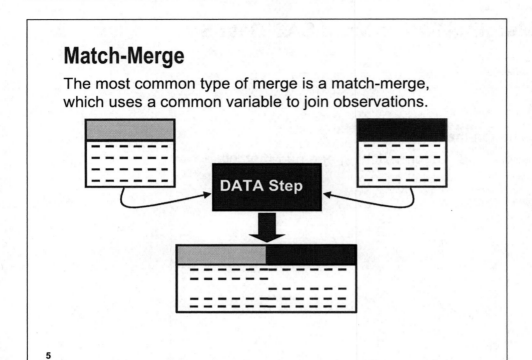

5

Match-Merging

When you match-merge two or more data sets, it is common to have

- repeated BY values
- non-matches.

6

Match-Merging

The data set **prog2.transact** contains an account number and information on transactions for a week. The data set **prog2.branches** contains an account number and the branch location for that account.

Act Num	Trans	Amnt
56891	D	126.32
56891	C	560
57900	C	235
58876	D	14.56
59987	C	371.69

Act Num	Branch
56891	N. Lincoln
56900	S. Cicero
58876	W. Argyle
59900	N. Damen
59987	E. Wacker

7

Desired Output

The bank manager wants to see reports based on three data sets.

Goal: A data set named **newtrans** that shows this week's transactions.

Act Num	Trans	Amnt	Branch
56891	D	126.32	N. Lincoln
56891	C	560	N. Lincoln
58876	D	14.56	W. Argyle
59987	C	371.69	E. Wacker

8

Desired Output

Goal: A data set named **noactiv** that shows accounts
with no transactions this week.

```
Act
Num        Branch

56900      S. Cicero
59900      N. Damen
```

9

Desired Output

Goal: A data set named **noacct** that shows
transactions with no matching account number.

```
Act
Num        Trans         Amnt

57900        C            235
```

10

The MERGE Statement

You can use the MERGE statement to combine observations from two or more SAS data sets.

General form of the MERGE statement with a BY statement:

```
DATA SAS-data-set ... ;
    MERGE SAS-data-set-1 SAS-data-set-2 ...;
    BY BY-variable-1 ...;
    <additional SAS statements>
RUN;
```

11

There is no limit on the number of data sets that can be merged in one DATA step.

The SORT Procedure (Review)

When you use the BY statement with a MERGE statement, the data set must be sorted or indexed according to the BY variable(s).

You can use the SORT procedure to sort the data.

General form of a PROC SORT step:

```
PROC SORT DATA=SAS-data-set1
            <OUT=SAS-data-set2>;
    BY <DESCENDING> BY-variable ...;
RUN;
```

12

If you merge a SAS data set with a DBMS table from another database, the DBMS table does not have to be sorted.

DATA Step Merge

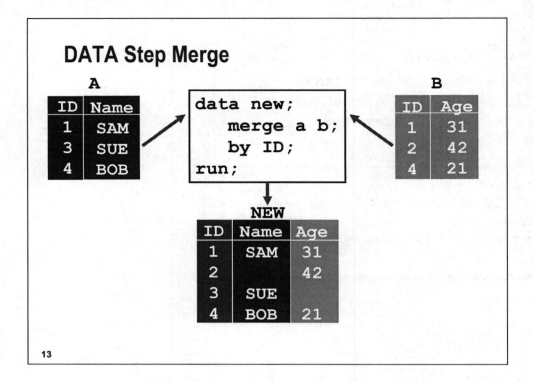

A

ID	Name
1	SAM
3	SUE
4	BOB

```
data new;
   merge a b;
   by ID;
run;
```

B

ID	Age
1	31
2	42
4	21

NEW

ID	Name	Age
1	SAM	31
2		42
3	SUE	
4	BOB	21

13

Identifying Data Set Contributors

When you read multiple SAS data sets in one DATA step, you can use the IN= data set option to detect which data set contributed to an observation.

General form of the IN= data set option:

> *SAS-data-set*(IN=*variable*)

where *variable* is any valid SAS variable name.

14

The IN= Data Set Option

variable   is a temporary numeric variable with
a value of

    0   to indicate false; the data set did **not**
contribute to the current observation

    1   to indicate true; the data set **did**
contribute to the current observation.

Variables created using IN= are automatically dropped
from the output data set.

15.

Using the IN= Data Set Option

```
data newtrans
     noactiv (drop=Trans Amnt)
     noacct  (drop=Branch);
   merge prog2.transact(in=InTrans)
         prog2.branches(in=InBanks);
   by ActNum;
   <additional SAS statements>
run;
```

16

If the Observation Is a Match

prog2.transact and **prog2.branches** both contributed to the observation.

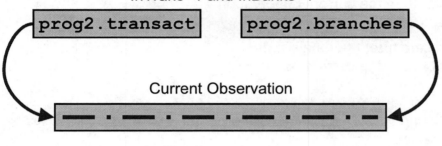

17

If the Observation Is Not a Match

prog2.branches contributed to the observation.
prog2.transact did not. (The account had no transactions this week.)

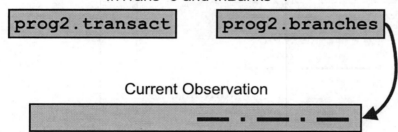

18

If the Observation Is Not a Match

`prog2.transact` contributed to the observation.
`prog2.branches` did not. (A transaction occurred,
but the account number was invalid.)

InTrans=1 and InBanks=0

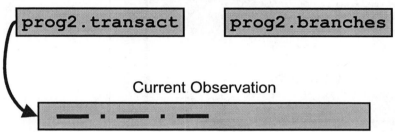

Current Observation

19

Using IN= to Identify Matches and Non-Matches

```
data newtrans
     noactiv (drop=Trans Amnt)
     noacct  (drop=Branch);
   merge prog2.transact(in=InTrans)
         prog2.branches(in=InBanks);
   by ActNum;
   if InTrans and InBanks
      then output newtrans;
   else if InBanks and not InTrans
      then output noactiv;
   else if InTrans and not InBanks
      then output noacct;
run;
```

c08s1d1.sas

20

Identifying Data Set Contributors: Compilation

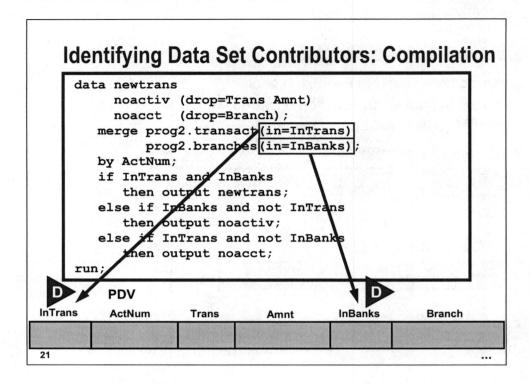

```
data newtrans
    noactiv (drop=Trans Amnt)
    noacct  (drop=Branch);
    merge prog2.transact(in=InTrans)
        prog2.branches(in=InBanks);
    by ActNum;
    if InTrans and InBanks
        then output newtrans;
    else if InBanks and not InTrans
        then output noactiv;
    else if InTrans and not InBanks
        then output noacct;
run;
```

D   **PDV**

InTrans	ActNum	Trans	Amnt	InBanks	Branch

21

Identifying Data Set Contributors: Execution

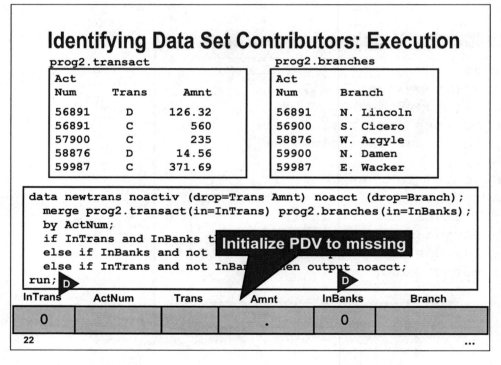

`prog2.transact`

Act Num	Trans	Amnt
56891	D	126.32
56891	C	560
57900	C	235
58876	D	14.56
59987	C	371.69

`prog2.branches`

Act Num	Branch
56891	N. Lincoln
56900	S. Cicero
58876	W. Argyle
59900	N. Damen
59987	E. Wacker

```
data newtrans noactiv (drop=Trans Amnt) noacct (drop=Branch);
  merge prog2.transact(in=InTrans) prog2.branches(in=InBanks);
  by ActNum;
  if InTrans and InBanks t
  else if InBanks and not
  else if InTrans and not InBa        en output noacct;
run;
```

Initialize PDV to missing

InTrans	ActNum	Trans	Amnt	InBanks	Branch
0			.	0	

22

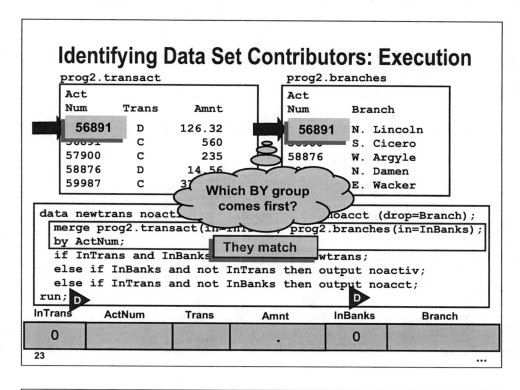

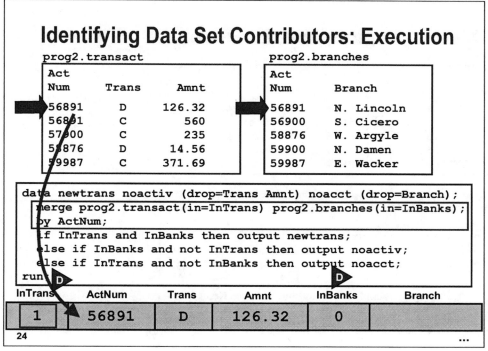

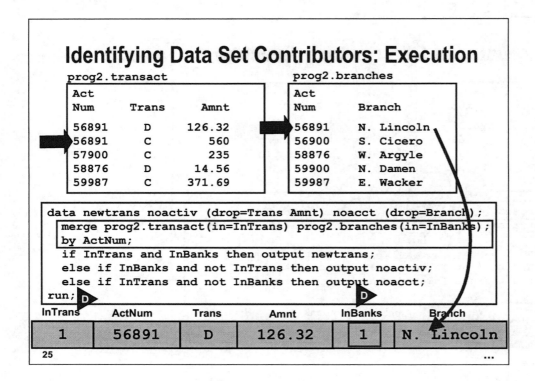

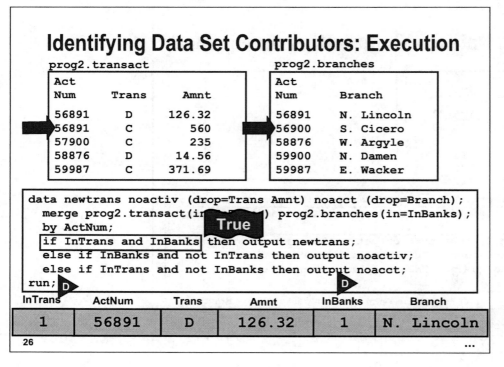

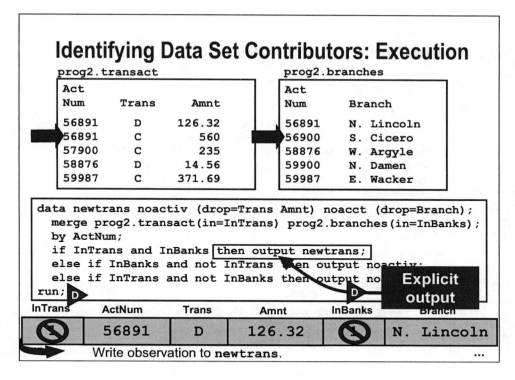

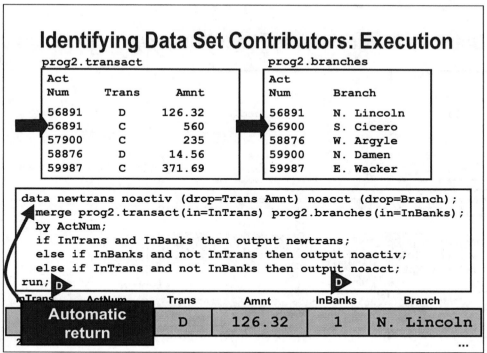

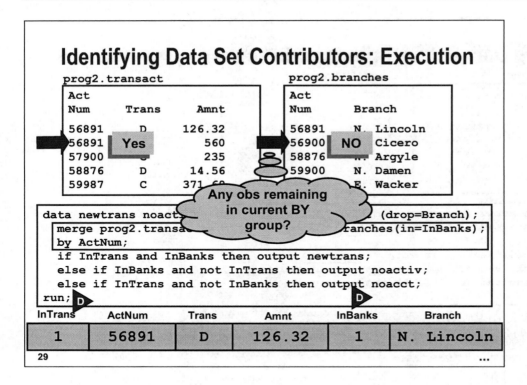

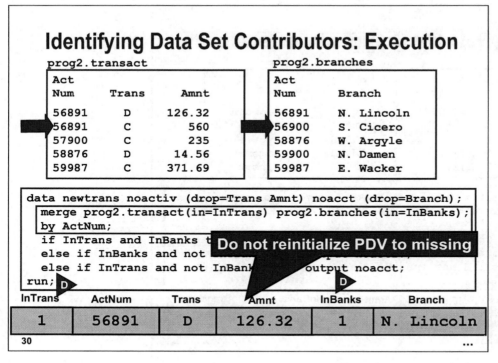

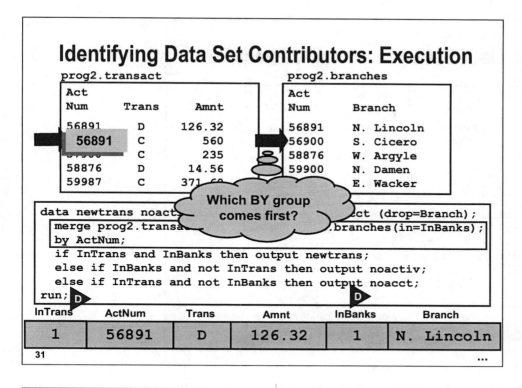

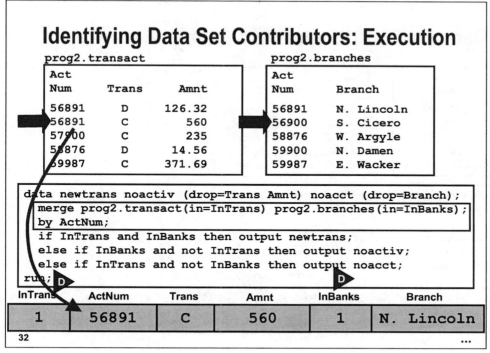

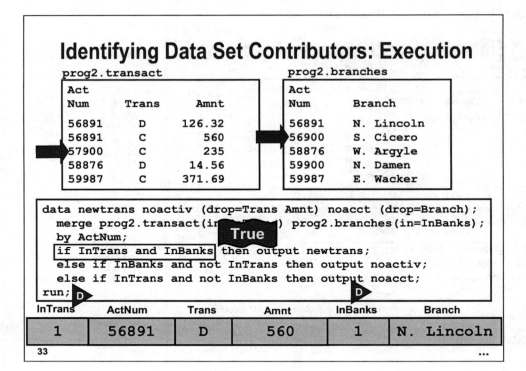

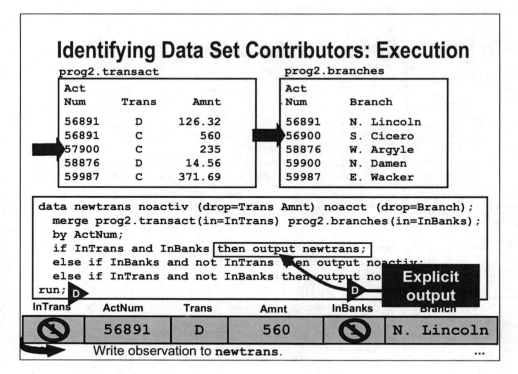

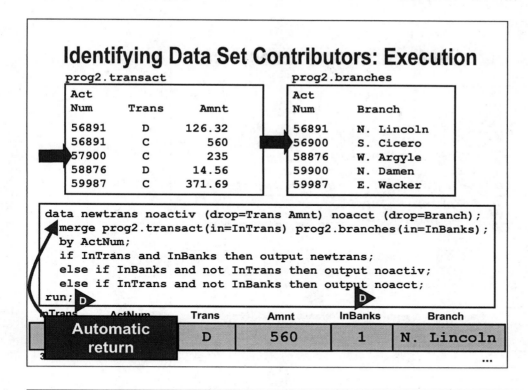

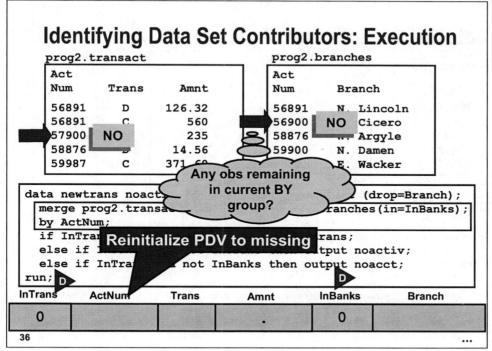

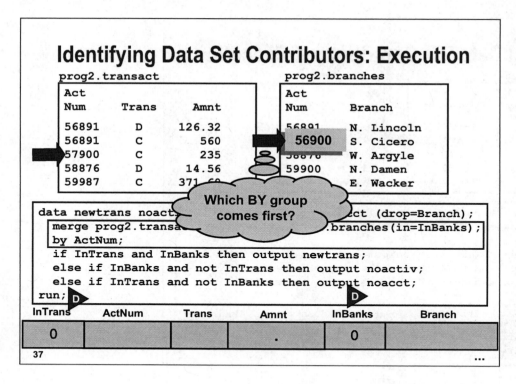

Identifying Data Set Contributors: Execution

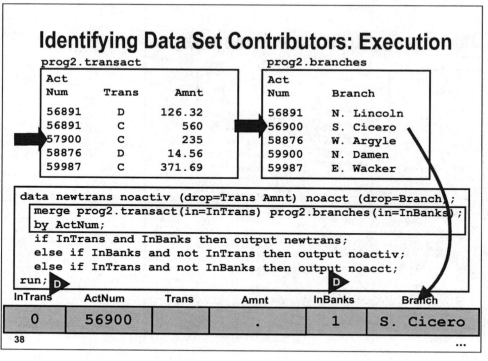

Identifying Data Set Contributors: Execution

prog2.transact

Act Num	Trans	Amnt
56891	D	126.32
56891	C	560
57900	C	235
58876	D	14.56
59987	C	371.69

prog2.branches

Act Num	Branch
56891	N. Lincoln
56900	S. Cicero
58876	W. Argyle
59900	N. Damen
59987	E. Wacker

```
data newtrans noactiv (drop=Trans Amnt) noacct (drop=Branch);
  merge prog2.transact(in=InTrans) prog2.branches(in=InBanks);
  by ActNum;
  if InTrans and InBanks then output newtrans;
  else if InBanks and not InTrans then output noactiv;
  else if InTrans and not InBanks then output noacct;
run;
```

InTrans	ActNum	Trans	Amnt	InBanks	Branch
0	56900		.	1	S. Cicero

38

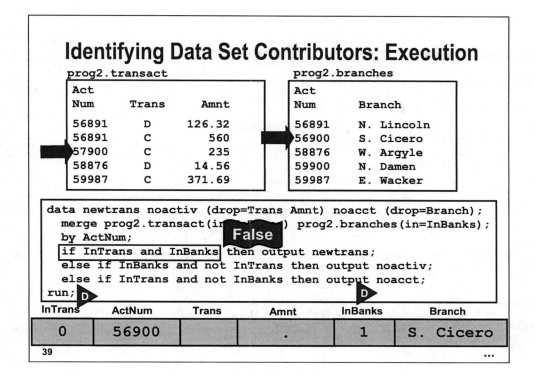

Identifying Data Set Contributors: Execution

prog2.transact

Act Num	Trans	Amnt
56891	D	126.32
56891	C	560
57900	C	235
58876	D	14.56
59987	C	371.69

prog2.branches

Act Num	Branch
56891	N. Lincoln
56900	S. Cicero
58876	W. Argyle
59900	N. Damen
59987	E. Wacker

```
data newtrans noactiv (drop=Trans Amnt) noacct (drop=Branch);
  merge prog2.transact(in=       ) prog2.branches(in=InBanks);
  by ActNum;
  if InTrans and InBanks then output newtrans;
  else if InBanks and not InTrans then output noactiv;
  else if InTrans and not InBanks then output noacct;
run;
```

False

InTrans	ActNum	Trans	Amnt	InBanks	Branch
0	56900		.	1	S. Cicero

39   ...

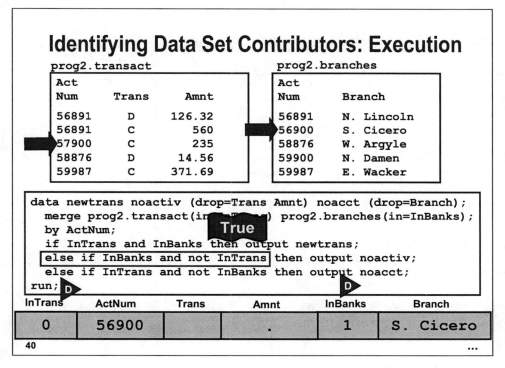

Identifying Data Set Contributors: Execution

prog2.transact

Act Num	Trans	Amnt
56891	D	126.32
56891	C	560
57900	C	235
58876	D	14.56
59987	C	371.69

prog2.branches

Act Num	Branch
56891	N. Lincoln
56900	S. Cicero
58876	W. Argyle
59900	N. Damen
59987	E. Wacker

```
data newtrans noactiv (drop=Trans Amnt) noacct (drop=Branch);
  merge prog2.transact(in=       ) prog2.branches(in=InBanks);
  by ActNum;
  if InTrans and InBanks then output newtrans;
  else if InBanks and not InTrans then output noactiv;
  else if InTrans and not InBanks then output noacct;
run;
```

True

InTrans	ActNum	Trans	Amnt	InBanks	Branch
0	56900		.	1	S. Cicero

40   ...

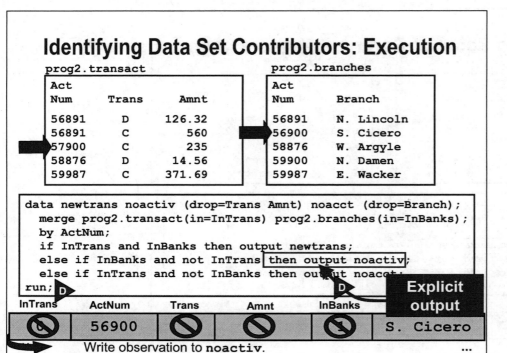

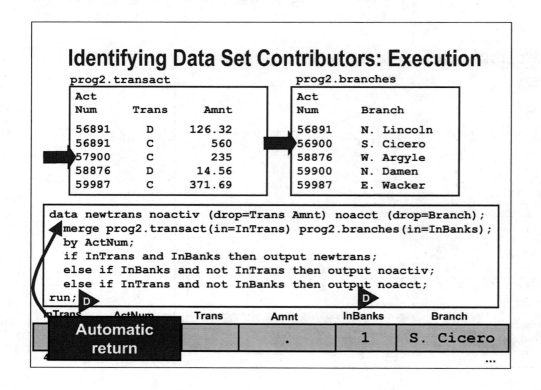

Identifying Data Set Contributors: Execution

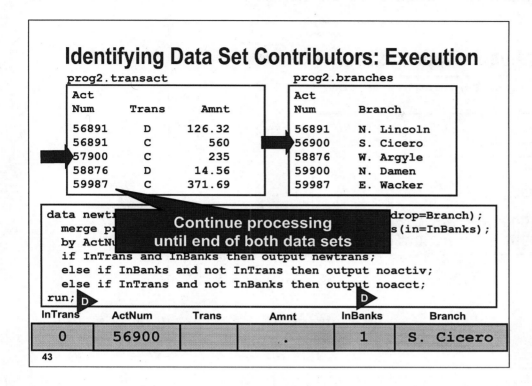

```
prog2.transact
Act
Num      Trans       Amnt
56891    D           126.32
56891    C           560
57900    C           235
58876    D           14.56
59987    C           371.69
```

```
prog2.branches
Act
Num      Branch
56891    N. Lincoln
56900    S. Cicero
58876    W. Argyle
59900    N. Damen
59987    E. Wacker
```

```
data newt                                    drop=Branch);
  merge p                                     s(in=InBanks);
  by ActN
  if InTrans and InBanks then output newtrans;
  else if InBanks and not InTrans then output noactiv;
  else if InTrans and not InBanks then output noacct;
run;
```

Continue processing until end of both data sets

InTrans	ActNum	Trans	Amnt	InBanks	Branch
0	56900		.	1	S. Cicero

43

Viewing Only the Matches

```
proc print data=newtrans noobs;
run;
```

PROC PRINT Output

Act Num	Trans	Amnt	Branch
56891	D	126.32	N. Lincoln
56891	C	560	N. Lincoln
58876	D	14.56	W. Argyle
59987	C	371.69	E. Wacker

44

Non-Matches from prog2.branches

```
proc print data=noactiv noobs;
run;
```

PROC PRINT Output

Act Num	Branch
56900	S. Cicero
59900	N. Damen

45

Non-Matches from prog2.transact

```
proc print data=noacct noobs;
run;
```

PROC PRINT Output

Act Num	Trans	Amnt
57900	C	235

46

c08s1d1.sas

 **Exercises**

1. **Match-Merging Two Data Sets**

   The data set **prog2.prices** is a master data set containing a product code (**ProdCode**) and a unit price (**Price**) for each product sold by a particular company. The SAS data set **prog2.todaysales** contains a product code and quantity sold for each sale made on a given day.

   Partial Listing of **prog2.prices**

Prod Code	Price
17237	89.64
29978	114.47
10496	128.99
08849	12.23
33060	162.99
05846	107.74
27731	140.75
30967	38.73
16344	181.51
11220	160.49

   Partial Listing of **prog2.todaysales**

Prod Code	Qty
17237	5
15078	23
10496	15
33060	1
33060	23
33060	16
33060	30
05846	13
05846	13
05846	10

   The two data sets are not sorted.

Create **three** data sets:

- A data set named **revenue** that contains the product code (**ProdCode**), the price (**Price**), the quantity sold (**Qty**), and the revenue generated from each sale (**Revenue**). **Revenue** is a new variable that is equal to **Price*Qty**.

- A data set named **notsold** that contains the product code (**ProdCode**) and price (**Price**) for each product that was not sold.

- A data set named **invalidcode** that contains the product code (**ProdCode**) and quantity (**Qty**) for each observation in the **todaysales** data set that does not have a corresponding product code in the **prices** data set.

The data sets should contain 39, 7, and 4 observations, respectively.

Partial Listing of **revenue** Data Set (should have 39 observations)

Obs	Prod Code	Price	Qty	Revenue
1	05288	53.26	16	852.16
2	05288	53.26	19	1011.94
3	05846	107.74	13	1400.62
4	05846	107.74	13	1400.62
5	05846	107.74	10	1077.40
6	08766	40.96	13	532.48
7	10496	128.99	15	1934.85
8	11220	160.49	13	2086.37

Listing of **notsold** Data Set (should have 7 observations)

Obs	Prod Code	Price
1	04333	114.36
2	08849	12.23
3	11211	69.16
4	17183	164.82
5	29978	114.47
6	30339	31.74
7	30967	38.73

Listing of **invalidcode** Data Set (should have 4 observations)

Obs	Prod Code	Qty
1	11465	13
2	12556	7
3	15078	23
4	26278	10

8.2   Simple Joins Using the SQL Procedure (Self-Study)

Objectives

- Perform an inner join using the SQL procedure.

49

The SQL Procedure

The SQL procedure enables you to write ANSI standard SQL code within the SAS System and use it to process SAS tables.

50

 This section covers basic SQL syntax for an inner join. To learn more about the SQL procedure, see the SAS documentation. SAS Education also offers an SQL course titled SQL Processing with the SAS® System (http://www.sas.com/apps/wtraining2/coursedetails.jsp?course_code=sql&ctry=us).

PROC SQL versus the DATA Step: Benefits

The SQL procedure enables you to

- join tables and produce a report in one step without creating a SAS data set
- join tables without sorted data
- use complex matching criteria.

By default, PROC SQL returns a report, not a SAS data set.

51

PROC SQL versus the DATA Step: Costs

In general, the SQL procedure requires more CPU time
and memory than a DATA step merge.

52

Joining Two Tables with PROC SQL

Act Num	Trans	Amnt	Act Num	Branch
56891	D	126.32	56891	N. Lincoln
56891	C	560	56900	S. Cicero
57900	C	235	58876	W. Argyle
58876	D	14.56	59900	N. Damen
59987	C	371.69	59987	E. Wacker

The table **prog2.trans** contains an account number
and information on transactions for a week. The table
prog2.branches contains an account number and
the branch location for that account.

53

Desired Output

The bank manager wants to see only the accounts that have valid transactions (only rows with matching values of **ActNum**).

ActNum	Trans	Amnt	Branch
56891	D	126.32	N. Lincoln
56891	C	560	N. Lincoln
58876	D	14.56	W. Argyle
59987	C	371.69	E. Wacker

54

The SQL Procedure: Syntax Overview

The PROC SQL statement signals the start of the SQL procedure.

```
PROC SQL;
```

55

The SQL Procedure: Syntax Overview

The QUIT statement ends the SQL step.

56

The SQL Procedure: Syntax Overview

Statements within the SQL step (also called *queries*) are made of smaller building blocks called *clauses*.

The following clauses are discussed in this section:

- SELECT
- FROM
- WHERE

There is one semicolon at the end of each query, **not** at the end of each clause.

57

The SELECT Clause

The SELECT clause identifies columns to include in the query result or table.

> **SELECT** *var-1, var-2 ...*

Columns listed in the SELECT clause are separated by commas. There is no comma following the last variable in the list.

> **SELECT** *

To select all columns read, use an asterisk in place of the column names.

58

The FROM Clause

The FROM clause identifies the SAS table(s) from which to read.

> **FROM** *SAS-data-set ...*

59

Using PROC SQL to Join Tables

To join two or more SAS tables, list them in the FROM clause separated by commas.

General form of an SQL join:

```
PROC SQL;
    SELECT var-1, var-2...
        FROM SAS-data-set-1, SAS-data-set-2...
    ;
```

60

✎   You can use PROC SQL to join as many as 256 data sets.

SQL Joins without a WHERE Clause

An SQL join specified without a WHERE clause results in a Cartesian product. All possible combinations are output.

```
proc sql;
   select *
      from prog2.trans,
           prog2.branches
   ;
quit;
```

61

SQL Join without a WHERE Clause

Partial Output

Act Num	Trans	Amnt	Act Num	Branch
56891	D	126.32	56891	N. Lincoln
56891	D	126.32	56900	S. Cicero
56891	D	126.32	58876	W. Argyle
56891	D	126.32	59900	N. Damen
56891	D	126.32	59987	E. Wacker
56891	C	560	56891	N. Lincoln
56891	C	560	56900	S. Cicero
56891	C	560	58876	W. Argyle
56891	C	560	59900	N. Damen

62

The WHERE Clause

In a join, the WHERE clause specifies the join criteria,

    WHERE *expression*

where *expression* is any valid SAS condition.

63

Joining on a Common Variable

The join in the scenario requires only matching values
of **ActNum**.

ActNum from **prog2.branches** =
ActNum from **prog2.trans**

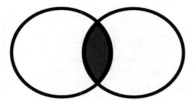

64

Identifying Variables with the Same Names

```
proc sql;
    select trans.ActNum, Trans,
           Amnt, Branch
        from prog2.trans, prog2.branches
        where trans.ActNum=branches.ActNum
    ;
quit;
```

You do not need to use the table name as a prefix
if the column name appears in only one table.

65

 Conceptually, SAS selects matching rows from the Cartesian product. However, when the code is actually processed, SAS uses the WHERE criteria to optimize the join.

Because the join outputs only rows where the values of **ActNum** match, you can select **ActNum** from either table.

```
proc sql;
    select Branches.ActNum, Trans, Amnt, Branch
        from prog2.trans, prog2.branches
        where trans.ActNum=branches.ActNum
    ;
quit;
```

Assigning an Alias for a SAS Table

You can also specify an alias for a SAS table. The alias replaces the table name as the column prefix.

> **FROM** *SAS-data-set-1 <AS> alias-1,*
> *SAS-data-set-2 <AS> alias-2 ...*

An alias can be any valid SAS name.

66

Assigning an Alias for a SAS Table

```
proc sql;
   select T.ActNum, Trans,
          Amnt, Branch
      from prog2.trans as T,
           prog2.branches as B
      where T.ActNum=B.ActNum
   ;
quit;
```

c08s2d1.sas

67

Usually, the table alias is used as a convenience. If you join two tables with the same table name but different library references, you **must** specify an alias.

Inner Join with PROC SQL

Act Num	Trans	Amnt	Branch
56891	D	126.32	N. Lincoln
56891	C	560	N. Lincoln
58876	D	14.56	W. Argyle
59987	C	371.69	E. Wacker

c08s2d1.sas

 **Exercises**

2. **Performing Simple Joins Using PROC SQL (Optional)**

The SAS table **prog2.rduschedule** has one row representing each time a flight attendant or pilot is scheduled to fly into RDU airport. It contains the flight number, the date of the flight, and the employee's identification number.

Partial Listing of **prog2.rduschedule**

FltID	SchDate	EmpID
IA03600	03JAN2000	E00075
IA03600	03JAN2000	E00434
IA03600	03JAN2000	E00481
IA02400	16JAN2000	E00082
IA02003	20JAN2000	E00082
IA02003	20JAN2000	E00485
IA02005	23JAN2000	E00481
IA02402	07FEB2000	E00364

The SAS table **prog2.fltspts** is a master table of all the flight attendants and pilots in the company. It contains each employee's first name, last name, identification number, and job code.

Partial Listing of **prog2.fltspts**

FirstName	LastName	ID	Job Code
DOROTHY E	MILLS	E00001	FLTAT3
J. KEVIN	COCKERHAM	E00024	FLTAT3
DESIREE	GOLDENBERG	E00031	PILOT3
ALEC	FISHER	E00033	FLTAT2
NORMA JEAN	WIELENGA	E00043	PILOT3
GREGORY J.	GOODYEAR	E00046	FLTAT1
HANS	ECKHAUSEN	E00047	FLTAT3
JOHN K.	MELTON	E00052	FLTAT2
ANNE	WHITE JR.	E00055	PILOT3

Use PROC SQL to produce a report showing all the information for the flight attendants and pilots scheduled to fly into RDU.

Partial Output

EmpID	FirstName	LastName	Job Code	FltID	SchDate
E00434	KATE	SMITH	PILOT2	IA03600	03JAN2000
E00481	BETTY A.	YANG	FLTAT2	IA03600	03JAN2000
E00481	BETTY A.	YANG	FLTAT2	IA02005	23JAN2000
E00377	DONALD T.	SZCZEPANSKI	PILOT1	IA02000	16FEB2000
E00207	ANNE H.	YANG	FLTAT2	IA02405	17FEB2000
E00432	SANDRA	SCHOBER	FLTAT2	IA02405	17FEB2000
E00052	JOHN K.	MELTON	FLTAT2	IA03400	03APR2000
E00247	CARRIE D.	DODGE	PILOT2	IA03400	03APR2000
E00120	PEGGY H.	DUNLAP	FLTAT2	IA02000	05APR2000
E00248	DAWN B.	EDWARDS	FLTAT3	IA02000	05APR2000

Hint: SQL joins do not require key columns to have the same name.

8.3   Solutions to Exercises

1. Match-Merging Two Data Sets

```
   /*Each data set must be sorted by ProdCode before merging*/

proc sort data=prog2.prices out=pricesort;
   by ProdCode;
run;

proc sort data=prog2.todaysales out=salesort;
   by ProdCode;
run;

data revenue
   NotSold(keep=Price ProdCode)
   InValidCode(Keep=ProdCode Qty);
   merge PriceSort(in=InPrice) SaleSort(in=InSales);
   by ProdCode;
   if InPrice and InSales then do; /*Matching Prodcodes*/
      Revenue = Qty * Price; /*Only necessary to
                            calculate revenue for matches*/
      output revenue;
   end;
   else if InPrice and not InSales then
      output notsold;
        /*Product not in TodaySales data set. */
        /*It has not sold this week*/
   else
      output invalidcode;
          /*Product in TodaySales that is not
             in the master price list.*/
run;

proc print data=revenue;
run;

proc print data=notsold;
run;

proc print data=invalidcode;
run;
```

2. Performing Simple Joins Using PROC SQL (Optional)

```
proc sql;
   select EmpID, FirstName, LastName,
          JobCode, FltID, SchDate
      from prog2.rduschedule, prog2.fltspts
      where EmpID=ID   /* SQL does not require
                          key variables
                          to have the same name. */
   ;
quit;
```

Chapter 9   Learning More

9.1 Where Do I Go From Here?

Objectives

- Explore which SAS training courses are appropriate after you complete SAS® Programming II: Manipulating Data with the DATA Step.

3

Suggested SAS Training Courses

SAS® Programming III: Advanced Techniques includes topics that you can use to broaden your programming skills.

SAS® Macro Language includes topics on building complete macro-based systems using the SAS macro facility.

4

SAS Certified Professional Program

Consider taking a certification exam to assess your knowledge of SAS software. For a current listing of certification exams and registration information, visit **support.sas.com/certify**.

5

9.2   SAS Resources

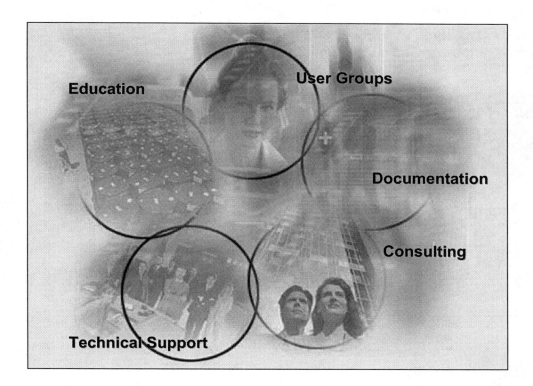

Education

Computer-based:
- e-Learning

Conferences:
- Data Mining Technology Conference

8

Education

Refer to the SAS Training Web site for more information on these classes and the broad curriculum of courses available.

support.sas.com/training

9

SAS Training Home Page

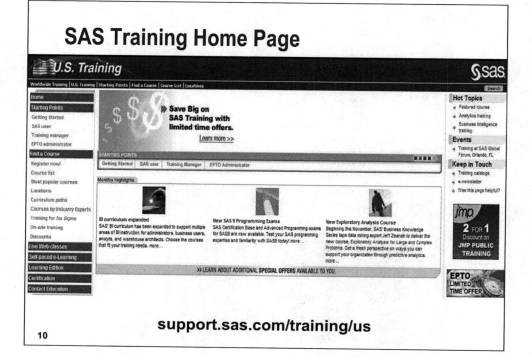

support.sas.com/training/us

10

100% Customer Satisfaction Guarantee

 100% Customer Satisfaction Guarantee

At SAS Education, satisfaction is 100% guaranteed.

 "At SAS Education we take great pride in the fact that our customers consistently rank our training as excellent. That's no accident. From the moment you register, during your training, and even after you're back at work, we strive to provide you with the highest level of customer care possible. Our goal is to help you learn how to use SAS more effectively. So, if you're not satisfied with your training experience, let us know and we will make things right. I promise."

Dr. Herbert J. Kirk, SAS Education Vice President

11

Value Beyond the Classroom

More than 2,100 SAS students who took training in the first three months of 2006 were surveyed to determine the impact of SAS training on their job performance. The survey was given between 60 and 120 days back on the job to allow a fair judgment on how SAS training might have helped them. Here are some results:

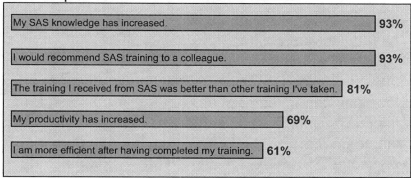

My SAS knowledge has increased.	93%
I would recommend SAS training to a colleague.	93%
The training I received from SAS was better than other training I've taken.	81%
My productivity has increased.	69%
I am more efficient after having completed my training.	61%

12

Consulting Services

Services provided include the following:

- knowledge transfer
- application development
- analytical consulting
- implement business solutions

13

Technical Support

Goals:

- Provide support to SAS users to solve any problems that they encounter when using SAS software.
- Free unlimited support.
- Local support at each site with a designated SAS consultant.

World Wide Web Services:

- Report/resolve problems
- Frequently asked questions
- SASware Ballot suggestions/results
- Download zaps/fixes/patches
- Upload code/data
- Search SAS notes
- Alert notes

14

Technical Support (North America)

Problem Tracking System

Telephone: 9:00 a.m. until 8:00 p.m. Eastern Time
Monday–Friday
(919) 677-8008

E-mail: support@sas.com – report problems
suggest@sas.com – software suggestions

Web: **support.sas.com/techsup/**

15

Documentation

Documenting SAS:
- Reference Guides
- Getting Started Guides
- User's Guides
- Operating Environment Companion Guides
- Changes and Enhancements

Current products and services:
- Publications Catalog
- SAS Press
- Online Documentation

16

Documentation

Reference guides:

- SAS online documentation
- Delivered on a CD-ROM
- Shipped free with software
- Single copies available
- Hard-copy books to purchase

support.sas.com/documentation

17

SAS Publishing

support.sas.com/publishing

18

User Groups

Benefits:

- Enhance your understanding of SAS software and services.
- Exchange ideas about using your software and hardware most productively.
- Learn of new SAS products and services as soon as they become available.
- Have more influence over the direction of SAS software and services.

19

International Users Groups

SAS Global Forum (formerly SUGI)
> Annual conference held March or April in North America

SAS Forum International (formerly SEUGI)
> Annual conference held May or June in Europe

SUGA (SAS Users Group of Australia)
> Annual Conference held August or September in Australia

20

Regional User Groups

SESUG   Southeastern United States

NESUG   Northeastern United States

MWSUG   Midwestern United States

SCSUG   South-Central United States

WUSS   Western United States

Regional conferences are usually held in September or October.

21

Other Users Groups

Local   City or area user group. Often hold multiple meetings per year.

Special Interest Industry-specific user groups.

In-house   Single organization or company user group.

Worldwide   Most countries have their own users groups.

support.sas.com/usergroups

22

Newsgroups

There is a newsgroup named **comp.soft-sys.sas**. This is a bulletin board for users to post questions, answers, and discuss SAS software.

To view this newsgroup, use any newsgroup viewer, such as **groups.google.com**.

23

Newsgroups

The newsgroup is also gated to a listserv. To subscribe to the listserv, send e-mail to any of the mail servers:

- listserv@listserv.uga.edu   University of Georgia
- listserv@vm.marist.edu   Marist University
- listserv@listserv.vt.edu   Virginia Polytechnic University
- listserv@AKH-WIEN.AC.AT   University of Vienna

The subject line is ignored and the body should contain the command: `subscribe sas-l your name`. For example, `subscribe sas-l Tom Smith` is how Tom Smith would subscribe.

24

Additional Information

Access the SAS Web site at **www.sas.com** to learn more about available software, support, and services and to take advantage of these offerings.

25

Wrap-Up

Do not forget to do the following:

- fill out your evaluation
- deposit your name badge in the container provided by your course coordinator
- pick up your diploma

26

Thank you for attending
SAS® Programming II:
Manipulating Data with
the DATA Step.

27

Appendix A Index